# Moving beyond Theoria toward Theosis

# Moving beyond Theoria toward Theosis

## The Telos of Plato's Cave and the Orthodox Icon

Justin A. Davis

LEXINGTON BOOKS
*Lanham • Boulder • New York • London*

Published by Lexington Books
An imprint of The Rowman & Littlefield Publishing Group, Inc.
4501 Forbes Boulevard, Suite 200, Lanham, Maryland 20706
www.rowman.com

86-90 Paul Street, London EC2A 4NE, United Kingdom

British Library Cataloguing in Publication Information Available

**Library of Congress Cataloging-in-Publication Data**

Names: Davis, Justin A., author.
Title: Moving beyond theoria toward theosis : the Telos of Plato's cave and the Orthodox icon / Justin A. Davis.
Description: Lanham : Lexington Books, [2024] | Includes bibliographical references and index. | Summary: "Moving Beyond Theoria Towards Theosis focuses on the telos of man as understood in Plato's theoria, envisioned in the allegory of the cave, and early Christian reinterpretation of theoria as theosis. Central to this is the place of icons in the Orthodox Church"—Provided by publisher.
Identifiers: LCCN 2024009489 (print) | LCCN 2024009490 (ebook) | ISBN 9781666949551 (cloth) | ISBN 9781666949568 (epub)
Subjects: LCSH: Plato's cave (Allegory) | Teleology. | Icons. | Devotional objects—Orthodox Eastern Church.
Classification: LCC B398.C34 D58 2024 (print) | LCC B398.C34 (ebook) | DDC 246/.5308828—dc23/eng/20240430
LC record available at https://lccn.loc.gov/2024009489
LC ebook record available at https://lccn.loc.gov/2024009490

To Theo, Matilda, Gwen, and Sy, *the living icons I encounter every day.*

# Contents

# Preface

I regularly teach philosophy classes at Boise State University, and I often open one of those classes by asking students to get out a piece of paper and divide it into four boxes. I then do the largely unprecedented thing of asking philosophy students to draw. This alone both intrigues and frightens a number of students, but there is a point to this otherwise odd exercise, the same point I wish to tease out in this book. I instruct my students to draw in the first box a picture of themselves. I remind them that they spend hours every day looking at themselves. Between the mirror, selfies, and going to social media posts, they know what they look like better than anyone else. I give them four to five minutes to complete this daunting task. In the second box, I ask them to draw a stick figure representation of themselves, a project that is much easier than the first and for which much less time is needed.

Once completed, I ask them if one picture is more accurate than the other. While some students believe the first has some quality that makes it somewhat more precise than the first, most students do not see a quantifiable difference between the two. Both serve only as a representation of them, and both are not genuine reflections of "reality." This excludes the ten percent or so of students who drew a stick figure of themselves in the first box as well.

In the third square, I ask them to draw a chair. I tell them they can draw any chair they wish to draw—it does not matter if it is the chair they are in right now, their favorite armchair or barstool, or their spot at the kitchen table. I then ask them to draw in that same box a person with the chair. Roughly two-thirds of the students draw a person sitting in the chair, and many more say that they felt inclined to do so but could not due to artistic ability. I then ask them a clear question which begins to get the philosophy students more engaged, "Why would you put the person in the chair?" The simple answer is also the most correct one. Namely, that is what the chair is for. It is what makes the object a chair. Regardless of what type of chair the student drew, the chair takes on its "chair-ness" through its ability to be sat upon. There is an idea which is connected to the image, that objects can convey reality through representation. The "sat upon chair" is also somehow more real than an isolated chair.

In the fourth box, I challenge them to draw "something real." I try to stretch them to represent reality, something really real, something they can convince their fellow students is real. Given the nature of the class many just give up after thinking about it for a few minutes and doodle something nice, but not "real." Others go a different direction and write mathematical formulas.

I stress that we should not blame the lack of reality on artistic ability. I point out that a photograph does not always reflect reality, and "good art" depicts reality though it may not be exactly accurate. Michelangelo's *David* is an example of great art that depicts something very real but is not at all accurate. The statue is famously not proportioned correctly, as the perspective was intended on being much different than how most approach it. Furthermore, Michelangelo never met David. He did not have a series of photographs and measurements to tell him what David actually looked like. Yet he caught the "spirit of David," and that makes the statue real. We connect with it in a way that a casual photograph or series of measurements never could. We get David as the innocent shepherd, not the military leader or king. Michelangelo gave us the author of the Psalms in the statue, not an autocrat who had too much blood on his hands to construct a temple to God, and so we connect with David through the marble.

This is of course what art does, or what it should do. It takes us beyond appearances and brings us to reality. Art becomes a symbol. The word symbol comes from the Greek *symbolon* which means to draw together. Items are brought together in a symbol. The converse Greek term *diabolos* means to tear apart. We see with the Greek terms that art in all of its forms brings things together. The primary thing that it unites is idea and form. The concept that the artist wishes to convey is made manifest in the medium of their construction. This idea existed originally independent of the art and then is combined in such a way that it has meaning for others who encounter it. Art in all of its forms is not about mere appearance, but about conveying a reality behind that appearance.

This difference between appearance and reality is what Plato's Allegory of the Cave is all about. It is what this book attempts to demonstrate about icons and the Orthodox Christian's understanding of reality when encountering an icon. In doing so, this book should also broadly convey the power of religious art in general and the reality found in all sorts of symbols that are used for the making of meaning. The power is also found in the telos (τέλος) or end of the object. The telos for Michelangelo was uniting his marble with the conception he had of David and bringing a religious connection between the observer of that art and God. The telos for Plato and for later Platonists is a concept known as *theoria* (θεωρία). *Theoria* is contemplation of these ideas. Roughly speaking for Platonic cosmology, especially under the Middle Platonists, the universe is threefold. At the center is God, then the realm of ideas or forms, and then the material world. For Platonists, the telos is to move from the material realm to the realm of ideas.

The telos for Orthodox Christians is *theosis* (Θέωςις), often translated as divinization. It is best understood as union with the uncreated energy of God. As Vladimir Lossky, the preeminent Russian Orthodox scholar of the twentieth century, states, "Here union means deification. At the same time, while intimately united with God he knows Him only as Unknowable, in other words as infinity set apart by His nature, remaining even in union, inaccessible in that which He is in His essential being."[1] The cosmology is roughly the same as with our Middle Platonists, but *theosis* is more than just escaping to the world of forms. *Theosis* is a union with God, who is the source of all. It is also an affirmation of the material world. Borrowing from Andrew Louth for Orthodox Christianity, "The Platonic doctrine of contemplation is left behind; it is beyond theoria, in the darkness of unknowing, that the soul penetrates more and more deeply into the knowledge and presence of God through love."[2] *Theosis* is beyond *theoria*, as Louth reminds us. It is this concept from which this work derives its title.[3] Orthodox Christians expect the resurrection of the dead, that the material world is not accidental or a temporary holding place before the soul is liberated but is central to what we are. *Theosis* therefore includes not only union with God, but a union with ideas and matter. As Norman Russell in his work on *theosis* states, "It is both a theological theme and a spiritual teaching, both the *goal* of the divine economy and the *process* by which the economy is worked out in the believer."[4] Or as stated by Dionysius, *theosis* is "the attaining of likeness to God and union with him so far as possible."[5]

For the Western audience to understand symbols, art, meaning, and icons requires a break in our normative approach to these topics. Roughly from Plato until Descartes, Western civilization accepted that real life existed beyond our base perceptions of reality, that we have the world we can see, and there is a mystery behind it which we cannot fully understand, but that truly exists. The bifurcated universe of the meaningful and the mundane is both profound and terrifying. Plato anticipates the trepidation of accepting this universe in *The Republic*. Socrates's dialogue partner Glaucon, in the famed Allegory of the Cave, states that most people would choose to endure anything rather than such a life outside the cave. Life outside the cave has texture, color, and depth. These are things that can be seen and appreciated but not grasped or held onto. In the attempt of Descartes and many others to identify exactly what can be known through systematic doubt, this world was abandoned, seeking instead only a world of shadows. The post-Enlightenment West flattened the universe, removing mystery for quantifiable, measurable, predictable outcomes. The groundwork for this disenchantment was laid early. Before Descartes, the iconoclasm of the Protestant Reformation removed mystery in artistic depictions. The messy symbolic and depicted universe was discarded for an orderly and neat world where rational treatment of text grew ascendent.

It is this messiness that this work seeks to address. It is not uncommon when addressing any work about Christianity, in general or Orthodox specifically, to draw connections with Plato. Many of the dominant philosophical voices in both the East and West were familiar with Plato parallels and connections are appropriate depending on the context and audience of each of these works. Andrew Louth,[6] Richard Temple,[7] and Vladimir Lossky have gone into detail concerning the impact that Plato's philosophical speculation had in Orthodox Christianity. Louth's work masterfully explains the understanding of mysticism as the Christian application of and correction to Plato's cosmology. Temple stresses the distinction between the inner and outer world as advocated by Plato. Temple maintains that this dual-natured Platonic world is the source for Christian understanding of their place in the cosmos. Furthermore, Temple connects this concept to the icon "but the idea of image or reflection also has a spiritual meaning that goes back to the cosmological world-view of early Christian philosophers in the third and fourth centuries."[8] It is Lossky, however, who states that with regard to the Platonism of the Church Fathers, it is "limited to outward resemblances which do not go to the root of their teaching, and relate only to a vocabulary which was common to the age."[9]

Both Louth and Temple's works have their limitations and oversights. For example, Louth in his brilliant work addresses the philosophical development of Christianity and the relationship between mysticism and philosophy. The next step where this philosophy speaks about the telos of Orthodoxy, as opposed to Platonism through the use of symbolism, meaning, and icons, is left untreated. Instead, the work is primarily concerned with the use and rejection of Plato in the first five hundred years of Christian history.

Temple's work draws out the connection between Plato and mysticism like Louth does, and he applies this to the notion of icons. Yet Temple's work stresses the origins of mysticism as rooted in Plato more than the issue of meaning derived from the icon for the Orthodox Christian. Temple fails to grasp what Lossky states concerning Orthodox understanding of mysticism, that "the eastern tradition has never made a sharp distinction between mysticism and theology; between personal experience of the divine mysteries and the dogma affirmed by the Church."[10] Lossky points out that within the tradition of Orthodoxy there is no mysticism without theology, and no theology without mysticism. Both have the same end, which is the same end of the Christian in general, that being union with God, *theosis*. Temple's understanding of Christian mysticism is reduced to Platonic mysticism. According to Temple, Christianity "holds that it is only in the inner world, in his spiritual world, that a man can become what he truly is."[11] Temple connects the language used by early Christians to Plato but does not see how the telos differs. In my estimation, Temple fails to properly understand how Christianity utilized the language and system of Plato as Louth and Lossky demonstrate. Temple does illustrate how this mysticism is connected to icons. Both mysticism and Platonic language provided the genesis for this piece.

This work ventures to explain how symbolism must be understood with telos, how Plato's philosophy and his Allegory of the Cave address the issue of meaning and that this meaning for Platonists is *theoria*. This work will also address the use of Plato's language for Orthodox Christians and the use of icons. The synthesis of these help to demonstrate the telos of Orthodoxy is *theosis*. In explaining the distinctions between *theoria* and *theosis*, I will draw on my background in religious studies and history, as well as my experience teaching philosophy. In addition to my academic study of religion, history, and philosophy, I have recently supplemented my PhD with additional coursework in Orthodox Studies from the Antiochian House of Studies. These academic pursuits, as well as my personal engagement with Orthodox Christianity, allows me to speak to the subject from multiple vantage points, both as an insider and as a scholar.

I will draw heavily upon the methodologies of religious studies scholars including Mircea Eliade, Pierre Bourdieu, J. Z. Smith, Émile Durkheim, Marshall Sahlins, Bronislaw Malinowski, and others. I will also use the the writings of iconographers Leonid Ouspensky, Jonathan Pageau, Aidan Hart, Solrunn Nes, and Fr Matthew Garrett and their treatments throughout this work. I will supplement their voices with luminaries of the Orthodox church, including Metropolitan Hilarion Alfeyev, Protopresbyter Alexander Schmemann, Protopresbyter Thomas Hopko, and a number of saints who speak on icons, such as Saint John of Damascus, Saint Theodore the Studite, Saint Basil the Great, Saint Nektarios Kefalas, and Saint Porphyrios, among many others. These voices will help explain the nature and telos of icons and Plato's philosophy that will add to the voices of existing literature already referenced. By incorporating contrasting fields and authors, the work should present an interdiscipinary approach to the question of meaning and telos for both Plato and Orthodox Christianity. It is from these and many other authors that I have developed my approach to the topic, and the synthesis of such is found here.

With such a synthesis, I am aware that the audience for this book will be mixed. There are scholars of religion who should expect a strong dose of methodology applied to an oft-neglegted group. The historian of ideas and philosopher can see how Plato's conception of the universe was iconically materialized and transformed by a Christian audience, and resulted in new debates and conceptions of matter and images that went well beyond anything Plato could have envisioned. The Orthodox Christian who seeks to better understand the nature of icons and their role in *theosis* should find both development and examples of application in this work. While these three audiences are distinct, each should find something valuable in the present synthesis. I hope that the material is presented in such a way that properly incorporates the needs of each audience and can provide a bridge to unite scholars and active learners of different fields.

## NOTES

1. Lossky, Vladimir. *The Mystical Theology of the Eastern Church*. Crestwood, NY: St. Vladimir's Seminary Press, 1944, 38.

2. Louth, Andrew. *Origins of the Christian Mystical Tradition: From Plato to Denys*. Oxford: Clarendon Paperbacks, 1981.

3. In addition to a conversation I had about this work with Eric (Nicholas) Nelson.

4. Russell, Norman. *Fellow Workers with God: Orthodox Thinking on Theosis*. Crestwood, NY: St. Vladimir's Seminary Press, 2009, 21.

5. Russell, *Fellow Workers with God*, 21–22, citing Ecclesiastical Hierarchy 1.3, 367A.

6. Louth, *Origins of the Christian Mystical Tradition*, 97.

7. Temple, Richard. *Icons and the Mystical Origins of Christianity*. Longmead, UK: Element Books, 1990.

8. Temple, Richard. *Icons: A Sacred Art at the Temple Gallery*. London: Temple Gallery, 1989, 4.

9. Lossky, *Mystical Theology*, 32.

10. Lossky, *Mystical Theology*, 8.

11. Temple, *Icons and the Mystical Origins of Christianity*, 5.

# Acknowledgments

I would like to first acknowledge Christ as the telos of this work, who separates mere speculation and divine life. Next, I would like to express my deepest gratitude to Fr Matthew Garrett for the use of his icons in this work. His support and feedback about the art and experience of making an icon were instrumental.

The faculty, staff, and my peers at the Antiochian House of Studies demonstrate a rigorous dedication to understanding and living an Orthodox life and provided much encouragement. To this end, I would also like to acknowledge the priests and other clergy I have been blessed to encounter.

Thank you to my children for their patience with me while I endeavored to write this work. Finally, I would like to thank my wife for her love, dedication, and assistance with this work and the many others along the way.

# Introduction

It is not enough for humans to survive. We must be a part of something bigger than ourselves. Meaning must be established to something that transcends mundane existence. We represent this meaning through artistic endeavors that demonstrate significance. The earliest example we have of this endeavor is the Chauvet Cave in Vallon-Pont-d'Arc France. More than 30,000 years ago, people started representing their world. Art varied from handprints and geographic shapes to animals. The practice of signifying oneself and one's world continues to be discovered with pictographs and petroglyphs done by nomadic people for thousands of years. Anywhere people have lived, they have left a series of markers and symbolic representation of their cosmos. Often the only thing we discover about ancient peoples is the art that they left behind. Art depicts the value assigned to daily life and culture through symbols, that is through depictions that are intended on bringing and demonstrating meaning to their culture.

Today we continue to represent what is meaningful to us through the pictorial representations that we create and surround ourselves with. We take hundreds or thousands of pictures every year trying to frame a shot in just a certain way that captures the essence of a moment or person. "A picture is worth a thousand words," even while they are silent. To try to ensure that the right words are spoken, hours are spent not only setting the stage for the photo, but in editing photos through adjusting filters and lighting and other software that is used to airbrush out perceived imperfections. Pictures are used to prove that something happened. One will often hear disputes about something being resolved with the phrase "pics or it didn't happen." Other photos are put together into endless memes. These memes are used to satirize, vilify, or honor and glorify people, nations, movements, and ideologies.

Our culture today intuitively knows that pictures hold meaning. We express this meaning by sending these photos around for amusement or to express love. Far too often, one's self-worth is tied to how their artistic rendering of the universe is received by their "friends and followers." We anticipate recognition; the image is not intended on being static, but in eliciting a response. We also respond to images of people, treating the image as if it is the person depicted. Images are burned, distorted, or destroyed publicly or ceremoniously to show our distaste for the subject. These include political leaders, world figures, past and present, as well as personal images of romantic trysts gone awry. We kiss photos of loved ones. We instinctively connect images with what they represent to us and for our community. If we love and admire a person, that love is passed onto the image. Similarly, if we revile another, that enmity is expressed toward the image.

We approach people and their relationship to an image from various fields of study. Sociologically, we see images in two- and three-dimensional objects representing people. Durkheim famously addresses the totem as the symbol for the clan. E. E. Evans-Pritchard discusses the symbolism connected with items standing for one another. "They are statements not that something is other than it is but that in a certain sense and in particular contexts something has some extra quality which does not belong to it in its own nature; and this quality is not contrary to, or incompatible with, its nature but something added to it which does not alter what it was but makes it something more, in respect to this quality, than it was."[1] Psychologically, Sigmund Freud addresses the taboos surrounding items and this imposition upon our ego from the outside. Philosophically speaking we can of course address Plato's forms, as well as Anselm and a whole host of others that see image and the connection between metaphysics and ontology. This began with the Stoics' concept of microcosm. Man himself is the image of the universe. Lossky argues that "for the Stoics in particular, if the human being is superior to the cosmos, this is so because he summarizes it and gives it meaning; for the cosmos is a large human being just as man is a small cosmos."[2] Images are microcosms of reality, and reality is found and interpreted through the image.

This notion of microcosm is the basis for theological understanding as well. Bonaventure's *Journey of the Mind into God* constantly makes connections between the microcosm of the self and the macrocosm of the universe. Saints Irenaeus, Basil the Great, Gregory of Nyssa, and other Church Fathers use the concept of mankind imaging God as the basis of theological reflection. Lossky maintains that this connection of a person to a personal God allows for them to "personalize" the world.[3] Understood properly, the connection between man as a microcosm of the cosmos is not to eliminate them in the vastness of the universe, nor to exalt them into a solipsistic sociopath, but to bring relation and bridge the connection between the seen and the unseen.

This connection is the purpose of the Orthodox Christian's use of images. They are to convey meaning and beauty. Fr Eugene Pentiuc paraphrases Fyodor Dostoevsky, saying, "Christ's beauty will save the world."[4] Beauty is something seen that shows us more than what is in front of us. This beauty comes in many forms, including acts of kindness, moving prose, music, and images. Pentiuc separates truly beautiful images, which inherently have a spiritual dimension, as they move one beyond oneself, from profane images. "Christian art has two enemies: the ugliness of a violent world that tempts us with the slogan 'Beauty is unreal,' and the seductive art that makes the human being prisoner of its basic instincts and desires."[5]

By moving outside of ourselves, an image becomes an icon. As John Baggley articulates, "'The icon is a door' . . . and a door is meant to be passed through, to be the threshold across which we pass into a different place."[6] The door is the link between the microcosm of the self and the macrocosm of the universe, and theologically toward God. This is why images have been used throughout the history of the Church. Not all images qualify however, as those that deny beauty or are seductive are rejected. The prohibition in the Second Commandment applies to these images; it is not a universal prohibition against all images. Shortly after the issuing of the Decalogue, God commands Moses to make statues of cherubim. God commands that the tabernacle is not only constructed as a visage of a heavenly tent, but that it is finished with beautiful decorations, ornate lampstands, vested priests, and utensils for service. The grandeur of these elements was to draw the Hebrews closer to God in worship. God also commanded other images for the healing of body, not only the soul. God instructed Moses to construct a brass serpent to heal those stricken by snakes.

These examples from Exodus are material representations building off of the visions and dreams that we have in Genesis. As Fr Pavel Florensky posits, "dreams are the images that separate the visible world from the invisible— and at the same time join them."[7] Dreams and other visions were primarily image without form, idea without matter. The duty of the Patriarchs was to connect the vision to their people. This was done through the physical construction of the tabernacle and later the temple. What was on earth reflected what was in heaven.

Solomon's temple and the vision Ezekiel had of the future temple[8] also continued this theology of image. Solomon ordained the temple with cherubim and pomegranates. Ezekiel's temple had animals, angels, man, and nature scenes. The images found in the tabernacle and temples are mirrored in synagogues during the Second Temple Period. Mosaics and other depictions of biblical scenes and heavenly images are found in Jewish settlements throughout the Mediterranean by communities that could financially afford to so, demonstrating the bridge between the visible and the invisible. As Fr Stephen De Young states, "Iconography continued to exist in synagogues, as continues to be revealed by archeological excavations in Galilee and elsewhere."[9] When Christianity emerged, the use of images to convey a deeper reality was already well established. What developed was a style, medium, and standardized symbolism, not the use of images in worship.

The earliest icon is known as "the image of Christ made without hands," the holy Mandylion. This was a cloth that contained the image of Christ and was given to the King Abgar of Edessa as recorded by Eusebius. The Mandylion was moved to Constantinople and subsequently lost in 1204, taken by the crusaders. Tradition holds that Luke was the first iconographer. While there are a few icons that are accredited to Luke in existence today, many are understood to be based on the original and not the original itself. Other early examples of Christian iconography include those found in the catacombs. Catacomb art survives and connects notion of images and relics of saints to corporate worship of God.

These artistic depictions are inherently liturgical, and as Mircea Eliade points out, they connect the image with its prototype. "The church is conceived as imitating the Heavenly Jerusalem, even from patristic times; on the other, it also reproduces Paradise or the celestial world."[10] Images play as crucial of a role as music and order in facilitating the realization of Paradise. The image is an intuitive element that conveys meaning beyond the intellectual comprehension. When one sees the endurance of a saint, it strengthens the parishioner. The image is more than a static decoration, it becomes a symbol for the communicant and the community.

When understood as the mediation between the microcosm and the macrocosm, images are symbols which bring the devotee and God together. As mentioned in the preface, the word symbol itself helps convey this message. Symbols are two things that are made one. The icon is not an item by itself, but it holds religious and cultural significance. There are different levels of meaning that can be understood, not only with the image but with ourselves as well. As Baggley conveys, "Symbols become the focal point at which the material and the spiritual, the ordinary and the extra-ordinary, the human and the divine converge in human perception."[11]

As symbols bring two disparate things together, there are multiple types of symbols beyond the image. Symbols exist at all levels of religious and social meaning. There are symbols of the law, which are further divided between spiritual and corporeal law. While the notion of the law exists in many spheres, the differentiation between divine law and civil law has been enshrined in Western consciousness. Yet both the religious and secular authorities will borrow the understanding of the law from the other's authority when necessary to draw a point. Statues of religious lawgivers are erected over courthouses, and the earthly judge as a metaphor for God is used regularly by Evangelical and Calvinist pastors in delivering a message of judgement and repentance. Symbols exist also to convey grace and freedom. Often as symbols are incorporated by a community, greater nuance develops. This nuance results in additional levels of representation found in the symbol.

As the symbol becomes more complex, typologies form. Mary is a symbol of herself, and a type for others to emulate. Light becomes a symbol of truth, purity, revelation, and goodness, while darkness takes on the opposite meaning. Older images are understood through the lens of the new. For instance, Bogdan Bucur reveals that the blood sacrifice in Isaiah is understood as a type of Christ's passion while also having the significance as the relation between the world and Moses's tabernacle.[12] This is why Elizabeth Theokritoff and many others can tell us that, "This is the prime way in which the Church reads the Old Testament as a book about Christ."[13]

A tension arises in how one should understand the layers of typology. Traditionally this is understood as the tension that existed between the two great centers of ancient Christianity, Alexandria and Antioch. Alexandria used an allegorical lens while Antioch preferred a literal interpretation. As Jean Danielou explains the conflict, "Whereas Alexandria remained a great centre of speculative theology and allegorical exegesis, Antioch developed in the direction of pastoral theology and scientific exegesis."[14] As we will demonstrate later, while both cities held importance in the Roman Empire, Alexandria was the philosophical hub, surpassing Athens within the first few centuries of its founding. It is also undisputed that the main philosophical and theological trends that emerged from Alexandria utilized allegory more in interpretation than any other. This standard method of Alexandria and Antioch, being fairly monolithic in their approach to interpretation, has undergone further consideration in the last few decades. The tension between one pole of allegory and the other of literal interpretation still exists. Regardless of philosophical schools, images by their nature as symbols bring together the depiction of events or people with culturally and personally significant meaning.

Since images are symbols, the treatment of images is not limited to Orthodox icons. Modern and abstract art exists on this plane of meaning. Scholars in the field of religious studies have a long history of treating images as symbols that are used to convey meaning. As Eliade says, "the historian of religions is preoccupied uniquely with religious symbols, that is, with those that are bound up with a religious experience or a religious conception of the world."[15] Sometimes this meaning is known to the religious practitioners. As Victor Turner identifies the Milk Tree as the object which shapes the consciousness of the group, that society knows it functions in relation to the tree and its meaning for them is something explicitly known. Similarly, both Durkheim and Freud acknowledge that the totem, with its prescribed duties and prohibitions, is understood by the group. There is not a denial of the materiality of the totem, rather it is known and interpreted by devotees as a symbol. William James understands symbols as an expression of faith. Therefore, "in the religious life the control is felt as 'higher'; but since in our hypothesis it is primarily the higher faculties of our own hidden mind which are controlling, the sense of union with the power beyond us is a sense of something, not merely apparently, but literally true."[16]

A key difference exists in the conception of a sign versus a symbol for the religious devotee. Susan Langer's contention is that "the fundamental difference between signs and symbols is the difference of association, and consequently of their use by the third party to the meaning function, the subject; signs announce their objects to him, whereas symbols lead him to conceive their objects."[17] In many ways, Langer's use of sign and symbol amplifies Clifford Geertz's definition of religion as this system of symbols. While understood as a symbol for something greater, William James asserts that "as soon as any one of these things stands for the idea, the latter seems to be more real."[18] For the devotee, when the image serves as a symbol, ideas possess a "living reality."[19] An outsider may not approach the object as something worthy of veneration or respect and will therefore miss the meaning that it possesses for the insider.

For these scholars and many more, religion is to be understood through the interplay of signs and symbols. Religious meaning for the practitioner is made by their knowledge and relation to symbols. Eliade reminds us that "From this point of view, symbolism appears to be a 'language' understood by all the members of the community and meaningless to outsiders, but certainly a 'language' expressing at once and equally clearly the social, 'historic' and psychic condition of the symbol's wearer, and his relations with society and the cosmos."[20] The symbol is interpreted through the devotee and the identity they consciously internalize in relation to the symbol. This language of the symbol is spoken by the community as an expression of their understanding of the deeper reality that the symbol represents or communicates.

Sometimes symbols are only something that can be understood from an outsider's perspective. As Peter Berger articulates concerning the way we accept what surrounds us, "Social world intends, as far as possible, to be taken for granted. Socialization achieves success to the degrees that this taken-for-granted quality is internalized."[21] The greater degree of socialization occurs around any given symbol, the more intrinsic its meaning is and the less it is taken for granted as an object of devotion or religious practice. Simple acts such as lighting candles and votive lamps can be understood in this way. While deeply symbolic, the illumination that came from these pious acts was something practical when initially brought into use. Marshall Sahlins understands these objects as "a set of historical relationships that at once reproduce the traditional cultural categories and give them new values out of the pragmatic context."[22] The logic of symbols is internalized by the practitioner and understood only from the outsider. Eliade articulates, "This logic goes beyond the sphere of religious history to rank among the problems of philosophy."[23]

Even still other things are only properly grasped through the lens of a scholar. The scholar of religion is both an outsider and someone who understands the vocabulary of the devotee. As such the scholar can tease out what is seen and what is taken for granted. As Wendy Doniger discusses in her work *The Implied Spider*, webs of meaning are everywhere and "we must believe in the existence of the spider."[24] The spider is the experience behind the myth, the webs, the taken for granted, and the why. To properly understand a symbol, multiple levels of analysis often must take place, utilizing comparative approaches. Wilford Cantwell Smith maintains, "Neither religion in general nor any one of the religions I will contend, is in itself an intelligible entity, a valid object of inquiry or of concern either for the scholar or the man of faith."[25] I. M. Lewis demonstrates this in relation to the concept of possession. From the insider's perspective, possession is something unique but understandable. From the outsider's perspective, possession may fulfill a functionalist purpose to alleviate a social stress or inequality. Still, the scholar following Lewis can understand that "possession is a culturally normative experience."[26] Actions which are profound from various levels of engagement should be understood as an expression of normative behaviors. We should always keep in mind Eliade's argument that "whatever its context, a symbol always reveals the basic oneness of several zones of the real."[27]

One such scholar who can help us navigate the connection between the icon as a symbol and community is Eliade. Specifically, his treatment of the "hierophany," this being his preferred term for a manifestation of the sacred. Eliade argues that "the symbol is carrying further the dialectic of the hierophany: everything not directly consecrated by a hierophany becomes sacred because of its participation in a symbol."[28] The sacred as understood by the community is susceptible to becoming a symbol. Because they bridge the realm of the divine and mundane religious, images are inherently symbolic. Eliade maintains that the symbol is not only important because it furthers the manifestation of the sacred, but because it "is able to carry on the process of hierophanization and particularly because, on occasions, it is itself a hierophany—it itself reveals a sacred or cosmological reality which no other manifestation is capable of revealing."[29] The symbol itself is what it portrays. The encounter of the divine manifested through the artistic medium is revered, not simply because it portrays the sacred, but because it is encountered itself as holy.

Unfortunately, the industrialized and modern West has abandoned its understanding of image holding inherent meaning following the Protestant Reformation. The disenchantment of the world that follows the theology of

Ulrich Zwingli and Calvin gave birth the philosophical systems of Descartes, Hume, and Kant. Jordan Peterson argues that "prior to the time of Descartes, Bacon and Newton, man lived in an animated, spiritual world, saturated with meaning, imbued with moral purpose."[30] For Peterson, the purpose was revealed in stories. For our goal, we can include images as storytelling devices as well. The Western mind, trained by centuries of early modern scholasticism, differs from its medieval counterpart. The medieval tried to understand the place of humanity in the cosmos within an older cosmology. Enlightenment thought questioned that cosmic structure. From George Berkeley's assertion that only the mind and ideas exist, that there is no matter in the traditional sense,[31] to Kant's distinction between the phenomena which are knowable unlike the noumena which is unknowable;[32] the belief that we can truly know a thing that we perceive is lost. Even the pragmatist William James added to this skepticism when he asserts "among the sensations themselves all are not deemed equally real."[33] James adds by diminishing the image itself and not only sensations, that to many "photographs of lost ones seem to be fetishes."[34]

Today we take this for granted; even the medieval philosophers from Bonaventure to Saadya discounted our senses, as they could fail and deceive us. Yet for those premoderns there was still a reality that could be known and passed down to us. Tradition held value was found through teachings, stories, and symbols. As Eliade affirms, "the symbol always has an important part to play in all societies."[35] Today our connection to the symbolic world is severed. Leonid Ouspensky contends that only recently, following the emancipation of the theology of modern scholasticism, is the attitude toward these symbols and images reasserting itself.[36]

Recently the value of the symbol has been reassessed. Symbols are no longer being dismissed as archaic forms of representation. The symbol is once again interpreted as the key to understanding meaning for a growing number of scholars and people in general. For those who have a new interest in the symbolic world, they understand that the symbol is inherently meaningful in itself. The symbols are not being treated as a talisman, but as a key to unlock a world where greater meaning is found. As Peterson states, "The cosmos described by mythology was not the same place known to the practitioners of modern science—but that does not mean it was not real. We have not yet found God above, nor the devil below, because we do not yet understand where 'above' and 'below' might be found."[37] We are learning to look in other places for above and below, to understand them not as special coordinates, but as directional casts. The myth is a story which tells us what we need to know about our place in the world even when it looks different than how we approach the world. The popularity of Jonathan Pageau and others who introduce us to a symbolic world testifies to the growing interest in a world that exists not through our perceptions but beyond our perceptions. In many ways, this is the return to Plato's cave and drawing out the world which exists beyond casual observations.

Today the place that the image as symbol is clearest to see reasserting itself is the Church. While images have proliferated throughout our lives in social media, texts, and memes, these images are only engaged with for a moment. Hours may be spent in crafting the perfect image to convey a simple message, the message is quickly "liked" or dismissed. The lasting impact is nullified by the reproduction of another to take its place. Oddly enough in the dynamic fast-paced world where images move all around us, the images that resonate are the ones that are static and call for personal and corporate engagement.

This personal and corporate engagement with meaningful symbolic images is housed in a place set apart for this engagement. This is one of the functions of the Church. As Eliade points out, "the interior of the church is the universe. The altar is paradise, which lay in the East. The imperial door to the altar was also called the Door of Paradise. During Easter week, the great door to the altar remains open during the entire service; the meaning of this custom is clearly expressed in the Easter Canon: 'Christ rose from the grave and opened the doors of Paradise unto us.'"[38]

Early modern historian Susan Karant-Nunn identifies icons in the church as "the ubiquitous tangible symbols of God's present action among his follow-ers."[39] She expands by telling us that, "the artistic representations that filled the late-medieval churches were often designed to arouse more than aware-ness of the story of this or that martyr-saint."[40] The level of awareness moves us toward contemplation, engagement, and action. J. Z. Smith underscores this contemplation, engagement, and action by observing the cyclic nature connected to it. As such, "repetition is the human mode of articulating abso-lute reality."[41] The actions associated with symbols are not isolated events but movements that are repeated on a regular basis. Ideas are internalized through habitualized routine, what is often identified as ritualistic engagement with tangible symbols. James suggests that the level of engagement has as much to do with our belief in an object's reality as to any other principle.[42] It is with this engagement that the Church makes the image a symbol and a living myth.

The language of the symbol is spoken through regular encounters and manifested through tradition. Images, while appearing as static, speak to the individual and the community. They relay stories. These stories are embodied myths. Myths should not be embraced as taken in the vernacular conception, but how they are understood by the scholar of religion. Myths are epic stories that are intended on conveying deep truths. As Peterson states, "Myth is not primitive proto-science. It is a qualitatively different phenomenon."[43] Rather it is an aspect of reality, as they connect a society through a shared culture by providing a shared experience. Traditionally this experience is enacted through the telling of the story. This story needs not be verbally expressed. It can be conveyed through images, that is through interpretation and understanding of the symbols. Religious images can be treated the same as myths, in that their portrayal and reception are understood as symbols.

With the reassessment of symbol, our key to understanding their significance lies in earlier treatment of religion by scholars. While most discussed what they called "primitive" religion, many of their statements apply to religion and societies at all different levels of organization. What they called primitive we should understand as people who are connected to the symbolic world. Since the West is only recently rediscovering a symbolic understanding, we must venture to put aside the prejudice of modernity and humbly learn from cultures which maintained this symbolic link. We can see the connections scholars of religion made about these cultures and apply them to our discussion, as fundamentally the needs of individuals and groups in relation to each other and the divine is not different.

For both the "primitive" and for the modern who is rediscovering symbolic value, the worldview is one that is open to meaning beyond the mundane. Mythic stories and religious art are overlapping symbols where the world is constructed. As Peterson states, the "prevailing religious viewpoint was not merely one compelling theory among many."[44] Rather it is the lens through which all events are understood, interpreted, and acted upon, a world where there is more to be understood than what is quantifiable. A world where more than shadows exist but light and texture. A world that is filled with beauty. A beauty that comes from a source outside of individual aesthetic valuation. This is why Dostoevsky can say that beauty will save the world. Beauty is given to the world. Once understood as given, the response is to accept the beauty. One becomes beautiful through accepting this gift found through the symbol. One can only become beautiful through this encounter. Temple concludes that "an important aspect of mystical Christianity, which it shares with all spiritual traditions, though it is not stressed in the doctrinal teachings, holds that it is only in the inner world, in his spiritual world, that a man can become what he truly is."[45]

In becoming what one "truly is," the world is constructed through the symbol and the actions associated with it. Anthony Wallace identifies these religiously interpreted meaningful acts as mazeways. Much like the webs spoken about by Doniger, or the notion of habitus addressed by Bourdieu, mazeways are the internalized operations of the socially constructed world. Unlike Bourdieu's habitus where the structuring structures are "Objectively 'regulated' and 'regular' without being in any way the product of obedience to rules,"[46] mazeways can be consciously rejected. For Wallace, this is done when chronic physiological stress presents itself and the mazeway is incapable of rightly addressing the cause of that stress. This results in a revitalization movement.[47] This revitalization brings both the individual, and the collective that cooperates with the revitalization, relief from the chronic pressure.

One could observe the periods of iconoclasm as examples where the system was changed as religious images came under attack, having lost the symbolic value they once had, and taking on a new one. As Peter Berger maintains, "Religions over time lose character as a symbol for the community, thus they will either accommodate or refuse."[48] The revitalization movement is one way to accommodate the character as symbol for the community. And as J. Z. Smith points out, "Social change is preeminently symbol or symbolic change."[49] The rejection of symbols was the creation of a new symbolic world, even if what this new world signified was an absence of the transcendent.

In a similar way the current revaluation of transcendent symbols in general and religious images in particular signifies the failures of this modern iconoclastic project. Modernity was built upon a rejection of a former system and believed that the preeminence of the word alone could suffice. For a period of time, it did. Before too long the solidarity of those gathered around the solitary word began to fail. Much like Orwell's critique of socialism, that "socialists did not really like the poor. They merely hated the rich,"[50] the iconoclasts disliked the system confirmed by the image and had not come to terms with the symbol as such. J. Z. Smith points out why this is ultimately doomed to fail, as he defines man as a "symbol-producing animal and society or culture as a symbol-system."[51] Or as Peterson states it, "Beliefs make the world, in a very real way—that beliefs are the world."[52]

We produce symbols because they provide meaning. We believe in the symbol because it is through this belief that the world is meaningful. Eliade says it this way, "Symbols awaken individual experience and transmute it into a spiritual act, into metaphysical comprehension of the world."[53] The spiritual world operates on meaning, it produces action that is meaningful, and it is habitualized, thus allowing for greater understanding of the symbol and what that symbol brings together.

Matthew Pageau explains symbolism as the ancient and universal language which combines the cognitive processes of generalization and specialization. Here, "Abstract principles are grasped from tangible experience, and multiple experiences are seen as instances of a single principle. In this manner, spiritual reality is united with corporeal reality to form symbols."[54] It is for this reason that the place of symbols is not only the domain of the scholar of religion but also the devotees themselves.

The medieval philosophical systems were built upon the tension between faith and reason. Neither denying faith nor reason, the question was how to hold the two in concert, where one will serve the other or provide the basis for acting upon the other. The questions emerged from classical philosophical interrogations to theological concerns inherent within the tradition. For the West, the main question was concerning sin and how to overcome sin. For Augustine, Anselm, and Aquinas the means of sin mitigation shaped their philosophical speculation. For others, such as Albert the Great and Meister Eckhart who interpreted Dionysius's speculative or mystical theology more than Augustine, the question of meaning grew dominant. For both sides of the West following Augustine, or those who read Dionysius, the question was also about action and consequences of that action. These consequences were both here on Earth and in the life to come.

In the Christian East, medieval philosophy is often viewed as following the mystical developments of Dionysius beyond the levels of Albert and Eckhart. Dionysius is read as the corrective to Neoplatonic thought and the triads are understood through relationship with the divine. This provides a basis for Orthodox theology, which is addressed in chapter 7. For contemporary Orthodox theologians, the place for symbols and meaning is understood through the mysteries. Symbols are liturgical and sacramental. The use of symbols is the medium to *theosis*, or unity with God. With symbols, ultimate place understood as the means of union, Alexander Schmemann maintains that "it is this unitive principle, whose absence is felt so strongly and the search for which dominates modern thought, that is given the name symbol."[55]

The aim of this work is not only to understand meaning and its relationship to the symbolic world, but how one relates to this meaningful world. With a different meaning there is a different telos. To approach this concept as understood both by Plato and by Orthodox Christianity and how it applies to the icon, this work can be roughly divided into four sections. The first chapter speaks about the philosophical schema that both Plato and early Christians approach the world with. Ancient philosophy was expected to provide the framework for action. As discussed in chapter 1, Plato and his Allegory of the Cave serves as an introduction to a world beyond mundane observations. The action that Plato envisioned was the reason for writing *The Republic*, where we find the Allegory of the Cave. Here we will discuss not only Plato's Allegory of the Cave, but also the philosophical landscape that Plato responded to and the trajectory of philosophy following Plato. This will lead us to the Christian response in chapter 2. As Lossky and Louth demonstrate, in the first three centuries Christianity used the language and landscape of Plato but ultimately rejected his teleology that terminates in *theoria*.

In the second section of the work, comprising chapters 3 and 4, we turn our attention directly to the icon itself. In chapter 3, we look at the theology behind the icon as maintained by Saints John of Damascus and Theodore the Studite, how icons are used as a symbol, and what an icon is as an image. Chapter 4 speaks about the telos of the icon as an instrument in the Church.

This will include the kinetic aspects of veneration, icons use in prayer, and their place as holy objects.

The third section of the work will focus on the historical controversies concerning icons. Chapter 5 addresses the history between the Quinisext Council and the Triumph of Orthodoxy. It was during this time that the Later Roman Empire had its two periods of iconoclasm. Having already addressed the theological responses given by John of Damascus and Theodore the Studite, this chapter concentrates more on the events than the theology of the icon. Chapter 6 looks at the various forms of iconoclasm that the Protestant Reformations produced and the reasons for iconoclasm in the West, highlighting the similarities and differences to the earlier Eastern iconoclasm. In these chapters, we can see how rejection of icons included a rejection of the telos attached to them.

The fourth and final section of this work will revisit the teleology of icons and their relationship to philosophy, what is revealed in icons, and the community formation around icons. In chapter 7, we return once again to Plato and his relationship with later Orthodox Christian thinkers. Here Dionysius and Maximus reassess Plato, but once again emphasize the telos of the Christian is *theosis*. This will be followed by a brief discussion of Western use of Plato and telos. In chapter 8, we turn our attention to specific icons. In this treatment we can see how symbolism, theology, and teleology are depicted in the icon.

Throughout these eight chapters, several strands of thought will be present. Obviously, Plato's cave will be one of them. His philosophy and its ramifications will be central to the interpretive model of icons and their use for Orthodox Christians. The theological and ecclesial conceptions of icons will be presented from both inside sources, faithful Orthodox Christians whose use of icons is understood in liturgical life, as well as scholars of religion and history. The three themes of Plato, religious scholarship, and that of the practitioner will provide a full picture of how icons are understood and provide meaning for Orthodox Christians.

The work will conclude by addressing community formation that exist in and through the icon. Icon comes from the Greek εικόν, meaning image. Today the term is used in an ordinary sense, but when applied to religious art, the meaning is far from ordinary. The image provides the basis for group formation and relationship with both the divine and members of that community. Since icons are not static, they produce reactions which have lived results. The telos of Orthodox Christianity is manifest through the icon, just as the telos of Plato is revealed in his written works.

Saint Maximus the Confessor reminds us that "the image returns to the archetype for which it now longs."[56] The symbol longs to fulfill its mission of bringing together. This is why Ouspensky proclaims that "the icon no longer represents only a cultural or spiritual value: it is a revelation of the Orthodox spiritual experience through artistic means, a 'theology in images.'"[57] Schmemann posits that the icon is "this unitive principle, whose absence is felt so strongly and the search for which dominates modern thought, that is given the name symbol."[58] Through the understanding of Plato's Allegory of the Cave and the significance of the icon, both secular and religious thought can help us to approach the symbol and what lies behind it.

## NOTES

1. Evans-Pritchard, E. E., *Nuer Religion*. Oxford: Oxford, 1956, 141.

2. Lossky, Vladimir. *Dogmatic Theology: Creation, God's Image in Man, and the Redeeming Work of the Trinity*. Crestwood, NY: St. Vladimir's Seminary Press, 2017, 85.

3. Lossky, *Dogmatic Theology*, 86.

4. Pentiuc, Eugen J. *The Old Testament in Eastern Orthodox Tradition*. Oxford: Oxford Univeristy Press, 2014, 264.

5. Pentiuc, *Old Testament in Eastern Orthodox Tradition*, 265–66.

6. Baggley, John. *Doors of Perception: Icons and their Spiritual Significance.* London: Mowbray, 1987, 4.

7. Florensky, Pavel. *Iconostasis.* Crestwood, NY: St. Vladimir's Seminary Press, 1996, 42.

8. Ezekiel 41

9. De Young, Stephen. *Religion of the Apostles: Orthodox Christianity in the First Century*. Chesterton, IN: Ancient Faith Publishing, 2021, 254–55.

10. Eliade, Mircea. *The Sacred & The Profane: The Nature of Religion.* San Diego: Harcourt Brace, 1987, 61.

11. Baggley, *Doors of Perception*, 33.

12. Bucur, Bogdan Gabriel. *Scripture Re-Envisioned: Christophanic Exegesis and the Making of a Christian Bible*. Leiden: Brill, 2019, 189.

13. Kimbrough, S. T. *Orthodox and Wesleyan Scriptural Understanding and Practice*. Crestwood, NY: St. Vladimir's Seminary Press, 2005, 81.

14. Danielou, Jean, and Henri Marrou. *The Christian Centuries: A New History of the Catholic Church, Volume One: The First Six Hundred Years.* New York: McGraw-Hill, 1964, 213.

15. Eliade, Mircea, and Joseph M. Kitigawa. *The History of Religions: Essays in Methodology*. Chicago: University of Chicago Press, 1959, 88.

16. James, William. *The Varieties of Religious Experience*. New York: Simon & Schuster, 1997, 397.

17. Langer, Susanne K. "Logic of Signs and Symbols." In *A Reader in the Anthropology of Religion*, edited by Michael Lambek, 131–38. Malden, MA: Blackwell, 2008, 136.

18. James, William. "The Psychology of Belief." In *Writings, 1878–1899*, by William James, 1021–56. New York: Library of America, 1992, 1042.

19. James, "The Psychology of Belief," 1042.

20. Eliade, Mircea. *Patterns in Comparative Religion*. Lincoln: University of Nebraska Press, 1996, 451.

21. Berger, Peter L. *The Sacred Canopy: Elements of a Sociological Theory of Religion*. New York: Anchor Books, 1967, 24.

22. Sahlins, Marshall. *Islands of History.* Chicago: University of Chicago Press, 1987, 125.

23. Eliade, *Patterns in Comparative Religion*, 453.

24. Doniger, Wendy. *The Implied Spider: Politics and Theology in Myth*. New York: Columbia University Press, 2011, 61.

25. Smith, Wilfred Cantwell. *The Meaning and End of Religion*. Minneapolis, MN: Fortress, 1991, 12.

26. Lewis, I. M. *Ecstatic Religion.* Middlesex and Baltimore, MD: Penguin, 1971, 65.

27. Eliade, *Patterns in Comparative Religion*, 452.

28. Eliade, *Patterns in Comparative Religion*, 446.

29. Eliade, *Patterns in Comparative Religion*, 447.

30. Peterson, Jordan B. *Maps of Meaning: The Architecture of Belief.* New York: Routledge, 1999, 5.

31. Berkeley, George. "The Principles of Human Knowledge." Edited by Jonathan Bennett. Earlymoderntexts.com, 2017, http://www.earlymoderntexts.com/assets/pdfs/berkeley1710.pdf.

32. Kant, *Critique of Pure Reason*, chapter 3.

33. James, *The Psychology of Belief*, 1042.

34. James, *The Psychology of Belief*, 1041.

35. Eliade, *Patterns in Comparative Religion*, 445.

36. Ouspensky, Leonid. *Theology of the Icon, Volume II*. Crestwood, NY: St. Vladimir's Seminary Press, 1992, 512.

37. Peterson, *Maps of Meaning*, 8.

38. Eliade, *Sacred and Profane*, 61.

39. Karant-Nunn, Susan C. *The Reformation of Feeling: Shaping the Religous Emotions in Early Modern Germany*. Oxford: Oxford University Press, 2010, 64.

40. Karant-Nunn, *Reformation of Feeling*, 65.

41. Smith, J. Z., *Map Is Not Territory*. Chicago: University of Chicago Press, 1978, 92.

42. James, *The Psychology of Belief*, 1044.

43. Peterson, *Maps of Meaning*, 9.

44. Peterson, *Maps of Meaning*, 5.

45. Temple, *Icons and the Mystical Origins of Christianity*, 5.

46. Bourdieu, Pierre. *Outline of a Theory of Practice*. Cambridge, UK: Cambridge University Press, 2008, 53.

47. Wallace, Anthony F. C. *Revitalizations and Mazewasys: Essays on Culture Change, Volume 1*. Lincoln: University of Nebraska Press, 2003, 12.

48. Berger, *The Sacred Canopy*, 153.

49. Smith, *Map Is Not Territory*, 143.

50. Peterson, *Maps of Meaning*, xiii.

51. Smith, *Map Is Not Territory*, 144.

52. Peterson, *Maps of Meaning*, xx.

53. Eliade, *Sacred and Profane*, 211.

54. Pageau, Matthieu. *The Language of Creation: Cosmic Symbolism in Genesis.* CreateSpace, 2018, 31.

55. Schmemann, Alexander. *For the Life of the World.* Crestwood, NY: St. Vladimir's Seminary Press, 2018, 174.

56. Maximus the Confessor, *On the Cosmic Mystery of Christ*, 54.

57. Ouspensky, *Theology of Icon*, 462.

58. Schmemann, *For the Life of the World*, 174.

*Chapter 1*

# The Platonic Universe
# and the Cave

To understand Plato's philosophy, we first need to understand how he understood the term philosophy and what it meant to him. The word philosophy comes from two Greek terms, *philo* and *sophy*. *Sophy*, a version of *sophia* (Σοφία) is best understood as wisdom, knowledge, or learning. This is opposed to notions of *doxa* (δόξα) which are teachings, opinions, or traditions. *Doxa* also took on the connotations of worship because it is the revealed tradition that has been learned by the community and is used in worship.[1] *Philo*, a version of *philia* (φιλία), is typically translated as brotherly love. Unlike other forms of love, brotherly love is one that is reciprocal. One loves something or someone and in return gets love back. It is not selfless, nor is it sacrificial, in that one will receive something from their beloved. It is also understood to be a love between equals, in that one party does not condescend to another. Philosophy, etymologically speaking, is a reciprocal love between the philosopher and wisdom itself. Wisdom is loved and prized as something outside the individual and yet something that gives back to the philosopher. The two approach one another as equals and both benefit through the relationship. The term was first credited to Pythagoras, who was once asked if he was a wise man. He responded that he was only a lover of wisdom. Following Pythagoras, ancient Greeks understood their relationship with wisdom as approaching a beloved partner.

The love of wisdom, and the discovery of what exactly wisdom is, was the concern of the early philosophers. In many ways, we can see the earliest philosophers as courting wisdom, learning about wisdom, and how best to woo it. From Thales of Miletus,[2] who is usually identified as the first philosopher, to Pythagoras and the other pre-Socratic philosophers, the questions that they asked of wisdom were metaphysical. What is the nature of the universe? What is its cause? What is it made up of? Later questions of our place in the universe were added to these metaphysical concerns. For Thales, the whole

17

universe was made up of water and was understood as alive. Parmenides tried to understand what actually existed. For him, reality properly understood would have a reason for it, and a good argument could be constructed to prove what is true. Parmenides is credited with introducing the philosophical "proof." Heraclitus believed that what undergirded the universe was a *logos*, but that this *logos* could never be understood. For Pythagoras, everything could be understood through numbers, which held the key to understanding and creation itself. God is symbolized by number as one, a monad. Duality begins creation.[3] This creation is of course imperfect in its complexity. The more complex, the further from perfection. Pythagoras continues by illustrating that through numerical division the immaterial gave way to the material. Richard Temple maintains that "the teachings of Pythagoras aimed to bring man's life into line with cosmic harmony."[4]

In many ways, the metaphysical analysis of these pre-Socratics was not only an attempt to understand the world but also a discussion as to the future orientation of the world, its telos. Metaphysics implied teleology. A telos, or direction for individuals and for the universe itself, was implied in its very formation. For Pythagoras, most clearly there exists a bifurcation of the universe between the spiritual and the material. The introduction of matter was an imposition that limited the unlimited spiritual universe. Pythagoras introduced the notion of the transmigration of souls to help compensate for the gap between the infinite world of numbers and the finite material world. His concerns were for becoming as much as cause.

This division beckons for unity. The material world exists from a more perfect spiritual realm and points toward that preexistent and more perfect reality. For Parmenides and Heraclitus, this meant that the sensory world was based upon an obfuscation or a lie.[5] If the worlds are as disparate as Pythagoras and the others maintained, then what can be done or how should we actually live? Ethical concerns were implied by this cosmology but not spelled out for the pre-Socratics.

Socrates was the first real philosopher to spend less time on metaphysical questions and more on ethical ones. Robert J. O'Connell, S.J., in his work *Plato on the Human Paradox*, maintains that Socrates was primarily interested in defining moral realities.[6] For Socrates, it was less important to know what exactly the universe is, and more important to know how we are to relate to it as such. As we read in Plato's *Phaedrus,* Socrates was skeptical as to how much we could actually know. "People imagine that they know about the nature of things, when they don't know about them, and, not having come to an understanding at first because they think that they know, they end, as might be expected, in contradicting one another and themselves."[7] Good counsel is hard to come by. People often have an overexaggerated view of their own understanding of the way the universe is and how things actually work. Socrates is admired both by Plato and philosophers today because he was open to being proved wrong. To prove he is wrong would dispel him of holding a position that is wrong. Instead of anger at a challenge, he reveled in the experience. Things could be known, and those things could be proven. The goal was not simply knowledge, but action following that knowledge. Wisdom needs to be acted upon.

Even with his eagerness to be proved wrong, Socrates attracted some powerful enemies. Socrates was called a stingray. He was tried and convicted of impiety and being a corrupter of the youth of Athens. Famously, he was ordered to drink hemlock tea as a form of execution when he was seventy. The charge that Socrates liked to confuse people is at least half right. We are told that he had a demon who instructed him. "Demon" did not hold the negative connotation it does for us today. Socrates's demon inspired him and enlightened him. This demon worked through Socrates by way of the dialectic.

In this dialectic, two or more people are engaged in a conversation. They try to understand the nature of a thing or how to act on that thing. Typically, Socrates begins by asking a question. Several answers are given, then a crisis emerges from the answers given. The interlocutor stumbles into the insufficiency of their beliefs. Socrates then presses them more on the fault, and then the answer to the problem is revealed. Throughout these five steps Socrates gets his opponent to confuse himself, whereby he realizes that the only solution is the one that Socrates believes is true. This Socratic method results in the participant teaching themselves. Socrates is not himself a teacher, but a dialogue partner. As Søren Kierkegaard says, Socrates is only the occasion.

> In the Socratic view, every human being is himself the midpoint, and the whole world focuses only on him because his self-knowledge is God-knowledge. Moreover, this is how Socrates comprehends himself, and in his view this is how every human being must interpret himself, and by virtue of that understanding he must approach his relation not to the single individual, always with equal humility and with equal pride.[8]

Socrates's humility was manifest in his ethical concerns. Socrates, like many of the Greek philosophies which followed him, was not only about ideas but application. The term "philosophies of life" is an appropriate reading of the systems following Epicurus, the Cynics, Stoics, and Skeptics. The term applies to the more rational systems of Plato and Aristotle. In the next centuries, the term is less applicable when compared to these others. For Socrates the passions, those impulses which drive us and to which we are subject to, arise out of desire and ignorance. We learn to overcome the passions and not be subject to them.

For Plato, the challenge that arose from the Socratic conception of philosophy was not only those who persecuted his teacher, but also the Sophists. The Sophists were the "practitioners of wisdom" rather than the lovers of it. They used logical techniques similar to Socrates but instead of trying to decipher what was true, they typically tried to dismantle other systems of thought. The Sophist used philosophy to parody or to disprove, to destroy rather than to construct. Gorgias was the greatest of the Sophists and for him we have no knowledge that can be known. Gorgias in fact "proved" that nothing exists, or if anything exists, that it is unknowable. The metaphysical analysis of the pre-Socratics was left with a naked materialism following the sophists. It was devoid of ground and consequence.

Robert O'Connell argues that the philosophical system that we connect with Plato was largely an outgrowth of this tension between Socratic morality and Sophist materialism. The answer comes by reintroducing Pythagorean dualism and providing a correction that harmonizes Pythagoras and Socrates. Plato sought to rectify the relative bifurcation of spirit and matter by introducing morals into the realm of ideas. This is essential because if there is no moral truth then the Socratic mission fails. Philosophy is left hollow and meaningless. Ethics becomes a tyranny against nature and reason, as Nietzsche says in part five of *Beyond Good and Evil*.

Plato accepts and adapts Pythagoras's divided universe. In *Phaedo*, we read that Socrates answers Cebes, "One day I heard someone reading, as he said, from a book of Anaxagoras, and saying that it is Mind [νοῦς] that directs [ὁ διακόσμων] and is the cause [or reason] of everything."[9] For Plato, it is the mind that will then direct us toward an object of knowledge. Andrew Louth presents the notion that while "we say, 'I think, therefore I am,' that is, thinking is an activity I engage in and there must therefore be an I to engage in it; the Greeks would say, 'I think, therefore there is that which I think—to noeta.' What I think is something going on in my head; what the Greek thinks, to noeta, are the objects of thought."[10] As much as our minds engage with a subject, it presupposes that that subject exists outside of our mind. *Theoria*, or contemplation, is the act whereby one engages with a reality beyond oneself. One could identify this outside source as spirit, and interpret this as a form of mysticism, but Plato simply identified the source of this knowledge as ideas. We will often translate this idea as form, or ideals as well. For Plato, man's telos is this *theoria*, this contemplation of the ideas as found in the realm of the spirit as articulated by Pythagoras.

Plato maintains Pythagoras's transmigration of souls as well as his belief in these disparate spheres. For Plato, the soul enters the material body bringing the eternal down to the material. This is of course a traumatic event. The consequence of this trauma is forgetting, or an obfuscation of the perfect vision of truth and beauty. Ideas are known but only vaguely and must be brought to recollection. As we read in *Meno*, the story of the slave boy announcing mathematical proofs without ever being instructed, we know we can access this vision.

Following Pythagoras, our material world is a limited shadow of the infinite world which houses the ideals. These ideals are the forms from which our sense-world emulates. The ideal is akin to the shadow that an object casts. It resembles the source and originates in part from that source, but it is not the source in any real way. What we find admirable in the material world has its essence in one of these forms. Things like beauty, goodness, and even being are all expressions of the world of forms. Different works of Plato emphasize these aspects as having their source in this realm. In *Phaedo*, Plato addresses the nature of being, the good is addressed in the *Republic*, and beauty is found in the *Symposium* and the *Phaedrus*.

Even ideas are shadows manifest upon our material existence. Ideas exist as a model as well as a standard that things measure up against. If one asks an artisan what they are making before it is complete, rarely would one get an answer of confusion. Instead, the artisans have an idea in their mind as to the project they are laboring over. The work is then evaluated by how closely the finished product resembles the image they had as their basis of the project. We too evaluate objects by how closely they resemble our expectation of them. A chair is called deficient if it does not provide a suitable place to sit; a tree is called useless if it fails to be either aesthetically or functionally useful. The realm of ideas can also be understood as the realm of archetypes. Plato argues that these perfect forms, the ideal, these archetypes, exist. In fact, we could never evaluate imperfection if these standards did not somewhere exist, and if we did not have at least a vague connection to them.

Our connection to the idea is not effortless. We must labor to see them. Part of the labor is in removing our subjective position to identify the objective reality that lays behind the imperfect material existence. While we may all have individual preferences, our separate taste does not equal the true, the good, the beautiful. At the same time our contrary tastes toward the true, good, and beautiful also let us know that these concepts exist as the common standard to which we evaluate these impressions.

Furthermore, the source of these ideals is not understood through how pious someone may be. In the *Phaedrus*, Plato refers to the realm of the forms as a place above the heavens.[11] Louth identifies that for Plato this realm is the divine world and the dwelling place of the gods.[12] Yet Plato does not connect the ideals with the Greek gods. Instead, the gods too dwell in this place and are in some ways subject to the forms as we are. We see that the gods are subject in the basic argument Plato articulates in the *Euthyphro*. "Is the pious loved by the gods because it is pious or is it pious because it is loved by the gods?"[13] Socrates, in this dialogue, shows that even the gods are subject to the ideas. This dilemma serves as a challenge to many divine command theorists today. Though the modern theist likely places God as the source of goodness, what Neoplatonists would identify as the One which goodness and this realm emanates from.

A cursory reading of Plato on the Greek gods does not leave anyone with the conviction that Plato was particularly devout. He clearly did not esteem these gods. The Greek gods are not paragons of virtue. When a modern audience reads of the escapades of Zeus or Apollo, they are shocked by the level of debauchery that was modeled by these divine figures. Similarly, when looking at the bloodlust of Ares and Athena, we see less justice than savage brutality. Socrates thought little different than we might. For him the gods were persons with minds and memories and wills of their own. They were powerful but possessed all the failings of the rest of us. Anyone reading Homer, the chief mythologist of the Greeks, can see that morality is not a concept inherent to the gods. If we rely upon the gods to be the source of our morality, we are left as unmoored as we were when finding the source of ethics within the sophists.

Consequently, we return to the concept of moral truth as the basis for Plato's philosophical system and the realm of ideas populating the material world with representations of itself. If we are to accept the ethics of Socrates and the worldview of Pythagoras, we must include in that immaterial world of ideas concepts such as truth, beauty, justice, and the cardinal virtues. Plato's cosmology, or an adaptation of it, is also necessary to some extent for anyone who wishes to advance a deontological view of normative ethics. A strict materialism can allow for the desire to advance a consequentialist model, but if something is inherently wrong it must have as its basis something that exists outside the self. Plato's solution is that these moral absolutes do exist, that we have access to them, but that we do not control them. O'Connell concludes that for Plato "those Ideals were real because they had to be real, and they had to be real if our universe was to make moral sense."[14]

With Plato's conception of the ideals so connected with morality, one would assume an exhaustive system in place to live a moral existence. Yet if we read the *Ring of Gyges*, Plato advocates for a form of ethical egoism. Charitably one could argue that Plato instead says that by our default we are psychological egoists. Plato's Academy is not as holistic as Cynicism, Epicureanism, or Stoicism in addressing the concerns of our material life. These philosophical schools have different answers to how we should live our lives, but they also are known for their concern with the practical and the mundane. Plato, and later Aristotle, concern their thoughts with governance and social formation. For Plato, this is to conform the material with the ideal.

Instead of a primary focus on practical concerns, Plato calls his adherents to ultimate contemplation of these forms. The concept of *theoria*, contemplation, becomes the solution to overcoming this great divide. *Theoria* is therefore not just thinking, rather it is a form of mysticism. We see this expressed in *Theaetetus* when Socrates states, "a man should make all haste to escape from earth to heaven; and escape means becoming as like God as possible; and a man becomes like God when he becomes just and pious, with understanding."[15] *Theoria* is a form of escape. It is an abandonment of the material world and participating in the virtues.

Louth connects Platonic *theoria* with mysticism by drawing a number of obvious parallels. First man lives in a world that he does not properly belong to. In the *Phaedo*, Plato argues that the soul shares its origin and identity among the forms. Further Plato maintains that the body exists in service to the soul and the real identity of a man is in the soul. Yet the body is also a prison for the soul. Plato's conception of the body is as a separate being from that of the soul. The soul is not simply the animating spirit of the body but something distinct from the body. Upon death, these disparate beings that were forcibly united are separated from one another. This of course is the goal for Plato. To liberate from the material realm, from the body and to return to the pure soul-ideal realm.

To return to the realm of ideas, the soul must purify itself from this world. Morality exists as the medium for liberation, and contemplation is the act whereby one discovers what is true and is capable of living morally. Plato differed with other Socratics concerning how one can be moral or not. Antisthenes believed that one could learn to be moral, Plato did not. For Plato one does not learn to be moral but connects with the virtues which exist in the realm of the forms. If one is born with an insufficient connection, nothing can help them to become moral. If one is sufficiently connected to the virtues then one must contemplate what is already known to them.

One cannot learn morality, but they can meditate on morals. Contemplation in all its forms, including morality, is the key to liberating the soul from the material world. Contemplation serves as the shortcut to this virtuous life, as greater participation in the realm of ideas liberates the soul from the concerns of the material body. Since the realm of ideas comes from a nondescript divine source and it is the manner in which union, even granting Plato's limited notion of union, is achieved, *theoria* is akin to a mystical encounter with the source.[16]

*Theoria* is mysticism because of the mystical conception of the soul. For Plato, this again grounds morality and telos with Pythagoras. Our world contains more than what is observable; it is more than material existence, but this mysticism is still a solitary mysticism. There is not a community that embodies *theoria*. It is not a moral community, as Émile Durkheim understands religion. Even the Academy is not this community in the sense that spiritual liberation from material form is shared. The divine realm of ideas is also not for Plato personified or shared with others. Early on in the *Republic*, Plato has Socrates give a vision to the masses to explain why some of them are inherently better than others, though they came from the same stock.

> You are, all of you in this community, brothers. But when god fashioned you, he added gold in the composition of those of you who are qualified to be Rulers (which is why their prestige is greatest); he put silver in the Auxiliaries, and iron and bronze in the farmers and other workers.[17]

The guardians and rulers are inherently different than the laborers. Instead of brotherly affection where people are treated as equals, Plato views the relationships that exist among people as fostering a *polis* that allows for *theoria*. It is not a community where obligations are shared and one's future is dependent upon their relationship with others.

For Plato, we interact not as a community dependent upon one another, but as a city-state. The goals of a city-state are different than the goals of a religious community. Justice is central. Justice should be understood and things being in their right place. Order is central to justice. Reason is necessary to know what order should look like. To ensure justice and moral standards are upheld, Plato, in the *Republic*, advocates for the governance of the city-state to be done by philosopher kings. After all, Plato tells us that "those who can reach beauty itself and see it as it is in itself are likely to be few."[18] It is therefore these select men who best understand the ideals, who are the best to govern the people. The closer to the ideal, the more just a society. Plato maintains that the average person has a limited conception of the ideal, and that the philosopher is the obvious choice to best bring the ideal into material existence. This naturally will create the most just society. As the goal of society is justice, the only reasonable way to produce a healthy society is the philosopher king. Louth explains Plato's position by telling us that, "A man who has seen the truth like that is the man who can help his fellow men, help them to order their lives."[19]

## THE CAVE

Having established the distinction between those qualified to be the rulers and the auxiliaries on one side and the workers on the other, Plato, at the heart of the *Republic*, gives three analogies. The first is the Simile of the Sun, then the Story of the Dividing Line. Finally, we are given the Allegory of the Cave. The purpose for these analogies is twofold. First, Plato uses these analogies to reaffirm the different quality of people. This leads us to the conclusion that it is the philosopher's right and duty to rule. Second, Plato reveals his philosophical construction of the universe through these analogies. We have already learned that for Plato the world is bigger than mere appearances, and that only a select few are capable of grasping this broader world, but this point is driven home in these three analogies.

The first analogy is the Simile of the Sun. Here the simile compares the form of the good to the sun. Plato draws a connection between objects in the visible world and their corollary in the realm of ideas. In the observable world, the sun is the source of light and growth, which in turn allows objects to be seen when combined with the faculties of the eye to produce sight. In the realm of the forms, the form itself, in this case the good, is the source of reality and truth. The form provides intelligibility to the objects. These forms, when combined with the power of knowing in the mind, produce knowledge. Through *theoria*, one returns to the forms and is a lover of wisdom. As Plato says, "Then what gives the objects of knowledge their truth and the knower's mind the power of knowing is the form of the good."[20]

For both the sun and the forms, the outside stimulus is internalized. There are two key ideas that must harmonize for any concept to be internalized following Plato. The first concerns the power of the outside source. Plato chooses the sun and the good because they are easily perceivable. Second is the issue of reception. The sun remains luminescent during the day but is dim or absent at night. Similarly, the ideas, including the good, are easy to recognize if one loves wisdom and seeks after it. For those who do not love wisdom, whose mind is clouded, the good is less easy to see. Both the sun and the good exist on their own but can be clouded by the recipient. The sun allows for sight and the ideas allows for knowledge. Later Neoplatonists will trace a similar trajectory in explaining how the forms themselves are brought into existence and how they relate to us.

The second analogy is the Story of the Dividing Line. With the dividing line, Plato sets up four divisions of how we understand objects. The four categories are intelligence, reason, belief, and illusion. The line divides the intelligible from the visible, or the forms from their material counterpart. The visible world consists of physical things and shadows and images. From the physical items themselves we have beliefs, and from the shadows we have illusion. Both belief and illusion provide the basis of *doxa* or opinions. These opinions are not incorrect knowledge but limited knowledge. Likewise, from the realm of the forms we have a division between the pure form and the shadow of the form. The shadow is what we can gather through the reasoning process, while the pure form is the basis for intelligence as expressed through dialectic. Dialectic is the most superior form of reasoning because "the whole procedure involves nothing in the sensible world, but moves solely through forms to forms, and finishes with forms."[21] Both dialectic and reasoning correspond to the concept of knowledge (episteme). While Plato's four categories of knowledge consists of a clear hierarchy, what we see is a progressive division through a form of obfuscation. The visible world is a confused copy of the intelligible realm.

These two analogies set the stage for the Analogy of the Cave. Plato has already demonstrated that different realms exist, that we learn through a progression from the forms to the sensible world. He then uses this last analogy to illustrate the goal of *theoria*, contemplation that exists and how it is then incumbent upon those who achieve liberation to return to lead the polis. The Allegory of the Cave therefore is a demonstration of Plato's entire philosophical venture of uniting Pythagoras with Socrates, preserving morality with a realm of forms that is clouded by layers of ignorance and slavery to one's passional nature. The allegory provides the telos of Plato's philosophy and the ethical requirements of life to achieve contemplative meditation once liberated from material existence.

The analogy opens by Socrates (Plato) asking Glaucon to imagine an underground chamber, a cave. This cave has a long entrance open to where there is daylight at the source but not recognized at the depths of the cave. Furthermore, we are asked to imagine men who are held prisoner in the depths of the cave and have been fettered so they cannot turn their heads to the side or look back toward the mouth of the cave. In front of them is a curtain which will be the only thing these unfortunate prisoners can see. Behind them is a fire, and between the fire and the prisoners is a road. The location of the prisoners, screen, fire, and road provides the prisoners with the only variation that exists in their mundane existence. Shadows are cast upon the curtain and as they move and interact. The prisoners perceive a puppet show and assume that it is real. Sounds that they hear from behind them are credited to the shadows, so convincing we are told that "in every way they would believe that the shadows of the objects we mentioned were the whole truth."[22]

Then Plato asks us to imagine what would happen if one of the prisoners was released from their bonds. When unfettered they are compelled to stand and turn around. Of course, "all these actions would be painful and he would be too dazzled to see properly the objects of which he used to see the shadows."[23] Even seeing the fire and the road would be uncomfortable. Liberation would not even be desirable. This prisoner is then forcibly dragged out of the cave and into the sunlight. This too would be painful. "When he emerged into the light his eyes would be so dazzled by the glare of it that he wouldn't be able to see a single one of the things he was now told were real."[24]

The bright light of the sun becomes indescribable and objects around him unknowable. Any explanation results in the prisoner sounding like a fool. Once familiar with the light and the unapproachable being approached, we are told the prisoner must return to the cave. The reason for this is "is not the special welfare of any particular class in our society, but of the society as a whole."[25] This will create a government where there are not struggles for political power, and where those with the least enthusiasm to govern will govern with tranquility. Plato seeks to create a government opposed to the current one where "the state whose rulers are eager to rule [are] the worst."[26] The philosopher king, who through contemplation arrives at a place of enlightened apathy, is the best one to govern. "For only then will you have government by the truly rich, those, that is, whose riches consist not of gold, but of the true happiness of a good and rational life."[27]

Now to contemplate the cave itself. Temple tells us that for Plato, as with the Pythagoreans, the symbol of the cave itself was a mystical medium whereby "enigmatic truths could be conveyed."[28] The cave by its very definition is an earthen body. It is swallowed up by matter and its concerns are only for the material. It is dark, and knowledge of what surrounds us in the cave is limited and often erroneous. The mission of anyone in a cave is to be freed, just as Plato advocates that the mission is to free our souls from the imprisonment in the material body. For both the cave as well as Plato's conception of our body, the realm revealed to us by sight is little more than a prison. Just like the prisoners who were fettered for their entire life, we too are constrained by believing that what we see in the sensible world is the totality of the world that exists. Socrates tells Glaucon that the light of the fire in the prison should be likened to the sun, "And you won't go wrong if you connect the ascent into the upper world and the sight of the objects there with the upward progress of the mind into the intelligible region."[29]

Connecting the cave to the earlier allegory of the dividing line we see the layers of confusion, where shadows are understood as real and only hint at what reality truly is. What we think of as real is only an offhanded way of referring to what we are used to; reality is far from it. Louth tells us that the purpose behind the Allegory of the Cave speaks to reality itself. "The soul, which really belongs to the divine realm of the Forms or Ideas, has made itself at home in this world of unreality revealed to us through the senses. Plato's concern, then, is with the soul's search for true reality."[30]

True reality is only understood when the restraints that bound us are released. This awakening is where we realize that we have confused *doxa* with *episteme*, opinion with real knowledge. Once we realize that our understanding was based upon convention and not deduction, we begin the process of learning based upon this corrected assumption. Louth's analysis of the cave leans upon Plato's *Phaedo*, where "the man who really wishes to attain to knowledge of reality must seek to purify himself—to purify himself from the body and become pure in himself."[31] To put the world back in order, Plato calls for moral purification following the chief virtues of justice, courage, prudence, and temperance. Each of these virtues requires wisdom. To know what is just, one must first understand how things have been wronged, what things are put out of place. Courage is not foolhardiness, but conviction based upon an understanding of the proper order of things. Prudence is choosing the correct course of action, and temperance is knowing how much to engage in any thing. In other words, the virtues are the what and the how of *sophia*, of wisdom, comprising knowledge episteme and action praxis, toward our telos that is *theoria*.

Along with moral refinement, one must have intellectual purification to be a lover of wisdom and to achieve this state of *theoria*. With both moral and intellectual faculties properly attuned toward the realm of ideas, beauty becomes one's guide. In the *Symposium*, we read that the form of beauty is the brother of beauty found in any manifestation. "Beginning from these beautiful things always to go up with the aim of reaching that beauty."[32] For Plato the realm of the ideas is not only manifest in material items to judge their relative value between an image and the archetype, but also in otherwise abstract qualities. Beauty is a form, just as the good is a form, as is the true. Through the beautiful, true, and good we have knowledge of the forms and participate in them. Louth adds that for Plato, "The Good is unknowable, and the soul can only touch it, or be united with it."[33] The actual form itself is beyond full comprehension, but through contemplation, *theoria*, one is capable of being united to it.

*Theoria* is the telos for Plato. This is the end of dialectic as the allegory of the dividing line illustrated. The goal is to remain entirely in the realm of thought and not based upon observation. *Theoria* is achieved only by engagement with the forms. One must rid themselves of concerns for this life. Plato points out that while we have grown accustomed to the minimal light of the cave, to the shadowy world paraded in front of us, we are unaware of what is real. In the cave all we can hope for is *doxa*, not episteme. When we are brought out of the cave we are blinded. The sun, the forms, are too bright for us. Yet persistence on the surface allows for contemplation to take root. It is only through continual training, best practiced with the use of dialectic, that the mind can focus on what is real and not on appearances. For those still in the cave the appearances seem normal. The one who returns to tell others about the light, about a world populated by color and texture, is seen as a madman.

For Plato, this perceived lunatic is the only one who truly knows the nature of things. They are the only one who can rule justly. They are the philosopher king. Their duty is to rule. They must return to the cave. They do not return out of love for their fellow convicts, as they know that they will be disparaged and treated poorly. Undoubtedly Plato saw the duty of Socrates and his premature death as flowing from the same illumination. The duty comes not from love but because they are simply the only one who can accomplish the goal. The task must be done, and they must be the one to do it. By returning to the material concerns, they demonstrate the validity of their knowledge. The virtues are not only about what to know, but what to do; one must act. Having emerged from the shadows, they must act upon the insights they received. To do otherwise is a rejection of the truth. It does not matter if one is successful or scandalized.

Plato's Allegory of the Cave, as understood in its proper context, is a call for action. This action is first to be aware that what we perceive is only shadows. A shadow has a connection with the truth but is only vaguely connected. We must move beyond perception to the prototype, the originator of the shadow. This will bring us closer and closer to the world which exists outside of ourselves. To connect this concept to the icon, one should learn that what is observable is not always what is understood as real. Shadows on a screen have a source. If one was free to turn their head and know that there is something there that is the cause of that image, a greater world would unfold. Plato is not calling to reject the images, but to look toward the source of those images, to understand the color and texture that exists at its source, to know the quality of a thing and not only that a thing exists.

## PHILOSOPHICAL TREATMENT OF
## PLATO AND THE CAVE

Philosophers have returned time and time again to Plato's cave and the ideas that can be found there. Different concepts can be mined out of this cave, and different lessons can be applied from a careful reading of Plato. Probably the greatest use of the Allegory of the Cave in modern philosophy is from Martin Heidegger. Heidegger, in his work *The Essence of Truth*, expands on Plato's Allegory of the Cave and what it can reveal to us about truth as such. For Heidegger, Plato's Allegory of the Cave is less about the rightful place of philosopher kings, or about the realm of ideals and the material world. It was not about synthesizing Socrates and Pythagoras in a bid to maintain a place for moral absolutes against the sophists. Instead, Heidegger's treatment of the cave is about the very notion of truth.

Heidegger opens his work with the question "Truth: what is that? The answer to the question 'what is that?' brings Us to the 'essence' of a thing."[34] For Plato, the essence is the form; a chair is identifiable as a chair because it contains "chairness." Heidegger responds that we discover what is universal by comparing particulars.[35] We understand through analysis of many what is true, and therefore what is correct. When we affirm that a particular thing is that thing which universally exists, Heidegger asserts,

We thus encounter something rather peculiar: not only do we know particular truths, but we also already know what truth is. Therefore, we already know the essence of truth. It is not just that we know accidentally and incidentally, as well as particular truths, also the essence of truth, but clearly we must necessarily already know the essence.[36]

We know the essence of a thing because we were able to identify an object not as a particular item, rather we identify the particular through its essence. Heidegger returns again to an essence which must exist outside of the object. While not identifying this as a form, idea, or ideal, he tells us that "Essence and essence-hood are also in this respect unintelligible."[37] Things are true because they have the essence of truth, even though we do not understand why we somehow know it to be self-evident.

This leads Heidegger to the next question. If it is self-evident to us, "Who are we then? How is it that come to regard ourselves as the court of appeal for deciding what is or is not self-evident?"[38] For Heidegger, we are united with the thing, with the object, with the claim of truth. There is unity already present even if we are unaware. We are justified in having the truth be self-evident because it is so. To clarify this, Heidegger addresses the Greek term for the truth (αλήθεια) and translates it as "unhiddenness." "Something true is αληθές, unhidden."[39]

According to Heidegger, for the Greeks, something that is true is something which is no longer concealed. It has been removed from the hidden world and given over to us. Something that is true does not take on a new character but loses one. It loses the feature of being hidden. For both Heidegger and for ourselves, "It is curious that 'true' means what something no longer has."[40] Truth then takes on a poetical character. It gains a relation to us by leaving its former relationship to itself.

Given the poetical nature of truth, Heidegger sees it as fitting that an allegory was used to reveal the truth, to unhide the concept that Plato tried to advance. Plato speaks in allegories and in so doing places us before a sensory image. This is why Plato speaks of the unhidden, τό αληθές, not just unhidden alone. It is objectified with the definite article. Heidegger states that, "The image is never intended to stand for itself alone, but indicates That something is to be understood, providing a clue as to what this is."[41] It is through the symbol, the bringing together two disparate ideas, that the truth is unhidden. The only way to unhide the object is by connecting it to another; this allows us to approach it.

Turning to the cave itself, Heidegger directs his attention to the fact that the prisoners have no relationship with the light. It is behind them, and they are unfamiliar with either its source or what differentiates it from the darkness. Furthermore, the prisoners do not have a choice in what is seen. They take what is presented and therefore are isolated not only from one another but themselves as well. The Allegory of the Cave takes on the existential character of knowing not only what is true in general, or true about the world, but also what is true about ourselves.

The first stage is this hiddenness where the prisoners have no relationships, and no distinctions are made. The next state is the unbinding. The shackles are removed. Heidegger asserts that now unbound, the prisoner sees the shadows as more unhidden than the world which is now being presented to them. While devoid of conscious choice and relations, the removal of the shackles produces a choice wherein the prisoner defaults to the shadow, even though it is not real.

> The unhidden can therefore be more or less unhidden. This does not mean more or less in numerical terms (that more shadows are unhidden), but that the things themselves are more unhidden, the things which the now unshackled prisoner, as he turns around, is supposed to see.[42]

Unhidden-ness then is not a static state but a relational one. It has levels, as the truth does. The whole truth varies from a partial truth, though each may have some elements the same. Heidegger asserts that the prisoner understands that beings exist in more or less the same ways as well. "There are 'beings that are more beingful.' Closeness and distance to beings changes the beings themselves."[43]

Beginning the process of relationships, the prisoner has a choice. This is the beginning of emancipation. The prisoner still is not free. They are not familiar with the truth; it is still hidden from them. The quality of themselves and others as beings is still rudimentary and needing further work. Heidegger points out that simply removing the binds, the prisoner sought its confinement once again. Liberation failed.

Genuine liberation is not external but internal. "Removal of the shackles is thus not genuine emancipation, for it remains external and fails to penetrate to man in his ownmost self."[44] For Heidegger, liberation can only exist when it is done for oneself and comes from their own essence.[45] This is achieved by exiting the cave and seeing the light of day. The sun becomes the source, and no artificial light is used. Once the prisoner has exited the cave, there is no longer any mention of trying to return to the shackles. Freedom is understood.

It is likely understood, because unlike the fire, the sun is all encompassing. The light of the sun is not managed or designed for utility; instead, it is brutal. "Attaining what is now unhidden involves violence, thus ἀγανακτεῖν, resistance, such that the one to be freed is forced up along a rugged path. The ascent demands work and exertion, causing strain and suffering."[46] This vicious emergence requires persistence. The sun blinds, and nothing is known. Then through determination all things become clear. Just as we read Socrates dialectical encounters were violent, but through persistence the truth was arrived at.

Heidegger then addresses Plato's own interpretation and pauses on the notion of idea and its relation to the light and to freedom. Plato calls for understanding beyond the shadows. This is where ideas are. The shadows are those things which daily occupy us. "Seeing is now a perceiving."[47] We are not only receiving what is given but engaging with the idea inherent in what is around us. "'Idea' is therefore the look of something as something."[48] "The look, ιδέα, thus gives *what* something presences as, i.e., what a thing *is*, its *being*."[49] Idea, beingness, and presence all exist when perceived, when taken in, and when unhidden.

While the prisoners knew nothing of the light, freedom is understood as being in this light. Heidegger tells us that it is not simply getting loose but stepping out into the light. "Unshackledness has no content in itself. He who has just been unshackled becomes insecure and helpless, is no longer able to cope."[50] It is therefore an imposition as well. "Genuine becoming free is a projective binding of oneself—not a simple release from shackles, but a binding of oneself for oneself, such that one remains always bound in advance."[51] There is always something to which we are attached—it is either for the illusion or the truth. For Heidegger, the truth is wrapped up in self-liberation and ideas inherent to the self. The more we are engaged with ourselves, the more we are free from others that constrain us. In many ways, both Heidegger and Plato do not place a priority upon relations with others as a key to freedom. Instead, it is a personal obligation to oneself or to the unhidden-ness of truth itself.

Heidegger interprets art as an expression of this unhidden-ness. Art, and in particular poetry, is the insight for the possible. "Poetry makes beings more beingful."[52] For Heidegger, knowledge is for beings and art in its various forms reveal this character; it reveals beings and ideas. It is the expression of the truth as such. Heidegger returns the question posed at the beginning of his work. What makes one qualified to assert something as self-evidently as true? It is self-evident because we have bound it to ourselves, removing the constraints of ignorance and choosing instead to rely upon ourselves. "Man is that being which understands being and exists on the basis of this understanding, i.e., among other things, comports itself to beings as the unhidden."[53] For Heidegger, this definition of truth is the confrontation that Plato engages with the whole of Western tradition.[54]

When addressing the return to the cave, Heidegger declares that we turn back to where we previously were, to what we know, to confirm tangible results. We return to ourselves as liberators of ourselves. In doing so we face death itself. The death comes from the cave-dwellers, who are not masters of themselves, yet impose conformity upon others. For Heidegger, "The philosopher must remain solitary, because this is what he is according to his nature."[55] One is alone to affirm idea and being over illusion and hiddenness. Truth then empowers, unhiding other ideas. Freedom is understood as progressive liberation. Truth begets truth, freedom begets freedom, even while it courts death.[56]

Like Plato, Heidegger affirms that truth is not isolated to the realm of thought but requires action. One must return to the hidden and unmask it. This is the telos to which freedom and truth abide. Once one has been illumined by the sun, they must make the hidden things visible. This is done first to themselves and then to others. Heidegger points out that knowledge corresponds to the sense of seeing, not any other. One perceives what is true and understand it as such. "We know that Plato, like the Greeks in general, understands genuine knowledge as seeing, θεωρεῖν (put together from θέα, look, and ὁρᾶν). Authentic knowledge of beings in their being is symbolized through sensory seeing, the seeing of the eyes."[57]

One sees the good. One sees being, ideas, and the truth. Heidegger concludes that "the proposition is true insofar as it conforms to something already true, i.e., to a being that is unhidden in its being. Truth in this sense of correctness presupposes unhiddenness."[58] Heidegger's treatment of Plato focuses on the conception of truth as unhidden-ness. This theme of revelation transforms ideas and beings insofar as they are revealed and seen. This also reveals the essence of man as a being which unveils to discover. There exists with Heidegger's treatment of Plato a form of Gnosticism, that the truth is experienced alone and is secret. While one may share it with others, like Plato, this is not done for their benefit but for oneself. Truth is not communal; it is not shared as something intimate but understood as a secret puzzle which one has uncoded to isolate themselves in a different way than before. The prisoner exchanges one prison for another, following Heidegger. They were alone while fettered and then separate themselves by binding themselves to themselves and not to others. One is not a disciple, or a devotee, one is alone. This freedom is tragic in its own way.

While Heidegger may be the most prominent philosopher of late to analyze, criticize, and utilize Plato's philosophy, he built upon a long history of philosophers. The first critic of Plato was his student Aristotle. Untold numbers of works have addressed the differences between Plato and Aristotle, whose system is superior, and which corresponds closer to our conception of reality and religious predispositions. For our purposes, Aristotle's criticisms of Plato come down to a few important points.

The first and most damning critique is that for Aristotle there is no world of ideals. For Plato, the reality of this realm was central to affirm a basis for morality and any true conception of meaning. For Aristotle, ideals are composites of abstract conceptions. Abstract ideas do not imply a reality that must truly exist. If we believe that these forms actually exist and give rise to manifestations in the observable world, we necessitate a useless duplication of reality. The contention that the sensible world participated in the realm of ideas is only an empty metaphor for Aristotle. Any appeal to the Pythagorean creation through the one and many, not only reduces metaphysics to mathematics, but also is something observable, thus not a realm independent from the material, but dependent upon it.

For Aristotle, we begin with what we observe. This was a vague copy of a copy for Plato but is the ground from which all knowledge could be derived from for Aristotle. Aristotle contends that we infer the nature of reality from the particulars, and from the items themselves. While we have chairs, and trees, and beauty, we do not have "chair-ness," "tree-ness," or beauty that exists independent from the person who characterizes something as beautiful. None of these qualities, nor any other, exist in a realm on their own. Instead, we abstract the idea of chair, tree, or beauty from the experiences we have of various items that we have identified as a chair, tree, or beautiful. Logic becomes the meaning of relating the general to particulars. Substances possess attributes in greater or lesser amounts.

Aristotle does not deny that something may be more or less of something, only that that quality does not exist independently or necessarily on its own. Aristotle agrees with Plato that things which change are composed of different things in different amounts. Aristotle's philosophy then follows from an argument of things existing in potentiality and in actuality. Movement between this is the growth of an item, the fulfillment of its telos. Since the quality of an item is inherent to it as well, Aristotle develops a distinction between those things which belong properly to an item and those things that exist as an accident. The distinction between substance and accidents, potentiality and actuality, challenged the metaphysical landscape that Plato advanced.

The final critique that Aristotle lays against Plato as it applies to this study concerns the soul. For Plato, the soul exists independently of the body. It exists as a bridge between the material and ideal. Since Aristotle accepted composite natures of things, the soul too could exist as a result of the composite nature of our body. There needs not be a substantial form to which the body is representative of. Rather the various elements of the body are arranged and organized into a thing which we call a person, just as matter is organized into a shape and purpose that we can identify as a chair.

Despite Aristotle's critiques, Plato's broad philosophical system dominated Hellenic thought, and then both migrated into the background. Today, we envision these two philosophers entering into a battle on these grounds and represented by different philosophers. Yet for the Romans who succeeded the Greeks, Plato and Aristotle seemed too otherworldly. Their focus was on concepts that broadly did not impact the day to day lives of average Romans. Instead, other philosophical systems grew ascendent such as Epicurean Hedonism, and Stoicism. These rival systems addressed the passions and provided a framework for life as a whole. It was only a select few who prized speculation that held onto the philosophy of Plato and Aristotle.

Of course, those speculative philosophers turned time and time again to Plato, especially in the fourth century, as well as the twelfth. In the twelfth century, the question of universals and how they should be understood reared its head. In many ways the various arguments on universals was a replay of the philosophical duel between Aristotelians and Platonists. The question was much the same as we have sought to clarify here. How much does our mental understanding of a thing indicate that there is a substance or form behind it?

In the eleventh century, with Anselm, the Platonic position was expressed, namely that grammar implied ideas and if the statement was true than the idea necessarily has a source for its truth. For Anselm, this inferred those ideas exists somewhere independent from the mind of the observer. This applied to universals as well as particulars. As such, the statement "Socrates is a man," if understood to be true, holds that not only is there a particular person called Socrates, but that there is a particular thing which we identify as man. Of course, Socrates exists, and he has a right to his name and his individual identity. The same is true about man, or humanity, or human nature. Since the statement is true, universals must exist in some capacity.

William of Champeaux, the founder of the School at St. Victor, proposed an extreme realism. For William, the nature of a thing was essentially and wholly present in every individual. Every person possesses all of humanity, just as every tree possesses the totality of "treeness." When challenged, Champeaux modified his position by adding an "indefferenter" so each individual has the status of the whole even though it may not contain the entirety of the whole. Champeaux, along with Anselm, maintained a Platonic conception of universals, one existing outside the thing, and the other existing within every particular thing, thereby universalizing its presence.

Peter Abelard, insisting on individual distinctions, was the one who forced Champeaux to change his position. For Abelard, it is impossible to predicate a thing about a thing. Abelard argued that only a name can be applied to a group. He proposed that the universal is a vocal sound (*vox*) and is then changed into a mental word (*sermo*). While the mental representation is more indistinct than the particular thing, it is used to express the nature of a thing. The mind makes these connections and classifies them together. For Abelard, there are no universal concepts. There are only inferences and words. Abelard is called the first nominalist by some. Properly speaking, he is the first great nominalist philosopher of the West.

Bernard of Clairvaux, who constantly challenged Abelard, returned to a more Platonic understanding of universals. In addition to God, eternal ideas of all created beings exist in the mind of God. Created ideas which are based upon these eternal ideas also exist, as does formless matter. Gilbert de la Porrée advanced Bernard's position a bit too far and hinted that all created things are a part of God. To avoid charges of Pantheism, he incorporated Boethius' distinction between substance and subsistence. Boethius was closer to Aristotle. Universals are subsistences but not existing substances. By the middle of the twelfth century, this middle ground dominated Europe. It incorporated some of Aristotle's critiques but maintained a largely Platonic conception of universals.

The distinctions concerning universals lasted roughly fifty years, at which time medieval philosophers looked less at Aristotle and Plato. That is until a resurgence of Aristotle emerged in the thirteenth century and philosophers wrestled with how much Aristotle could be synthesized into the philosophy of Western Europe. Largely the debate took place among the medicant orders of the Franciscans which included Roger Bacon and Bonaventure, and the Dominicans, including Albert the Great and Aquinas. Both Bonaventure and Aquinas introduced Aristotle to the University of Paris. Aristotle dominated the concerns of the thirteenth century.

When nominalism resurfaced in the fourteenth century, Aristotle was reinterpreted as the "old way." Still Plato remained and returned during the Italian Renaissance when Marsilio Ficino published the complete works of Plato in 1484. Nicholas of Cusa also connected Plato and Aquinas, attempting once again a middle way where Plato and Aristotle could be held together with an uneasy truce.

In the nineteenth century, some other Platonic ideas resurfaced. Schleiermacher produced his monumental translation of Plato into German. Kierkegaard also turned his attention in *Philosophical Fragments* to the conception of truth as held in *Meno*. Quoting *Meno*, Kierkegaard states that "a person cannot possibly seek what he knows, and just as impossibly, he cannot seek what he does not know, for what he knows he cannot seek, since he knows it, and what he does not know he cannot seek, because, after all, he does not even know what he is supposed to seek."[59] Kierkegaard's reading of Socrates communicates the fixed nature of knowledge. One cannot seek out knowledge; they cannot learn. They already possess all knowledge that they will ever have. Kierkegaard posits that "the truth is not introduced into him but as in him."[60] Everyone possesses the truth because they have experienced it before. For the Socratic position advanced by Kierkegaard, the truth is recalled. It is recalled from this eternal return.

Later Nietzsche expanded upon this idea in Plato's *Meno*, focusing on the idea of the eternal return. Nietzsche did not address the concept that ideas must exist outside of the self, nor how they are accessible through the faculties of the soul. Instead, Nietzsche saw the myth of eternal return inherent to the slave's recollection. The concept of eternal return poses the question of how we would respond if this life of ours was lived an infinite number of times before and will be lived an infinite number of times following. Nietzsche describes this life as "nothing new in it, but every pain and every joy and every thought and every sigh, and all the unspeakably small and great in thy life must come to thee again, and all in the same series and sequence."[61] He then asks if we would look favorably upon this life or would we ardently look for the end. The myth of the eternal return therefore has ethical ramifications. While we are free to do whatever we would like, our actions will continually laud or haunt us.

Eliade speaks of the eternal return in his work bearing that name, as well as in *The Sacred and the Profane*. In the later work, Eliade tells us that for the Pythagoreans, Stoics, and Platonists nothing was lost or created but existed within a cycle. In this cycle, "the same situations are reproduced that have already been produced in previous cycles and will be reproduced in subsequent cycles—ad infinitum."[62] In the former work, Eliade also treats the symbol in the eternal return. Here he maintains that all sacrality is a repetition of sacred creation. Just as all sacred points are simultaneously the highest point on earth, the navel, and a transformed profane space, all acts done in this sacred place are temporally transformed. All sacred rites participate in and are present in the acts of creation whereby chaos becomes cosmos.[63]

More recently Plato's work and the Analogy of the Cave is used in the realm of philosophical psychology and other self-help work. In his work connecting Plato to overcoming our imposed limitations, Ran Lahav suggests that the prisoners in Plato's cave are like us "because we too are enclosed in a limited understanding of the world, and we too assume that this is what reality is like."[64] The goal is to step out of the cave and use the skills developed as a philosopher to release others. Lahav does not call for a philosopher king but a philosopher therapist as it were. The cave is imposed by rigid patterns that are either psychologically or socially constructed. In this reading, the philosophy of Plato is therefore practical not speculative.

Plato's philosophical system to which the Allegory of the Cave belongs has found many different iterations since *The Republic* was written. Plato's attempt to explain a metaphysical universe populated by a material sensible world and a world of forms served the purpose to ground morality. Plato saw the assaults of sophists who increasingly doubted anything could be known for certain. If they emerged victorious then all morality was suspect. Dostoevsky, in the *Brothers Karamazov*, shared the concern of morality in a world unmoored from metaphysical underpinnings when he said every person "who believes neither in God nor in his own immortality, the moral law of nature ought to change immediately into the exact opposite of the former religious law, and that egoism, even to the point of evildoing, should not only be permitted to man but should be acknowledged as the necessary, the most reasonable, and all but the noblest result of his situation."[65] Dostoevsky maintained that "there is no virtue if there is no immortality."[66] Plato feared that without some form of permanence there is no virtue either. The philosopher who has journeyed to the place of virtue is therefore the only one who should rule. They are the only ones who can properly institute justice for the city-state.

A key difference between Dostoevsky's Christian morality and Plato's is not in the source of morality but the effect. For Dostoevsky and other Christians, morality is not simply a duty, but an expression of love, and found in the ecclesia. Heidegger and Plato view liberation from the cave as personally meaningful but still somewhat egoistic. As we will discover in the next chapter and the final chapter of this work, the Christian interpretation of Plato pushes the obligations outward. The trajectory looks similar to the telos of Christianity and goes beyond *theoria* to *theosis*. *Theosis* implies another. This distinction is key to understanding the Christian reception of Plato in the first five centuries in the East.

## NOTES

1. This term of worship is not the one reserved for God in Christianity, nor that of veneration.

2. 625–547 BC.

3. Temple, *Icons and the Mystical Origins of Christianity*, 23.

4. Temple, *Icons and the Mystical Origins of Christianity*, 23.

5. Maximus the Confessor, *European Philosopher*, 37.

6. O'Connell, Robert J. *Plato on the Human Paradox.* New York: Fordham University Press, 1997, 77.

7. Plato, "Phaedrus." Edited by Benjamin Jowett. Classics.mit.edu, n.d. http://classics.mit.edu/Plato/phaedrus.html (accessed 2022).

8. Kierkegaard, Soren. *Philosophical Fragments/Johannes Climacus.* Princeton, NJ: Princeton University Press, 1985, 11.

9. Maximus the Confessor, *European Philosopher*, 39.

10. Louth, *Origins of the Christian Mystical Tradition*, xv.

11. Plato, *Phaedrus* 247C.

12. Louth, *Origins of the Christian Mystical Tradition*, 2.

13. Plato. *Five Dialogues: Euthyphro, Apology, Crito, Meno, Phaedo.* Translated by GMA Grube. Indianapolis: Hackett Publishing, 1981, 14.

14. O'Connell, *Plato on the Human Paradox*, 96.

15. Plato. *Theaetetus.* Indianapolis: Hackett, 1992, 46. 176b

16. Louth, *Origins of the Christian Mystical Tradition*, 193–94.

17. Plato, *Republic*, 116.

18. Plato, *Republic*, 198.

19. Louth, *Origins of the Christian Mystical Tradition*, 16.

20. Plato, *Republic*, 234.

21. Plato, *Republic*, 239.

22. Plato, *Republic*, 241.

23. Plato, *Republic*, 242.

24. Plato, *Republic*, 242.

25. Plato, *Republic*, 247.

26. Plato, *Republic*, 248.

27. Plato, *Republic*, 248.

28. Temple, *Icons and the Mystical Origins of Christianity*, 20.

29. Plato, *Republic*, 244.

30. Louth, *Origins of the Christian Mystical Tradition*, 5.

31. Louth, *Origins of the Christian Mystical Tradition*, 7.

32. Plato. *The Symposium.* London: Penguin, 1999, 49.

33. Louth, *Origins of the Christian Mystical Tradition*, 13.

34. Heidegger, Martin. *The Essence of Truth: On Plato's Cave Allegory and the Theatetus.* London: Bloomsbury, 2022, 1.

35. The concept of universals intrigued Aristotle and a host of medieval philosophers, which we will discuss in the later part of this chapter.

36. Heidegger, *Essence of Truth*, 2.

37. Heidegger, *Essence of Truth*, 4.

38. Heidegger, *Essence of Truth*, 5.

39. Heidegger, *Essence of Truth*, 8.

40. Heidegger, *Essence of Truth*, 9.

41. Heidegger, *Essence of Truth*, 14.

42. Heidegger, *Essence of Truth*, 28.

43. Heidegger, *Essence of Truth*, 29.

44. Heidegger, *Essence of Truth*, 31.

45. Heidegger, *Essence of Truth*, 32.

46. Heidegger, *Essence of Truth*, 36.

47. Heidegger, *Essence of Truth*, 42.

48. Heidegger, *Essence of Truth*, 43.

49. Heidegger, *Essence of Truth*, 43.

50. Heidegger, *Essence of Truth*, 48.

51. Heidegger, *Essence of Truth*, 48.

52. Heidegger, *Essence of Truth*, 52.

53. Heidegger, *Essence of Truth*, 62.

54. Heidegger, *Essence of Truth*, 39.

55. Heidegger, *Essence of Truth*, 69.

56. Heidegger, *Essence of Truth*, 73.

57. Heidegger, *Essence of Truth*, 85.

58. Heidegger, *Essence of Truth*, 97.

59. Kierkegaard, *Philosophical Fragments*, 9.

60. Kierkegaard, *Philosophical Fragments*, 9.

61. Nietzsche, Friedrich. *The Gay Science.* Garden City, NY: Dover, 2020, 176 Aphorism 341, "The Greatest Weight."

62. Eliade, *Sacred and Profane*, 110.

63. Eliade, Mircea. *The Myth of the Eternal Return: Cosmos and History.* Princeton, NJ: Princeton University Press, 2005, 18.

64. Lahav, Ran. *Stepping Out of Plato's Cave.* Hardwick, VT: Loyev Books, 2016, 1.

65. Dostoevsky, *Brothers Karamazov*, 69.

66. Dostoevsky, *Brothers Karamazov*, 70.

*Chapter 2*

# Receiving Plato

## *Christianity and Platonic Thought*

Modern philosophers wrestle with how to utilize or reject Plato. This is nothing new. After Aristotle and well before the philosophical wrestling between Platonists and Aristotelians in the West, Plato's ideas underwent a metamorphosis that is essential to understand before approaching the Christian reception of Plato in the first few centuries. The question of how to understand Plato existed for all of Hellenic culture. Plato's Academy was first challenged by Aristotle, but then by others. Zeno's stoicism (336–265 BC) moved from the *stoa* to dominate discussion in Plato's Academy. By the time of *Chrysippus* (280–207 BC), a new intellectual movement of Skepticism seemed to have emerged. By the disintegration of the Academy in 88 BC, the elites' preference for Stoicism, Skepticism, or even Epicureanism was well known. After all, these systems provided more practical engagement with the struggle against the passions.

It would be a mistake to read the shifting tastes of Athens over this time as a rejection of Plato, though. Even when interest in Plato waned, his cosmo-logical adaptation of Pythagoras remained dominant. How to apply philoso-phy in a way to overcome the passions was central to the Stoics, Epicureans, and even the Skeptics and Cynics. Still the struggle to overcome these earthly concerns took place largely in Plato's cosmology. Plato's authority as a teacher was still valued. To one degree or another, they accepted the realm of ideas as the source for meaning. The reach to a world beyond perception was understood through the use of symbols and imagery. As Eliade said, "symbol-ism carries further the dialectic of hierophanies by transforming things into something other than what they appear to profane experience to be."[1] The mundane world continued to provide opportunities to reach beyond, to engage in something that was holy. This engagement with a spiritual world is the foundation of mysticism. This is why both Temple and Louth connect Plato with the origins of Christian mysticism. Plato provided the framework in his cosmology, a cosmology that was modified by both Christians and Platonists, but not entirely rejected by either.

Père Festugière the antiquity scholar is a little bolder in his assertion that the mysticism of the Church Fathers was essentially Platonic. "When the Fathers 'think' their mysticism, they platonize."[2] On one level, he is correct. Plato's cosmology, while decidedly not Christian, dominated Hellenistic culture before Christ and even after Christianity spread throughout the Mediterranean. As Platonic thought evolved from Plato through Middle Platonism and eventually into Neoplatonism, the cosmology grew to be the prevailing conception of the universe. Just as today most people hold some concept of the universe as articulated by Einstein, Newton, and Copernicus, people following Plato understood the universe as the Pythagorean world of the forms as expressed by Plato. Plato's cosmology replaced Homer's lore. Symbolism replaced myth as the dominant way of understanding.

Symbols grew. They incorporated mythos and *doxa*, reconciling what was previously taken for granted within itself. Reason, episteme also revealed itself through the populated symbolic world and new things would populate Plato's cosmology. Both episteme and *doxa* contributed. The arguments of Epicureans, Stoics, Skeptics, and Cynics could all fit into Plato's framework. The touchstone between Plato and the broader world was with the use of allegory. Plato's use of allegory not only provided us with the imagery from the cave, but it provided a basis for understanding outside of traditional myth. Stories, just like material objects, can have their basis beyond the profane sensible world. Symbolism was not new, as Eliade points out "symbols were pregnant with messages; they showed the sacred through the cosmic rhythms."[3]

In the first century, Christians had to choose how they wanted to address the philosophical system of Plato. How should they challenge and reshape the cosmic rhythms that were previously laid down? Thankfully for them the groundwork of how to use allegory was already laid by Jewish scholars such as Philo of Alexandria and the development of Middle Platonism. As Temple asserts, "the allegorical method of understanding scripture was central to the mysticism of such men as the Jewish philosopher Philo, the Christian Platonist Origen and his pupils St Basil the Great and St Gregory of Nazianzus."[4] Other concepts from Plato's cosmology are transformed into Christian theological concepts. For example, the use of the *logoi* (λόγοι), as the foundation of theological formation of Dionysius and Maximus is essentially the use of Platonic forms. Dionysius and Maximus will be addressed in chapter 7.

## MIDDLE PLATONISM

Sometime around 88 BC and the breakup of the Academy, Platonism entered a new phase. Today we refer to this period as "Middle Platonism." It is middle in the respect that it was not the same Platonism as Plato and the early days of the Academy, and it differs from the later form of Platonism known as "Neoplatonism." Plato's ideas spread from Athens and schools that taught his philosophical conception of the universe emerged in nearly every major city in the Roman Empire. Louth reminds us that central to Platonism in all of its expressions is the conviction that man is essentially a spiritual being.[5] By the time we arrive at Middle Platonism, the conception of a transcendent God, that Plato only hinted at, is further developed and matured.

*Theoria* was increasingly directed toward the God who was connected with the realm of the divine. This God was not like the gods found in the Greek pantheon. Plato and the Middle Platonists knew the folly of attaching virtue to them. Man as a spiritual being now sought union with this new divine being, the being who is the source of the forms. The forms became a middle road between the soul and the source. Bigg, in his treatment of Platonists in Alexandria, identifies these forms as God's agents who "create the ideas, and stamp them on matter."[6] Middle Platonists conceived of the forms as the thoughts of God; they existed in the mind of God. *Theoria* then is our participation in the divine mind since we contemplate the thoughts of God. *Theoriaic* union was not with the God but with the thoughts of God. For most Middle Platonists outside of Judaism and Christianity, this union was still rather impersonal.

Increasingly the center of thought and learning in the Roman Empire was Alexandria. The Egyptian capital had long been associated with wisdom and possessed the Great Library, and it was more cosmopolitan and essential for the empire than Athens. Some Egyptian scholars and intellectual historians today believe that philosophy may have first arisen in Egypt. They cite Ptah-hotep (roughly 2400 BC) as the first philosopher, as well as the time spent in Egypt by Athenian philosophers, including Pythagoras and Plato. Even if Egypt was the birthplace of philosophy, it was surpassed by Athens. Typically, the reason for this is due to the linguistic ability to express ideas in greater detail in Greek than Egyptian. Some also discuss the military shifts that favored Greece more than Egypt after the Persian conquest. By the time of the Roman occupation of Egypt, Alexandria had the linguistic and material resources as well as the cultural tradition to expand upon Plato. Baggley also maintains that the religious atmosphere affirmed the "sense of the reality and importance of the spiritual world; spiritual reality was more significant than the physical and historical aspects of human life, these latter being seen as mere shadows or pale reflections of reality."[7]

For Alexandria, the use of allegory became second nature. While central to Platonic and Pythagorian interpretation, the Stoics in Alexandria utilized allegory to interpret the world. Even the Greek myths of Homer were read as allegorical. This practice grew to the point that in the early second century Saint Irenaeus wrote that the Valentinians had Homer as their prophet.[8] Not just Homer, but all texts were interpreted through the use of allegory.

Alexandria also possessed a large number of diasporan Jews. Charles Bigg asserts that by the beginning of the first millennium the Jews in the city likely numbered around a million.[9] Judaism believed in many of the same tenets as Middle Platonism in general. Both affirmed a central God and a spiritual reality that is manifest in different ways with the material and sensible world. Many Jews at this time also began to use Greek wisdom to reconcile their beliefs with the broader Hellenic culture. The earliest clear example of this is the Septuagint, the translation of the Hebrew Scriptures into Greek.

Arguably the greatest of the Middle Platonists was an Alexandrian Jew by the name of Philo.[10] Philo was deeply engaged in the allegorical interpretation of texts of Alexandria. The bulk of Philo's writings were commentaries on parts of the Pentateuch, utilizing the translation of the Septuagint. Philo's scriptural work read as an apologetic piece, trying to reconcile Hellenic philosophy and Judaism. In his commentary on Genesis 2:8, we read, "Moses, who had early reached the very summits of philosophy and who had learnt from the oracles of God the most numerous and important of the principles of nature."[11] For Philo, Moses was not only a prophet and a religious teacher, but also a philosopher in the truest sense, because he loved wisdom that is found in God. The Middle Platonic conception of the divine as the source of wisdom and *theoria* was reinterpreted as not only contemplation but participation with God. For Philo, this was an easy fit. Philo argued that "Moses was speaking philosophically of the creation of the world,"[12] as the aim of philosophy is now some degree of participation with the divine.

Philo's adaptation of Platonic reasoning to scripture is found throughout his works. As we read in the *Commentary on Creation* 8.31, "And the invisible divine reason (θείου λόγου), perceptible only by intellect, he calls the image of God. And the image of this image is that light, perceptible only by the intellect, which is the image of the divine reason (θείου λόγου), which has explained its generation."[13] We see the major step for Middle Platonism is the use of the divine, yet the structure remains roughly the same as it did for Plato earlier.

Philo uses Platonic speculation about the utility of the body, "two eyes, an equal number of ears, two channels for the nostrils, and the mouth to make up seven, through which as Plato says, mortal things find their entrance, and immortal things their exit."[14] He also uses symbols in a Greek manner. Names are symbols. Moses becomes a symbol, not just a man or even a prophet. The name signifies the form and Moses is the one who is in touch with the divine Logos. Even the Patriarchs are understood allegorically. "Abraham, Isaac and Jacob represent different types of soul in pursuit of the life of virtue."[15]

Philo's conception of God resembles both Moses and the conception of the divine held common by Second Temple Judaism, but also Plato. Terms for God include the One, and He that is. Philo calls God not only the creator of all but also the "purest mind."[16] God is the "most righteous being possible."[17] Philo uses the Stoic notion of the *logos* as the fashioner of all things. Philo connects the Stoic *logos* as the being above the realm of ideas, as held by Plato. It is the *logos* that is the source for virtue. Louth contends that Philo's doctrine of the word is the outgrowth of this philosophical synthesis. Here the word is negotiated through meditation on scripture. The Torah becomes the focal point of *theoria*. Meditation on scripture is God's self-disclosure and the means of participation within the mind of God.[18]

Scriptural meditation is also the only way one truly understands God according to Philo. Philo articulates that "God is unknowable in his ousia and knowable in his dynameis."[19] God is unknowable in His essence but can be understood in His energies. This essence energies distinction becomes central in Orthodox Christian understanding of participation and interaction with God. It is key to the theology of Gregory of Palamas in the fourteenth century and the development of Hesychasm from at least the fourth century. We also see the importance of this essence energies distinction Apophatic or negative theology is therefore another outgrowth of Philo's Middle Platonism. This theological vantage point is expanded upon by both the Christian Dionysius and the Jewish Maimonides. The unknowability of God is also a break from any Stoic notions of God as the immanent *logos*. Instead, the Logos is the second power of heaven. The divine Logos is the mediator possessing both transcendent and immanent aspects, while remaining divine. The second power of heaven is also the demonstration of God's grace, and that which sustains creation.

It is Philo's distinction between God's essence and energies that prefigures the Christian conception of *theosis* as the telos of man. It also provides the language for the debate between Arius and his Alexandrian Bishops Alexander and Athanasius. *Theoria* for other Middle Platonists is only abstractly connected with the God who is the source of the forms. The forms exist as an expression of the God but are not divine in the same sense as the God is. Philo states that we can know God through his energy. By linking this with the second power of heaven, this is uncreated. By failing to see the distinction between created and uncreated energy one also fails to see the distinction between the second power in heaven, Christ as possessing the same essence as the Father. Arius' heresy is an outgrowth of an underdeveloped Middle Platonism that remains too close to Plato and not close enough to the Gospels. Athanasius and other Christians reject this half measure of Arius and begin the shift of the telos of man toward *theosis*. Using the same language as Philo, participation with God is possible through the second power of heaven, namely Christ and the uncreated energy of God.

Philo's conception of the soul is likewise a synthesis of Second Temple Judaism and Plato. Philo embraces the notion of the immortality of soul. He also speaks of the soul's dependence upon God. Its existence is a product of this divine grace, and there is a second death where one is separated from the divine. Philo also maintains in his *Commentary on Creation* 23.69, "Moses says that man was made in the image and likeness of God." And later in 23.71, "Moses has shown this by adding to the words 'after his image,' the expression, 'in his likeness,' to prove that it means an accurate impression, having a clear and evident resemblance in form."[20] The people are made in the image and likeness of God and this notion of image includes a connection to the form. Materiality is understood as a participation in a form that exists in God. This same notion of image and likeness will be applied by Christian theologians later on when discussing icons.

Philo, while the dominant figure of Middle Platonism as it applies to Christianity, was not the only interpretation of Plato in this period. For many of the same reasons why Middle Platonism was able to be applied to Second Temple Period Judaism, early Gnosticism also utilized Middle Platonism's cosmology. There is no single Gnosticism and therefore some could add into their system different interpretations of Plato. Primarily the dualist system of matter and spirit confirmed their cosmological construction. Adding to this, Plato's contention of the immortality of the soul, and the soul as the identity of a person provided a philosophical backing to the rejection of the material world for various gnostic sects. Unlike Philo, many Gnostics could embrace the mythology of Homer and other allegorical exegesis of Plato and the Neo-Pythagoreans. Some Gnostics, primarily those in Alexandria, even incorporated Philo's interpretations of scripture into their own.

While many Gnostics of the first and second centuries attempted to synthesize not only Plato, but also Philo into their disparate systems, the true heirs of Philo's Middle Platonism were many of the Church Fathers, such as Clement and Origen. Temple contends that through Philo these Alexandrian Fathers inherited "the allegorical method of interpreting the deeper meanings of sacred imagery in literature and art."[21]

The allegorical interpretation of art, as well as philosophy in general, was a core component of education. For Middle Platonists following Philo, and particularly for the Christian experience in Alexandria, *theoria* increasingly became associated with mysticism. Union with the divine was the aim, not simply contemplation of the forms. God as the source of the forms naturally became the end of speculation. Temple connects Plato's notion of *theoria* with the mysticism of the fathers. Others such as Protestant theologian Anders Nygren maintains that the whole of Christian mysticism appears "as a deviation or Platonic distortion of primitive Christianity."[22] Essential to this position is that the spiritual message of early Christianity was hijacked by Platonic philosophy.

This argument fails to connect the treads of thought existent in Second Temple Judaism as a whole, and the fact that notions of contemplation can differ wildly depending on the object and aim of contemplation. Lossky believes that

> contemplation is not the exclusive appanage of Platonism and if it were, Platonism in a broad sense would simply mean spirituality which tends toward communion with eternal realities . . . contingent. In this very broad sense almost all religious speculation would be an unconscious Platonism.[23]

It is also unrealistic to expect the language of Christian mysticism to have no overlap with the cultural expression of contemplation. As J. Z. Smith contends, concerning religious biographies and competition, "The solution of each group or individual so charged was the same: to insist on an inward meaning of the suspect activities. The allegedly magical action, properly understood, is a sign. There is both a transparent and a hidden meaning, a literal and a deeper understanding required."[24]

Religious competition centralizes on questions of meaning. Meaning is achieved through the formation of signs and the reinterpretation of common signs to be meaningful for the group. Using the sign of the broader culture is an apologetic tool, not the loss of the initial meaning by the dominant culture. As Eliade reminds us, "Symbols awaken individual experience and transmute it into a spiritual act, into metaphysical comprehension of the world."[25] The symbol of the contemplative world was refashioned by early Christian apologists. This refashioning included a different telos. For the Platonists *theoria* was still somewhat vague during this middle period. Contemplation of the forms was in part contemplation of an aspect of the divine, and they were used to achieve some sort of union with the divine. What this union looked like was ambiguous and differed depending on which type of Middle Platonist one encountered. Increasingly, the Christian telos advocated for a break in terminology. Instead of Platonic *theoria*, Christians preferred the concept of *theosis*. Lossky states,

> Unlike Gnosticism, in which knowledge for its own sake constitutes the aim of the gnostic, Christian theology is always in the last resort a means: a unity of

knowledge subserving an end which transcends all knowledge. This ultimate end is union with God or deification, the θέωςις of the Greek Fathers.[26]

Contemplation has to make way for union without any confusion for Christianity. *Theosis* is understood as a relation to a personal God, not a thing to be grasped or a concept to understand. *Theosis* as the telos cannot be limited to mere *theoria*.

In addition to the Middle Platonism of Philo and the broad overlap between Plato's *theoria* and mystical engagement, early Christians, along with others, believed that Plato had in fact read the Torah. For Middle Platonists, it was Plato who borrowed from the scriptural sources, not the other way around. Today most scholars believe this to be dubious, but early Christian apologists, including Irenaeus and Justin believed this to be the case. Justin connected Plato's time in Egypt as the basis for his philosophical ascendancy, as well as providing him with the teachings of Moses. "Plato accordingly having learned this in Egypt, and being greatly taken with what was said about one God, did indeed consider it unsafe to mention the name of Moses, on account of his teaching the doctrine of one only God."[27] Justin even draws parallels between the *Timaeus* and what God told Moses concerning creation. The Prophets are therefore the source for Athenian philosophy. Use of Plato or others would be akin to using any other commentary on scripture.

The apologists saw this as an easy connection. Plato, as an interpreter of scripture, anticipated union with God. It was now with the incarnation that contemplation was transformed into knowledge. Justin, and later Clement and Origen, sought to demonstrate that "true philosophy" was found in the Church. Lossky argues that "involuntarily they brought about a kind of synthesis, lending to Christian contemplation an accent of Platonic intellectualism."[28]

The greatest of the early apologists for the fulfillment of philosophy in the Church is Justin Martyr.[29] Justin is also known as Justin the Philosopher. His philosophy was primarily Platonic. Justin was born around the year 100. His formative years were spent studying Plato, and Justin eagerly sought after the vision of God that Middle Platonism connected with *theoria*. When a stranger encountered Justin around the year 130, instead of complimenting his philosophical acumen, the stranger chastised Justin as little more than a sophist. According to this visitor, Justin was a lover of words, not of action. His words were not based upon truth, but instead rhetoric. As a lover of philosophy, Justin understood how serious this challenge was. The stranger gave him a work, some believe it to be the prophecy of Isaiah, and told him that true philosophy was found with Christ. Justin dove into the work, and like the Apostle Paul, reasoned with the text to discover if this revelation was true. Before too long, Justin bade Plato, Pythagoras, and other philosophers farewell, believing them to be "half-philosophers."[30] He then embraced Christianity, which he understood to be the truest philosophy.

Justin began to reinterpret his former philosophical heroes according to their compatibility with Christ. He speaks of Pythagoras and his numbers being symbols to which he "entertained thoughts about the unity of God not unworthy of his foreign residence in Egypt."[31] Justin lauded Pythagoras's conception of God. Justin speaks of Pythagoras, maintaining that "God is one; and He Himself does not, as some suppose, exist outside the world, but in it, He being wholly present."[32] God is not terribly distant though; he is the first principle and father of all.

Justin also speaks of Plato along similar lines. "For Plato, with the air of one that has descended from above and has accurately ascertained and seen all that is in heaven, says that the most high God exists in a fiery substance."[33] Justin also draws out several triads that exist in Plato's cosmology, God, matter, and form, as well as three parts of the soul, the faculty of reason, affection, and appetite. In this, Justin demonstrates his preference for Plato over Aristotle.[34] While incomplete, Justin still had a positive view of his philosophical teachers.

Justin found little benefit in the Greek gods. He viewed them as morally deficient. Citing Homer as the chief teacher of religion, Justin points out that if anyone acted as the gods do, they would be either the cause of scandal or worse. If indeed these gods are true, they are not worthy of worship or veneration.

These gods are also impotent. Justin demonstrates that for the Greeks "the gods were made."[35] They were created after the material world. They are not the cause of the world but a consequence of it. Justin says of Plato that he never names these gods as creators, nor does he name the creator. There is a great chasm between these two, "For the creator creates the creature by his own capability and power, being in need of nothing else."[36] In his critiques of the gods, Justin remains within the growing trend of Middle Platonism, preferring a singular absolute God who would be the source of virtue. Unfortunately, the Greek pantheon falls short of this philosophical ideal.

Since *theoria* shifted from contemplation of the forms to contemplation of the source of the forms, Justin intended that his philosophy was not only a synthesis like Philo, but a philosophical proof that was demonstratable and knowable to any philosopher. Justin's Christological philosophy served as an apology for Christianity in general to the broader Hellenized world. Justin clearly advocates for the reasonableness of the Christian philosophy of life over and against Platonism, Stoicism, Epicureanism, and any other rival. "Do not suppose, you Greeks, that my separation from your customs is unreasonable and unthinking; for I found in them nothing that is holy or acceptable to God."[37]

Justin presents Christianity in philosophical terms familiar to any Platonist. Virtue is embodied by the Holy Ghost,[38] as it descends upon man, transforming them, not only so that they are virtuous but truly holy, and have the insight of Platonic *theoria*. Justin argues that Plato, having learned not only Jewish Scriptures in Egypt, but also their interpretation, applied the teachings concerning the Spirit of God to the concept of virtue itself. "I think, Plato having learned from the prophets regarding the Holy Ghost, he has manifestly transferred to what he calls virtue."[39] Virtue for both Plato, as interpreted by the Middle Platonists, and Justin, is understood as a gift that comes from the source. This source increasingly became identified as a single God. Justin concluded that "philosophy is the science of God and the knowledge of God."[40]

Justin's philosophical apology grew more insistent that true philosophy seeks the truth. Yet this truth must come by revelation and not by mere speculation or dialectic. Justin asks if Socrates, the pinnacle of speculative philosophy, "confesses that he knows nothing, how did those who came after him profess to know even things heavenly?"[41] True wisdom must come from a prophetic source and remain reasonable to its hearers. True wisdom must be revealed. Revelation concerning not only the structure of the universe, but also the structure of man should be addressed. Justin urged his readers to see which vision appears most reasonable and true.

Justin's conception of the soul was the first and more glaring difference between him and Plato. While Plato viewed the soul as the life and essence of a person, Justin maintained that "The fancies of your wise men, Plato and Pythagoras, are naught. The soul is not life itself, but is merely a partaker of life. The life is in God."[42] The soul is not wholly separate from the body. It is the life of the body; it is what animates it. Justin emphasizes that it partakes of this life from God. It is not its own eternal source. Justin further separates himself by asserting that soul does not gain anything through release from the body.[43]

The place of the body radically differs between Plato and Justin. Justin values the body, seeing it not only as a vehicle for the soul, but the created image of God. This distinction, while easy to pass over, is a key separation between the mysticism of Christian *theosis* and the *theoria* of Plato. For Plato, *theoria* involved only the soul. The body had to be abandoned. For Justin and Christianity, the body is essential. Mankind is created in the image of God, and it is this image that unites with God. *Theosis* includes not only an ascent to the realm of ideas, but union with the God who formed those ideas, and maintains that the material body is how we exist. The soul is the life of the body as it finds its source for life in God. *Theosis* is not only moving beyond *theoria* toward union with God, but an embodied union.

Justin's philosophy is one that is dependent not upon contemplative powers that separate one person from another, but upon the grace of God. For Christianity as maintained by Justin, "divine knowledge is not to be acquired by study nor by practice. No lecturer, no drill-master can impart it. To understand God, you must see Him. But to see God is the gift of God Himself."[44]

The image of God comes from the source, from God. It is given not because of what separates one person from another, but within an *ecclesia*, a congregation where people stand before God equally in need. Justin's philosophy is shaped by Paul's assertion that in Christ there is neither Jew nor Greek, slave nor free.[45] This claim was radical when it was made. For Justin, it serves as the common construction of mankind in relation to knowledge that is divine. This is another break from Plato who understood some people as inherently inferior to others.

The incarnation becomes the pivot for Justin's philosophy. The incarnation reveals God to mankind. Justin asserts, "the advent of our Saviour Jesus Christ; who, being the Word of God, inseparable from Him in power, having assumed man, who had been made in the image and likeness of God, restored to us the knowledge of the religion of our ancient forefathers."[46] Justin draws on Philo, and Genesis, where mankind is created in the image of God. The power of the image connects Plato's forms with Christian revelation. Real life exists beyond mere appearance since mankind is an image of God, there must therefore exist the idealized complete imager. This for Justin and for Christianity before and after him is Christ, as the Apostle Paul proclaims in Colossians 1:15.

Pythagoras and Plato, while incomplete, were still compatible with the truth according to Justin. Having believed that Plato learned from the prophets, the source for Plato's contemplation was still with God. Plato erred concerning the equality of people and the nature of the body and soul. Plato's cosmological system was still compatible with Christian revelation. Justin did not see him co-opting or synthesizing Christianity with Plato but explaining Christianity in Platonic language. Both Plato and Christianity sought to address the same reality, one was just clearer than the other. Plato was just a half philosopher, and only after Christ can anyone be a true philosopher.

Some early Christians did not believe that the two worldviews could be reconciled. Tertullian famously asked, "what does Athens have to do with Jerusalem?"[47] For Tertullian, philosophy was not only incomplete, it was ill suited for a Christian. Having studied Middle Platonism himself, he rejected Plato being closer to the Stoics. Tertullian eventually even rejected this.[48] The structure of speculative philosophy from either Plato or the Stoics relied too heavily upon human wisdom for Tertullian. For Tertullian, this human wisdom was either fantasy or demonic. Bigg's reading of Tertullian is that "Greek Science is the invention of devils, the bridal gift of the fallen Angels' to the daughters of men."[49] A plain reading of the text instead would be preferable to an allegorical reading inspired by Plato.

This plain reading was the exegetical model of Antioch. The Antiochene tradition emphasized literal reading instead of allegorical. It emphasizes the humanity of Christ as the knowable aspect of God that could serve as the beginning of deeper understanding. Baggly identifies their theology as written in "functional terms."[50] Danielou characterizes the Antiochians as "more matter-of-fact."[51] Wallace Hadrill goes so far as to say that, "Antiochene Christianity was in its essence unphilosophical."[52] This claim is a bit hyperbolic. Antioch traditionally represents the opposite end of the spectrum, preferring a typological approach instead of Alexandria's allegorical method that was deeply indebted to Plato.[53] For our purposes, it demonstrates that mystical expressions of reality, as found in Christianity, were not wholly dependent upon Plato, and that Platonism, even the more theistic Middle Platonism, was never universally accepted as a default orientation for Christianity.

Probably Platonism's biggest champion within the early Church came not from Justin but from Clement of Alexandria.[54] Like Justin, Clement grew up a pagan and spent a good portion of his life studying Greek philosophy. Clement's parents were likely wealthy well-connected Athenians. Clement used his family's wealth in travel. After a journey to Palestine, Clement went onto Egypt, where he encountered Pantaenus, the head of the catechetical school in Alexandria. Clement then joined Pantaenus and before too long became the archbishop of the city. Like Justin, Clement wrote apologetic works, such as his *Exhortation to the Greeks.* As the bishop and head of the catechetical school he also wrote various pieces instructing the faithful. Like Justin, Clement sought to unite Greek philosophy to the Church, with the understanding that the Athenian philosophers studied and were thus indebted to the prophets and their writings in the Christian Old Testament. Clement may have died a martyr's death during the persecution of Septimius Severus, though this is uncertain. He was forced to leave Alexandria and died without ever returning.

Clement understood the philosophical aim as wisdom. Wisdom was conceived along similar lines of what Justin recognized it to be, the *logos*. Uniting the notion of *logos* from the Stoics and Middle Platonists with Christianity, Clement saw true philosophy as the operation of the divine *logos*, who is Christ. For Clement, to deny the wisdom inherent in philosophical speculation was to deny God's revelation. Similarly, to deny the truth of Christianity is a denial of wisdom itself. Faith is the foundation of gnosis (knowledge). Faith is based upon the revelation of knowledge, not conjecture. Like Justin, Clement maintained that a true philosopher must be a learned Christian, and wisdom is a gift from Christ.

Clement's conception of gnosis was deeply indebted to Philo. It was through Philo that Clement recognized the wisdom of God was not only presented to Plato, who Clement understood as setting the greatest possible likeness to God as the aim of life, but also to the Jews in the Old Testament. Following Philo and the cosmological system of Middle Platonism, the source and aim of life is found in God. Just as philosophy was the operation of the divine *logos* revealing wisdom to men, so too was all revelation. Wherever knowledge flourished this was an operation of Christ, and the aim of this self-revelation of God is to bring all people back into union with God. Clement wrote that, "Although there is only one way to the truth, different streams flow into it, forming a river that flows into eternity."[55] Philosophy is one of these streams, that if done correctly strengthens faith and flows into revelation. Philosophy done poorly can separate us from true wisdom. Clement chastised those who held such erroneous positions, "atheism and daemon-worship are the extreme points of stupidity, from which we must earnestly endeavour to keep ourselves apart."[56] Clement never advocated for ignorance, but greater knowledge. Learning becomes the cure for the folly of both heretics and pagan philosophy.

Clement did not believe that everything could be known either. God was still infinite, and knowledge could only point toward the source of revelation, it cannot reveal all of it. Like Philo, there is a use of apophatic theology. Allegories and analytical speculation do not lead one to cataphatic statements but preserve God in God's essence as unknowable. Philosophy becomes the tool to understand revelation and even to approach it, but it can do nothing apart from the self-revelation of wisdom.

Clement understood the perfect state and telos of man through Plato's eternal realm and a Christianized *theoria*. In his *Exhortation to the Greeks*, Clement praises Plato: "Well done, Plato, you have hit the truth."[57] Clement believed that Plato's writings declared the true God to be the supreme God, yet Plato still fell short of perfect understanding. Clement did not admit the preexistence of the soul, eternity of matter, or the division of humanity inherent to Plato's system.

Clement saw the errors of Plato as being corrected in the Church. Like Philo and Justin, creation is understood as preserving the dignity of matter and people. Clement maintained that "image of the Word is the true man, that is, the mind in whom this account is said to have been created."[58] Christ is the true image of mankind, and the telos of man. Mankind is made as an image or icon of Christ. The ecclesia, which serves as the body of Christ, is the source of life in this world. "Through his understanding heart he is made like the divine Word or Reason, and so reasonable."[59] Creation is completed by union with Christ in His Church. Clement paraphrases Paul along the same lines as Justin, "Moreover, the whole Christ, so to speak, is not divided; there is neither barbarian nor Jew nor Greek, neither male nor female, but a new man transformed by the Holy Spirit of God."[60]

Clement's conception of Christ transforms not only matter, but all people. The aim then is beyond *theoria*, it is participation with Christ, it is *theosis*, though the term was not used yet. Clement used the terms to deify (*theopoieō*) and to apotheosize (*apotheoō*). It is only later in 363 that Saint Gregory of Nazianzus coins the term *theosis* in Oration 471. Clement's conception of deification incorporated concepts of the divine economy and God's organization and dispensation to mankind. Central to his notion is that this is accomplished through the work of Christ. "The Word of God became man so that you too may learn from a man how it is even possible for a man to become a god."[61]

Lossky states that for Clement, "The contemplation of God is presented therefore as the highest bliss, and this contemplation seems to involve man's intellectual faculty almost exclusively. Knowledge is beatitude."[62] Knowledge is beatitude following a careful reading of Plato, but one that is only fulfilled with the proclamation of the Gospel. Since Plato maintained that the soul had two movements, one following reason that seeks its end in the realm of ideas, and the other of the sensual world toward gratification of material desires. For Plato, the only solution is to rid one of their passionate nature to afford them the freedom to pursue *theoria*, the contemplative life. At its basis Plato advanced a philosophy of life akin to what the Stoics and Epicureans advanced, though not as complete in Clement's interpretation. For Clement, the system of ridding oneself of the passions is only completed when united with Christ and the Church.

Clement and Justin would argue that the true aim of the contemplative life cannot be contemplation alone but participation in the Body of Christ. This participation is also against the passional nature of life, which is identified as sin. Repentance is a learning whereby one grows not only to a place of self-mastery but also takes place in a communal life.

Beatitude, passionlessness, true *theoria*, and life in the Church are all identical with eternal salvation. Clement unites these themes in the following quote:

> I will say boldly that he who pursues gnosis for the sake of divine knowledge itself will not embrace it simply because he wishes to be saved. Intellect, in its proper use, tends always to be an activity; and this ever-active intellect, having become in its uninterrupted tension the essential feature of the gnostic, is transformed into eternal contemplation and exists as a living substance. If therefore we should suggest hypothetically that the gnostic choose between knowledge of God and eternal salvation, assuming that these two things are separate (in fact they are absolutely identical), he will without hesitation choose the knowledge of God.[63]

In his *Exhortation to the Greeks*, Clement connects the removal of ignorance and participation with the divine light as what is meant by the term "the new creation."[64] For Clement, Christ comes to make new, fulfilling the vision outlined by Plato, as well as Moses in Genesis.

## NEOPLATONISM AND CHRISTIANITY

Following Clement, Plato's teachings are revised further. This latest period of Platonism is known as Neoplatonism. Danielou maintains that Neoplatonism marked the end of classical thought.[65] Middle Platonism witnessed a movement beyond the realm of the forms by speaking about the source of the forms. The idea of a divine source was found in Plato but grew, lending itself to Second Temple Period Judaism of Philo and early Christian Apologists such as Justin and Clement. Neoplatonism continues this trajectory, bringing many of the hallmarks of a completed religious system. Broadly speaking, Neoplatonism incorporated the cosmology of Middle Platonism with Aristotle's Logic.

Neoplatonism also took advantage of the collapse of Stoicism and Epicureanism. Both of these other systems grew in part because of their emphasis on mastering the passions and their focus on material life. Their emphasis on life instead of metaphysical analysis made them more appealing to Greeks and Romans than the speculative philosophies of Plato or Aristotle. With the rise of Christianity, various forms of Gnosticism, and greater concern about the origins and destiny (metaphysics and telos) of humanity, a revived interest in Plato resurfaced. Neoplatonists did not view themselves as producing a new system but building off of what had existed beforehand.

The questions that gave rise to Neoplatonism are similar to those that produced Christianity. It should not be surprising that Neoplatonism resembles a religion. Especially if one follows Paul Tillich's definition of religion, where "faith is the state of being ultimately concerned. . . . Faith as ultimate concern is an act of the total personality. It happens in the center of the personal life and includes all its elements. Faith is the most centered act of the human mind."[66] Neoplatonism incorporates the materialist concerns of Stoicism and the metaphysics of Plato with a god akin to Philo, and the logic of Aristotle. In the mid-fourth century, Julian the Apostate even sponsors Neoplatonic thought, trying to advance it as the genuine religious expression of Pagan Rome against the Nicaean Orthodox Christianity.

Before the relatively short-lived imperial favor of Julian, Neoplatonism originated and grew out of Alexandria. The originator of Neoplatonism in many ways is the teacher of Origen and Plotinus, Ammonius Saccas. Saccas, like Socrates, never wrote anything down. Thus, many scholars identify Plotinus as the founder of Neoplatonism. Origen's Christianity seems to disqualify him as a cofounder for many of these scholars. Yet Lossky[67] and any reasonable analysis of early Neoplatonism demonstrates that what connected Origen and Plotinus was greater than what separated them. Their analysis and use of Plato serves as the foundation of Neoplatonism and points to Ammonius Saccas as the likely founder of the Neoplatonic analysis.

Origen[68] grew up in Alexandria, the son of Christians. As a teenager, when persecution of Christianity moved through the city in either 202 or 215, Origen's father Leonides was martyred. Stories circulate that Origen himself wanted to go with his father and be a martyr. Eusebius tells us that "his mother concealed his clothes to compel him to remain at home."[69] While Origen was willing to die as a martyr, he did not want to bring shame on himself or his family by parading himself through the town naked before his execution. Most accounts of the end of Origen's life indicate that he likely did suffer martyrdom in either Caesarea or Tyre in 254. Eusebius also records that "Such a passion for martyrdom possessed the soul of Origen, when still a youth, that he took pleasure in running risks, in leaping and throwing himself into the struggle."[70]

Origen was a brilliant and pious writer and teacher. Having grown up a Christian, he learned from some of the greatest Christian minds in the city, likely including Clement, who died around the same time as Origen's father. Eusebius states that "Origen, while yet a boy was one of his pupils."[71] If Origen did not learn directly from Clement himself, he undoubtedly learned from his writings. Origen is usually seen as the inheritor of Clement, as well as the Platonist Ammonius Saccas. Origen's piety and brilliance gave him the courage to lead the catechetical school, which many feared doing because it was this post more than any else that brought persecution. Teaching catechumens the faith was the main thing that Emperor Septimius Severus sought to put an end to with his edict against Christians in 202.[72]

Like Philo, the bulk of Origen's works are commentaries on Scripture. Danielou asserts that Origen uses "Philo's allegorical method in his moralising exegesis of Scripture."[73] This serves as the basis of Origen's exegetical work. Origen was also the father of textual criticism. His *Hexapla* compared various translations of the Old Testament. In this work not only could one read the different texts and translations but could also expand upon notions of meaning inherent to each translation. This provided the basis for Origen's systematic work. Many identify Origen as the first Christian theologian, the founder of Christian theology,[74] or more properly the first "Systematic Theologian." Origen was capable of dissecting thoughts and interpretations of ideas and extrapolating a broader meaning from that work. He was the first to attempt a systematic approach to scripture and the problems of the Church.

Until recently the only other Eastern Christian to do so with any level of depth akin to Origen was John of Damascus in the eighth century and possibly Photios the Great in the late ninth century.

Origen's genius resulted in broad statements and assumptions that are simultaneously humble and boastful. Origen was more than capable of recognizing the errors that exist as a part of any tradition. He demonstrated how some translations of works are poorer than others. He also viewed the allegorical method of interpretation that was common to Alexandrians as a personal gift more than a cultural inheritance.[75] Origen's allegorical interpretation of scripture, as well as his systematic treatment of its subjects was widely used over the subsequent centuries. The Cappadocians Basil the Great and Gregory the Theologian[76] compiled an anthology of Origen's works, and much of their theology is deeply indebted to Origen.

While the Cappadocians freely used Origen as their philosophical anchor, the use of Origen's conception of the soul was not accepted in its entirety. Origen's Neoplatonism is most evident in his conception of the soul and its movement. Like Plato, Origen conceives of a world inhabited by souls. These spiritual beings begin and end in a mode of contemplation for Origen. Like Plato's Allegory of the Cave and Dividing Line, we have the shadows of ideas producing and being the product of greater distance from the source. Origen conceives of these spiritual minds all growing tired of *theoriac* bliss and falling away from God. This falling away gradually transformed the mind into souls and ultimately into embodied souls. The bodies are sufficiently cooled and solid enough to arrest the falling away from God. Once embodied, these souls can begin the contemplative life to which they were initially created for and return to the ascent to God. Louth contends that, "For Origen, the 'real' world is the realm of spiritual, non-material beings: the drama of Fall and Redemption belongs essentially to this spiritual realm."[77]

While Origen's conception of the universe is very Platonic, there are some key differences. First the universe and all that is in it is created by God. Matter is created. *Theoria* is also essentially theistic. Meditation on the God who is revealed in the Bible is the act of contemplation. For Origen, contemplation is also not purely a mental exercise. Lossky tells us that for Origen, "Action and contemplation, practice and gnosis are united in a single act—in prayer."[78] *Theoria* is a manifestation of prayer.

Prayer is also completely natural for Origen. Since we preexisted in a state of prayerful contemplation, the act of praying is a return to that initial state. Prayer is a participation in Christ, the Logos of God, the only mind that did not fall away from God. Louth maintains that Origen diminished the incarnation in part because of his Platonic cosmology.[79] Instead, the aim is the mystical life, which realizes union with Christ in the Church as lived out through the sacraments. Ultimate truth is always mediated through the Church for Origen.

Origen's system also advocates that just as all preexisted, so too will all eventually return to resting in God. "We think that the goodness of God, through the mediation of Christ, will bring all creatures to one and the same end."[80] Origen's universalism is based upon this cosmic cycle and the telos for all being participation in God is a concept known as *apokatastasis*. Plato's *theoria* is combined with Christian notions of equality by Origen. Since all minds, save Christ's, fell from God, and all return through Christ, Origen believed that all eventually would return. Some Origen scholars today have advanced the notion that this return does not mean that all will necessarily enjoy divine contemplation. For those, contemplation of a God they have refused instead of embraced, becomes more akin to eternal torment than bliss. In any case, Origen's *apokatastasis* is not identical with *theosis*. The origin of souls differs from Orthodox Christianity, so too does the telos. Matter is minimized, yet a connection with the divine is stronger than is present within Platonic *theoria*.

Origen's incorporation of Platonic ideas has some fallout in the history of Christianity. Lossky points out how many of Origen's ideas are adopted by Arians, and there also appears to be a radicalization of his ideas that result in Origen being condemned at the Fifth Ecumenical Council. Thankfully for Origen, he was not alive at the council. Some maintain that what actually gets condemned at the council did not belong properly to Origen, but instead was the radicalization of his teachings. Origen and Origenism are not necessarily one and the same. Origen was rather cautious in many of his philosophical notions. He often left dogmatic questions unanswered instead of advancing his own opinion. When he did advance an idea where no clear dogmatic answer existed, he usually emphasized that it was only his personal opinion in. He intentionally attempted to diminish the fallout.

If we accept statements attributed to Origen to be genuine, then several notions, including those of preexistence, universalism, and the souls of angels inhabiting the sun, moon, and stars need clarification. Further notions of Christ also being incarnate in the entirety of the celestial hierarchy, and the resurrection consisting of spherical bodies are decidedly not Christian concepts, as Metropolitan Hilarion Alfeyev demonstrates.[81] Origen and beliefs connected with him have since the fifth century been treated as suspect and dangerous. *Apokatastasis* is not systematically addressed by Christians in the East or West until the Protestant Friedrich Schleiermacher discusses them in the nineteenth century.[82]

Neoplatonism was also formed by Ammonius Saccas's other student Plotinus.[83] Unlike Origen, Plotinus did not feel obliged to fit his Platonism into a Christian conception. Plotinus maintained a hierarchy of being, akin to Plato without any Christian notion of equality. Instead of a community of people engaged with one another and therefore dependent upon one another, Plotinus held that the best possible state is self-sufficiency, a principle emphasized in Stoicism. For Plotinus, the greatest of all beings would be self-sufficient, and following Pythagoras, also solitary. For Plotinus and Neoplatonism following Plotinus's conception of it, this is known as the One.

This Neoplatonic concept of the One goes beyond any concept of God that Plato had. Plato spoke of a divine realm, that clearly possessed a God more powerful than the Greek pantheon but did not give full expression to it. Plotinus identifies Plato's perfect deity as entirely consistent with Pythagoras, as the One. The One is beyond the forms and gives rise to the forms, though not as a creator, which would imply volition. Instead, the One simply is. The One possesses no attributes other than being the One. Any attributes would essentially create a duality and the One would no longer be the One but would be many, therefore imperfect.

From the One arise the virtues and the realm of ideas. From there we have the World Soul, which mediates between the world of ideas and the material world. To maintain the solitary nature of the One, the One is also understood as not one, since attributing oneness is a concept that would therefore create multiplicity in the One. Similarly, all things emanate from the One and do not, since we would add notions of the One being a source, and therefore add a characteristic and multiplicity to the One. The One is simply the One, for Plotinus and later Neoplatonists, though this One resembles a God and a source for the universe.

The use of apophatic philosophy of Philo is also essential when addressing the One as we have seen. The One is not a being, but beyond being, yet not even beyond, as that implies a relation. We have similar statements about the nature of God by Dionysius the Areopagite along with Maximus the Confessor. For these Christians God is beyond solitary, God is trinitarian. The Christian God is not isolated and self-sufficient but self-emptying. While on one level of analysis Plotinus's One is similar to Dionysius's God, the two are radically different in all manner of relations.

Plotinus is likely drawing on Christian and Jewish conceptions of God as the existing One, the One who is, the great I Am as revealed to Moses. The forms emanate from the One, akin to Pythagoras's notion of creation arising out of multiplicity. As with Pythagoras, one implies perfection, while multiplicity is further from perfection. The division from the single to the multiple, as mediated through ideas as the World Soul, continues creation for the Neoplatonist. For Plotinus, the material world is the product of this emanation and is also eternal. He argues, "We hold that the ordered universe, in its material mass, has existed forever and will forever endure: but simply to refer this perdurance to the Will of God, however true an explanation, is utterly inadequate."[84]

The material world, while having a connection to the realm of ideas, is also too weak. It barely possesses enough of a connection to survive and is nearly eliminated as it is almost non-being. The material world borrows its being from the world that it touches. The soul for Plotinus is similar to Origen's conception. It exists first in this other realm and is cooled off by further distance from its source. The telos of mind is to return to this source. In *the Enneads*, Plotinus states, "The elements of this sphere change; the living beings of earth pass away; only the Ideal-form [the species] persists: possibly a similar process obtains in the All."[85]

The aim is therefore a *theoria* akin to what Origen advanced. Like Origen, Plotinus holds the notion of emanation and return. He argues that in every state "Every living thing is a combination of soul and body-kind."[86] This body differs depending on the source and location. The key difference between the two is the relational aspect. Just as Origen's God is a relational God, so too is Origen's conception of *theoria*. For Plotinus, as is the case for Plato, *theoria* is a solitary quest. Instead of an ecclesia, there is solitary transcendence. Instead of a God who through love calls the person into community, Plotinus's One is impassible, and has no concern for people. There is no grace since the One does not care and could not care for the person along their journey. Furthermore, not all people are equally prepared for the task ahead of them. As a solitary journey the One cannot even elect to help anyone else. Louth maintains that, "These limitations, as we shall now begin to see, disclose a radical opposition between the Platonic vision and Christian mystical theology."[87]

While possessing the same teacher and having a shared cosmology, Plotinus and Origen produce two rather different interpretations of the cosmos. The difference is one of relationship and community. While the aim is the same, the methodology to achieve that aim is radically different. Origen also saw the labor of prayer as the conspirator with contemplation. For Plotinus, it is contemplation alone, as he says, "This celestial journey is accomplished not on foot."[88]

With a shared cosmos, it is easy to identify Neoplatonism as a rival religious system to Christianity, as Julian did in the latter half of the fourth century. As Danielou tells us of Julian's paganism, "His paganism, moreover, is very original and very different from that of ancient Rome; it is marked by the philosophic influence of Neoplatonism and especially by irrational elements of the occult and theurgy, which Neoplatonism tends more and more to patronise."[89] Man is material and spiritual, seeking redemption and freedom and restoration. Louth therefore calls Neoplatonism a "mystical philosophy."[90]

This mysticism is also engaged in a symbolic world. For Neoplatonism the material world is a symbolic construction mediated by the World Soul and revealed to us. Plotinus also borrows the language of archetype and image, as Temple points out.[91] This language is central for Plato's conception of the forms, as well as Christian notions of creation and icon usage. Other language and symbolic understanding are used by Neoplatonists in common with Christianity as well. There are even Trinitarian manifestations of Neoplatonism as it further develops. This "Platonic trinity" has no source in Plato, save uniting conceptions of God, the Ideas, and the World Soul. Bigg identifies "The genesis of the Platonic Trinity is one of the most perplexing questions in the history of philosophy."[92] This trinitarian concept is likely taken directly from Christian theology and incorporated into Neoplatonism as a way of allowing for any relational sense with the One.

While Origen's orthodoxy is at best suspect and Plotinus was in no way a Christian, the next philosophical expression of Platonism comes from Saint Athanasius the Great.[93] Athanasius was born over forty years after Origen's death and was more than conversant with some of his ideas that impacted Arianism. Athanasius represents a further shift in Alexandria away from Plato, in large part because of the conception of the soul as shared by Origen and Plotinus. Athanasius did not accept the notion of a pre-existent soul, nor a conception of universal salvation.

Like Plato and the Platonists, Athanasius believed that the soul is rational and immortal. The fact that the soul is rational is demonstrated by the ability to override the natural will of the body, that is the organs of the body and the desires and impulses of them. Athanasius also wrote that "The soul of man, being intellectual, can know God of itself, if it be true to its own nature."[94] As far as the immortality of the soul is concerned, Athanasius saw it as distinct from the body in some way, the source of motion, and possessing the power to go beyond the body in imagination and thought. Athanasius states, "Ideas and thoughts about immortality never desert the soul, but abide in it, and are as it were the fuel in it, which ensures its immortality. This then is why the soul has the capacity for beholding God."[95]

For Athanasius, this internal conception of God is what provides the basis of life. This can only be achieved by cleansing one's soul from sin.[96] It is immortal in that it is created as an image of God and transformed by the incarnation. This immortality does not exist apart from God, but only in connection with God. There is an interconnection between creation itself and the incarnation that results in the redemption and re-creation of humanity. This is why the aim is beyond *theoria*, in *theosis*. As Athanasius advanced, *theosis* is becoming god, through participation with God. Athanasius famously says in his fifty-fourth chapter of *On the Incarnation*, "God became man so man can become God."[97] This is not polytheism or pantheism but participation.

Fr David Hester defines *theosis* as "the gradual process by which a person is renewed and unified so completely with God that he becomes by grace what God is by nature."[98]

Athanasius's maxim encapsulates what we now call the "exchange formula." This idea was not new to Athanasius as it existed as early as Irenaeus of Lyon. Irenaeus, in the preface to *Against Heresies 5*, states that Christ "became what we are to make us what he is himself."[99]

The ideal for Athanasius is not the utopia dreamed of by Rome nor the flight of the Platonists. Instead, it is found in the Church and is modeled by the monastic life of Saint Anthony. It is communion with God. Lossky points out that,

> The contemplation of God in the Platonic sense of the word—and even the vision of God as the goal of the solitary life—seems completely alien to this spirituality of the desert. It is a spiritual environment altogether different from the intellectual world of Alexandria, the world of Origen and Plotinus.[100]

For Louth, Athanasius represents a "complete break with the Platonist tradition."[101] The basis for *theoria* as the goal is denied; the shift toward *theosis* is made complete.

The further separation between Plato and Christianity is played out throughout the fourth and fifth centuries. Since Philo the concept of *theoria* as simple contemplation of the forms was further developed to contemplation of the source of the forms. This contemplation was expanded upon by each subsequent generation of Christian Fathers. The aim moved less and less to contemplation as an end but toward the source of that contemplation. With this came a radical equality and *ecclesia* that cooperated with this divine contemplation. By the time of Athanasius *theoria* resembles a shadow of the new aim of *theosis* that is built upon the exchange formula. *Theoria* is the mystical hallmark of Platonic thought. This mysticism gradually developed through both Middle Platonism, and again with Neoplatonism. By the time we arrive at Athanasius, this concept is radically transformed. As Louth says, "The Platonic doctrine of contemplation is left behind; it is beyond theoria, in the darkness of unknowing, that the soul penetrates more and more deeply into the knowledge and presence of God through love."[102]

Theological mysticism subverts philosophical speculation. Central to this is the divine act of creation. Creation needs to be understood in two ways. First is the creation of the cosmos, and secondarily the specific creation of mankind. Both of these acts of creation force a separation between Plato's conception of the universe and Christianity.

Second Temple Judaism rejected Plato's account of preexisting matter. For Judaism and Christianity, God is the creator, and the doctrine of creation *ex nihilo* radically transforms the relationship between God and creation. God is not co-eternal with the universe, but its source. God does not need to figure out how to relate to this universe, but freely chose to participate with it. Louth posits that "the doctrine of creation ex nihilo implies that the most fundamental ontological divide is between God and the created order."[103] This means that ontologically the soul is not united to the source as it is a product of creation and not *homoousias* with the divine.

It is the second act of creation that unites the soul with the divine. God then chose to create not only a cosmos but also people. In the act of creation, God formed man in his image and likeness. Since man is created in the image of God, mankind now shares a foretaste of the divinity. Both Plato and Christianity believe that the soul desires to return to its source. For Plato, the soul was eternal and belonged in the eternal realm where god resides. For Christianity, God created the universe and then places in man divine likeness that desires to return. Ontologically, this allows for free will to exist while also providing a telos of union with God. Just as the completed acorn is the oak tree, and its will may be thwarted by natural distractions, the telos of mankind is united to a completion of this designed will toward likeness with the divinity.

Lossky unequivocally declares that after Origen, "It is pure theology, a theology of the Holy Trinity, where there is no room whatsoever for the God of the philosophers."[104] In many ways this decisive step was accomplished by the Cappadocian Fathers, who in combating a host of heresies, including Arianism, Apollinarianism,[105] and pneumatomachoi or Macedonianism,[106] relied less and less upon Alexandrian allegories and the Platonic notion of the universe. Increasingly important was the distinction made by Philo on the essence energies distinction in how one approaches God, in addition to continued development of *theosis*.

The Cappadocian Fathers studied Greek philosophy in Athens along with the future emperor Julian, who became the apostate.[107] Julian rejected Christianity and embraced paganism and supported Neoplatonist philosophy during his short tenure as emperor. Having received the same education, the Cappadocians preserved their faith and added to it knowledge of the world. In Basil the Great's *Address to Young Men on Reading Greek Literature*, Basil lays out the value of pagan literature, including poetry, history, and philosophy.

Throughout this short address Basil urges his readers "not to take everything without exception, but only such matter as is useful."[108] In each of the areas of literature there are things that are useful for Basil, primarily when addressing the issue of virtue. Basil borrows most of his philosophical language throughout this treatise from Plato but is not an apologist for Plato.

Plato, Pythagoras, and even Diogenes are held as models of virtue when they did not over esteem their bodies but sought spiritual benefits through virtue. Like earlier apologists, Basil in this address spends time criticizing the "adulteries of gods and their amours and their sexual acts in public."[109] Even these epics can be useful, since Basil maintains that,

> if there is some affinity between the two bodies of teachings, knowledge of them should be useful to us; but if not, at least the fact that by setting them side by side we can discover the difference between them, is of no small importance for strengthening the position of the better.[110]

Clearly for Basil the Christian position was better as it led to a firm theology that is reasonable and profitable.

Basil the Great's[111] theology was incarnational. He understood that the telos of man as envisioned by God necessitated the incarnation. It is through Christ's death that death itself is defeated. "Just as the death which is in the flesh, transmitted to us through Adam, was swallowed up by the Godhead, so was the sin taken away by the righteousness which is in Christ Jesus."[112] Having defeated death, man's progress to unity with God can be accomplished through the work of the Holy Spirit. "Through the Holy Spirit comes our restoration to paradise, our ascension into the kingdom of heaven, our return to the adoption of sons, our liberty to call God our Father, our being made partakers of the grace of Christ, our being called children of light."[113]

Basil also emphasized that God is unknowable in his essence. Our adoption is not one that makes man equal with God, but a recipient of God's grace. Basil states, "We know our God in his energies, we scarcely promise that he may be approached in his very essence. For although his energies descend to us, his essence remains inaccessible."[114] This distinction between God's essence (οὐσία) and energies (ἐνέργειαι) provides the means of understanding and unity with God. The energy of God resembles the emanations of the One, but for Philo, and especially Basil, this is understood as an act of volition from the divine. It is not a spontaneous byproduct of God's existence, but the manner in which God chooses to interact with creation.

Gregory of Nyssa[115] was the younger brother of Basil and the most Platonic of the Cappadocians. He was rather familiar with the Neoplatonic system of Origen and was in part partial to it. Many Christians accused Gregory of accepting some of the more questionable teachings of Origen. He was a teacher of rhetoric and philosophy until 370 when Basil induced him to become a bishop.[116] The points of departure from Origen and Plato demonstrate a conscious break in the further formation of Christian doctrine.

Gregory's debt to Plato is an often-discussed question. There are those like Harold Chemiss who believe that Gregory was first a Platonist and conceded to add Christian doctrine into his otherwise Platonic writings.[117] Others such as Jean Danielou and Catharine P. Roth maintain that Gregory was thoroughly Christian but he communicated in the expression of Platonic terminology since that was the scientific worldview of his time.

Gregory's conception of God was decidedly trinitarian. This basic conception of God not as a monad separates Gregory from the prevailing Neoplatonic conception of the One. Gregory speaks of God's creation ex nihilo, separating him from the preexistent Platonic matter. Gregory also uses the terms essence ούσία and energies ένέργειαι to address how one understands this God. In doing so he relies heavily upon not only the philosophy of Philo but the theology of Basil. In this development the gulf between the uncreated God and the created world is only overcome by God. He does utilize Plato's distinction between the intelligible and sensible worlds. Louth maintains that, "for Gregory the realm of the intelligible is divided into the uncreated and creative on the one hand and, on the other, that which is created—and this is the fundamental divide."[118]

*Theosis,* newly coined by the other Cappadocian Gregory, is also the aim of the creative God. Gregory's conception of *theosis* builds off of Athanasius, that in the incarnation God deified all humanity.[119] Christ became incarnate "so that by becoming as we are, he might make us as he is."[120] Gregory was more than familiar with Plato's *theoria but* interpreted this as a steppingstone to *theosis*. For Gregory the sensible world demonstrates the ideas behind them, but it is the energy of God that brings those images to all intelligible creatures. As Lossky states, "the celestial journey of the soul (a common theme in all Platonic writings) is interiorized, there is an interior ascent: the soul finds its native land—what is conatural with itself—within itself, by recovering its primitive state."[121]

There is no notion of ecstasy attached with *theoria*, but union with God. The process of union also requires work, as Origen maintained. The labor of prayer and ridding oneself of the passions that ensnare them, as Clement maintained, is the process whereby the image of God is clarified. This is also assisted by God's grace and is thoroughly relational. *Theosis* is understood as the mingling of "our god-formed mind and our divine reason with what is properly its own and the image will return to the archetype it now longs for."[122]

The soul is this god-formed mind that survives after death, as both Plato and Athanasius maintained. Gregory does not see the soul as eternal in the Platonic sense. Instead, it is not material nor immaterial. "If it is material, it will be dissolved along with the body if it is immaterial, it cannot be contained in the elements."[123] The soul is the life of the body but has its source in God who gives life. They are not created before the bodies and the notion of transmigration of souls is rejected. The soul is also not created after the body but is the animating spirit of the body.[124]

Plato's conception of an eternal preexistent soul is reduced to "the futile talk of unbelievers."[125] "Therefore we shall abandon the Platonic chariot and the pair of horses yoked to it, which pulled unequally, and the charioteer controlling these horses, through all of which Plato presents symbolically a philosophy concerning these faculties in relation to the soul."[126] In rejecting Plato's conception of the soul Gregory lays out the argument that man is the union of body and soul, following Saint Irenaeus and against any gnostic or Manichean conception of humanity. The Christian conception of *theosis* is material and spiritual and fully realized with the resurrection.

Lossky confirms this shift away from Plato after Gregory when discussing Cyril the Great.[127] Cyril of Alexandria, the champion of the Council of Ephesus, moves past any notion of *theoria* as the aim. Even a Middle Platonist position, where perfect knowledge of God is understood as *theoria*. Instead, *theosis*, "the spiritual world of delights" τρυφῆς δέ τρόπος πνευματικός,[128] is the goal for Christianity. The Coptic Orthodox rite of midnight praises quotes Saint Cyril, "He took what is ours, and gave us what is his."[129] This clear shift in aim from the Alexandrian bishop confirms that while Plato played an important role in development of the cosmological structure of the universe, this structure has undergone serious revision and correction to fit within a Christian mold by the fifth century, not vice versa.

With Athanasius and the Cappadocians, as well as clearly evident by the time of Cyril, Christianity becomes the dominant philosophy of the Roman Empire. Christians are not consciously Platonic. Instead, Plato's realm of the forms is understood in connection to a spiritual reality where God and the heavenly hosts are present. As Plato's cosmology grew to be the default conception of the universe, Christians following the metaphysical addition of the supreme god of Middle Platonists such as Philo saw no reason to reject Plato entirely. Patristic theology worked within the rational systems of Hellenistic culture, correcting it when necessary and using the existing philosophical language to express Christianity to the Roman world. From the beginning the most Platonic Fathers, Justin and Clement, still departed from Plato when necessary.

Plato provided the framework but not the conclusions. Bourdieu tells us that Plato must be taken literally when he says, "The philosopher is a mythologist."[130] The mythology of Plato is not the same as the Christian one, nor is its religious expression. Platonic mysticism was dependent upon the telos of man being *theoria*, a simple return to the contemplative life of the forms. When Plotinus advanced a more theological conception of *theoria* it was outright rejected by the Cappadocians and later Christianity. As we will discuss in chapter 7, both Dionysius and Maximus return to the theocentric cosmology of Neoplatonism, but they do not accept the system; rather, they provide a correction to the faults in a similar way Justin and Clement did for Middle Platonism.

Platonism's vision was an isolated withdrawal from the material world and ascend to the realm of ideas. Christians instead begin their ascent not in isolation but by the grace of God. Alexander Schmemann identifies this change as essential in understanding Christian development. "That which we propose here is immeasurably far from the abstract doctrine of freedom. For the liberating truth about which Christ speaks is not a new philosophy or ideology, but rather Christ himself, who said of himself: *I am the way, the truth, and the life* (John 14:6)."[131] Schmemann continues saying that the revelation of God through the incarnation contains the telos of man, the freedom of man, and the means for which man can ascend to God. This God is beyond the One, but love, life, and freedom.

The act is also not private but communal. Danielou comments that "the soul's ascent is never presented as a solitary ascent. The soul ascends surrounded by a retinue of other souls who are attached to her."[132] The ecclesia partners with this ascent which moves beyond *theoria*, and toward *theosis*. Notions of love permeate Christian mysticism in a way that is foreign to Plato and even in Neoplatonism. The love of Christ becomes the telos and the means of this communal life. This is not a community of intellectual elites, a cabal of philosopher kings; instead, it is the body of Christians, who are all made equal in this encounter.

Plato did not conceive of people as equals. In *The Republic*, he states, "when god fashioned you, he added gold in the composition of those of you who are qualified to be Rulers, . . . he put silver in the Auxiliaries, and iron and bronze in the farmers and other workers."[133] People were formed with different values. As such only a few could live the contemplative life. Christianity, by focusing on the image of God in man, has lasting ramifications. Not only is the *ecclesia* made up of people from all walks of life and all abilities, but how one is called to approach every member of this body is also different. Plato insisted that when those of bronze or iron in their makeup are present, they must be assigned their proper value and be degraded "to the ranks of the industrial and agricultural class where it properly belongs."[134] Instead, the soul's ascent is available to all, and each person is indebted to others. As Danielou confirms, "The graces of sanctification which she receives she receives not for herself but that she may sanctify the others."[135]

These graces inherent to the image of God in man are what provides the basis for the Christian conceptualization and utilization of icons. Icons as image maybe understood through a Platonic lens, but the lens that was corrected by Christianity over the first four centuries. It is to this treatment that we will turn our attention in the subsequent chapters.

## NOTES

1. Eliade, *Patterns in Comparative Religion*, 452.

2. Louth, *Origins of the Christian Mystical Tradition*, 191.

3. Eliade, *Sacred and Profane*, 137.

4. Temple, *Icons and the Mystical Origins of Christianity*, 7.

5. Louth, *Origins of the Christian Mystical Tradition*, xiv.

6. Bigg, Charles. *The Christian Platonists of Alexandria*. Forgotten Books, 2012, 13.

7. Baggley, *Doors of Perception*, 48.

8. Danielou, *The Christian Centuries*, 135.

9. Bigg, *Christian Platonists of Alexandria*, 2.

10. Roughly 15 BC–50 AD

11. Philo. "On Creation." *Earlychristianwritings.com*, n.d. http://www.earlychristian writings.com/yonge/book1.html (accessed 2023).

12. Philo of Alexandria, *The Works of Philo*. Peabody, MA: Hendrickson, 1993, 327.

13. Philo, *Commentary on Creation*.

14. Philo of Alexandria, *Works of Philo*, 17.

15. Baggley, *Doors of Perception*, 49.

16. Philo of Alexandria, *Works of Philo*, 327.

17. Philo of Alexandria, *Works of Philo*, 328.

18. Louth, *Origins of the Christian Mystical Tradition*, 30.

19. Louth, *Origins of the Christian Mystical Tradition*, 21.

20. Philo, *Commentary on Creation*.

21. Temple, *Icons and the Mystical Origins of Christianity*, 29.

22. Lossky, Vladimir. *The Vision of God*. Crestwood, NY: St. Vladimir's Seminary Press, 1963, 48.

23. Lossky, *Vision of God*, 64–65.

24. Smith, J. Z., *Map Is Not Territory*, 194.

25. Eliade, *Sacred and Profane*, 211.

26. Lossky, *Mystical Theology*, 9.

27. St. Justin Martyr, *Saint Justin Martyr Collection*. Philadelphia: Aeterna Press, 2016, 208.

28. Lossky, *Vision of God*, 65.

29. 100–165.

30. St. Justin Martyr, *Collection*, 233.

31. St. Justin Martyr, *Collection*, 205.

32. St. Justin Martyr, *Collection*, 205.

33. St. Justin Martyr, *Collection*, 191.

34. St. Justin Martyr, *Collection*, 192–93.

35. St. Justin Martyr, *Collection*, 206.

36. St. Justin Martyr, *Collection*, 209.

37. St. Justin Martyr. "Discourse to the Greeks." In *Ante-Nicene Fathers, Volume 1*. Edited by Alexander Roberts, James Donaldson, and A. Coxe Cleveland. Translated by Marcus Dods. Buffalo, NY: Christian Literature Publishing, 1885.

38. St. Justin Martyr, *Collection*, 220.
39. St. Justin Martyr, *Collection*, 220.
40. St. Justin Martyr, *Collection*, 235.
41. St. Justin Martyr, *Collection*, 223.
42. St. Justin Martyr, *Collection*, 235.
43. St. Justin Martyr, *Collection*, 235.
44. St. Justin Martyr, *Collection*, 235.
45. Galatians 3:28
46. St. Justin Martyr, *Collection*, 226.
47. Tertullian. *The Prescription Against Heretics, Volume 3: Ante-Nicene Fathers.* Grand Rapids, MI: Eerdmans, 1951, 246.
48. Danielou, *The Christian Centuries*, 156.
49. Bigg, *Christian Platonists of Alexandria*, 50.
50. Baggley, *Doors of Perception*, 48.
51. Danielou, the Christian Centuries, 212–13.
52. Hill, Robert C. *Reading the Old Testament in Antioch.* Leiden: Koninklijke Brill, 2005, 8.
53. Bucur, *Scripture Re-envisioned*, 260.
54. 160–215.
55. Met Hilarion Alfeyev, *Orthodox Christianity, Volume 1.* Yonkers, NY: St. Vladimir's Seminary Press, 2011, 36.
56. Clement of Alexandria. *Clement of Alexandria Collection.* Philadelphia: Aeterna Press, 2016, *Exhortation to the Greeks*, 51.
57. Clement of Alexandria, *Exhortation to the Greeks*, 155.
58. Clement of Alexandria, *Exhortation to the Greeks*, 215.
59. Clement of Alexandria, *Exhortation to the Greeks*, 215.
60. Clement of Alexandria, *Exhortation to the Greeks*, 239.
61. Russell, *Fellow Workers with God*, 39.
62. Lossky, *Vision of God*, 53.
63. Lossky, *Vision of God*, 53.
64. Clement of Alexandria, *Exhortation to the Greeks*, 243.
65. Danielou, the Christian Centuries, 181.
66. Tillich, Paul. *Dynamics of Faith.* New York: Harper & Row, 1957, 4.
67. Lossky, *Vision of God*, 67.
68. 185–251.
69. Eusebius, *Ecclesiastical History.* Translated by C. F. Cruse. Peabody, MA: Hendrickson, 1998, 192. VI 6,2,5.
70. Danielou, *The Christian Centuries*, 140.
71. Eusebius, *Ecclesiastical History*, 197. VI, 6,6.
72. Danielou, the Christian Centuries, 141.
73. Danielou, *Christian Centuries*, 129.
74 . Met Hilarion Alfeyev, *Orthodox Christianity Volume 1*, 37.
75. Bigg, *Christian Platonists of Alexandria*, 145.
76. Their Platonism is treated later in this chapter.
77. Louth, *Origins of the Christian Mystical Tradition*, 61.

78. Lossky, *Vision of God*, 66–67.

79. Louth, *Origins of the Christian Mystical Tradition*, 70.

80. Origen, *Sacred Writings of Origen.* Altenmünster: Jazzybee Verlag, 2016.

81. Met Hilarion Alfeyev, *Orthodox Christianity Volume 1*, 40.

82. Davis, Justin. *Schleiermacher and Palmer: The Father and Mother of the Modern Protestant Mindset.* Eugene, OR: Pickwick Publications, 2019, 51.

83. 205–270.

84. Plotinus, "Plotinus: The Six Enneads." *Internet Archive*, n.d. https://archive.org/details/in.ernet.dli.2015.460836 (accessed 2023).

85. Plotinus, *The Six Enneads.*

86. Plotinus, *The Six Enneads.*

87. Louth, *Origins of the Christian Mystical Tradition*, 51.

88. Lossky, *Vision of God*, 67.

89. Danielou, *The Christian Centuries*, 237.

90. Louth, *Origins of the Christian Mystical Tradition*, 36.

91. Temple, *Icons and the Mystical Origins of Christianity*, 75.

92. Bigg, *Christian Platonists of Alexandria*, 248.

93. 296–373.

94. Tyson, John R. *The Great Athanasius: An Introduction to His Life and Work.* Eugene]: Cascade, 2017, 12.

95. Athanasius of Alexandria. *Saint Athanasius of Alexandria Selection.* Philadelphia: Aeterna Press, 2016; *Against the Heathen*, section 33, 33.

96. Saint Athanasius of Alexandria. "Against the Heathen." In *Saint Athanasius of Alexandria Selection*, by Saint Athanasius of Alexandria, 3–46. Philadelphia: Aeterna Press, 2016, section 34.

97. Athanasius. *On The Incarnation.* Yonkers, NY: St. Vladimirs Seminary Press, 2012; *On the Incarnation*, 107. 54:3 "he was incarnate that we might be made god."

98. Shuttleworth, "Theosis: Partaking of the Divine Nature." *Antiochian Orthodox Christian Archdiocese of North America*, n.d. http://ww1.antiochian.org/content/theosis-partaking-divine-nature (accessed 2023). Quotes from Hester's booklet "The Jesus Prayer."

99. Russell, *Fellow Workers with God*, 23.

100. Lossky, *Vision of God*, 70–71.

101. Louth, *Origins of the Christian Mystical Tradition*, 78.

102. Louth, *Origins of the Christian Mystical Tradition*, 97.

103. Louth, *Origins of the Christian Mystical Tradition*, 77.

104. Lossky, *Vision of God*, 98.

105. Those who denied that Christ had the mind of a man.

106. Those who denied the divinity of the Holy Spirit.

107. St. Basil the Great. "Letters." In *St. Basil Collection.* By St. Basil the Great, 259–735. Philadelphia, PA: Aeterna Press, 2016, 395. Letter XLI.

108. St. Basil the Great. "Address to Young Men on Reading Greek Literature." In *St. Basil Collection.* By St. Basil the Great, 738–54. Philadelphia': Aeterna Press, 2016, 749.

109. St. Basil the Great, "Address to Young Men," 745.

110. St. Basil the Great, "Address to Young Men," 744.

111. 330–378.

112. Morris, John W. *The Historic Church: An Orthodox View of Christian History.* Bloomington, IN: AuthorHouse Publishing, 2011, 59.

113. Morris, *The Historic Church*, 60.

114. Lossky, *Vision of God*, 78.

115. 335–395.

116. St. Gregory of Nyssa, *On the Soul and Resurrection.* Crestwood, NY: St. Vladimir's Seminary Press, 1993, 9.

117. St. Gregory of Nyssa, *On the Soul and Resurrection*, 11–12.

118. Louth, *Origins of the Christian Mystical Tradition*, 80–81.

119. Morris, *The Historic Church*, 63.

120. Russell, *Fellow Workers with God*, 39, citing Refutations 11.

121. Lossky, *Vision of God*, 86–87.

122. Maximus the Confessor, *On the Cosmic Mystery of Christ*, 62.

123. St. Gregory of Nyssa, *On the Soul and Resurrection*, 15.

124. St. Gregory of Nyssa, *On the Soul and Resurrection*, 21.

125. St. Gregory of Nyssa, *On the Soul and Resurrection*, 29.

126. St. Gregory of Nyssa, *On the Soul and Resurrection*, 50.

127. 376–444.

128. Lossky, *Vision of God*, 99.

129. Gergis, Emmanuel. *Cyril of Alexandria's Christological Dialogue on the Incarnation of the Only Begotten.* Oradea: Agora University Press, 2020, vi.

130. Bourdieu, *Outline of a Theory of Practice*, 158.

131. Schmemann, Alexander. *A Voice for Our Time: Radio Liberty Talks, Volume 1.* Yonkers, NY: St. Vladimir's Seminary Press, 2021, 274.

132. Louth, *Origins of the Christian Mystical Tradition*, 201.

133. Plato, *Republic.* Translated by Desmond Lee. New York: Penguin Classics, 2007, 116.

134. Plato, *Republic*, 117.

135. Louth, *Origins of the Christian Mystical Tradition*, 201.

# Chapter 3

# A Revelation in the Icon

Alexander Schmemann reasons that "the concept of the person can be grounded only in a religious worldview."[1] This statement is not very far from Eliade's conception of man as *homo religiousis*. Man is by its nature a religious being. The structure of the cosmos as understood through religion invariably molds everything else. In the first chapters, we addressed the cosmos as understood by Plato. For Plato, the structure preserved a duality between appearance and reality. This preserved moral absolutes and provided a basis for government and understanding. Cosmology implied a teleology for Plato just as it did for Socrates. The telos for Plato was *theoria*, an escape from the material world into a meditative concentration upon the forms.

In chapter 2, we moved onto the Christian inheritance of Plato and the rejection of *theoria* as the telos of man. Like Plato, the Christians understood everyday life as something permeated by a spiritual presence. As for the Middle Platonists, material reality is connected to God and animated by God. While this is connected to Plato's realm of the forms, the spiritual reality as understood by Christianity goes well beyond that. Christianity also concretely affirmed material reality, not as simply a shadow of the forms but as something good. The language of Plato's cosmology was shared, but the words took on a different meaning. So too did the telos change and with it the concept of *theoria* was not only transformed under Justin and Clement but eventually it was dropped as insufficient and too limited by its Platonic past.

*Theosis* replaced *theoria* as the telos of man. The new term was used to convey an older concept. We see it in the writings of second-century Christians like Saint Irenaeus, who in *Against Heresies 5* states, the Son of God "became what we are in order to make us what he is himself."[2] As Norman Russell articulates, *theosis* is "more than redemption or salvation. It is not simply the remedying of our defective human state. It is nothing less than our entering into partnership with God, our becoming fellow workers with him (I Cor 3:9) for the sake of bringing the divine economy to its ultimate fulfillment."[3]

In the fifth session of the Seventh Ecumenical Council, the concept of *theosis* was enshrined by the church, stating, "God re-created man in immortality, thus bestowing upon him a gift which could no longer be taken away from him. This re-creation was more godlike and better than the first creation; it is an eternal gift."[4] It is fitting that this enshrinement of *theosis* took place at the Seventh Council, which dealt with icons and what it means to be made in the image of God. It was in this council that we have the firm rejection of the telos of Plato in favor of the telos of Christianity, as affirmed by the writings of Irenaeus, Athanasius, and Cyril.

From the first century, Christianity affirmed that reality is found in the material world through images, not just in the forms or spiritual realm. Today we accept the fact that some images are not merely representations of an item but are symbols of something else. The object and its message, when analyzed from an outside perspective, may appear arbitrary or mysterious. An illumined red hand at an intersection tells pedestrians to stop, as does a red octagon. The hand could mean peace or illustrate openness as it does in other cultures. Yet it is not understood that way when we approach it. If it was taken to mean there are peaceful ways ahead, the pedestrian would be just as likely to get hit by an oncoming car as not. If they were spared by the car, the driver would likely yell out something akin to, "Why didn't you stop, you see the light is red." The expectations of social interactions are based upon the symbol provided.

Similarly, there is nothing inherent about red that means danger. For many cultures it is representative of blood and power. Victor Turner tells us that it is often symbolic of all women. He adds it is also the power of a man, and of animals.[5] It can be purifying and yet it also stands for death and witchcraft. That we understand it as a color associated with us arresting our locomotion is arbitrary. While arbitrary, however, it is not capricious. It is a culturally meaningful symbol. Once again, a symbol is something that brings two disparate things together. In the case of the red hand, it unites the meaning of stopping with the image present. The image does not itself possess this meaning; it only has this meaning when understood as a symbol. This symbol is one that most westerners take for granted, but it could be otherwise and often it is. The basic symbolic conception of street signs does not have lasting significance. They should demonstrate though, that even in our flat materialistic conception of the universe, we can understand that symbols have physical actions and social interactions associated with them.

Just as the color and shape of the symbol have meaning, so too is the artistic skill that is utilized in the presentation of this symbol. Some symbols are ornate, but more often than not, a symbol at its basic level is reduced over time to its bare necessities, and then the skill of the artisan builds upon the symbol just enough to reveal the message. This, along with some degree of their skill, is how we see symbols as an expression of beauty. Symbols are therefore not reflexively complicated, even though they are complex.

For Plato, symbols were a clear connection to the idea that lay beyond the material object. For many of us it is a representation of social convention and normative practices in that society. When the symbol turns its attention toward the religious, it takes on a new character. This character is more akin to the theology behind *theosis*. It affirms the matter while looking to the animating spirit behind the material image. It moves beyond recognizing the beauty and unites the material with the spiritual and ideally to the divine as well. John Baggley argues that when we approach an icon "we are entering a world where a different language is used: the non-verbal language of visual semantics, the symbolic language of form and colour. To people accustomed to naturalistic art the learning of this different language of silence can be a hard task."[6] Archimandrite Vasileios amplifies this when he says, "Through the icon, an everlasting and unchanging reality speaks without words; a reality which, in the clarity of silence and in tranquility, raises up from the deepest level that which unites everything in man."[7]

Baggley believes that realism loses symbolic value to naturalistic art.[8] For both Baggley and Arch. Vasileios, the language of silence inherent to the symbolic world is shouted over by literalism. Metropolitan Hilarion Alfeyev maintains that there is a place for both. "Images of a symbolic character appear together with completely realistic painting; Christian and antique subjects coexist in harmony."[9] Symbolism is easier to see when the aim is for symbolic value instead of realism. Here we begin to see the difference between religious art in general and symbolic art, which includes icons.

## WHAT IS AN ICON? THE THEOLOGY OF JOHN OF DAMASCUS AND THEODORE THE STUDITE

Religious art is nothing new or anything particular to Eastern Christianity. All religions, regardless of one's definition of religion, possess some art that is an expression of their religion. Buddhism, which advocates impermanence, not only has sand mandalas which are created and then destroyed, but also statues. Islam, while typically understood as iconoclastic, has ornate paintings and uses calligraphy to adorn sacred places. Ancient Judaism was also not nearly as iconoclastic as the casual observer believes was the case today. While the Second Commandment prohibited the making of graven images and worshipping them, this was not a universal prohibition against images and their use. As mentioned in the introduction, Solomon's temple had carvings of not only things on earth but things in heaven. Pomegranates and cherubim are found in the temple. The temple was modeled on the tabernacle, which also possessed this earthly and heavenly imagery.

As Judaism developed, so too did its religious art. Pentiuc advances Weitzmann's thesis that suggests that illustrated copies of the Hebrew Scriptures existed in Second Temple Judaism.[10] While we do not have any of these lost illustrated manuscripts, this does not make the thesis untenable. First, given the fact that manuscripts are written on mediums, typically sheep skins, that are not likely to survive more than two hundred or so years.[11] Second, as Rabbinic Judaism emerges, it increasingly becomes iconoclastic and would have destroyed any surviving illustrated manuscripts. Finally, we have evidence of artistic representation in other forms by Second Temple Jews.

The clearest example of sacred art by Second Temple Jews are the myriad of decorations in synagogues that date to this period. The Dura-Europos synagogue for example has frescoes depicting subjects from the Old Testament, including representations of people. Moses's birth, the visions of Prophet Ezekiel, the Israelites crossing the Red Sea, Prophet Elijah standing up to the false prophets of Baal, Elijah raising the widow's son from the dead, and others are all present.[12] Other representations of vegetation and the Jewish Zodiac are also found in synagogues of this period. Temple reminds us that this style "goes back several centuries before the lifetime of Christ and which continues until the beginning of the fourth century AD."[13] One of the latest depictions found in Jewish Synagogues is in Sepphoris, where a mosaic dubbed the "Mona Lisa of the Galilee" is dated to some point in the fourth century.

Earlier relief work is found throughout the Middle East and is identified as more legendary than realistic. Mystical cults flourished as rivals to Judaism, and some degree of syncretism is often used to explain the use of religious art in these synagogues. While the styles changed, mirroring the surrounding cultures, the fact that Ezekiel's prophecy and Moses's tabernacle have religious art depicting things in heaven above and earth below should indicate that Judaism until fairly recently was not opposed to religious imagery. The adoption of images in places of worship is not an example of religious syncretism or paganism leaking into an iconoclastic religion.

This is important because religious images do not exist on their own. The source of the image and how it is used is mediated by cultural and religious expectations. Icons develop not only from within the Christian tradition but also as an inheritance of earlier Jewish usages. The meaning inherent in Jewish images prior to the incarnation shaped the Christian reception of images in the first century.

Probably the earliest Christian usage of imagery came from funeral pictures. This was a practice prevalent in Egypt and the Middle East by the first century. Christians at this time coexisted within Jewish synagogues or in their own churches. In the first few centuries, the Christian churches were often smaller and less wealthy than their Jewish counterparts. Beautiful mosaics were usually sponsored by a wealthy member of the community as an act of piety and public works. Given the smaller resources for Christians at this time, we have relatively few churches with mosaic work, but we do have funeral pictures.

Funeral pictures were typically encaustic paintings. Encaustic paintings utilize beeswax and pigment. They are labor intensive but not permanent fixtures. These paintings were placed in the home or at the gravesite. It is at the gravesites that we also see larger paintings by Christians. The catacombs are some of the earliest surviving art. When looking at the catacombs, they are more symbolic than literal depictions. Frescoes exist dating to the second century, though typical conception of the style associated with icons does not emerge until about the fourth century. There is also evidence of early Christian symbols of the cross, fish, and the sator square in Pompeii, thus dating the use of these images as early as 79.[14]

When discussing the use of Christian icons in liturgical service and devotion, scholars often talk past one another. There are those that say that the first iconographer was Saint Luke. Today there are icons which are either accredited to Luke himself or are believed to be modeled after one of Luke's encaustic paintings of the Theotokos. For these scholars, mosaics and other religious art from the first three centuries are icons.

There are also scholars that see the stylistic difference as a difference in kind. For these, often Protestant scholars, early religious art is something different than icons as used in Orthodox Churches today. Not only do these scholars place the advent of the icon into the latter half of the third century, but the existence of mosaics in places like the catacombs are interpreted as art akin to funeral pictures of pagans. They remove the symbolic meaning of the image, because of their own implicit iconoclasm.

What is misunderstood is that there was virtually no art that was secular in the ancient world. Even depictions of the emperor or military victory are understood in a religious context. The victory and following triumph were used by pagan Rome to demonstrate divine favor or the divinity of the emperor. Funeral art was used as a connection to the deceased person represented in a religious context.

For the ancient world, whenever art exists and in whatever style it is found, it had deep religious significance to it. The style may have changed to one degree or another but the substance behind it did not. Connecting this with Plato, the image represented the idea, which exists beyond the sensible world; it is a call toward *theoria*. For Christians, it was the affirmation of matter, as well as the union of the spirit and a call for deification. This is not only a philosophical concept but a religious one that permeated the Hellenized world and beyond.

In the catacombs and elsewhere we also have depictions of Christ and the events of the Gospels represented. In the Catacombs of Via Dino Compagni, Christ is found speaking with Saint Photini the Samaritan woman. In the Catacombs of Saint Domitilla, we have a depiction of Christ raising Lazarus from the dead and Christ among his disciples.[15] Christ is easily recognizable even in these early depictions because his head is surrounded by a halo that has a signifier next to it. In many of the catacombs, the signifier is the Greek letters A alpha and Ω omega. In later iconographic work, the letters are placed inside the halo and are Ὁ ᾽ΩΝ. Fr Steven Bigham tells us that "these letters form the present participle, ὤν, of the Greek verb to be, with a masculine singular definite article, ὁ. A literal translation of Ὁ ᾽ΩΝ would be 'the being one.'"[16] The being one or the existing one is a reference to the name of God revealed to Moses at the Burning Bush.

It is clear that before Constantine, Christians had religious art that identified Christ and other figures from the Gospels and Christian history. Even Eusebius, who was not in general a supporter of icons, mentions in the fourth century that he has "seen a great many portraits of the Savior, and of Peter and Paul, which have been preserved up to our time."[17] One of these icons that Eusebius speaks about is "the icon made without hands" given to King Abgar of Osroene, as mentioned in the introduction. This miraculous icon was taken from Edessa in the tenth century before disappearing with the crusades. Stories connecting religious imagery with miracles are also found before the Roman Empire adopted Christianity. Any argument that the use of religious art in homes and churches is the result of a "Constantinian fall of the Church," as popularly spouted by Protestants from Calvin through the nineteenth century, is without merit.

Under imperial patronage we do have an explosion of religious art. The reason for this was less imperial influence than the legal status allowing for more permanent church structures. Prior to Constantine, churches were routinely seized by local governors. In response, art, along with the Gospels and other liturgical items, were kept outside the church. These sacred items were typically held in the residence of the bishop or a deacon. With the permanent settlement of churches, icons could be made on the walls themselves instead of panels that were placed on the walls. Frescoes are permanent transformations that forever identify the building as a church. The use of frescoes likely built off of the same tradition that was found in the catacombs. Christian churches, also having received imperial patronage, were wealthy enough for mosaic work. Mosaics were placed not only on the floor, as seen in Jewish synagogues, but also on the walls and ceilings.

The high point of mosaic work came under Justinian's reign.[18] This period is known as the first golden age for the Later Roman Empire. Imperial patronage for the arts moved beyond Constantinople and Palestine into the rest of Asia Minor, Syria, Sinai, Egypt, North Africa, Italy, the Balkans, and Greece.[19] Church architecture also changed with the construction of the Hagia Sophia. The Hagia Sophia came to Justinian in a dream where he had a vision of a large unsupported dome on a square building. This architectural marvel had never occurred before but transformed religious architecture throughout the Middle East and Europe. The dome becomes identified specifically with Orthodox Church architecture and typically at the high point of this dome was an icon of Christ known as the Pantocrator, or all powerful, the ruler of all. The first Pantocrator icon was preserved at Saint Catherine's monastery in Sinai. Justinian sponsored its founding along with a number of other monasteries.

The Middle Byzantine period, or the Macedonian Renaissance,[20] saw another development of Christian art with a number of illumined manuscripts. With the Palaeologian Renaissance[21] the peak of Byzantine art was achieved. The following century saw the disintegration and eventual loss of the empire itself in 1453. While the empire's borders shrunk, a greater emphasis was placed upon religious imagery and the belief that a greater world existed beyond mere perceptions.

It was Justinian II who called for the Quinisext Council, also known as the council in Trullo. This council in 692 spoke about what was appropriate in Orthodox iconography. This council is not considered an ecumenical one, as it spoke mostly on issues of dogma, laying out canons on various subjects. It was also never accepted by Rome. In the council icons are recognized as the mirror of grace and truth. The council, in canon 100, condemned anything that was deceitful or that corrupted the intelligence by exciting the passions.[22] Icons are not intended to be theatrical but contemplative.

Canon 73 also said that holy images, including the cross, should not be placed on the floor as had been done before, since they could be treated with disrespect. In canon 82 specific decrees were made against imaging Christ as a lamb, since Christ is the good shepherd, not one of the lost sheep. The practice of depicting Christ as a lamb ended in the East. It continued in the West, often illustrating Christ as a lamb led to slaughter.

As the disagreement of what a lamb could reasonably signify, we see the difficulty in establishing some specific formulations as to what can be depicted at all. Depending on the historical and cultural understanding, what is taken for granted or a sign of disrespect, could be polar opposites. As Bourdieu tells us, habitus is "history turned into nature."[23] Habitus is the structuring structure, something that regulates society without the need of a regulator. Theology, as embodied in specific canons, is the expression of a reality as represented to safeguard against oppositional notions. Mosaics with Moses and other prophets were found on the floors of synagogues. Christian churches had carved crosses and mosaics of crosses on the floor before the council, but these historical realities shifted. Instead of contemplative ornamentation, standing on them was understood as disrespectful. The symbol remained, but how one interacted with it varied.

For both East and West, icons as symbols took on a different connotation than what was envisioned. Therefore, icons were rejected, a practice known as iconoclasm that will be addressed in chapters 5 and 6. For Orthodox Christianity, the discussion of veneration and the image is best understood through the two major theological responses to the iconoclastic controversies in the eight and ninth centuries. John of Damascus and Theodore the Studite presented the theological basis as understood today for Orthodox iconography. While apologetic in nature, they faced critiques and concerns that still exist in the mind of some today. Once we understand their main theological tenets concerning icons, the why of icons, their connection to Christian anthropology and cosmology, should come into place.

The first wave of iconoclasm was led by the iconoclastic emperors Leo III the Isaurian and his son Constantine V in the eighth century. The iconodule position was articulated by the greatest systematic theologian of the Eastern Church, Saint John of Damascus.[24] John had the distinct advantage of being outside of the borders of the Later Roman Empire. Even though he was a devout Christian, he held a prominent position in the Umayyad Caliphate before in 730. In 730, he retired to the Mar Saba monastery near Jerusalem, where he wrote his *Exposition of the Orthodox Faith* and his *Three Treatises on the Divine Images*. While not present in Constantinople, he saw the abuses of the Isaurians and wrote several tracts against them in support of icons. In his support of icons, John lays out several reasons why the veneration of icons is appropriate and beneficial for the Christian.

The easiest response supporting the maintenance of icons is their place in tradition. John shares the story of Abgar the king of Edessa receiving "the image made without hands" of Christ,[25] as well as the conversion and life of St Mary of Egypt drawing close to Christ through the icon of the Theotokos.[26] He quickly refutes the notion that an icon is a violation of the Second Commandment by demonstrating that an icon is not an idol. An idol is a false image that is used to take worship away from God, and icon of Christ, and by extension the saints are legitimate images as they are used to bring worship to God. John also demonstrates that the prohibition was not universal in the Bible. Shortly after Moses receives the Ten Commandments, God orders Moses to create two carved Cherubim for the Arc of the Covenant.[27] John argues that the broad prohibition against images in the Old Testament had more to do with the condition of the Jew than the image. The proscription was "legislated for the Jews . . . because of their inclination toward idolatry, but not for Christians, who serve God alone and have . . . a perfect knowledge of God."[28] It is only after Christ has revealed Himself that the inclination toward idolatry can be abated by imaging what is revealed instead of what one speculates. John clearly disagrees with Plato's conclusion in the allegory of the Dividing Line.

One of the key distinctions that John makes is in explaining the distinctions between worship λατρεία (*latreia*) and veneration ηροοκύνησις (*proskynesis*). Worship belongs to God alone: "The veneration of worship is one thing, veneration offered in honor to those who excel on account of something worthy is another.[29] He further expands on the discussion between the image and the archetype, that the iconoclast Constantine V advanced. Unlike Constantine, John argues that an image is "a likeness depicting an archetype but having some difference from it; the image is not like the archetype in every way."[30] It is the difference that makes the image separate from the archetype, but it possesses the same name and therefore the divine grace is communicated through it. John does not see a problem with venerating an image, since following Basil the Great "the honor given to the image passes to the archetype."[31]

Icons also serve a practical purpose. John stresses that words and images are on equal footing. "What the book does for those who understand letters, the image does for the illiterate; the word appeals to hearing, the image appeals to sight; it conveys understanding."[32] Icons are books for the illiterate who can teach those who can see them.

Finally, John discusses the transformation, that we can approach images within light of the incarnation. Since Christ took on matter, we are not depicting something that is unknown. "Of old, God the incorporeal and formless was never depicted, but now that God has been seen in the flesh and has associated with humankind, I depict what I have seen of God."[33] We hold matter in respect because the God of the universe took on matter. We receive the bread of life and the cross, which are material not purely spiritual experiences. John articulates that "I do not venerate matter, I venerate the fashioner of matter, who become matter for my sake, and in matter made his abode, and through matter worked my salvation. 'For the Word became flesh and dwelt among us.'"[34] Affirming the incarnational aspect of Christ is not a Monophysite or Nestorian trap as Constantine V postulated, but we see that in the icon the two natures of Christ's humanity and divinity are acknowledged without confusion, change, division, or separation as Chalcedon affirms. Saints, as well as holy objects, also share in this since they are sign posts to Christ and not receiving worship themselves.

Theodore's theology focused on the specific concerns of the second-wave iconoclasts, as will be addressed in chapter 5. He begins his first treatise on icons rather clearly, that the object of all veneration does not equal worship.

"Worship is unique, and belongs to God alone; but other kinds of veneration belong to others. We venerate kings and rulers, servants venerate their masters, children venerate their parents: but not as gods. Although veneration has the same outward form, it varies in intention."[35]

Theodore grants the iconoclasts objection concerning the uncircumscribable nature of God. "It is obvious to everyone that the Godhead is incomprehensible and uncircumscribable."[36] Yet he demonstrates that this only applies to the Godhead and not entirely when addressing the hypostatic union of Christ. "We must admit that Christ, is circumscribed. . . . At the same time we must also admit that He is uncircumscribable, if indeed He is God made man."[37] To deny that Christ is circumscribable denies the incarnation, to deny that he is also uncircumscribable denies his divinity. Christ as both God and man, contains both the essence of God and the essence of man. This is the great mystery of the incarnation and to deny this in relation to icons denies the incarnational nature of the divine. Theodore concludes, "Therefore, if anyone denies that our incarnate Lord Jesus Christ is circumscribed by the flesh, while remaining indescribable according to His divine nature, he is a heretic."[38] This position on the incarnation also helps to explain the concept of *theosis*, since matter is transformed when Christ assumes it.

For Theodore, the attack on icons is an attack on Christ's incarnation. We must affirm the entire human nature was assumed, not just a single body as the Apollinarians or Nestorians argued. Christ also remains fully divine without confusion or mixture of these natures, as opposed to the Monophysites. The earlier theological claims of Constantine and the iconoclastic council fall short. Theodore clearly affirms, "In depicting the Saviour, we do not depict either His Divine or His human nature, but His Person in which both these natures are incomprehensibly combined."[39]

Presenting Christ in the icon is an affirmation of Chalcedon. "If Christ's human nature is not changed or confused with His divine nature, then He must be able to be portrayed like any human being. If His two natures are not separated, then the one portrayed must be the incarnate God, even though the divine nature itself cannot be portrayed. Indeed, it is not a nature which can be portrayed, whether divine or human, but a hypostasis."[40] Therefore an image of Christ is not the same as an idol to an unknown spirit. Christ's image directs us to Christ himself. An idol moves one to worship what is not real and that which is not present. The prohibition against idols does not apply to icons. Theodore exclaims, "Would you please stop ignorantly dragging out scriptural verses to use against us, taking the words spoken against the pagans in regard to the forms of idols, and misapplying them to the icon of Christ? For what person with any sense does not understand the difference between an idol and an icon? That the one is darkness, and the other light? That the one is deceptive, the other infallible? That the one belongs to polytheism, but the other is the clearest evidence of the divine economy?"[41]

When addressing the distinction between the image and the prototype, Saint Theodore builds on Saint John and Saint Basil. "The honor given to the image passes over to the prototype."[42] Eliade would say that in acts of veneration the icon becomes the axis mundi, the center of the world where creation comes about, where order is brought out of chaos. For Theodore, the order is brought about through the hypostatic connection between the image and archetype.

Theodore adds that the image differs in essence but bears the likeness of the hypostasis of its prototype. The image does not need to contain the same essence as the prototype but only a likeness. In fact, it must not be identical, for then it is not an image but the original. In the eucharist is the essence of Christ and is not an image of Christ. The Eucharist is Christ. Christ is truly present.

In icons the image and prototype are identical not in essence but in name. "In every case the copy is called by the name which signifies the prototype. This principle also applies to Christ and His icon."[43] Therefore when we venerate the icon, the nature of the thing, wood, paint, etc. is not what receives the veneration but the prototype.

## ICONS AS SYMBOL

Having encountered the main theological responses to iconoclasm in the East, the foundation for mystical understanding of icons should be clearer. Central to the theology of John and Theodore is the notion of symbol. Icons are symbols in the classic sense. They depict reality by bringing two things together. In this case it is the material object and the spirit behind it. Icons must be received as a symbol, connecting these two notions. If it does not communicate to the recipients what is intended, then the symbol is just art. Dennis Sardella says that anyone who approaches an icon only as beauty and fails to see the theology of the icon "misses the greater and most important part of their raison d'etre."[44] Icons are not art simply for the sake of adding beauty, but the transformation that should correspond with that beauty. Archimandrite Vasileios expounds by saying that "A religious picture is an altogether different thing from a liturgical icon. The one is the creation of someone's artistic talent, the other a flower and reflection of liturgical life."[45] For Vasileios, the icon unites the image with not only meaning but a life lived in the Church.

Since all symbols are culturally mediated, icons are specially an expression of Orthodox spirituality. Historically the West separated themselves from the symbolic understanding of icons with Charlemagne, and the development of a different artistic style to connect Western Christians with the divine. Ouspensky maintains that "the *Libri Carolini* dissociated artistic creation from the catholic experience of the Church."[46] The West chose a more naturalist approach to religious art that has value in the West but is foreign to Orthodox Christianity. When Peter the Great tried to assimilate Western art into Russia, it was largely rejected by the people. Its symbolic value was lost or obscured. If the icon is approached only as art it can only lead one to *theoria*, and not toward *theosis*. Icons as received symbols are the basis for spirituality for Orthodox. They possess the theological expressions as revealed in the councils and the Church Fathers as well as the beauty associated with the Church.

As symbols, icons do four different things for Orthodox Christians. First, they affirm the incarnation. As a result of the incarnation, icons also adjust the Christian's understanding of anthropology. What it is to be a man is transformed by Christ. Third the cosmology of the Christian breaks away from the Platonic world that only prizes the forms and affirms matter as well. Finally, icons are essential in how a Christian relates to God through worship that has been transformed by the incarnation.

As argued by John of Damascus and Theodore the Studite, central to the theology of icons is the incarnation. In the incarnation, God assumed humanity by taking on flesh. The immaterial assumed materiality, not through any fault in contemplation as Origen and Neoplatonists maintain, but voluntarily. The Seventh Ecumenical Council grounded the icon in the incarnation. Rejection of icons is a Christological heresy, not a cultural preference. Ouspensky tells us that the council repeatedly "referred to the veneration of icons as unbroken since the time of the apostles, that is, to the uninterrupted succession of the apostolic tradition."[47] Icons are incarnational and traditional. Later Ouspensky states that the "dogma of the veneration of icons is an answer to all heresies."[48] This is because rejection of the icon is a rejection of the Christological conception inherent to the proclamation of all councils.

Following the incarnation, the cosmology of Christianity was fleshed out. For Orthodox Christians the body cannot be limited to the vehicle for the soul as Plato affirmed. Neither can the soul be reduced to an activity of the brain, as a materialist may affirm. Henry Boosalis, a dogmatic theology professor at the Orthodox seminary St. Tikhon's, tells us that, "The soul has life not only as an activity but also as its essence, since it is self-existent; for it possesses a spiritual and noetic life that is evidently different from the body's and from what is actuated by the body. Hence when the body dissolves, the human soul does not perish with it."[49] This is in keeping with the conception of the soul advanced by Gregory of Nyssa addressed in the previous chapter.

Typically, the Christian concept is that man in the singular is the union of body and soul, or body, soul, and spirit. The spirit is a function of the soul, thus the discussions of man as dipartite or tripartite is really a modern academic exercise. Maximus the Confessor affirms that "The rational and intellectual soul given to man is made in the image of its maker and through desire and intense love it holds fast to God and participates in the divine life."[50]

John Meyendorff argues that, "On this point, the Biblical view decidedly overcame Platonic spiritualism; by the same token, the visible world and its history were recognized as worthy of salvation and redemption."[51] Man is truly man because he is the union of a created body and a created soul. As Lossky states, "Not only the soul but the body of man is created in the image of God."[52] Christian anthropology consistently affirms the union of soul and body. There is not room for a "Christian Materialism" that rejects the soul, nor a Gnosticism that rejects the material body.

It could be argued that icons serve as the body of the one presented, while not losing the connection the saint has with their material body. The ancient Christian conception of body differs from our modern materialist ideas. Bodies differ not only among particulars, for no two people's bodies are exactly the same. Bodies also differ according to kinds, a human body is not the same as the body of a dog, or the body of a tree. Similarly, the human body differs from the body of an angel or other celestial being.

Fr Stephen De Young defines body in this ancient sense, as a "nexus of powers and/or potentialities."[53] The body as the nexus of powers and potentialities serves to strengthen the spiritual senses. Man as body, has a body that is in service to the soul and the aim of union with God. This again helps to differentiate between *theoria* and *theosis* as the telos of mankind, since *theoria* is understood only in this gnostic spiritualized sense, whereas *theosis* necessarily incorporates the body as well.

Bodies understood in this way belong to people in different ways depending on how they are interacting with them. Icons can serve as the body of a saint because they are present in the icon; their power *dynamis* or energy ἐνέργειαι is present. Symbolically, the icon serves to bring together the life of the saint with their image. As bodies are different, it is not about the material, but the presence of these powers. Maximus the Confessor states, "The body is an instrument of the intellectual soul of a man, and the whole soul permeates the whole body and gives it life and motion."[54] Similarly when veneration is given to a saint through their icon, the veneration passes from the image to the archetype in part because the *dynamis* of the saint is made present in the icon. The icon is not "possessed," nor does it somehow trap the saint in itself. Rather it provides the means of communion where the saint is truly present in the interaction.

How a saint can be present in an icon demonstrates a further break with Plato, and a cosmology that is transformed by a symbolic union of spirit and matter. Eliade reminds us that symbolic thought "makes it possible for man to move freely from one level of reality to another."[55] This movement of thought is interpreted differently at different times and locations. Symbols identify, assimilate, and unify different levels of realities that are otherwise incompatible.

In this symbolic union of life man is understood as a microcosm. As Meyendorff maintains, "as image of God, man is lord of creation and 'microcosm.'"[56] Microcosm, initially used by Platonists, was transformed by the Cappadocian fathers. The body is a microcosm because it unites the intelligible and sensible; it also has a telos. It is through symbols that we have both the unity and telos most present. Man as a microcosm is also a symbol of the cosmos, just as an icon is the symbol of the saint.

The clearest representation of man as microcosm is seen in the story of creation. Matthew Pageau asserts that "to understand the book of Genesis and its ancient cosmology, we must posit a universe founded on meaning and language instead of mindless mechanical causality."[57] Adam can be understood as a particular man, but as Lossky points out the name Adam suggests it is universal as well.[58] Adam means man, and in the story serves as the universal man. Connecting Orthodox cosmology with the incarnation, Adam is created in the image of Christ. The story of Adam is an occasion where we can envision ourselves as Adam, created in the image of God. Since Adam is the beginning of creation, a connection with Adam therefore brings us back to Eliade's conception of sacrality, returning to the moment of creation.

Still, Adam's creation is a failed creation. The fall allows for chaos to remain if not grow. Therefore, the archetype for Christians cannot be Adam but must be Christ. Following the fall, Lossky states, "Now there is only one nature common to all men, . . . the body of Christ."[59] In Christ, human nature is singular though the persons are many. This is not an act of creation but of re-creation or a new creation as Paul speaks about. Simeon the New Theologian articulates it such that, "Man, such as God had created him, ceased to exist in the world; it was no longer possible for anyone to be like Adam was before his fall. But it was indispensable that such a man exist."[60] This union is the reason for the incarnation and the recreation of man through the incarnation.

Man as microcosm also has this telos toward union with God. Icons help model this telos. As images of sanctified people, they invite the practitioner to engage with that sanctity. As Peterson states concerning maps, "The future is an image or partial image of perfection, to which we compare the present, insofar as we understand its significance."[61] The behaviors that go along with this require formation and transformation. Ouspensky states that the greatness of man can only consist as a microcosm of the universe with a defined telos. "It is inherent in his destiny because it is his calling to become a great world in the little one, a created god. This is why everything in the icon focuses on the image of man."[62]

This telos is understood by the Church Fathers in the dialogue by God preceding creation. The creation of man was accomplished not only as a union of body and soul but also in the image and the likeness of God. The concept of image and likeness helps us approach the meaning and theology behind the icon. After all, the word image (ἡ εἰκών) is the same word that is used for icon. According to Genesis man was created in the image of God, or as an icon of God. Boosilas clarifies this point: "Christ is the natural image of God, while man is created according to this image."[63] It has been argued, especially by nineteenth and early twentieth century scholars of religion such as Max Muller, Edward Tylor, and Sigmund Freud, that Judaism and later Christians anthropomorphize God. Instead, it would be best to say that Christians have a theanthropic view of humanity. God is not made in man's image, but man is made in God's image.

Christian apologists first spoke in the philosophical language of the Greeks to explain this mystery to their fellow Greeks. As discussed in chapter 2, the early apologists Clement and Justin criticized Plato and broader Hellenic thought, calling them half-philosophers. The telos fell short in part because of this rejection of the material, and therefore a rejection of both the cosmos of Christianity and the use of icons to help navigate this cosmos.

Jonathan Pageau tells us that "Iconography is just a very powerful exemplary of how the patterns—the same patterns we find in Scripture, find visual form in icons, but it's there all over the place. The world is made this way. It's basically the structure of reality."[64] The icon as such is the revelation of truth. Truth must correspond to what is known about both the nature of people and their universe. As Christianity affirms the incarnation, material patterns aid in ways that contemplation cannot. *Theoria* has to make way to *theosis* because of the presence of the icon. Material, physical communion with an object is made incarnate. Carnal reality mediates spiritual concepts. For Orthodox Christianity the icon confirms creation and the conception of mankind as a union of body and soul.

The icon not only confirms the Christian conception of the universe as a harmony of matter and form, but it also confirms this reality over and again. The icon is an essential component in Orthodox worship of the divine. They are both a sign and a symbol. They signify the object present while also being the bridge to that object. They are personal not abstract. In the liturgy, people are collectively and individually encountering the object of veneration or worship. As Schmemann says, "We do not symbolize the presence of the angels; we *do*, however, join them in their unceasing glorification of God."[65] This is accomplished because time and space are transformed in the symbol.

The icon, especially with its use in the sacrament, is thus somewhat sacramental. How icons are used in veneration and their liturgical function will be further discussed in chapter 4. Concerning the sacraments, it is important to know that unlike the West, Eastern Christians do not hold a set number of sacraments. In the history of the Church many acts were confirmed as sacraments by one community and not conceived of as such by another. Orthodox Christianity allows for a more fluid conception of sacrament. Orthodox prefer to use the Greek term *mysterion* as opposed to Latin *sacramentum*.

For Maximus the Confessor's theology, the symbol is "inseparable from, and for all practical purpose, subordinated to the central notion of mystery, *mysterion*, which, at least in its application to the liturgy, refers to the mystery of Christ and to His saving ministry."[66] Mystery therefore is the content of faith, the knowledge of that content. It is an act of revelation, something given and mediated by Christ. Schmemann tells us that the mystery's action and its very presence in the liturgy privileges the symbol. "The Symbol is thus the very reality of that which it symbolizes. By representing, or signifying, that reality it makes it present, truly represents it."[67] Symbol must be properly understood in the context of bringing things together and mediating the presence of a saint, as understood in the liturgical life of the Church and its members. There are many Orthodox scholars, such as Pavel Florensky, and iconographers, such as George Kordis, who maintain that there is nothing symbolic about the icon. I believe their reading of symbol is limited to the notion of representative rather than what I am arguing here that a symbol unites both realities together.

Eliade throughout his works speaks of sacred spaces. The Church by its nature constitutes a break in the profane space of the world and is transformed into a sacred location. In this sacred location space is transformed. Actions that are done in the liturgy are transformed because they happen in heaven not on earth. The practitioners are heavenly participants, not earthly spectators. Icons allow one to engage with this sacred space and can only be understood in this light. Andrew Louth reminds us that "we can only fully understand an icon by seeing it as part of an iconic world, a world whose symphonic harmony is established and manifest in the manifold relationships and reflections that link everything together."[68] If one denies the iconic world, then the icon has no meaning.

If the cosmos is a harmony of the present moment and space with the eschatological unfolding whereby all things are healed and restored, then the icon is the medium for this. The icon creates the sacred space, as it differentiates one sphere from another. Icons not only bridge the sacred and profane but unite the fragments that are disintegrated in the profane world, joining them in the sacred with an idealized representation to which we all strive. As Arch. Vasileios states, "The icon is the new pillar of fire that leads the new Israel to the Promised Land. It is a new star leading to the King of peace."[69] Icons thus represent perfection. They are only made perfect though because of the theology of the incarnation and the engagement by the practitioner in a symbolic world where matter and form are united.

Because icons are proclamations of the incarnation, all icons are therefore to one degree or another icons of Christ. Even when Christ is not depicted, he is recognized as the source of sanctification and the means of communion. Jonathan Pageau tells us that "Out of the icon of Christ appears the icons of the saints, the feasts, and the vast church programmes which grace our long history."[70] The icon presents the pattern for the reality and the Church, as both are understood as being one. As Schmemann says, "The whole point of the eschatological symbolism is that in the sign and that which it signifies are one and the same thing."[71]

As a union of sign and signifier, icons always point to the archetype. Just as Plato's conception of the forms is hidden, the material representation makes present the form behind it. Aidan Hart, an iconographer, states what is understood by all Orthodox Christians when they approach an icon, "an icon is always pointing beyond itself to its archetype, to what it depicts."[72] Daniel Clendenin goes a step farther, telling us that "Since the person depicted is a bearer of divine grace, the icon must portray his holiness to us; Otherwise, the icon would have no meaning."[73]

We can add to this worship and veneration associated with icons as well. This time is the fullness of time both before creation and at its completion. Time in this symbolic sense stops. Secular time is transformed into something different through participation and engagement in the sacred space. Matthew Pageau says that "that 'time' may be considered the opposite of 'space' in ancient cosmology. Of course, in this context space is defined as a stabilizing power against the transformative forces of time."[74] Sardella adds that "icons invite the religious viewer to transcend physical time and place and enter into sacred time and space, in effect serving as metaphorical conduits to the divine."[75] For both religious insiders and outsiders, scholars and practitioners of religion, time and space are not understood in the profane materialist way. Instead, time along with space are made more real through contact with the sacred and the icon.

While present with the icon, time itself is made sacred. Eliade speaks of the concept of sacred time in multiple works. In the *Myth of the Eternal Return*, he speaks of this time as a mystical return to creation. We have seen a similar argument made by Matthew Pageau. In *The Sacred and the Profane*, Eliade discusses how sacred time is different within a liturgical Christian context. Eliade picks up on the incarnational nature associated with Christian worship in the liturgy. "Christianity radically changed the experience and the concept of liturgical time, and this is due to the fact that Christianity affirms the historicity of the person of Christ. The Christian liturgy unfolds in a historical time sanctified by the incarnation of the Son of God."[76]

This sacred time is beyond what Plato envisioned with the realm of ideas. Plato hinted toward a greater fulfillment of reality present, but not this level of transformation. Just as *theosis* is a step beyond *theoria*, symbolic engagement with the idea is transformed into a different reality. Plato's *theoria* is akin to standing before a natural image instead of a sacred one. Clendenin provides an illustration when he says that "Like worship itself, the icon is a revelation of eternity in time. This is why in sacred art the naturalistic portrait of a person can be only a historical document; in no way can it reflect the liturgical image, the icon."[77]

Both in the liturgy and at home, icons provide the means of transformation and affirmation. They transform a space into sacred space. They also affirm the Christian understanding of the cosmos as shaped by the incarnation. Icons establish the Orthodox understanding of religion. Boosalis tells us that, "The image of God in man is not limited to one specific quality or characteristic of human nature. Rather, it emanates as through a prism, throughout the whole of human existence."[78] This may be why Eliade defines man as *homo religiousis*, or Saint Nektarios says, "Without religion, man distorts his god-like character and destroys the beauty of his image, which can only become manifest in him through likeness to the image of God."[79]

## ICON AS IMAGE

To fully comprehend how icons serve as a symbol, we must also decipher the idea of image as understood in this iconic sense. This approach has key practical concerns to how the Orthodox Christian understands their religious duties. To begin, we commonly say that a son is the image of the father, or a daughter is the image of the mother. They image their parent not only in how they may look but the mannerisms and how they act resembles their parent. An image is not based upon the physical resemblance alone, but in how that resemblance interacts with its surroundings.

Images are also something seen. We expect to look upon an image, not to hear it, but we also know that we can see beyond what is just physically present. We tell people that we can see what they are up to, speaking about their motivations or desires. These two conceptions of imaging something presuppose a relationship exists between the person seeing the image and the image itself.

Image necessarily is a relational term. Man by being an image of God is a person who relates to a personal God. Louth maintains that "Being in the image means being a rational, or intelligent, being with free will."[80] Being an image of God, we can extrapolate that man is a person. Beyond that the person is one that resembles its source. Since God is described as love in John's First Epistle, Orthodox Christians are assumed to be love as well, or are called to image this love. God is also free, thus to image God includes free will, as Louth mentioned. As Lossky states, "The image is the personal being of man in his freedom."[81]

This freedom allows for greater or lesser resemblance of the image to the imager. The possibility exists to obscure the image. This condition theologically is known as sin. The goal of this freedom according to Gregory of Nazianzus is "that good might belong to him as the result of his choice."[82] This free choice to grow closer to the image of God is fulfilled in the second portion of the creation description, the likeness of God.

In Greek, the term likeness is *homoiosis*. The ending implies an ongoing state not a completed one.[83] This ongoing state implies motion, and a telos to that motion. St Irenaeus conceives this aspect of creation to imply that man was created immature with an opportunity to approach the divine. Likeness is understood as potentiality to attain spiritual perfection. Saint Nektarios Kefalas adds to this that God "created him also as a moral being."[84] "That by making continual progress in virtue he may be perfected and truly conform to the 'image and likeness of God.'"[85]

Virtue, both moral and spiritual, become the means of growing into the likeness of God, a key idea to understanding *theosis*. Likeness in creation was in a state of potentiality. It is here that Aristotle's philosophy of potentialities and actualities can be of some use, but the actuality has an infinite dimension. Christ is the only one who is fully like God, in that He is God. Paul affirms that Jesus is the image of the invisible God.[86]

For man to grow into the likeness of God is not only the act of creation but of re-creation. It is achieved only through the new creation. The new creation restores the image of God in man, transfigures man and "makes him no longer just potentially godlike—in the image of God—but actually godlike in likeness of being,"[87] as Saint Sophrony tells us. The notion of *theosis* is the goal and likeness established in growing into the likeness of God. This requires participation. As Lossky says, "A single will for creation, but two for deification. A single will to generate the image, but two to make the image into a likeness."[88]

The icon represents a foretaste of *theosis*. It depicts the saint as having arrived. One should not see this arrival as full or complete. The epistemological difference between God and man remains infinite. Even with eternity the process is never complete. The icon shows the state of partaking in the energy of God, not just contemplation of God. The icon tries to depict divine beauty as the action of God through the saint. God is beauty, as Dostoevsky states. The icon must show beauty in man to depict them as partakers of this likeness of God. Saint Theophan the Recluse urges parents to set icons before their children because of their beauty. "The beautiful, which on one side is essentially bound up with the forms of the senses and the imagination, will attract him not otherwise than under sacred forms."[89] The beauty of the icon will draw the child to seek the beauty of God. Hart says, "one role of beauty is to give us a foretaste of that for which we suffer and labour. Aesthetic beauty intimates the prize of our asceticism. It shows us the trophy for which we compete."[90]

Hart continues by differentiating Platonic beauty, which consists in balance and order, with Christian beauty. "Christian beauty is ultimately rooted in something more personal; beauty is perceived primarily as a quality of persons, as a radiance of a relationship."[91] Beauty is relational because it is an aspect of God, it bears witness to God.[92] Furthermore it unites people together as an affirmation of the beauty in others. The beauty of the icon also affirms human creation as something good. While fallen and free to reject beauty, man was created in the image of a beautiful God.

Icons are beautiful to aid in the transformation that we are all called to. Icons confirm the Christian anthropology and the cosmology. Man is created in body and spirit and as the image and likeness of God. They show beauty because God is beautiful and created man beautiful. Icons reveal the telos of man embodied in Christ, called to be created and continually to be re-created, to image Christ more and more.

A materialist approach to an icon is one that removes its teleological meaning. If we eliminate the prototype from the image, the icon becomes an imaginative act not a religiously significant one. Daniel Sahas prefers to avoid the connection between image and icons entirely. For him image, from *imago*, "implies a depiction out of one's imagination; an image compared to an icon is a *desideratum*, not a statement."[93] Yet icon as image, in the more Platonic and traditional usage, connects closer to the representation in a mirror. St Ephrem the Syrian says man "having purified the eyes of his heart, always discerns the Lord in himself, as in a mirror," and "transforms himself into the same image."[94] The image is not imaginary but participatory. This is why many icons include a name. They are not images but instead are identified with the person presented. Jamey Bennett tells us, "When we signify an icon with a name, we transfer the honor to the prototype; by embracing it and offering to it the veneration of honor, we share in the sanctification."[95]

When an icon is made, it is not an expression of individual artistic talent. Rather it is a product of the eccelsia for itself as a lived community. The concept of icons and community formation will be discussed in chapter 9. Icons portray more than the subject matter, but Christianity in its entirety. The icon makes present the archetype of the image, making present Christ and His saints. Ouspensky expresses, "What is shown in the icon becomes reality, as first-fruits, in the eucharistic essence of the Church."[96]

The icon as a symbol is the means of communion. In this communion the icon is also the pedagogue. It teaches the spiritual truths inherent to it. Since icons, to be an icon, are received as this spiritual bridge, symbolic interpretation is guided by symbolic knowledge. Meaning and truth are then interpreted and understood through both the image and the community that embodies it. This is why Orthodox Priest Andrew Damick constantly affirms that "doctrine matters."[97] "Here is a fundamental truth about all religious practice: What you believe and what you do make a difference. If this is true, and I think it's obvious that it should be, then there is also a corollary we have to accept: If you change what you believe and what you do, you will get different results."[98] The naturalistic style of icons advanced by Peter the Great resulted in abandonment of the icons. In the nineteenth century, this resulted in the intelligentsia abandoning the Church. In Russia, this led to the "Old Believers" schism and other struggles in the Russian Church.

What is depicted and how it is depicted forms how it is received and what it is to then be an icon. Western realism was not received by the Church in Russia or elsewhere as naturalism removed symbolism. A portrait differs from an icon as a story differs from a myth. Both can be true, both can be beautiful, but only the latter conveys something infinitely more. Infinitely more is what separates icons and myths from good art and good storytelling. Not all art or stories need to be religious to convey meaning. There are wonderful pieces of art and stories that deeply touch someone, yet it is at the level of *theoria*, of Platonic contemplation. Icons and mythic stories connected with scripture and the lives of the saints seek to convey *theosis*. They seek to convey not only the contemplative realm but the very source of that contemplation, and to unite that divinity in material existence. What is depicted in an icon is not just a saint but the source of their sanctity.

Temple states, "The icon was an image in matter of an event or person whose reality was actually in a higher, invisible and non-material world."[99] This is also why icons are not overly complex. Cities are often represented by one or maybe two buildings, and vast crowds are represented by a handful of additional unnamed people. Intentionally icons have empty space. There are not typically more people than necessary to convey the message, often it is a solitary image. The focus is on the transformation of both the saint and the observer of the icon.

This is one reason why the face is central in icons. An overly complicated icon runs the risk of obscuring the face of the saint. Icons must be personal. The English term person derives from both the Greek *prosopon* and the Latin *persona*. These terms originally meant mask, the expressive face of the character performing in the amphitheater. It is this face put on the performer that identified them to their audience; it also revealed something about that character. The face is the central identifying part of a person. It is how we identify a person and how we envision them.

The face of the icon is directed toward the viewer. Even when it would be natural to depict someone facing away or in profile, they face the observer of the icon. This is not incidental; it often produces more work for the iconographer to turn the face away from the central action of the icon. In doing so the icon puts the action not in the depiction but in the relation between the icon and the devotee. Icons present the face of Christ and His saints because this is how we relate to people. Icons are relational and not static. They remind us that what we long for is not bare walls, where *theoria,* or observance to a law code and morality is the goal, but a transforming face-to-face relationship with the divine that does not leave the spectator as they were before the encounter.

By seeking an encounter, icons avoid becoming an ideological tool. When people encounter one another, we identify the other not as an ideology but as a person. The same exists even with God in the icon. In icons we see God and interact with God. Depictions of Christ are, as John of Damascus and Theodore the Studite remind us, pictures of God. While God is uncircumscribable, the incarnation circumscribes God, it en-fleshes God and gives God a face that we can see and relate to. This is done in and through personal transformation. We must seek out God in the icon; this requires our participation. Mariamna Fortounatto and Mary Cunningham remind us that, "The idea that the faithful may be given the grace to see God in fact has biblical authority. 'He that has seen me has seen the Father,' says Christ to Philip in John 14:9, and again, in the Beatitudes, he says, 'Blessed are the pure in heart, for they shall see God'" (Mt 5:8).[100]

Icons reveal the face of God and also the face of Christ the man. The union of God and man in Christ is the cornerstone in accepting icons by the Church. The creation of icons is participation in this incarnational act. The materials used to make icons are matter, objects derived from the earth and created for spirit. Regardless of the medium, painting or mosaic, the material for icon creation is a union of matter and form. Life is given to lifeless matter and made present through the face of a person. For the Church, the beginning of the pursuit of God is the conviction that Christ defines humanity. Not only does the understanding of the divine begin by learning from Christ, but so too does the concept of what it is to be a man. This is the conclusion of the council of Chalcedon, that Christ is perfect man. Accordingly, we learn about what it is to be human through participation with Christ. By identifying Christ as the archetype of man while being God, the Church affirms that religion is something eminently personal.

The notion that religion is personal lay behind many nineteenth-century religion scholars' conclusions about the origins of religion. These scholars sought to identify the first religion, what they called the ur-religion. They attempted to find the simplest religious expression and apply that concept to religion going forward. For Muller, this was a slow evolution of naming objects and actions and eventually agency was given over to the name. Religion formed around a personal connection between people and these personified objects. For Tylor, the ur-religion was animism, and the fundamental belief that there were spiritual beings behind natural forces. Both Tylor and Muller understand religion as beginning a connection with something that is outside of the individual person. The Church affirms these statements but does not see this as an evolutionary process, rather a revealed one. There is a name and an archetype behind these forces, and it is Christ.

For Durkheim, the ur-religion is totemism. The totem is the symbol which represents the clan or people. For many the totemic animal was the source of the people as well. They are in fact descendants of and related to the totem. Orthodox Christians would therefore have no problem relating the icon to the totem. Archpriest and "Elder" by the Alaska Federation of Natives Michael J. Oleksa has edited a list of sources connecting Orthodox missionary activity in Alaska from the eighteenth and nineteenth centuries.[101] One theme that runs through the work is how Orthodox Christians found ways of correlating traditional Orthodox beliefs with the pre-Christian beliefs and customs of the Alaskan natives. Image as totem and as source for life is something that is present in pre-Christian societies and confirmed with Christian claims and understanding of the incarnation. For Orthodox Christians, Christ is the totem of the family of Christians, and Christians are members of the family owing its origins to this totem.

The aim and telos is what makes an icon different than traditional art. As Arch. Vasileios says, "the icon is a life-giving presence. It brings before you the transparency of transfigured history and matter: it brings you to the wedding of the created and the uncreated."[102] It seeks to connect the immaterial with the material, to give a face to God, and to present God's face in others. Icons must therefore be the expression of a lived tradition and not the imagination of an iconographer. This was expressly stated in the seventh session of the Second Council of Nicaea. "The making of icons is not an invention of the painters but an accepted institution and tradition of the Catholic church."[103]

This tradition is typically handed down from one iconographer to another. They are taught and different forms and understanding of the tradition are learned. Pentiuc tells us that "only in relatively modern times was this iconographic tradition fixed in writing."[104] The manuals are compiled by Dionysios of Fourna (1730s), Fotis Kontoglou (1895–1965), and Leonid Ouspensky (1902–1987).

Central to manuals and inherent to the oral tradition of iconography is that icons are first an expression of piety. Icons, while art, are also images of prayer. A beautiful icon can be rejected if it does not embody this prayer. Likewise, a crude icon may be embraced because it has the quality of prayer. Because icons are objects of prayer even with their creation there is no need to consecrate them. They are consecrated with their creation, and they remain a consecrated item in their function. The icon's main function is found in the liturgical and sacramental life of the Church. How they are used will be addressed in the subsequent chapter.

Since an icon's main function is found in the liturgical and sacramental life, they are found everywhere. Icons are found at homes to consecrate a space for prayer. They are found in the catacombs and other places where the dead are buried. Most clearly icons are found in churches where they provide a pedagogical and practical function. Many of the Church Fathers called icons the Gospel for the illiterate. Their use was to illustrate the teachings of scripture to those who enter the church. Saint Gregory the Great, Pope of Rome wrote, "Images are used in churches so that those who do not have literacy, at least, looking at the walls, may read that which they are not able to read in books."[105] John of Damascus confirms this when he says, "If one of the heretics comes to you saying, show me your faith, you take him to the church and place him before various types of holy images."[106]

Being placed in front of various images in the Church reveals the meaning of the icon. The Divine Liturgy itself is a movement of ascent. It begins with the Liturgy of the Word.[107] It then moves directly into the Liturgy of the Faithful. The culmination of the first is the Gospel reading, the culmination of the second is the Eucharist. The first has the little entrance, where the Gospel is brought out; the second has the great entrance where the gifts are processed. The cyclical nature of the liturgy builds from one layer onto another, from *theoria* to *theosis*. Contemplation makes way to experience of the divine. This experience transforms the person spiritually and materially as they are engaged in physical acts of worship.

The physical layout of the church is similarly arranged. Icons are used to highlight the transformation of one space to another, and to draw focus ultimately to the activity of the altar. Participation in the church requires movement. Like all things in the church, movement is both physical and spiritual. There are icon stands throughout the church. Not every Orthodox church is exactly the same. There is great variation between nationalities, localities, and relative wealth and sizes of a parish. Every Orthodox church, from the grandiose where icons cover every surface, to a simple mission parish uses icons to demonstrate the teachings of the Church. The icons on the walls typically depict various saints or events from the scriptures. The saints present are to remind the Christian that they are surrounded by a great cloud of witnesses (Hebrews 12:1).

On the ceiling of the church, typically housed in the dome is a large icon of Christ, known as the Pantocrator. Typically, this is the largest icon in the church. This icon shows Christ as the Lord of all. The dome itself has taken on symbolic value. A dome is understood as movement from the top to the bottom, and it covers the church. Christ, in the center of the dome, symbolizes Christ covering the people in the church and being present with them. Often the dome is contrasted with Western use of a steeple. The steeple represents man's ascent to God. The directional cast between the Orthodox and Western Christians is one of movement. In the East, the focus is on God's descent upon His people. In the West, the movement is of the people toward God. Neither is inherently superior to the other, but the symbolic interpretation of church architecture impacts and mediates the experience.

In the front of an Orthodox church exists an icon screen, known as an iconostasis, that separates the altar from the nave. The development of the iconostasis is a long one in Christian history. Early on icons were placed in front of the nave on a low wall. As time went on, this low wall grew in the East, as it did in some places in the West, notably in England where it developed into the rood screen. The low wall was the demarcation between the holy place and the holy of holies, as early churches were modeled after Moses's tabernacle and Solomon's temple.

The basis of the low wall is still present today, just with larger icons typically present. The wall has an opening in the center, known as the royal doors. These doors have an icon of the Annunciation on them, demonstrating that even while closed, the way is being prepared for union between man and God. Only clergy at certain times are allowed to pass through these doors. In Constantinople the emperor would also go through these doors to receive communion. Other doors, often called deacon doors, are on the outer part of the wall where clergy at other times will enter and exit the altar along with various altar servers.

From the royal doors looking out, Christ is on the left (looking ahead directly to the right of the doors). On the other side of the doors is an icon of the Theotokos. To her right, the icon of the church is present. Churches are named after either a saint or a feast of the Church and the icon of that saint or feast is what is depicted in this place. Next to this is an icon of the archangel Michael. To the left of Christ is an icon of John the Baptist. Next to John the Baptist is an icon of the archangel Gabriel. The icons of Michael and Gabriel are typically the altar doors. This holds other symbolic meaning, as Michael is understood to be the one who brought Adam and Eve out of paradise, and Gabriel announces the return to paradise through the Annunciation. If the iconostasis is wider than these six panels, additional saints are usually depicted.

Depending on the architectural needs, these saints may be on either side of the angelic deacon doors.

Thomas Hopko has also commented about the two main icons to the right and left of the royal doors. He has said that there is a second way to identify the icons of the Theotokos and Christ that adds another level of meaning to the icon screen. The icon of the Theotokos is actually an icon of Christ's incarnation. In almost every Orthodox icon of Mary she is holding Christ and points to her son. The icon of Christ is understood not as Christ as he came but as he will come. Following this interpretation, the icons are of the first and second coming in addition to the Theotokos and Christ. If one takes this reading, then the location of the altar in the center of the doors has a revealed meaning. Here in the preparation of the Eucharistic gifts we have Christ present now among His people.

From this low wall, additional layers were slowly constructed on top of it. This was done first in Russia, where icons were placed in higher and higher rows above the iconostasis. These rows vary both in number and composition greatly between churches. If present, they may contain the twelve great feasts of the Church, the twelve apostles, various saints or Old Testament prophets. The number varies from none to as many as the five-tiered Rublev iconostasis. There are no rules that limit or define what is on these additional layers of the iconostasis.

The variation that exists in the construction of the iconostasis is permitted as long as the basic theology behind the iconostasis remains. First it needs to be stressed that countless theologians and commentators insist that the icon wall is not a barrier separating the altar from the people. Instead, it is understood as a meeting point, a link as Baggley says.[108] Since icons are the medium to deeper understanding, the existence of the iconostasis is there to intensify a spiritual reality not to remove the clergy or the gifts from the people. It indicates the integration of earthly participation into heavenly worship. Florensky goes so far as to say, "Destroy the material iconostasis and the altar itself will, as such, wholly vanish from our consciousness."[109]

The iconostasis, like the icon itself, holds tremendous significance and symbolic meaning. On the other side of the wall the altar is present. Unlike Protestant churches that may or may not have an altar, the altar is the focus of the liturgy. The altar contains the divine gifts. The priest also faces the altar not the people. For Luther, Zwingli, and Calvin, this was an outrage that did not make sense. They believed that the celebrant facing away from the people muted the message. For Orthodox Christians, the priest is leading the congregation in worship. The church is constructed as a ship, with the nave being where the work of the people is done and the altar at the bow leading the people forward. The priest is in the heavenly place leading his people, not abandoning them.

Over the apse in the front of the altar is typically the second largest icon of the church. This is an icon of the Theotokos with her arms spread wide in prayer. In front of her is an icon of the Christ child giving a blessing. This icon is known as Panagia Platytera or the Virgin of the Sign or Our Lady of the Sign. The sign is a reference to Isaiah 7:14, that a virgin will conceive. Platytera means wider or more spacious. It conveys the idea that Mary's womb is more spacious than the heavens, that all of creation cannot hold God, yet Mary held God within her. The purpose of the icon again is to affirm the incarnation and bring about union.

Essential to Orthodox understanding of icons is that icons are not just objects. Icons are symbols that affirm the incarnation and call the Christian to a life of *theosis* not *theoria*. The icon also has other ramifications in how the Orthodox approaches people. As mentioned in the previous chapter, Athanasius famously said that "God became man so man can become God."[110] Even with the aim of *theosis*, Orthodox do not see themselves as gods, or equal with God. Instead, the goal is to grow to be like God, and to partake of what God is by nature through God's grace, to become icons of Christ.

With the ambition to be icons of Christ, and with this as the consequence of the incarnation, Orthodox Christians see icons everywhere. People are living icons. This is how all people, regardless of their level of piety, are expected to be treated. If every person is made in the image of God, then all people are God's living icons. Eliade interprets this as a product of religious experience. This experience makes it "possible for man himself to be transformed into a symbol."[111] Mankind becomes the symbol as the symbol takes on more value. This is accomplished through participation, and the greater the recognition of the image of the icon is to God, the greater the recognition of everybody as an icon of God.

Icons become an experience of the holy which therefore transform and contextualize every other experience. This is experienced liturgically, when "the priest censes all the icons in the church; not only those on the iconostasis and the walls, but the living icons, clergy and congregation."[112] Orthodoxy affirms that all people can become saints and can be venerated as imagers of God. Prayer before an icon reaffirms the belief that those other people they may encounter maybe saints and are worthy of veneration. This includes all people, not just the bishop, but also the beggar. This equality of man before God is a departure from Plato but is the outcome of an iconic understanding of the world.

If the Orthodox Christian sees other people as living icons, they must also understand themselves to be an icon as well. The goal is to grow and conform the will into the likeness of God. This understanding requires a great degree of self-knowledge. Saint Nektarios Kefalas states that,

Self-knowledge is the first and foremost obligation of every person. Man . . . is
destined to become like God, in whose image he was fashioned, and to become
a partaker of divine goodness and blessedness. But in order to become like
God—good and blessed—and in order to commune with Him, he must first of
all know himself.[113]

Following Saint Nektarios, knowledge of self is a prerequisite for knowledge of God. One must recognize what in themselves is like God and what
is opposed to God. Then, what is antagonistic to God must be abandoned
through the things of God. Because of our innate intelligence of freedom, we
can choose to do this. Saint Nektarios continues, "When God fashioned man
according to His image, He made him so that he might seek Him, know Him,
love Him, and draw near Him."[114] These abilities are given for sanctification.
Saint Nektarios is not alone with this understanding. Clement of Alexandria
states, "If you desire to know God, you must first know yourself."[115] St John
Chrysostom echoes Clement by stating that "Ignorance about ourselves is
more grievous than the worst pitch of madness and insanity."[116]

Deception of who we are, either through egoism and self-love or
self-loathing, distorts the image of God in man. It not only violates the
symbolic understanding of the icon but also humanity. Nektarios agrees
with Plato in Cratylus who said, "There is nothing worse than self-decep-
tion."[117] Therefore there is a benefit to Plato's contemplation. *Theoria* forces
one to look beyond the mundane world and into the ideas behind it. It con-
strains the person by telling them there is more. Icons do the same but tell
people that there is more than just self-knowledge and contemplation, there
is union with God.

Icons as understood from the Orthodox perspective reveal the value of the
material world. Icons therefore incorporate the symbolic world by not resting
in Platonic contemplation but collapsing the cosmos into the source of sanctity. This collapse includes the person as well. This union does not cause a
loss of identity but provides an identity beyond materialism, mere existence,
or contemplative isolation. Understanding of self and neighbor as image of
God transforms how one interacts with the world around them. This will be
the topic of the next chapter.

Icons stress not only the incarnation of Christ but also the transfiguration. As Christ revealed his divinity, he reveals the telos of mankind. S.
T. Kimbrough proclaims that, "The Byzantine icon in particular reveals
how matter, in fact the whole of creation, human beings and nature alike,
can be transformed: not just to the original harmony and beauty they possessed before the Fall, but to a much greater glory they will acquire in the
eschaton."[118] This calls to mind the story of a Russian intellectual who once
asked the priest why there were not more doctrinal teachings laid out in the

church. The priest casually responded that "Icons teach us all we need to know."[119] The Orthodox church has relatively few systematic theologians, but it has many icons. As William James says, "Moral and religious truths come 'home' to us far more on some occasions than on others."[120] The theology is expressed and known simpler from icons than disputations. The saints reveal theology in a profound way through their lives and works. It should be no surprise then that over the last century a resurgence in interest among icons is taking root in not only traditionally Orthodox areas, but also the West.

## NOTES

1. Schmemann, *A Voice for Our Times*, 247.

2. Russell, *Fellow Workers with God*, 38.

3. Russell, *Fellow Workers with God*, 36.

4. Clendenin, Daniel B. *Eastern Orthodox Theology: A Contemporary Reader.* Grand Rapids, MI: Baker Academic, 2003, 39.

5. Turner, Victor. *The Forest of Symbols: Aspects of Ndembu Ritual.* Ithaca, NY: Cornell University Press, 1967, 70.

6. Baggley, *Doors of Perception*, 78.

7. Archimandrite Vasileios, *Hymn of Entry*, 81.

8. Baggley, *Doors of Perception*, 77.

9. Met Hilarion Alfeyev, *Orthodox Christianity, Volume 3.* Yonkers, NY: St. Vladimir's Seminary Press, 2014, 114.

10. Pentiuc, *Old Testament in Eastern Orthodox Tradition*, 276.

11. Dr. Michael Wingert in a Lecture delivered May 8, 2023, *On the Dead Sea Scrolls.*

12. Met Hilarion Alfeyev, *Orthodox Christianity, Volume III*, 109.

13. Temple, *Icons and the Mystical Origins of Christianity*, 16.

14. Met Hilarion Alfeyev, *Orthodox Christianity, Volume III*, 110.

15. Met Hilarion Alfeyev, *Orthodox Christianity, Volume III*, 112.

16. Bigham, Steven. "On the Origin of Ὁ ὪΝ in the Halo of Christ." *Orthodox Arts Journal*, June 2016.

17. Forest, Jim. *Praying with Icons.* Maryknoll, NY: Orbis, 2017, 3.

18. R. 527–565.

19. Pentiuc, *Old Testament in Eastern Orthodox Tradition*, 277.

20. Roughly 870–1025.

21. 1234–1360.

22. Forest, *Praying with Icons*, 9.

23. Bourdieu, *Outline of a Theory of Practice*, 78.

24. 675–749.

25. St. John of Damascus. *Three Treatises on the Divine Images.* Crestwood, NY: St. Vladimir's Seminary Press, 2003, 41.

26. St. John of Damascus, *Three Treatises on the Divine Images*, 55.

27. St. John of Damascus, *Three Treatises on the Divine Images*, 28.

28. Pelikan, Jaroslav. *The Christian Tradition, Volume 2: The Spirit of Eastern Christendom (600–1700)*. Chicago: University of Chicago Press, 1974, 215.

29. St. John of Damascus, *Three Treatises on the Divine Images*, 25.

30. St. John of Damascus, *Three Treatises on the Divine Images*, 25.

31. St. John of Damascus, *Three Treatises on the Divine Images*, 35

32. St. John of Damascus, *Three Treatises on the Divine Images*, 31.

33. St. John of Damascus, *Three Treatises on the Divine Images*, 29.

34. St. John of Damascus, *Three Treatises on the Divine Images*, 70.

35. St. Theodore the Studite, *On the Holy Icons.* Crestwood, NY: St. Vladimir's Seminary Press, 1981, 19.

36. St. Theodore the Studite, *On the Holy Icons*, 20.

37. St. Theodore the Studite, *On the Holy Icons*, 23.

38. St. Theodore the Studite, *On the Holy Icons*, 39.

39. Ouspensky, Leonid, and Vladimir Lossky. *The Meaning of Icons.* Crestwood, NY: St. Vladimir's Seminary Press, 1982, 32.

40. St. Theodore the Studite, *On the Holy Icons*, 11.

41. St. Theodore the Studite, *On the Holy Icons*, 27.

42. St. Theodore the Studite, *On the Holy Icons*, 13.

43. St. Theodore the Studite, *On the Holy Icons*, 51–52.

44. Sardella, Dennis J. *Visible Image of the Invisible God: A Guide to Russian and Byzantine Icons.* Brewster, MA: Paraclete Press, 2022, 5.

45. Archimandrite Vasileios, *Hymn of Entry*, 81.

46. Ouspensky, *Theology of Icon*, 488.

47. Ouspensky, *Theology of Icon*, 482.

48. Ouspensky, *Theology of Icon*, 483.

49. Boosalis, Harry. *Person to Person: The Orthodox Understanding of Human Nature.* South Canaan: St. Tikhon's Monastery Press, 2018, 103.

50. Maximus the Confessor, *On the Cosmic Mystery of Christ*, 66.

51. Meyendorff, John. *Byzantine Theology: Historical Trends and Doctrinal Themes.* New York: Fordham University Press, 1979, 140–41.

52. Lossky, *Dogmatic Theology*, 86.

53. De Young, Stephen, and Andrew Stephen Damick. "Bodies and the Bodiless." *The Lord of Spirits.* Chesterton, NY: Ancient Faith Publishing, 2021.

54. Maximus the Confessor, *On the Cosmic Mystery of Christ*, 71.

55. Eliade, *Patterns in Comparative Religion*, 455.

56. Meyendorff, *Byzantine Theology*, 142.

57. Matthew Pageau, *Language of Creation*, 21.

58. Lossky, *Mystical Theology*, 120.

59. Lossky, *Mystical Theology*, 121.

60. Clendenin, *Eastern Orthodox Theology*, 39.

61. Peterson, *Maps of Meaning*, 28.

62. Ouspensky, *Theology of Icon*, 497.

63. Boosalis, *Person to Person*, 94.

64. Pageau, Jonathan. "The Inevitability of Re-enchantment." Edited by Ancient Faith. *Orthodox Engagement*, 2021.

65. Schmemann, Alexaner. *Liturgy and Tradition: Theological Reflections of Alexander Schmemann.* Edited by Thomas Fisch. Crestwood, NY: St Vladimir's Seminary Press, 1990, 127.

66. Schmemann, *Liturgy and Tradition*, 122.

67. Schmemann, *Liturgy and Tradition*, 122–23.

68. Walker, Andrew, and Costa Carras. *Living Orthodoxy in the Modern World.* Crestwood, NY: St. Vladimir's Seminary Press, 1996, 167.

69. Archimandrite Vasileios, *Hymn of Entry*, 87.

70. Pageau, Jonathan. "Iconography Shows us the Pattern of Reality." *Orthodox Arts Journal*, 2020.

71. Schmemann, *Liturgy and Tradition*, 127.

72. Hart, *Beauty Spirit, Matter*, 96.

73. Clendenin, *Eastern Orthodox Theology*, 48.

74. Matthew Pageau, *Language of Creation*, 116.

75. Sardella, *Visible Image of the Invisible God*, 135.

76. Eliade, *Sacred and Profane*, 72.

77. Clendenin, *Eastern Orthodox Theology*, 49.

78. Boosalis, *Person to Person*, 100.

79. St. Nektarios Kefalas. *Collected Works, Volume 7: Know Thyself.* Jerusalem: Virgin Mary of Australia and Oceania, 2022, 75.

80. Louth, Andrew. *Introducing Eastern Orthodox Theology.* Westmont, IL: IVP Academic, 2013, 85.

81. Lossky, *Dogmatic Theology*, 90.

82. Lossky, *Dogmatic Theology*, 87.

83. Louth, *Introducing Eastern Orthodox Theology*, 84.

84. St. Nektarios Kefalas, *Know Thyself*, 74.

85. St. Nektarios Kefalas, *Know Thyself*, 11.

86. Col 1:15.

87. Boosalis, *Person to Person*, 99.

88. Lossky, *Dogmatic Theology*, 88.

89. St. Theophan the Recluse. *The Path to Salvation: A Concise Outline of Christian Ascesis.* Safford, AZ: Holy Monastery of St Paisius, 2006, 48 Westmont, IL 49.

90. Hart, "The Nature of Divine Beauty."

91. Hart, *Beauty Spirit, Matter*, 130.

92. Forest, *Praying with Icons*, 16.

93. Sahas, Daniel J. *Icons and Logos: Sources in Eighth-Century Iconoclasm.* Toronto: University of Toronto Presso, 1986, 17.

94. Ouspensky, *Theology of Icon*, 486.

95. Bennett, Jamey. "Should Orthodox Christians Get Their Icons Blessed?" *Ancient Faith*, September 26, 2013. https://blogs.ancientfaith.com/orthodoxyandheterodoxy/2013/09/26/should-orthodox-christians-get-their-icons-blessed/ (accessed 2023).

96. Ouspensky, *Theology of Icon*, 498.

97. Damick, Andrew Stephen. *Orthodoxy and Heterodoxy.* Chesterton, IN: Conciliar Press, 2011, 11.

98. Damick, *Orthodoxy and Heterodoxy*, 9.

99. Temple, *Sacred Art*, 4.

100. Cunningham, Mary B., and Elizabeth Theokritoff. *Cambridge Companion to Orthodox Christian Theology.* Cambridge, UK: Cambridge University Press, 2008; Daley, 141.

101. Oleksa, Michael J. *Alaskan Missionary Spirituality.* Yonkers, NY: St. Vladimir's Seminary Press, 2010.

102. Archimandrite Vasileios, *Hymn of Entry*, 90.

103. Pentiuc, *Old Testament in Eastern Orthodox Tradition*, 271.

104. Pentiuc, *Old Testament in Eastern Orthodox Tradition*, 272.

105. Met Hilarion Alfeyev, *Orthodox Christianity, Volume III*, 211.

106. Met Hilarion Alfeyev, *Orthodox Christianity, Volume III*, 212.

107. Sometimes called the Liturgy of the Catechumens.

108. Baggley, *Doors of Perception*, 91.

109. Florensky, *Iconostasis*, 63.

110. Athanasius, *On the Incarnation*, 107. 54:3 "he was incarnate that we might be made god."

111. Eliade, *Patterns in Comparative Religion*, 455.

112. Walker and Carras, *Living Orthodoxy in the Modern World*, 14.

113. St. Nektarios Kefalas, *Know Thyself*, 7.

114. St. Nektarios Kefalas, *Know Thyself*, 8.

115. St. Nektarios Kefalas, *Know Thyself*, 9.

116. St. Nektarios Kefalas, *Know Thyself*, 9.

117. Plato, *Middle Platonic Dialogues: Cratylus, Euthydemus, Menexenus, Meno, Parmenides, Phaedo, Phaedrus, Republic, Symposium, Theaetetus.* Translated by Benjamin Jowett. Independently published, 2021, 40. Cratylus 428 D

118. Kimbrough, *Orthodox and Wesleyan Scriptural Understanding and Practice*, 33.

119. Clendenin, *Eastern Orthodox Theology*, 33.

120. James, *Writings, 1878–1899: The Psychology of Belief*, 1044.

## Chapter 4

# The Telos of an Icon

The theology behind icons is wrapped up in the words of Saint Basil the Great, that the honor paid to the image is passed along to the prototype. This honor is one that presupposes a relationship, a community, and actions. An isolated icon is not an icon. It only becomes an icon when engaged with by someone for the purpose of spiritual practice. Icons serve not only as models of reality but also models for reality. Following Clifford Geertz's understanding, icons as models for reality are not theories; rather, they are cultural patterns that have a double aspect, "they give meaning, that is objective conceptual form, to social and psychological reality by shaping themselves to it and by shaping it to themselves."[1] It is in this interaction between the icon and the devotee that icons are agents of action. This, not surprisingly, involves active participation by the practitioner. It is fitting to look at this oft overlooked aspect of icons in Orthodox worship, namely how they are used, and how this use helps us understand the symbolic meaning of icons. The telos of an icon is directed toward transformation, toward *theosis*. Only by looking at how icons are used can we understand what it means for the Orthodox Christian to escape from the confinement of Plato's cave. It is not enough to leave the cave; the experience in the open has significant value. In this chapter, we will address the use of icons in practice for Orthodox Christians.

The meaning of an icon is found when they relay their meaning to people. What J. Z. Smith articulates concerning myth can also be applied to icons. Icons serve not only as a narrative, "the analogue to the limited number of culturally determined objects" but also as application that "represents the complex interaction between diviner, client, and situation."[2] It is in this way that Richard Temple's assertion that "it is not icons themselves that we study so much as their meaning. Icons exist to convey the highest cosmological, philosophical and theological ideas"[3] should be understood. The function of icons is this interaction. In this interaction, meaning for oneself is understood, as well as meaning for the universe. In this way, interaction with icons is sacramental. Its use of the material world points to a reality which exists beyond the mundane, and a world that is ordered and shaped by the divine.

These complex interactions between the Christian and the icon begin with the act of veneration. Veneration is not a passive act. One must engage on some level to offer veneration. The most obvious form of veneration to an outside observer is the bowing of one's head. This simple and easily observable action relays significance to the person or object that is being venerated. As Bourdieu posits, agents of ritual action reveal themselves as significant through the movements or postures of the human body.[4] Hart, in his treatment of icons, expresses veneration as a continuation of human nature being an image making being. Veneration by men and women is the use of "all his five senses to express love. He wants to move toward the objects of his love, to touch them and not simply see them."[5]

The first step in understanding veneration is that it is a physical act which reveals desire for the object. Given the medium and setting, the object that is desired is personal transformation and holiness. The second step in understanding veneration is that it does not need to be performative or grandiose. While bowing is probably the easiest act to recognize as veneration for Orthodox Christians, simple observance can be an act of veneration. We are visual creatures, and we understand our world through objects we see even when we do not understand. This is the starting point of Eastern Christian understanding of the world. Henri Nouwen states, "Whereas Saint Benedict, who has set the tone for the spirituality of the West, calls us first of all to listen, the Byzantine fathers focus on gazing."[6]

Once looked upon. the desire for the object, in this case holiness, takes root in the practitioner. This produces an immediate effect. Specifically, the effect is prayer. Consciously or not the door is opened to prayer, to interacting between the two disparate worlds. To return to Plato's Allegory of the Cave, gazing upon the icon is akin to being released from the constraints that limited the ability to turn one's head and being brought to the mouth of the cave and perceiving the light from outside. This experience reveals that there is more, but not yet what that is. Further action is required to understand what this freedom means, and what this glimpse of light truly does.

Perceiving an icon is only a glimpse of the sacramental life. It beckons for further interaction. Icons are also not easy to see in this respect. The point is not to stir the emotions. Rarely are the colors so vivid as to tantalize the senses. They are subtle and inviting. This is also why icons are mediums for veneration and not worship. The invitation is to move forward in building a relationship with the sanctified image.

Once the invitation is accepted, veneration of the icon can take on a deeper relationship. It is at this point that emotions and desire can come into play. As Saint Gregory of Nyssa remarked, "he could not see an icon of Abraham with Isaac 'without tears.'"[7] Just as a parent responds differently to their child's call than to another child's, so too will people who have developed a relationship with the saints.

It may appear odd to many in a Western audience, especially if they are Protestant or nonreligious, to hear about a relationship emerging between a person and an icon. Yet this is exactly what an icon signifies. It is not art, but the door to a spiritual understanding, where the object portrayed is present and interacting back. For most throughout history, the *koinonia* or fellowship includes those materially present and those who are spiritually present. This spiritual presence is taken for granted and not dismissed or rationalized away. When Saint Paul addresses the Corinthians and prohibits them from eating food offered to idols, this was not because of any materialist understanding. Rather the prohibition was because eating food offered to idols had the real result of "having communion with demons by participating in these meals,"[8] as Fr Stephen De Young and other scholars of this period have pointed out.

Unlike the materialist conception of reality, Orthodox Christians take for granted the connection between spiritual and material, that spiritual acts have material effects, and material objects have spiritual effects. This is key to the conception of *theosis* that Orthodox Christians aspire to. The material world participates with the spiritual world. The two spheres are not distinct as Plato conceives of them, but there exists a mutual dependence and a symbiosis between them. Actions and interactions are not limited to one sphere. This is why Metropolitan Hilarion can say that, "Icons grow out of prayer and without prayer an authentic icon cannot be made."[9] Icons also train prayer. The slight bow or the gaze is only the first step in venerating an icon and in understanding veneration. Further exertion is needed. Saint Porphyrios tells us that, "Bodily exertion causes the body to protest and complain and react, but it is unable to make the soul lax in prayer."[10] Bodily activity becomes a part of veneration. The protests of the body invite spiritual action. Physiology affects psychology and vice versa.

The tension between the body and the soul reveals the primary purpose of veneration is engagement in prayer. As Boosalis reiterates, "The whole man, body and soul, is created for holiness. Our entire person—body and soul—participates in prayer."[11] The body is exerted to begin prayer. Prayer is the beginning or continuation of fellowship. Ultimately the purpose of this fellowship is salvation; this is understood through the concept of *theosis*. Father Zinon sums it up thusly, "You need to feel the Holy Spirit. You can feel icons only during prayer."[12] Body and soul are used in prayer; icons as physical objects are only understood spiritually in prayer.

Ouspensky and Lossky see "the icon is both the way and the means; it is prayer itself."[13] Eliade's treatment of sacred stones applies rather well to this conception of icons as prayer itself. For Eliade, "The cult is not, then, directed toward the stone as a material thing, but rather to the spirit that animates it, or the symbol that makes it sacred."[14] Veneration of the image passes to the prototype. The object becomes sacred not because of what it is but because of the symbolic value. Eliade's perception of man was that he is *homo religiosus*, that we are all religious, yet Father Alexander Schmemann advances this understanding by calling man *homo adorans*.[15] For Schmemann, we are worshippers, those who pray, those who venerate. It is the action not just the impulse that separates Eliade from Schmemann. Following this the act of veneration is what makes man, man.

While bowing the head and gazing upon an icon are the first steps in kinetic worship, the most characteristic act and the one most performed and unique to Christianity is the sign of the cross. This simple act is done all the time. Gillian Crow expresses what is common to all Orthodox, conscious or not, that, "The sign of the cross is used as a physical way of praying the 'amen' at the conclusion of prayers, of dedicating one's life to the Trinity, of literally putting one's weight behind one's words."[16] Anytime someone could say amen, they cross themselves. Beyond a physical punctuation to a prayer, the sign of the cross is a prayer in itself. Upon hearing of good or bad news Orthodox Christians reflexively will cross themselves. No words are given, no thoughts expressed, but a physical action is realized. The body at this point reaches out in prayer before the mind has even processed why the prayer is uttered.

The sign of the cross is what begins the liturgy. Separating the matins service from the liturgy, the priest holds up the Gospel over the altar and traces the cross over the antimension, stating "blessed is the kingdom." The signing of the cross transforms time going forward. Just as it transforms time in the liturgy, the signing of the cross also transforms the Christian. The sign of the cross is imprinted upon the Christian at all of the initiation services. During the naming prayers of the infant on the eighth day it is prayed, "let the cross of thine only-begotten Son be signed in his (her) heart and thoughts so that he (she) may flee from the vanity of the world and every evil plot of the enemy."[17] Before even this, the priest makes the sign of the cross on the infant three times. Before any words are expressed to the initiate, the cross is signed over them. At the churching the priest signs the cross over the mother and the infant before they enter the church. The water for baptism is crossed. When this is done, the priest proclaims, "let all adverse powers be crushed under the tracing of the sign of thy cross."[18] This statement, often overlooked, is the key to understanding why the signing of the cross is performed so regularly and unconsciously. Whenever adverse powers are present, they are crushed by the signing of the cross. Whenever a blessing is received the cross signals that. The signing of the cross is an act pregnant with meaning.

The signing of the cross is also done in connection with icons. When someone enters a church, they begin a journey throughout the church, approaching key icons and crossing themselves. This journey mirrors the spiritual journey from the material world to union with God. The church therefore is a physical manifestation of the telos of the Christian. The telos is played out beginning at the very entrance of the church in the part referred to as the narthex. The narthex serves as a border between this world and the next. Symbolically it is connected to the world, the world outside the church, but it is here that icons are first encountered. This reminds people that icons are in the church and in the world. Present in the narthex are the things used to prepare for entrance into the church proper, holy water, candles, and information about the church can usually be found. Here you will frequently find the festal icon of the church. Typically, the sign of the cross is done here.

Then, entering into the nave (the body of the church), the cross is signed at the threshold. Often, another icon may be present at the threshold. This icon is connected to the liturgical cycle and is connected to the commemorations for that day or week. The Christian will cross themselves here and proceed to icon stands or the iconostasis at the front of the church. Beginning on the right side the devotee will venerate and cross themselves before Christ. Then move toward the center, crossing themselves as they pass the altar. From here they will venerate the icon of the Theotokos. At this point it is not uncommon for one or two more bows and crossings to take place. The first would be toward the congregation, the second would be toward another icon found in the church. If the Christian is familiar with parish and the myriad of icons present, they may seek out another icon. This would be the final act of veneration before joining their fellow congregants.

The typical way the sign of the cross is done holds tremendous symbolic value. The hand itself conforms to this symbolic reality. Unlike in Western churches, where the position of the fingers does not carry deep consequence, every finger is made to symbolize a spiritual truth and holds significance. On the right hand, as crossing is always done with the right, the index and middle finger along with the thumb extend outright. These three fingers represent the Trinity. The ring finger and the pinky reside in the palm of the hand. They represent the two natures of Christ: His humanity and His divinity. They are placed into the palm demonstrating the incarnation, that Christ has come down to earth, as the fingers have come down to the hand. Some will also point out that this places the ring finger into the round portion of the palm connected to the thumb. The palm envelops a portion of the finger. This portion of the palm represents the Theotokos, Christ taking His humanity from her.

With the hand properly formed, the signing of the cross begins with the forehead, then knees, and each shoulder. Unlike the West, the first shoulder touched is the right shoulder, then the cross is "pushed" over the heart and rests on the left. It is not uncommon when one is crossing themselves to then rest their hand lightly over their heart.

When standing before an icon the cross is usually done three times. A short prayer accompanies the crossing. Typically it is not verbally expressed, but is connected to whatever is being venerated. Before Christ would be a "Lord have mercy," and in front of the Theotokos or a saint, a call for intercession. At some point in the three crossings, a deeper bow and kissing of the icon is done. The icons throughout the church become the template of religiously significant places, events, and people that usher the participant from the outside world into a world inhabited by saints and one ready to worship God. This journey from outside the church to their place in the nave echoes and anticipates the spiritual journey where the telos is participation with God among the saints.

Bronislaw Malinowski can identify this procession throughout the church as a public performance of religious dogma. He calls this indispensable for the maintenance of morals. Yet Malinowski believes that every article of faith which wields moral influence must be universal. "The endurance of social ties, the mutuality of services and obligations, the possibility of co-operation, are based in any society on the fact that every member knows what is expected of him; that, in short, there is a universal standard of conduct."[19] We see with Malinowski that key to public religious performance is universal adaptation. While the performance, if one wishes to call it that, is public, it is far from universal in the Orthodox Church. How things are done varies from jurisdiction to jurisdiction, from church to church, and even from person to person.

Rules for dogma are spelled out rather clearly for the Orthodox Christian, and many of the rules for praxis. Yet even in the conformity of common worship variations exist and these variations are not incorrect. Some are expressions of personal piety unknown to anyone else and generally not corrected or investigated. Frederica Mathewes-Green, in her short article "12 Things I Wish I'd Known," reveals what appears to be chaos to an outsider when visiting an Orthodox Church. This chaos exists in the "inconsistencies" from person to person when crossing themselves before an icon. She points out that, "Some people cross themselves three times in a row, and some finish by sweeping their right hand to the floor."[20] Other people do not sweep the floor with their hands but bow, and others place their hands on their hearts. Even the number of times someone crosses themselves varies. Sometimes people will cross themselves three times in a row before departing. Others will cross themselves only once. Still others will cross themselves twice then kiss the icon and then cross themselves one more time. Contrary to Malinowski's expectations, nothing is clearly known to all. Rather with the chaos of action, the body is used only to mediate a personal experience. Sister Gabriela writes that, "The most direct way to form an image of God is through the heart, the meeting place between God and man, but this remains a personal and hidden form. There is a visual path to the heart, which is the way of the icon."[21]

Saint Porphyrios articulates his understanding of what is done in the signing of the cross. "First I made the sign of the cross, striking my fingers on my forehead, then on my knees and then on each of my shoulders." This is the typical signing. He continues by demonstrating his actions that follow. "Then I touched the ground with my hands and rose up swiftly. Then I would rest my knees briefly on the ground each time. Do you see how body and soul participate in the worship of God? Mind and heart are with Christ and the body too is with Christ."[22] For Porphyios a quick bow where his knees hit the ground is also used. The whole body can be used, not only the hands or arms.

Saint Porphyrios leads us to insight concerning the body's total participation in veneration. When one enters an Orthodox Church, especially in traditional Orthodox countries, they will be struck by the lack of pews, chairs, or anywhere to sit. The only visible chair looks like a throne and has an icon of Christ above it. This is for the bishop and if the bishop is not present it is vacant. This lack of seating is not incidental or an oversight. It is a long-held custom from the Ancient Roman world, where only the teacher would sit, and the disciples would stand around him. Our culture today has moved away from that model. Typically, when an American student attends classes they expect to sit and have their instructor stand. We see vestiges of this older practice in other arenas where we encounter those in authority. The judge sits while the prosecutors and defendants stand before them. When an important person enters a room, we typically rise up, even if we are not meeting them. The same idea applies to the liturgical setting. Orthodox Christians are not passive participants but active. The lack of chairs is not a bug but a feature. It forces alertness and demonstrates that what is happening is worthy of their respect. The proper posture for prayer is not sitting but standing.

Standing as a default also allows for prostrations. The act of a prostration is typically connected with the Greek term μετάνοια (*metania*). The word *metania* literally means a change of mind.[23] It is the word that is used for repentance in Orthodoxy. Repentance is understood differently in the East than in the West. It is not only a turn away from sin in general, or one specific sin in particular, but an ongoing act. Repentance is akin to a course correction for a ship or steering a car. At very few points can a captain not think about where the ship is to go. When driving one constantly adjusts the wheel slightly one way or the other to keep the vehicle in the center of the lane. Sometimes radical adjustments are necessary, but other times small modifications are all that is needed.

Repentance is the change of mind that moves from focusing on oneself to approaching God. It is also a physical act of bowing. "Our body is created for prayer. We pray bowing our heads and bending our knees; by prostrating and crossing ourselves. We pray kneeling and standing."[24] The *metania* is understood as a physical act as well as a spiritual one. A "full" *metania* usually includes a bow that incorporates touching one's knees and forehead to the ground while making the sign of the cross. Lesser *metanias* include a full bow from the waist, or a slight bow. These also incorporate the signing of the cross or a simple hand over the heart.

The typical penitential act in the West is kneeling. This is done in Orthodox Churches as well, but not on a Sunday. The canons from the First Council of Nicaea prohibit kneeling on Sundays and other periods when the resurrection is celebrated. Kneeling as an act of contrition reveals something beautiful. Saint Isaac the Syrian writes, "Whenever you find it delightful to kneel in prayer, do not be carried off by the thought to put an end to it. Would that this were never cut short for as long as you are in this life!"[25] This symbol of a contrite heart may even include laying fully prone on the floor.

In whatever manner these prostrate acts are done the heart remains central. A full *metania*, kneeling, or laying prostrate should all be done to show respect, just as standing can do. Other than a few prohibitions against kneeling at certain times, or prescription for kneeling at other times, how and when these acts are performed are acts of individual piety. They are times where the Christian is humbling their body to ask for divine grace to come upon them. Eliade states that, "The ideal of the religious man is, of course, that everything he does should be done ritually, should, in other words, be a sacrifice,"[26] while ritually done. None of these actions are viewed as meritorious for Orthodox Christians. Again, Saint Porphyrios can be our guide when he says, "we add anything to Christ with the worship which we offer Him."[27] Elsewhere he states, "The person with faith displays his love, his devotion and his adoration of Christ in tangible ways. That's why bodily exertion is made. That's why we make prostrations. Not to gain anything, but because your love for Christ doesn't allow you to do otherwise."[28] While they may be difficult to do, especially with longer services, he urges us, "Before complaining about your bodily exhaustion, start praying."[29]

There is probably no place where the body is more exhausted than during the Great and Holy Lent. Often the most trying time of Lent is the very beginning when the fast is new and the intensity of prayer increased. For many Orthodox Christians the first day of Lent, known as "Clean Monday," is a strict and complete fast. Some will continue this fast until Wednesday night. It is also at this time that the penitential Canon of Saint Andrew of Crete is chanted. This is an allegorical poem that addresses the sinful thoughts and deeds of characters in the Bible, used to focus on the sins of each of us.[30] The choral refrains also include a full prostration after each line. Due to its length, only portions of the canon are usually chanted until the fifth week of Lent when it is done in its entirety. When done in its entirety over 350 prostrations are made.

While not meritorious, these actions are still required to be done as an act of piety. Porphyrios posits, "Perhaps someone will say, 'I have love in my heart.' That's all very well, but prostrations and all the other exercises are still required, because, although they are external forms, through those formal actions we are able to penetrate to the substance."[31] Just as the icon is a physical object used to bridge to the soul, so too are physical actions used for the benefit of the soul. Both in mediums and actions Orthodox Christians constantly affirm salvation exists for body and soul, and that man is material and spiritual. There is no place for dualism. *Theoria* is incompatible with the telos of Christianity. Icons, and the kinetic worship performed in and around them, demonstrate the telos of Orthodox Christianity. *Theosis* includes the material, spiritual, and divine.

Orthodoxy affirms the material world visually and with actions it also affirms the entirety of the material world. This means that interactions between the spiritual and material use all five senses. This sensual experience applies to icons as well. It is easy to see how the visual senses are engaged with icons. After all, they are primarily a visual medium. We have demonstrated how the body engages with the icon through making the sign of the cross, *metanias* and other physical activities. The ear is engaged with icons as well. Songs are sung to Christ, dedications to various saints and feasts as well. Many of these songs are incorporated only for a few services a year and they are an auditory reminder of the icon that greeted the parishioner when they entered the Nave. When the hymns are sung, prayers are uttered, and the image is made real. In concert the song and image transport and transform the devotee, bringing closer union with the prototype. One can almost hear their words as the songs are sung about them. Iconographer Aidan Hart points out that, "Most traditional art is likewise intended to function together with the word."[32] Iconography goes hand in hand with hymnography; one fulfills the other.

Smell is also engaged with veneration of icons. When one enters into an Orthodox Church, they are struck by what some in the West call a "high church" service. As the Orthodox Liturgy developed from a synthesis of the High Church of the Hagia Sophia in Constantinople with the monastic disciplines, the result for the last millennia or so is that there is no "low church" service. Even when different versions of the Liturgy are celebrated, be it Basil or Chrysostom, one still gets the full accoutrement associated only with "high church" services in the West. The "smells and bells" are commonplace. The use of incense is a practice found in the book of Exodus. Moses was commanded to mix a special blend of incense that no one else should try to copy. In the tabernacle there was an altar of incense. Fr De Young points out that the incense "altar was actually used more than the altar of burnt offerings, because . . . the incense offerings were the basis of the daily cycle, at morning and evening, with prayers."[33] Prayer throughout the Bible and church hymnography is likened to incense rising from censer and covering the people as a pleasing aroma before the Lord. We see this explicitly in Revelation 8. Icons are censed in the church. The smoke and smell covers and surrounds each icon and fills the building.

Today the amount of incense that is used varies with each presiding priest, as well as the mix of incense. Both of these become matters of personal taste, but the use of incense at specific times is explicitly prescribed in every liturgical manual. Its use is not optional. It provides the covering and the preparation for sacrament. It is with the Eucharist that the sensation of taste is reserved for. One does not taste anything beforehand. The Eucharist will be received before icons, often with the refrain of Psalm 34:8, "Taste and see that the Lord is good," being sung in a church that has been filled with smoke and the pleasant aroma of incense.

With the whole body engaged in spiritual worship a tactile connection is established with icons. However, the veneration of an icon takes place, one bow or three, a simple cross or full prostration, icons are typically kissed. Many outside observers see the act of kissing an icon not as an act of veneration but of worship. This is an excusable misunderstanding. The kiss is how Christians are instructed to greet one another. Paul commands that we greet one another with a holy kiss in his epistles.[34] Just as one person may kiss a parent, child, or friend in a holy embrace so too are icons received. Seventh-century bishop Leontius of Neapolis tells us that, "We Christians, by bodily kissing an icon of Christ, or of an apostle or martyr, are in spirit kissing Christ Himself or His martyr."[35] There is no substantive difference. Christ or the saint are present in their icon. Thus the kiss is just as personal. In kissing the icon, one also confirms the unity of the church, that different people are united and brought alive together in Christ.

There are some general rules when kissing an icon. Usually, the face itself is not kissed. If the image contains the full person, the hands or the feet are the object that receives the veneration. This allows for respect and piety to dictate the kiss. If only the face exists in the icon usually a corner of the icon will be kissed, still avoiding the face for this reason. If multiple saints are depicted in an icon some will kiss each saint, while others will choose to only kiss the "main" saint found in the icon. Typically, whenever Christ is present with a saint, Christ is kissed first. This practice is broken when approaching icons of the Theotokos. In nearly every icon of the Theotokos she is holding Christ. Yet it is she who receives veneration first. This is done for a few reasons. First, Christ was likely venerated moments ago and the prayer before the icon was directed toward the Theotokos. Secondly, Christ will still be venerated as the conclusion of the prayer cycle.

Todor Mitrovic, a Serbian iconographer, has done extensive research on icons and points out that the practice of kissing icons "was not a regular part of liturgical practice during the first millennium of Christianity."[36] Before this, the ritual kissing of the laity was more common than it is done today. As one practice waned the other practice waxed. It is also important to note that the rise in kissing of an icon coincided with the Triumph of Orthodoxy and the defeat of iconoclasm, as we will discuss in chapter 5. As icons are affirmed as central to Orthodoxy, a pious practice of greeting the icon as one would any other person grew to take on a central part of liturgical worship. Through the kissing of icons Orthodox Christians are able to connect with the holy persons depicted in the icons. Christ and the saints are properly honored.

Another way that icons are used in liturgical practice and veneration is the lighting of candles. Candlestands are located near many prominent icons in the church. It is typical that along with the bowing and kissing of an icon a candle is lit at one or all of the icons visited. The lighting of candles is another physical expression of prayer. If one were to ask an Orthodox Christian why they light candles, they may give a reason different from what you are expecting, usually centered on their motivation for lighting that particular candle. They may mention a loved one, or help with a particular difficulty coming up, or as a celebration, an offering of thanks. Rarely will they give you an answer as to why to light candles at all. If this answer is given, it will usually connect the light of Christ to their prayer or connect it to Christ's parable about lighting a lamp and putting it out for all to see instead of hiding it. Saint John of Kronstadt provides probably the most complete theological reason for lighting candles:

> The candles lit before icons of the saints reflect their ardent love for God for Whose sake they gave up everything that man prizes in life, including their very lives, as did the holy apostles, martyrs and others. These candles also mean that these saints are lamps burning for us and providing light for us by their own saintly living, their virtues and their ardent intercession for us before God through their constant prayers by day and night. The burning candles also stand for our ardent zeal and the sincere sacrifice we make out of reverence and gratitude to them for their solicitude on our behalf before God.[37]

Still for most, the action itself holds more personal meaning than it does a corporate meaning. As Saint John points out, it comes from our ardent zeal and gratitude. Just as with incense we have commands about lampstands and lights in the book of Exodus connected with the tabernacle, in many ways this tradition has continued, even when not necessary to illumine a space.

These and other physical gestures are incorporated into Orthodox worship as a matter of learned habit. Many of these learned habits are formed in liturgical practice and are not connected with icons. As a part of general acculturation, people begin to take on the gestures of those in authority. In church when a priest is directed to lift their hands at certain moments in the liturgy, the people may do the same. This is probably easiest to see during the recitation of the Lord's prayer. Many parishioners will lift their hands to about shoulder height with palms upward. Crossing one's arms over their heart where their hands rest on the opposite shoulder is a traditional posture while waiting to receive communion and at a few other times in the liturgy.

The kinetic worship of Orthodox Christians appears to be a ritualistic dance. Bourdieu points out that, "Practice has a logic which is not that of the logician. This has to be acknowledged in order to avoid asking of it more logic than it can give thereby condemning oneself either to wring incoherences out of it or to thrust a forced coherence upon it."[38] Why things are done is often simply because they are done that way. We learn through doing and cannot explain the why behind what we do. In these cases, there is little benefit of knowing the answer to the question of why. By doing these prescribed or normative acts, the world of the devotee is organized. Just as Freud states "the basis of taboo is prohibited action, for performing which a strong inclination exists in the unconscious,"[39] the unconscious also shapes what is to be done in relation to the holy.

Jordan Peterson states, "The world can be validly construed as forum for action, or as place of things."[40] The church also serves as a forum for certain actions, which by participating in them demonstrates a connection with the group. The icon has a socioculturally determined status in the church. Peterson continues that the status, in this case for icons, "consists of its meaning—consists of its implication for behavior."[41] As stated in the introduction to this chapter, the icon has meaning because of its use, not apart from it.

Its use in the church resembles modern performance art. Each gesture has a meaning known or unknown but used to convey a deeper meaning and a deeper reality. The icon is one part of this larger ritualistic act, the use of music and movement keep the timing of the dance moving along. Fortounatto and Cunningham argue that icons are "not intended to leave us passive and, indeed, they are not themselves passive." They quote Metropolitan Philaret of Moscow, who says that we are not passive spectators, "but we present our soul to the luminous face of Jesus Christ, like a mirror to receive his light."[42]

The icon as something that requires action resembles Durkheim's notion of the totem. For Durkheim, "the totem is not merely a name; it is an emblem."[43] This emblem shapes those connected with it, both in how they conceive of the emblem but also in how they construct their understanding of themselves and others. Freud characterizes Durkheim's notion of the totem as "the visible representative of social religion among the races concerned: it embodies the community, which is the true object of their worship."[44] No Orthodox Christian would reject this analysis of an icon of Christ embodying their community. Christ as embodied and depicted in the icon is worshipped. When a saint is depicted, it is pointing toward Christ, not themselves. Worship passes along from the community through the saint and ultimately to Christ.

Peterson points out that the same principle applies to nonreligious icons as well. While we may be impressed or terrified to stand before anyone who embodies our personal or cultural aspirations, the same effect can arise from a mere image of them. "We do not even need the person to generate such affect. The icon will suffice. We will pay vast sums of money for articles of clothing worn or personal items used or created by the famous and infamous of our time."[45] In this way meaning is created for both the object and for ourselves in relation to that object. When an Orthodox Christian venerates an icon in whatever physical way they choose, they confirm their place in the community, as well as the place of the icon and others.

## ICONS AND PRAYER

As mentioned in chapter 3, Orthodox Christians see other people as icons of Christ. It is not only two-dimensional objects that can contain a spiritual reality deeper than what appears, but also other people surrounding them. It is in this light that the notion of the priesthood of all believers, so central to Luther and other Protestant Reformers, can best be understood by the Orthodox. "The Church is the gathering of the *laos*, the whole people of God. A lay person is not, as in the popular usage of the word layman, an amateur or an ignoramus."[46] Each person, regardless of their ecclesial or social status, is an image of God and thus a living icon. This message is fundamental to the Christian worldview that see all people as equal before God. There are no barbarians, no *non-persona*, because they do not hold the right citizenship, or are racially or ethnically different. Instead, all people share this image from creation, and have the status as icons. Even those who do not accept the image, are images, and should be approached as such.

Those whose image has grown more toward the likeness of Christ are no more images than others. They are simply images that are clearer. The priest is a clearer image of Christ, not because of a superior position but because he stands at the head of the congregation and represents the laity before Christ. Liturgically this is why the priest leads the people in prayer facing east, the same direction they are facing, and not toward the people. This reason was lost to Luther and Protestants who viewed the priest facing away from the people as an obstacle. Rather they are the lead example of piety and worship.

From an ecclesial point of view this is also important, as the priest still remains a member of the laity; they never lose that status. In practice, "Christ remains the only celebrant, just as he remains the head of the Body and the head of the Church."[47]

Along with physical acts of veneration, the Orthodox Christian also connects their body to worship in regular periods of fasting. While there may be no obvious connection between fasting and icons, several do exist. First, all people are icons of Christ, including the practitioner as well as the painted icon they encounter in church. The expectation is that icons are to reveal holiness in all their manifestations. The body of the practitioner must conform through practices to the likeness of God. Since Christ fasted, so too should His icons in the Church. Furthermore, the artistic style found in icons is usually one that exaggerates the physical conformity of the subject to a likeness of Christ. In the practice of self-denial, a greater connection is made to the image portrayed in the icon. Arch. Vasileios amplifies this connection of kinetic worship with feasting on the icon. "You stand before the icon with fear, yearning and joy. You stand before it. You venerate it. You receive life. You suck from it, you drink it in. You feed insatiably on it. What nourishes you now can never be exhausted."[48]

The Orthodox Church has a fairly standard cycle of feasting and fasting. This cycle is used to integrate the person into the community that is the Church, as well as to conform the body to the soul of the individual. Fasting is not simply dieting but restricting foods for the purpose of spiritual enrichment. As a quick aside, pastorally every priest will instruct that one should always fast in accordance with their ability and needs. Certain people have different dietary restrictions or needs that correspond with medical needs. Fasting should always be done with consultation with one's priest or spiritual father. With that said, the Orthodox Church has maintained a general fasting rule from antiquity. A strict fast constitutes no meat, eggs, dairy, fish, wine, or oil. This is not too far removed from a typical vegan diet. A complete fast is done only when one is preparing for the Eucharist (midnight hour forward), or on a few occasions connected with the Lenten cycle.

The Church prescribes a strict fast on Wednesdays and Fridays to commemorate the betrayal and crucifixion of Christ. There are four weeks of the year when these fasts are relaxed.[49] Further, a strict fast is called for throughout the forty days of Lent and Holy Week and comprises most of the time during the other three prescribed fasting periods.[50] In all, Orthodox Christians fast from meat for a third to a half of the year. The cycles of fasting are used to punctuate normal time and to bring the church life home. When one fasts, they are not doing so only in church, but it serves as a reminder throughout the day that their bodies are icons of Christ and should conform to His likeness. Christ also connected prayer and fasting in the Gospels. A life of prayer is one that also includes a life of regular fasting.

Saint Matthew the Poor tells us that, "Fasting by itself is not a virtue. It is nothing at all. Without prayer, it becomes a bodily punishment that induces spiritual aridity and bad temper. The same is true of prayer; without fasting, it loses its power along with its fruits."[51] All fasting must be accompanied by an increase in prayer. Often this prayer includes time standing before icons. The hunger in the stomach and tiredness of the body shows our dependence upon God and therefore we must live out this dependence by praying.

Fr Thomas Hopko sees this dependence as greatest during the fast of Great and Holy Lent. During this time, the "Lenten spring is consecrated to prayer and fasting. The practice of abstinence is at the very heart of the effort. The Church has declared a solemn fast. All are commanded to join in the action, making their prayers and prostrations with the 'persecution of the stomach.'"[52] Just as fatigue sets in with prostrations and we are urged to move forward, so too should our determination to keep the fast. Both are only truly accomplished if done with the corresponding prayer.

As Saint Matthew the Poor continues to explain, "Fasting is not a deprivation from certain kinds of food, but a voluntary abstinence from them.—It does not humiliate the flesh, but refreshes the spirit.—Nor does it fetter or imprison the senses; it releases them from all that hinders the contemplation of God."[53] For Saint Matthew, fasting frees one to pursue other obligations. Similarly, Saint Isaac the Syrian sees a full stomach as bondage that hinders this progress when he delivered his homily on fasting, "There can be no knowledge of the mysteries of God on a full stomach."[54] Saint Seraphim of Sarov tells us that, "Fasting calms the impulses of the flesh and quenches the fire of passion."[55]

The quenching of our passion provides the opportunity to look at the icon in a new light. Ouspensky asserts that, "Only the icon can portray what it means 'to fast with our eyes' and what this allows us to attain."[56] The icon provides the corrective lenses to the tantalizing world around us. It calms the passions and works in a symphonic harmony with the fasting. As Lossky says, "This is the root principle of asceticism; a free renunciation of one's own will, of the mere simulacrum of individual liberty, in order to recover the true liberty, that of the person which is the image of God in each one."[57]

In this way, fasting serves as a physical exaltation of the message inherent in the icon. Both are done to affirm our humanity. Lossky, Schmemann, and others throughout the history of the Church have pointed out that mankind fell through eating. It was through food that sin entered the world. It is also through food, the Eucharist, that we find salvation. By denying food that appears pleasant to the eye and seeking food that is food indeed, we find ourselves. We find ourselves in community with others. This is also why the Orthodox Church does not do individual liturgies; there are no private masses. The Eucharist, the bread of life, is meant to be shared. A priest cannot serve a liturgy alone.

The cycle of fasting and its corresponding eucharistic feast affirms not only our humanity but the humanity of those around us. Once again, we are brought to the realization that icons are necessary for worship. Icons in this case being other people, and it is only possible to partake of communion if one views those partaking with them as icons of Christ. If not, it is done to our condemnation. The act of fasting, with its corresponding prayer, provides a space for us to recognize other people. As Louth tells us, fasting is "a kenosis, a self-emptying, that enables us to make space for the others, and in that space allowed by the others to find ourselves."[58] The saying of a desert monk, and most recently attributed to Saint Seraphim of Sarov, tells us, when asked why they were so severe on their bodies, "If I don't kill it, it kills me."[59] Orthodox are not Gnostics who reject the material world. Instead, the material world and the body are used as service to the spiritual reality that we all participate in.

The final and possibly most important physical act that is done connected with the Orthodox understanding of icons is the act of silence. Orthodox spirituality is wrapped up in the development of Hesychia. This is the spiritual practice of silence as developed by such prominent Orthodox saints as Saint John of the Ladder, Saint Symeon the New Theologian, Saint Gregory Palamas, and arguably Saint Sergius of Radonezh.

Saint John Climacus tells us that, "Intelligent silence is the mother of prayer."[60] The first step in approaching an icon resembles the final step, both approach it in silence. One, while on the threshold, unsure as to what the icon is to tell them. In the final step one approaches the icon and has learned to listen to what it says. Saint Matthew the Poor proclaims that it is at this point "When you are completely alone with God, sitting in his presence in holy silence, you shall see your own image in the mirror of God."[61] The disparity between ourselves and God then urges us back to worship of God through *metanias*, repentance, and prostrations. The more light that is shown, the easier it is to see the path forward and the corrections become clearer. Our sin becomes more apparent, as does the love of Christ. This is why sanctity and inner perfection is characterized only by silence.[62]

Icons are more real in many respects because they demonstrate this holy silence. Saint Symeon the New Theologian says that the icon expresses the theme of Holy Saturday, all mortal flesh keeping silent. "Everything here is subordinate to the general harmony which expresses peace, order, and inner harmony. For there is no disorder in the kingdom of the Holy Spirit."[63] The silence of an icon should not be confused with emptiness or a void. Instead, the silence is an invitation to still your heart and conform your will, to pray with all of your body. As Saint Ignatius of Antioch states, if we have purified our-selves and encountered Christ, we "can ever hear his silence."[64] Metropolitan Anthony Bloom tells us that real silence "is something extremely intense, it has density and it is really alive."[65]

In the same way the icon, though silent, is alive. It represents this ideal of the Church. There are no icons that depict someone speaking, all remain silent. Even those whose message is central to the icon itself are kept silent, instead they hold a scroll or maybe make a gesture. The icon is also a model for our participation in the heavenly realm and not only a dialogue partner engaging with us. The icon serves as a pedagogical tool as to what sanctity looks like for us.

With holy silence being key to Orthodox spirituality, one is struck by the constant noise filling the nave of any thriving Orthodox Church. There is a great commotion as people enter the church, venerate icons and take their place standing alongside their fellow parishioners. People often show up late, and while this is frowned upon, it is rather common and accepted. When someone shows up late, they too move forward and venerate the icons. The deacon is constantly in motion between the altar and the Nave, praying lita-nies or censing the icons on the wall and the people. The choir sings while the priest is praying in the altar. Doors open and close. The cacophony of activity and noise hardly seems to fit an ecclesiology whose theological imperative is to cultivate silence. Nonetheless, this is exactly where we can understand the value of holy silence. Several times the priest or deacon tells the people "in peace let us pray to the Lord," yet the world is as chaotic as the church is. Our minds are not at peace, still this is the directive. The Church is a micro-cosm of the entire universe. Christ and the saints are present in the Eucharist and the icons. People are running into each other and making life difficult for others while also providing them with an opportunity to learn, pray, and repent. The goal of holy silence belongs not only in monasteries but in a full and dynamic parish. Silence and peace are not platitudes but encouragement. Once again, we see that icons reveal a world beyond what is visible and show us the greater things.

The use and veneration of icons provides the opportunity for salvation of soul and body. The noise and chaos of the church is the testing ground for piety and endurance. As Saint Porphyrios says, "Without exercise nothing is achieved. Subject yourself to a spiritual programme, for example, a rule of prayer, a cycle of church services, and so on, and do not diverge from it."[66] With this act of veneration, salvation can be found.

Malinowski may identify an icon therefore as an object of magic. Magic being the quality of the thing or "the relation between man and the thing, for though never man-made it is always made for man. In all tradition, in all mythology, magic is always found in the possession of man and through the knowledge of man or man-like being."[67] The physical icon and possession of it holds totemic value. It is material. Icons are matter that possess a quality that is made manifest in relation between man and it. Louth's reply to this objection that icons are matter and therefore either not spiritual or magical is "to concede the point—icons are just matter—but to refuse to accept it as an objection."[68] The material nature of the icon instead confirms the incarnation of Christ, as addressed in chapter 3. To paraphrase Saint John of Damascus, matter is not worshipped, but Christ who became matter for our sake. It is not accidental nor is it magical, but intentional.

As icons affirm the incarnation, the true meaning of an icon is revealed. Louth continues his defense of the image in matter by relating Christ to the Platonic forms. "The Platonic Forms that exist in the mind of God and are the models of everything that has come to be as a result of God's will. This Platonism has, however, been modified in that Saint John sees this second type of image as the idea in God of what is to come."[69] Icons, while real and relational, continue to serve as the prototype of redemption and the second coming. As Saint Dionysius calls these images and paradigms *prohorismoi*, or predeterminations, that connect what exists in the will of God. As Maximus the Confessor connects the notion of the *logoi* of man with the Logos that is Christ. This is how we learn love.

This reality coming through the icons is shared by a story about Saint Seraphim when he was a young hierodeacon. He was standing by the royal doors and a brilliant light suddenly shone on him. Seraphim saw Christ surrounded by angels enter the doors of the Church and approach Seraphim on the ambo.[70] Christ then blessed all those praying and entered his icon on the iconostasis.[71] The response was silence. After being taken back into the altar he remained in a sense of spiritual ecstasy for three hours. Later he became the famed monk and continued to develop the light he partook of on this day through prayer and asceticism. The fact that Christ entered his icon reveals that for the devout Christ remains there, present in all his icons.

Given their significance, it is easy to see how icons are used in public life for the Orthodox Christian. In Letter 105, Pope Gregory the Great advocated for the place of icons in churches so those "ignorant of letters may at least read by looking at the walls what they cannot read in books."[72] Pedagogically they reveal much more than simple Bible stories. Gregory's often cited example about the use of icons was not intended as an exhaustive list. One of the greatest lessons taught by icons is not found in any single icon but in their broader public and private use. Churches are filled with them. There are many Orthodox churches that do not have a blank spot on any wall. Every inch is covered. This reinforces the theological lesson that the Christian is surrounded by a cloud of witnesses.[73] The Christian faith is not an individual act but one that necessitates the incorporation of others.

The clearest example of an icon's place in the church is in their role in the Divine Liturgy. It is here that we see the church as a microcosm of the universe. The purpose of the liturgy is to reveal heaven while we participate on earth. The altar of every church becomes the center of this universe. As Eliade points out, the center is itself a sacred zone; anything which represents the sacred becomes a symbol for the center as such.[74] Icons help usher the person into this center and the symbolic purpose inherent in this place. Hieromonk Gabriel Bunge argues that, "Icons by their nature . . . are in no way images intended for personal pious reverence."[75] Since their purpose is for worship their place is public and not hidden away. Similarly, Met Hilarion Alfeyev argues that, "Outside the context of the Church and the liturgy, icons lose their meaning to a considerable degree."[76]

During the liturgy, the icons serve a similar role as the Gospel book, crosses, and other sacred objects. They are instruments to facilitate the spiritual progress of the Christian during the eucharistic rite. During the liturgy, the priest, deacon, and altar servers exit the altar on a number of occasions. Each one has a specific purpose in advancing the rite. The Gospel book is brought out as the fulfillment of the liturgy of the word before the epistle and gospel are read. This is commonly known as the little entrance. Later the great entrance takes place, where the bread and wine which will shortly become the body and blood of Christ, are brought through the church. Historically these two entrances were the medium of bringing the gospel or elements from another location to the altar. Today they exit and return to the altar. At other times censing takes place, and the priest or deacon will leave the altar, this time to cense the icons of the church. The place of the icons on the walls heightens the engagement of the people with the icons. They are showed to be objects of reverence just as the elements or gospel are. The church building itself embodies the liturgy and is intended on showing the symbolic value of everything therein.

The symbolic value of icons and the incorporation of others is brought home. Just as the Church is a microcosm of universe, the home becomes a microcosm of the Church. Met Hilarion Alfeyev expands his position that the proper context of icons is the Church and the liturgy when addressing icons in the home. He argues that, "Of course, every Christian has the right to hang icons in his home, but he has this right insofar as his home is an extension of the church and his life is an extension of the liturgy."[77]

The home too serves a liturgical purpose; it is an extension of the Church. The icons at home are extensions of the icons at church. The meaning is not lost or changed simply because it is not at church, but the liturgical center, as Eliade highlights, moves with the Christian. At home icons are the center of prayer and include many of the same externalities found in the Church. The icons are honored with prostrations; they are kissed, candles are lit before them and often times incense is lit in the home during these times of prayer. As Elissa Bjeletich Davis and Caleb Shoemaker wrote about in the book aptly titled *Blueprints for the Little Church*, the home is a little church. Icons in the home are placed in a central location. Usually this is called a prayer corner, but it is not necessary in a corner. Rather it is the corner piece of the home altar. The number of icons usually grows, but will begin with an icon of Christ, then the Theotokos and then typically patron saints of the family. A cross is usually found somewhere in the home altar. Under the home version of the iconostasis, other items connected to the spiritual life of the home are typically kept. This would include holy water, sacred oil, prayer books, and other items that help facilitate home worship. As the prayer corner develops, candles, vigil lamps and incense are added. In other words, the home begins to look like a church that awaits the entrance of the holy mysteries. If at all possible, the prayer corner is structured to look like one found in any church. Ideally it would be on an eastern-facing wall, and the layout will have Christ on the right and Mary on the left from the vantage of the observer.

Since "Icons are like the markers on our path to the new creation,"[78] as Ouspensky reminds us, we will see icons throughout the house as well. Often times there are icons of the Hospitality of Abraham or Saint Euphrosynos the Cook of Alexandria in the kitchen. Children's rooms will contain a few icons, usually including their patron saint. Saint Theophan the Recluse encourages this, "and so, let the child be surrounded by sacred forms, objects of all kinds, and let everything that can corrupt in examples, depictions, and things, be put away."[79] The home filled with icons becomes formative and transformative. It is for this reason that icons are also found everywhere among the Orthodox. Small icons are placed in cars, stands are erected outside to shelter icons, trails are marked with icons. In an odd reversal, icons are found everywhere, thereby sanctifying everything. Since following Eliade, the icon becomes the center of the world. Their proliferation reshapes our notion of sacred geography.

While icons adorn the walls of the churches, homes, and everywhere else that have significance for the Orthodox Christian, they retain other specific connections within the Church outside the liturgy or typical church services. Since icons are so central to the life of the Church, it has become increasingly common for icons to be brought to the church to be blessed. This practice is fairly new and somewhat debated among the Orthodox.

Many Orthodox Christians will have a priest bless the icons once they have them before displaying them in their home or elsewhere. Priests will usually recite some prayers over them and then sprinkle the icon with either holy water or anoint them with holy oil. To save time some icons are even packaged as being "pre-blessed."[80] Icons are also brought behind the iconostasis and kept in the altar for forty days to bless them. These forms of blessings transform a piece of art into a sanctified image.

While it is not harmful to have an icon blessed, it is not theologically necessary. Since traditionally icons are made as objects of prayer, with prayers said over them while they are painted or otherwise constructed, they already have a spiritual purpose, and a sacred disposition. Historically since they are created as an expression of prayer there is no need for an additional blessing. "What the artist makes is worthy of veneration; it is not something 'common or worthless' that needs to be blessed."[81] Still for many, bringing the icon, recognizing that it is already a blessed object, into the church serves as an offering to God. The icons return to them as an object that belonged to the Church and as a reminder that it belongs to the Church still, though its home is found in the little church of their house.

Icons also have a sacramental importance during confession. Traditionally confession is given before the icon of Christ with the priest standing to their side. Orthodox Christians visibly are confessing to Christ, and the priest is there for guidance and prayers. The ancient church did public confession in front of the whole congregation. This practice evolved into confession before the priest, who assumed the role of the congregation. In every case, it is Christ who forgives sins, but it is the priest's job to mediate this sacramental repentance. The placement of confession before the icon of Christ, and the priest's words at the beginning of confession confirm this: "Behold, my child, Christ standeth here invisibly, and receiveth thy confession." The priest continues, "Lo, His Holy image is before us and I am but a witness, bearing testimony before Him of all things which thou doest say to me."[82]

Icons are also processed in the church. There are a number of feast days when icons may be processed around the church, both inside and outside. The greatest procession is done on the first Sunday of Great and Holy Lent, known as the Sunday of Orthodoxy. Here the celebration concerns the icon itself and the procession is a victory parade. Processions have also taken place in times of trouble. There are several instances where icons were paraded around a city before a battle and used as intercession.

One such example took place in the seventh century, where an icon of the Theotokos was paraded around the city of Constantinople as the city was besieged and the majority of the forces were still a way off. The Theotokos protected the city, and a hymn[83] was written to commemorate the event. Russia has had several events when icons were used to protect its cities from foreign invasion. The first was connected with the icon of the Sign. Here the icon of the Theotokos was taken from the Church of the Savior in Illyn and protected the city of Novgorod. The Kazan Mother of God protected Russia from the Poles in 1612, the Swedes in 1709, and Napoleon in 1812. Even the Soviets encouraged the procession of the icon in 1944 with the siege

of Leningrad. The Theotokos, through the Kazan Icon, has the title Holy
Protectress of Russia.[84]

As icons are used to protect cities and countries, they are also used as a
blessing for married couples and the newly baptized. Often icons are given as
a present by the sponsors of these events. For the newly baptized, it is usually
an icon of their patron saint, and for the newly married couple, it may be an
icon that has both saints present or another one that may have significance
for the couple or sponsors. For both the newly baptized and newly married,
the icon connects the sacrament and brings home the blessings of the Church
and community.

Icons are also found in church halls and are faced toward and prayed
toward at the conclusion of church and beginning of fellowship. Called various things, agape meals, coffee hour, Orthodox Christians after liturgy will
eat together. Before doing this, the priest will bless the food and once again
the icon becomes the focus of prayers. Icons are thus hung in church halls and
wherever people may gather and give thanks to God.

## HOLY ICONS

While all icons serve as an opportunity to encounter the divine, some icons
like the Kazan Theotokos and others are viewed as miraculous since they
provide tangible and observable signs of the blessings of God. Many such
icons are called wonder working icons or miracle working. The miracles
vary from large-scale survival during a war to personal healings. Gillian
Crow defines miracles thusly, "Miracles are understood as occasions when
by the grace of God the conditions of the kingdom are fulfilled; when human
faith, compassion, and love are joined to the divine, allowing God to bring
his healing power to restore part of his creation to its intended splendour and
wholeness."[85]

Some wonder-working icons are constantly producing miracles, some
do so sporadically, and yet many will be remembered for one particular
encounter. The majority of the miracle-working icons are of the Theotokos
but not exclusively. One common category of miraculous icons are known
as myrrh-streaming icons. Myrrh is a fragrant oil that is used in church services and in making of perfume and traditional medicines. While some wish
to downplay this category of miraculous icons, their presence is certain and
not able to be explained away. Met Hilarion Alfeyev asks, "How are we to
consider this phenomenon? First of all, it is necessary to say that cases of
myrrh-streaming icons are an indisputable fact and have been recognized
repeatedly."[86] The answer as to how we are to approach these is with wonder
ourselves.

The number of icons that fall into this category is too many to list, especially since the vast majority are not brought to greater attention than the local bishop, and cease producing myrrh after a short period of time. Equally amazing to the number of icons that exude myrrh is the fact that the style of icons is not consistent. Some icons are handmade with egg tempera, others are made with acrylic paints, and still others are prints. Even some icons made on postcards have been known to exude myrrh.[87]

Today there are three prominent icons that Orthodox Christians encounter. The first is known as the Iveron or "Montreal" icon. The story of this icon begins with José Muñoz, a Chilean convert to Orthodoxy in Canada who went to Mount Athos on a pilgrimage. Here he saw an icon and was immediately attracted to it. The iconographer made this copy of the Iveron icon and was hesitant to give it away and unwilling to sell it. Still, after some discussion, the iconographer relented and gave it to Muñoz. When Muñoz returned home, he noticed that the icon began to produce myrrh. This icon continually produced myrrh and healing of soul and body for those who encountered it. Unfortunately, José Muñoz was murdered in 1997, and the icon was lost.[88] There are many who view brother José, the protector of the icon, as a saint. In November 2022, a print of the Iveron icon produced copious amounts of myrrh at the anniversary of his martyrdom at Saint Tikhon's in Jordanville, New York. This print is known as the Hawaii myrrh streaming Iveron icon. This print of the copy of the Iveron icon has streamed myrrh off and on for over a decade. In both of these cases, the reason why the icon produces myrrh is unknown, but the quantity is tremendous. Vials are filled and gathered and distributed to churches and people. Both of these icons have traveled the globe and been witnessed by millions of people.

Another well-known icon present today is the icon of Saint Anna. On Mother's Day 2004, this icon streamed myrrh. This icon produced myrrh until the fall of 2012, when it suddenly stopped. It still smells fragrant. The icon is also known for helping women who have difficulty getting pregnant to conceive and give birth. Miraculous icons are wonderous, but they are not wonder-shows. Some miraculous icons are brought all around the world, but not as evidence to confirm a point. They are not apologetic pieces to prove that the faith is real. The icons are brought around to share a blessing. They exist as an expression of the community and as an object of solidarity.

The question of why these miracles exist remains. As the icon becomes a symbol of the people, they contain, as Eliade would say, "in itself all the manifestations of sacred power."[89] But these miracles are not psychosomatic or any form of wish fulfillment. They are specific and observable even by skeptics. The church has never pursued a "miracle for the sake of a miracle." Rather it boldly proclaims that a miracle happens in every Orthodox Church every Sunday with the Eucharist. Met Hilarion Alfeyev tells us that, "In order to acknowledge the meaning of these miracles spiritual eyes are needed, but myrrh-streaming icons, visible to the physical eyes, are given to those whose eyes are darkened by sin."[90] Matthew Pageau adds that "from a spiritual perspective, explaining a miracle with mechanical causality would be the equivalent of detailing the steps required to construct a written word with marks, which is hardly relevant at all."[91]

The explanation, whatever it may be, will always be found lacking. Miracles in general are experienced as examples of divine grace but are not "proof." Changed lives are supposed to be the "proof" for the world, not visible signs. So how are these visible signs interpreted? Some postulate that they are there to encourage the faithful before a cataclysm, while others see a myriad of personal reasons, each unique to those who experience it. In any case, just as the Orthodox Church continues to engage the other world with icons, and to make saints, miracles continue to bridge the material and spiritual realms.

One final note, an icon is not made by the miracles associated with it. These icons are no more "real" than others. The effects are more visible, but their status is no different than any other icon received as such. Any icon that is used in prayer and veneration is just as much an icon as one that protects cities or exudes vials of myrrh that are then circulated among the faithful. The distribution is for the healing of body and soul, and is used for protections and blessings. The oil becomes another means of grace separate from but connected to the icons themselves.

As icons are made real by their pious reception, icons do not belong in museums. Met Hilarion Alfeyev proclaims, "It is ridiculous to think of icons in museums. An icon is not alive there, but exists only as a dried flower in a herbarium or as a butterfly stuck by a pin in a collector's box."[92] While they are beautiful artistic expressions, icons are more than that, as addressed in the previous chapter. To the casual observer, icons may appear as beautiful pieces of abstract art, yet the icon goes beyond abstraction. Temple affirms this position: "Icons are, in a real sense, abstract art. Their forms, rhythms, and harmonies are not intended to reflect the natural world, rather they try to convey to us the supernatural, or supersubstantial world."[93]

If icons remain a piece of art, the best they can do is help one contemplate life. Contemplation, Plato's *theoria*, is not an insignificant goal. Most artists would be honored if their art spoke to the audience and helped them to some contemplative truth about their lives and the lives of others. This is not the telos of the icon. Icons seek to convey God and produce a change in everything. The aim of the icon, as mentioned in the previous chapter, is *theosis* not *theoria*. They are created for community formation not contemplative isolation. They are intrinsically kinetic, not static images, an image that requires one approach others not just themselves.

Treatment of icons as primarily pieces of art is what led to the iconoclastic controversies in the East and West, as will be addressed in the subsequent two chapters.[94] Peter the Great instituted artistic reforms which led to schism in Russia as well as disenchantment and the rise of the Soviet Union. The Renaissance style worked to convey a religious image in the West, but these are not icons as understood in Russia or the rest of the Orthodox world. If icons are treated primarily as works of art the spirit is lost. Icons are created to be seen and interacted with, not admired as a static object. Prince Eugene Trubetskoi pointed out a distinction that is profound in its simplicity. Icons are "holy images," not "holy things."[95] Images are objects that are to be seen and interacted with. Icons are no more a museum piece than they are a talisman. Eliade credits symbols for uniting primitive man to real existence. Interaction with art instead of icon destroys the symbolism. For Eliade, the loss of the symbolic value led to "the broken and alienated existence lived by civilized man to-day."[96]

Icons are created for veneration and connection with the divine. If this connection is moved to a museum, then they are no longer seen in the way that they are supposed to. They are not venerated. They lose their connection as an object of prayer and meditation. They are held behind velvet ropes and cannot be kissed. Museums prevent the interaction that icons are made for—as such, they lose their sacramental character. Father Zinon, speaking with Jim Forest about icons in museums, expressed this sentiment clearly: "They should all be put back in the churches they were taken from. . . . They are not civil paintings. They aren't for museums. They aren't decorations. They are a reflection that God became man. They are holy doors."[97]

Icons are holy doors. If they are not intended or received as such, they are isolated themselves. Eliade says, "This lowering of the metaphysical significance from the 'cosmological' to the 'aesthetic' is in itself an interesting phenomenon."[98] It is a phenomenon of diminishment and loss. Transcendence is lost. As Michael Pomazansky says, when revered objects are treated as mundane, the result is death. "For example, there was the 'Ark of the Covenant,' the very touching of which without special reverence could cause death."[99] Death is not understood only in a physical way but a spiritual death as well. When one fails to treat an icon as a window to heaven or a holy door, they separate themselves from the holy. This is the second death which is understood as far worse than the first. It brings about alienation and loss.

Veneration, as understood by Orthodox Christians, brings about life. Not only is there a harmony created between the Christian and the saint depicted, but also God, and ultimately neighbor. Icons transform and create culture. Louth states, "Historically conceived, Byzantine culture, and the Slav cultures derived from it, are distinctive in being cultures that have evolved an explicit understanding of the place of visual art."[100] The icon becomes the cultural expression of Orthodox lands and when taken seriously allows the culture to thrive.

This is why Schmemann declares, "It remains an absolutely indisputable fact that great art is always, one way or another, connected with religion, and even atheists are forced ultimately to show people cathedrals and icons, have them listen to Bach—in short, point to the spirit as the source of creativity."[101] Religious art is art that seeks to move beyond contemplation into a place of connection.

Truly seeing an icon means interacting with it. Veneration is done with the whole person. The body is affirmed, as is the community that surrounds it. One engages with the icon through the liturgical life of the Church and the sacrality of that is brought home through icon corners. Culture is transmitted and transformed. By keeping the icon as an object of sacred veneration, it prevents man from a life of static and isolated *theoria* at best or worshipping themselves at worst. As we will see in the subsequent chapters, the destruction of icons results in the destruction of community as well.

## NOTES

1. Geertz, Clifford. *The Interpreptation of Cultures.* New York: Basic Books, 1973, 93.

2. Smith, *Map Is Not Territory*, 300.

3. Temple, *Icons and the Mystical Origins of Christianity*, 182.

4. Bourdieu, *Outline of a Theory of Practice*, 118–19.

5. Hart, *Beauty Spirit, Matter*, 25.

6. Nouwen, Henri J. M. *Behold the Beauty of the Lord: Praying with Icons.* Notre Dame, IN: Ave Maria Press, 2004, 13.

7. Damick, Andrew Stephen. "What John Calvin Really Thought about Icons in the Church." *Ancient Faith*, 2017. https://blogs.ancientfaith.com/orthodoxyandheterodoxy /2017/10/10/john-calvin-really-thought-icons-church/ (accessed 2023). (PG 46:572)

8. Damick, Andrew Stephen, and Stephen De Young. "Eating with the Gods." *Ancient Faith*, 2021. https://www.ancientfaith.com/podcasts/lordofspirits/eating_with _the_gods (accessed 2023).

9. Met Hilarion Alfeyev, *Orthodox Christianity, Volume III*, 234–35.

10. St. Porphyrios, *Wounded by Love: The Life and the Wisdom of Saint Porphyrios.* Translated by Sisters of the Holy Vocenant of Chrysopigi. Limni: Denise Harvey, 2018, 168.

11. Boosalis, *Person to Person*, 29.

12. Forest, *Praying with Icons*, 26.

13. Ouspensky and Lossky, *Meaning of Icons*, 39.

14. Eliade, *Patterns in Comparative Religion*, 220.

15. Forest, *Praying with Icons*, 35.

16. Walker and Carras, *Living Orthodoxy in the Modern World*, 15.

17. Najim, Michael, and Patrick B. O'Grady. *Services of Initiation into the Holy Orthodox-Catholic and Apostalic Church.* La Verne, CA: Antiochian Orthodox Institute, 2017, 14.

18. Najim and O'Grady, *Services of Initiation*, 56.

19. Malinowski, Bronislaw. *Magic, Science, and Religion and Other Essays.* Long Grove, IL: Waveland Press, 1992, 67.

20. Mathewes-Green, Frederica. "12 Things I Wish I'd Known." *Ancient Faith*, 2020–2023. https://blogs.ancientfaith.com/frederica/12-things (accessed 2023).

21. Anderson, Christabel Helena. "Painting as Prayer: The Art of A. Sophrony Sakharov." *Orthodox Arts Journal*, 2021.

22. Porphyrios, *Wounded by Love*, 170.

23. Clendenin, *Eastern Orthodox Theology*, 57.

24. Boosalis, *Person to Person*, 29.

25. Boosalis, *Person to Person*, 30.

26. Eliade, *Patterns in Comparative Religion*, 460.

27. Porphyrios, *Wounded by Love*, 169.

28. Porphyrios, *Wounded by Love*, 169.

29. Porphyrios, *Wounded by Love*, 168.

30. Hopko, Thomas. *Lenten Spring.* Crestwood, NY: St. Vladimir's Seminary Press, 1983, 42.

31. Porphyrios, *Wounded by Love*, 169.

32. Hart, *Beauty Spirit, Matter*, 191.

33. Damick and De Young, "Eating with the Gods."

34. Romans 16:16, 1 Corinthians 16:20, 2 Corinthians 13:12, and 1 Thessalonians 5:26.

35. Leontius of Neapolis Bishop (in Cyprus), seventh-century hagiographer.

36. Davydov, Philip, and Olga Shalamova. "Interview with Serbian Iconographer Todor Mitrovic: on the Dialogue between the Sacred and Secular Arts." *Orthodox Arts Journal*, 2016.

37. Bjeletich Elissa, and Caleb Shoemaker. *Blueprints for the Little Church: Creating an Orthodox Home.* Chesterton, NY: Ancient Faith Publishing, 2016, 79.

38. Bourdieu, Pierre. *The Logic of Practice.* Stanford, CA: Stanford University Press, 199086.

39. Freud, Sigmund. *Totem and Taboo.* New York: W. W. Norton, 1950, 41.

40. Peterson, *Maps of Meaning*, 1.

41. Peterson, *Maps of Meaning*, 2.

42. Fortounatto and Cunningham, *Cambridge Companion*, 137.

43. Durkheim, Emile. *The Elementary Forms of the Relegous Life.* New York: Free Press, 1965, 134.

44. Freud, *Totem and Taboo*, 141.

45. Peterson, *Maps of Meaning*, 3.

46. Walker and Carras, *Living Orthodoxy in the Modern World*, 19.

47. Walker and Carras, *Living Orthodoxy in the Modern World*, 20.

48. Archimandrite Vasileios, *Hymn of Entry*, 90.

49. Bright week (the week following Pascha), the week of the Publican and the Pharisee (before Lent), the week following the Nativity, and the week following Pentecost. The Antiochian jurisdiction also relaxes all fasting between Pascha and Ascension.

50. Nativity, Dormition, and the Apostles Fast.

51. Matthew the Poor. *Orthodox Prayer Life: The Interior Way.* Crestwood, NY: St Vladimir's Seminary Press, 2003, 229.

52. Hopko, *Lenten Spring*, 109.

53. Matthew the Poor, *Orthodox Prayer Life*, 230.

54. Matthew the Poor, *Orthodox Prayer Life*, 230. (St. Isaac the Syrian, Homilies 4, in Ascetical Homilies, p. 33.)

55. Matthew the Poor, *Orthodox Prayer Life*, 229.

56. Clendenin, *Eastern Orthodox Theology*, 57.

57. Lossky, *Mystical Theology*, 122.

58. Louth, *Introducing Eastern Orthodox Theology*, 92.

59. Hopko, *Lenten Spring*, 109

60. Climacus, John. *The Ladder of Divince Ascent.* Mahwah, NJ: Paulist Press, 1982, 158. Step 11.

61. Matthew the Poor, *Orthodox Prayer Life*, 198.

62. Clendenin, *Eastern Orthodox Theology*, 53.

63. Clendenin, *Eastern Orthodox Theology*, 55.

64. Met Hilarion Alfeyev, *Orthodox Christianity, Volume II.* Yonkers, NY: St. Vladimir's Seminary Press, 2012, 57.

65. Forest, *Praying with Icons*, 44.

66. Porphyrios, *Wounded by Love*, 169–70.

67. Malinowski, *Magic, Science, and Religion*, 75.

68. Walker and Carras, *Living Orthodoxy in the Modern World*, 164.

69. Walker and Carras, *Living Orthodoxy in the Modern World*, 166.

70. The place in front of the royal doors on the solea.

71. Met Hilarion Alfeyev, *Orthodox Christianity, Volume I*, 185.

72. Damick, "What John Calvin Really Thought about Icons in the Church."

73. Heb 12:1

74. Eliade, *Patterns in Comparative Religion*, 437.

75. Met Hilarion Alfeyev, *Orthodox Christianity, Volume III*, 225–26.

76. Met Hilarion Alfeyev, *Orthodox Christianity. Volume III*, 226.

77. Met Hilarion Alfeyev, *Orthodox Christianity, Volume III*, 226.

78. Clendenin, *Eastern Orthodox Theology*, 63.

79. St. Theophan the Recluse, *The Path to Salvation*, 49.

80. Bennett, "Should Orthodox Christians Get Their Icons Blessed?"

81. Walker and Carras, *Living Orthodoxy in the Modern World*, 163.

82. "Confession/Absolution." EasternOrthodoxChristian, April 16, 2023. https://www.easternorthodoxchristian.com/confession (accessed 2023).

83. O Champion Leader (sometimes translated General).

84. Sardella, *Visible Image of the Invisible God*, 125.

85. Walker and Carras, *Living Orthodoxy in the Modern World*, 17.

86. Met Hilarion Alfeyev, *Orthodox Christianity, Volume III*, 236.

87. Met Hilarion Alfeyev, *Orthodox Christianity, Volume III*, 236.

88. "25th Anniversary of Martyrdom of Br. José Muñoz-Cortes Commemorated at Jordanville." OrthoChristian.com, n.d. https://orthochristian.com/149240.html (accessed 2022).

89. Eliade, *Patterns in Comparative Religion*, 452.

90. Met Hilarion Alfeyev, *Orthodox Christianity, Volume III*, 236–37.

91. Matthew Pageau, *Language of Creation*, 27.

92. Met Hilarion Alfeyev, *Orthodox Christianity, Volume III*, 226.

93. Temple, *Sacred Art*, 4.

94. Walker and Carras, *Living Orthodoxy in the Modern World*, 163.

95. Baggley, John. *Festival Icons for the Christian Year.* Crestwood, NY: St. Vladimir's Seminary Press, 2000, 3.

96. Eliade, *Patterns in Comparative Religion*, 456.

97. Forest, *Praying with Icons*, 26.

98. Eliade, *Patterns in Comparative Religion*, 439.

99. Pomazansky, Michael. *Orthodox Dogmatic Theology.* Platina, CA: St. Herman of Alaska Brotherhood, 2021, 322.

100. Walker and Carras, *Living Orthodoxy in the Modern World*, 163.

101. Schmemann *A Voice for Our Times*, 30.

# Chapter 5

# Iconoclasm and the Iconodules

Thomas Hopko declares, "The icon is Orthodoxy's highest artistic achievement. It is a gospel proclamation, a doctrinal teaching, and a spiritual inspiration in colors and lines."[1] Yet this masterpiece of faith has undergone many trials throughout the history of Christianity. There have been many who distort, discredit, or destroy the sacred images of the Church. Known as iconoclasts or iconomachs,[2] these sacreligious actions are found througout the history of the Church in the East and the West. This chapter will address the two Iconoclastic periods of the Church in the East during the later half of the eighth and beginning half of the ninth centuries. The next chapter addresses the iconoclasm of the West.

While many Protestant scholars of today wish to paint icons as a later invention of the Church, something that came along with Constantine and a "Paganization" of the Church, Holy Tradition and archeology have pointed out that there was wide use of images by Christians throughout the world by the second century. Saint Nektarios demonstrates that, "Engraved monuments and murals found in the chambers of the cemeteries of the catacombs and the evidence therein, and wherever worship was performed, confirm the use of the images in the Church."[3] We also have ample evidence of the proper veneration of icons by saints such as Maximus the Confessor, who kissed the Gospels, cross, and icons of Christ and the Theotokos after his debate in Bizna with Monothelites in 656.[4] Furthermore, the Quinisext Council of Constantinople in 692, also known as the Council in Trullo, specifically affirmed the propriety of venerating icons of Christ, though laying out some stipulations concerning how Christ should be depicted, as we spoke about in chapter 3.[5] While the See of Rome never adoped the council, during Justinian II's[6] early reign the relationship with Old and New Rome remained strong.

It is therefore surprising that within thirty years of the Quinisext Council, iconoclasm would be declared the law of the land in Constantinople and all Roman lands. Much of this radical reversal of fortunes had to do with the political rather than the religious atmosphere of the Later Roman Empire.

After the Council, Justinian II lost the throne to Leonitus,[7] who promptly cut off Justinian's nose in an attempt to prevent his return to the throne. Following Leonitus's absence, Tiberius III[8] reigned. Justinian, with a newly fashioned golden nose, reassumed the throne and upon his return his reign was rather brutal. During the next six years, Justinian II lost most of the support that he once had and was executed in 711. The fates of many of Justinian's successors were not much better. Rebellion and regicide were common. Five of the six emperors during this period had their reigns cut short through violence. Furthermore, the worsening state of the emperors increased the appetite of the political foes, including the Arabs, Bulgars, and Lombards. It appeared that Rome underwent similar trials as it faced during the third century. In light of this growing threat, the unprepared Theodosius III abdicated the throne in 717, and he and his sons retired to a monastery.

## FIRST ICONOCLASTIC WAVE

It should therefore come as no wonder that a strong general should rise to power and attempt to right the ship, akin to Diocletian's ascension in the third century. In the spring of 717, the general who adopted this task was a man called Leo,[9] often known as "the Isaurian." Emperor Leo III's[10] first act as emperor was to strengthen the defensive measures of Constantinople. This was just in time, as during the summer of the same year the Caliph's brother marched through Asia Minor with an army of 80,000 men. The Arab army was complemented by 1,800 ships in September. The city of Constantinople was under a full siege. Fortunately, in the next year, the navy was reduced to a handful of ships due to the unique weapon of Greek fire, and with the assistance of prayers to the Theotokos, the massive Arab army was reduced in numbers to the point that they could no longer sustain the siege. Leo followed this success with a few more military achievements against the Arabs from 726 to 740.

With the Muslim threat so powerful, it might have seemed like a prudent decision to find a nonmilitary way of appeasing them. In 721, Yazid II,[11] the Caliph of the Umayyad Empire, issued the first iconoclastic decree in his lands. During the next decade Leo imitated this Islamic decree, but scholars are uncertain why. J. M. Hussey points out that "there is no evidence of direct contact between Leo and Yazid."[12] Knowledge of this decree likely found its way into Constantinople, and some believe it was for political reasons that Leo chose to act this way. His Orthodox opponents clearly saw a connection, as they called him the "Saracen-minded."[13] Others believe it was due to the influence of Judaism, though this explanation is less likely. Historians such as John Julius Norwich believe it was a connection to Monophysite belief[14] found in the eastern regions of Anatolia where Leo originated from. There were also many accounts of clear abuse of icon veneration during the reign of Leo, as Met Hilarion Alfeyev admits, including some icons that were "made godparents at baptisms, and paint scraped from icons was mixed with the wine used for the eucharist."[15]

With the presence of such abuses, a corrective was necessary. Instead of pressing upon the clergy to speak to the errors, Leo took it upon himself. Leo believed that all veneration of icons was idolatry, and this needed to be uprooted from society. The military failures of his predecessors and the violence of their reigns only proved God's displeasure in Leo's mind. The solution was to remove the idols as King Hezekiah did in the Old Testament.[16] Leo was not a priest, though he assumed this position. Steven Runciman states that "On certain feasts he preached the sermon in Saint Sophia."[17] While the Saracen-minded Emperor sought reform, he looked at the simple prohibition of images in the Second Commandment and saw icons as a violation. To him, there was no difference between an icon of Christ and idolatry. Therefore, they must be removed.

The first step in enacting Leo's "reform" was taken in 726. The golden image of Christ over the Bronze Gate of the emperor's Great Palace in Constantinople, known as the Chalke, was the largest icon in the city. It was the primary target. Leo tore the icon down and replaced it with a cross. During the next few years, icons of Christ, the Theotokos, and the saints were destroyed throughout the empire. Most of them were replaced by a cross, an empty throne, or in direct opposition to the Council in Trullo, a lamb. Leo sought not only to destroy icons from the public sphere, but from churches and even in some cases in private worship. In 730, this culminated in Leo's edict prohibiting icons,[18] dispossessing Patriarch Germanos and a local council that forbade the veneration of all images.[19] The reaction by the populace was outrage. "The commander of the demolition party was set upon by a group of outraged women and killed on the spot."[20] There were also demonstrations and mutinies in the army and navy. The objection was most severe in the European portions of the empire, yet the worst was still to come.

In 741, Leo III's reign came to an end and a new dynasty emerged. Instead of chaos determining who would succeed him, we have the birth of the Isaurian dynasty.[21] This did not bring stability to the empire, though. Constantine V,[22] the son of Leo, was appointed the successor and Constantine had more zeal for iconomachy than his father did. Partly as a result of this predisposition to warring against icons, there was a brief reign of Constantine's older brother-in-law Artabasdus in 742. Artabasdus proclaimed himself to be the emperor and restored the icons. The quantity of icons that was produced or uncovered during this brief reign indicate that the people never subscribed to Leo's iconoclasm. Artabasdus was defeated sixteen months after his ascension by Constantine, who took his revenge on not only Artabasdus but his sons,[23] Patriarch Anastasius[24] who crowned Artabasdus, and the lovers of icons as well. Patriarch Anastasius was flogged, stripped, and paraded backward on a donkey around the Hippodrome.[25] To the shock of the people, after this humiliation he was reinstated, though properly chastised and more compliant with the emperor.

Constantine V, Copronymus, or dung named, as he became known due to his defecation during his baptism, launched the most brutal attack against the icons during his nearly thirty-year reign as emperor.[26] Unlike his father, who primarily wanted to dissuade people and remove icons from the public sphere, Constantine V sought to remove them from every aspect of society. His iconoclasm included the only real broad anticlericalism that we can see during the Later Roman Empire. Since monks and clergy opposed iconoclasm, Constantine's attack was also against the institution of monasticism. For Constantine, the population needed its resources and it needed to reproduce. In his eyes, monastics took away from both of these needs, in addition to their opposition to his imperial policies. He forbade the taking of novices, closed several monasteries, and transported monks to Cyprus to diminish their numbers in and around Constantinople.

While Leo may have illicitly adopted the duties of a priest on occasion, Constantine viewed himself as the theologian of the iconoclasts.[27] Moving beyond the simple criticism of icons derived from a poor reading of the Second Commandment, Leo developed a sophisticated theological approach concerning icons. He argued that an icon, if it were to be a true image, must be consubstantial with the person that depicted.[28] Since Christ is both human and divine and the image is only material, it can only speak to the humanity of Christ and not to his divinity. If icons are maintained, since the divinity cannot be portrayed, we either confuse the divinity with the human nature, which is Monophysitism, or we separate the two natures, which is Nestorianism. Therefore, according to Constantine, all images, even of Christ, are false and must be removed. Furthermore, the image cannot contain the same essence as the prototype when speaking of Christ and it is therefore a false image according to Constantine and those who followed him. Along this line, he was broadly opposed to the cult of saints but did not persecute them. He did refuse to use the title holy or saint as that connected a spiritual reality conferred upon a material person. Leo's theology was far closer to affirming a Platonic duality than anything advocated by the church up until this time.

To ensure his theology was adopted, Constantine called for an "ecumenical" council in 754 to condemn the making of and veneration of icons. The council sat 338 bishops and was recognized as ecumenical by the emperor but not by the Church at large. Until the final session, none of the Patriarchs were present, and then only the Patriarch of Constantinople. The Sees of Rome,

Alexandria, Antioch, and Jerusalem were entirely absent from the council and would have opposed the findings if invited. The council's theology largely followed the dictates of Constantine concerning what is represented in the icon. It added a stress on God being uncircumscribable. God was therefore unable to be captured in any form with the exception of the Eucharist. The iconoclasts believed this was the only true image of Christ.

The minutes of the council have been lost, but we know that three iconodules[29] were anathematized by the iconoclastic council, including Patriarch Germanus, George of Cyprus, and Mansur "the Saracen-minded," also known as John of Damascus. These condemnations had little effect, especially on John of Damascus since he was outside of imperial territory. The result of the council is that it gave support for the iconomachs. They not only continued to break and burn icons but also anything that may have contained an image of Christ, the Theotokos, or saints. This included furniture, vestments, and reliquaries. Martyrdom followed for the iconodules including Stephen, abbot of the monastery of Saint Auxentius, who was stoned to death in the street, as well as thousands of other monks and nuns who were mutilated or killed in the defense of icons. As a result of these atrocities, the following decade is known as the "decade of blood." So brutal was this time that Florensky posits that the lines were clear, "people knew precisely what they were struggling for, and they knew clearly who was friend and who was enemy; plainly, there were icon-smashers and icon-worshippers."[30]

The iconoclasts consisted primarily of the emperor, those in the imperial household, and the military since the two iconoclast emperors saw military success during their tenure. The iconodules consisted of the monks and the general population. Saint Nektarios maintains that "icons have been around since the beginning, and the honour given to them was [already] deeply rooted in the hearts of the faithful."[31] We can also see a general regional breakdown, where the Asiatic population of the empire was more willing to accept Constantine's iconomachy, while the European portions of the empire were staunch iconodules.[32] Akin to Diocletian's great persecution of the Church which he used to shore up the empire, iconoclasm and the subsequent persecution was the tool of the Isaurians. The result of both persecutions was to grow the faith in opposition to the government oppressors. The most beneficial result of this period came in the form of theological reflection from some of the brightest minds the Church has offered.

The main theological response to Leo and Constantine came from John of Damascus.[33] John was well connected, holding a prominent position in the Umayyad Caliphate before his retirement to the Mar Saba monastery near Jerusalem in 730. Saint John of Damascus's theological response to Leo and Constantine was discussed in chapter 3. John spoke to each of the concerns raised by the Isaurians and masterfully demonstrated how their theology was flawed at best. John constantly articulated the reasons why veneration of icons is appropriate and beneficial for the Christian.

As we can see with John of Damascus and the popular unrest against iconoclasm, the Isaurian dynasty was not likely to maintain its iconomachy indefinitely, regardless of Constantine V's hard handed and brutal measures. In 775, when Constantine died, his son Leo IV[34] ascended the throne. Leo was the eldest of six sons and one daughter from the thrice married Constantine. He shared his father's disposition against icons but did not need to prove his military might in the same manner, since, in 750, the Umayyad Dynasty collapsed and the Caliphate moved to Baghdad. The newly formed Abbasid Empire were for a time more interested in fighting Persia and Afghanistan than territories in the west. Europe is where Leo focused his attention, primarily when choosing a wife. For some unknown reason, he chose an Athenian woman by the name of Irene to take as his wife. Irene[35] was stunningly beautiful, but her family had no wealth or position. To complicate things further, Irene's stance on icons was opposed to the Isaurian position. This likely did not matter much in the eyes of Leo, since Irene, as a woman, theoretically would have had little effect on the government's official position. That is until the summer of 780 when Leo came down with a violent fever. He died on 8 September 780. Thankfully for Irene they had produced a son, Constantine,[36] who was not ten years of age.

After a brief five-year reign, Leo IV's death left the rule of the empire to his wife. At less than ten, Constantine VI needed a regent to rule, and Irene took the opportunity. She was a competent ruler for the empire for the next eleven years. Many men in the army in Anatolia tried to rebel and elevate someone else but it was futile. Irene was smart, determined, and not willing to relinquish power. Eventually this would prove her undoing, but in her early reign it proved a valuable asset.

Irene took the lead and tried to right the broken relationships with the broader Orthodox world that were caused by iconoclasm. By reversing the stance on iconoclasm, not only did Irene advance an issue she believed was important theologically, but it also arrested the fears and trepidation of the Constantinople populace who had grown tiresome of the hard hand of Constantine V. This measure likely earned her much more support in the capitol and influential areas. Furthermore, it strengthened the position of Constantinople in relation to Rome, as Rome had opposed the iconoclastic decrees from their inception. In 787, this culminated in an invitation to Pope Hadrian I to have a genuinely ecumenical council concerning icons, unlike the iconoclastic council of 754. Some have cynically wondered why Irene did not invoke a council earlier to address the issue. Likely it was due to Patriarch Paul IV, the New.[37] Paul was elevated during the days of iconoclasm and was largely silent concerning icons. He may have himself been an iconoclast at the beginning of his tenure, but after seeing the martyrdom of the Orthodox he secretly supported the iconodule position. He was also a rather quiet, old, and timid man. While he pushed for a council, he was not capable of making a strong position for the case. When he retired to a monastery in 784, a former civil servant, Tarasios,[38] assumed the patriarchate, in part on the condition of holding a council to resolve the issue. Tarasios was wise and understood the diplomatic road that would be necessary to ensure an end to iconoclasm. Both Paul and Tarasios are counted as saints for their support of icons and their connection to their restoration.

In September 787, at the church of the Holy Wisdom in Nicaea, with a firm and well-spoken Patriarch of Constantinople, the support from Papal legates, and representatives from all three of the Eastern Patriarchates, the Seventh Ecumenical council began, also known as the Second Council of Nicaea. The council was in Nicaea instead of Constantinople because of a few iconoclastic soldiers who tried to disrupt those arriving at the council. Irene decided it was best to both relocate the soldiers and the council to a safer venue, ensuring the peace and stability of the council.

The council followed the theology as was laid down by John of Damascus. His eloquent exposition of the faith resounded. Using the phrase from Basil, that the image passes to the prototype, the case was clearly made that we worship the God of matter, and Christ took on matter for our sake, and not matter itself. Icons were given ηροοκύνησις reverence, but God alone receives λατρεία true worship. The veneration of icons was proclaimed:

> Venerable and holy images, in painting and mosaics, as well as in other appropriate materials, should be set forth in the holy churches of God, and on the sacred vessels, and on the vestments and on hangings, and in pictures both in houses and in public places. These holy images should depict the figure of our Lord God and Savior Jesus Christ, and of our spotless Lady, the Mother of God, and of the honorable Angels and of all Saints, and of all pious people.[39]

Unlike the iconoclastic council, the condemnations issued at the Seventh Ecumenical Council were fairly minor. Standard anathemas were issued, "Anathema to those who do not venerate the holy and venerable images. Anathema to those who call the sacred images idols."[40] Furthermore, Gregory, Bishop of Neocaesarea, who was one of the few bishops that participated in the illicit council, was subject to reading out the *Horos* of that synod with each paragraph being refuted. There was no real persecution of those who participated in iconoclasm. A good amount of time was spent on how to receive the penitents back. In essence, as long as they did not maltreat iconodules, they were received back. Maltreatment also required some proof and not simply an accusation.[41] The effect was that icons and those who adore them were recognized as belonging firmly within Orthodox Holy Tradition.

The Western response to all of this set the stage for the later years in Irene's reign and the relationship between Constantinople and Rome from then on. The Popes of Rome had consistently condemned the iconoclasm of the Isaurians. From the beginning, Gregory II[42] publicly condemned iconoclasm and even wrote to Leo that he should refrain from defining dogma. Later popes followed suit. Since the Isaurian dynasty clung to iconoclasm, the papacy was distanced. The relationship of the Emperor and the Pope was strained, and the popes could also get away with more abuses, most notably the various abuses that surrounded Pope Leo III.[43] They also did not believe that Constantinople could come to their aid after the Lombards sacked Ravena in 751, and they relied more heavily upon the rising Carolingian Franks.

Charlemagne[44] chose to call for his own council in response to the Seventh Ecumenical council in Frankfort in June 794. He then sent his Carolingian Books (*Libri Carolini*) to Pope Hadrian I.[45] The Franks concluded that "The iconoclasts had been wrong in rejecting all cult of images, and the iconodules had been wrong in ascribing too much to the images but both had been wrong in ignoring Rome."[46] The Frankish reading of the council was poor, largely due to a bad translation from the Greek to Latin, where the key distinction of *Proskynesis* ηροοκύνησις veneration and *latreia* λατρεία worship was confused. This also provided Charlemagne more fuel to advance his cause in Rome over and against Constantinople. This culminated in his coronation as the Emperor of the Romans on Christmas Day 800.

The title Emperor of the Romans was already held by Irene, but the West, following the old Salic tradition, did not recognize a woman's right to rule. To resolve this issue, marriage was proposed to Irene, who contemplated it against the advice of many in her court. With the elevation of Charlemagne, Irene's problems only increased. She was unwilling to relinquish her throne to her son Constantine VI. Those supporting Constantine revolted in 790. This resulted in a brief two-year reign for Constantine before Irene was invited back to help his failing rule. Irene took advantage of this and began to assume her old role. Constantine also found himself wanting a divorce. His proposed remarriage in 795 was opposed by half of the clerics in Constantinople. This is known as the Moechian Controversy. The result of the divorce was that it created two branches of iconodules, and their position was subsequently weakened. Irene continued to reign and overthrew her son in 797. She had him blinded so he could no longer rule. This was done so brutally that it may have resulted in his death.[47]

The later rule of Irene was fraught with challenges, and she found herself more and more isolated from her subjects. Additionally, there were repeated military failures against both the Arabs and Bulgars. Potential marriage with

Charlemagne looked appealing but dangerous to those who wanted Irene deposed. Finally, in October 802, an assembly in the Hippodrome declared Irene deposed. She was arrested and accepted her deposition with dignity. She was then exiled to Lesbos, where she died a year later.

Irene's successor was Nicephorus I,[48] the mastermind behind her deposition. He firmly opposed the idea of calling any Carolingian the "Emperor of the Romans." That title was reserved for him and those in New Rome. He admitted that Charlemagne might be an emperor, but not of the people that he claimed in his title to rule. No other ruler would even concede this, typically referring to these German rulers with the title rex.[49] Nicephorus was the former Logothete of the Treasury and revived many of the economic problems facing the empire. Unfortunately, he was also not a great military tactician. In a battle against the Bulgars, he believed he had routed them only to find that he fell into a trap. On his long march back, he and his soldiers were unprepared for the ambush that they walked into. He was lost in battle and his body was retrieved by Kahn Krum[50] with his head impaled on a stake. Later, to add more indignity, his skull was mounted in silver and used as a drinking cup for the Bulgarian Kahn. The next emperor did not fare much better.

Stauracius[51] was there with Nicephorus and tried to dissuade the emperor from his poorly planned attack. Those who survived saw this judgment and acclaimed him to be the emperor on 28 July 811. His claim was supported by his services as co-emperor since 803, but this was always under Nicephorus's shadow. Stauracius was in no shape to reign. As a result of the battle, he suffered many ailments, that upon his return to Constantinople resulted in him being paralyzed from the waist down. He was also paralyzed by those who did not recognize him as the emperor and rumors of plots. To try to insulate himself from this, since he did not have any children, there was a thought of making his wife Theophano his lawful successor. Unfortunately, the final years of Irene made this less palatable. Instead, most people supported his sister Procopia's husband Michael (I) Rhangabe.[52] Michael was the will of the people and the clergy, but Stauracius desired his wife to rule. On 1 October, Stauracius planned to blind Michael to keep him from ruling, which increasingly seemed inevitable. Instead, on 2 October, the coup was successful, and Michael was proclaimed the emperor. The Patriarch Nicephorus[53] told Stauracius that this was done not out of treachery but concern for his health and the health of the empire. Stauracius lived only another three months before the infection from his wound resulted in his death.

Michael Rhangabe[54] looked very promising upon his elevation. He had the support of the people and the Church. He was a good-natured man and was very admirable by most accounts. Unfortunately, the broad consensus is that he was not prepared to rule. His only qualification was his marriage. Critics said he was weak willed and easily led, often a puppet of the

Patriarch Nicephorus and Theodore the Studite.[55, 56] These criticisms have some basis in reality. Michael was devout and listened to the prominent clergy of his day. He was also not adequately prepared for what was about to come his way. Some of the remaining iconoclasts tried to replace him with one of Constantine V's sons in the middle of a conflict with the Bulgarians. Michael seemed capable of dealing with Krum, even winning several engagements in 813. Unfortunately, when it was time for the decisive battle of Versinikia[57] near Adrianople, several of his troops abandoned him, following their generals, notably Leo the Armenian.[58] The result was a catastrophic loss and upon his return to Constantinople, Leo assumed the throne. Instead of fighting Leo, Michael opted to retire to a monastery along with his sons, whom Leo castrated to prevent from pursuing the throne. Michael had lost his military forces while Leo maintained his and Khan Krum was preparing to lay siege to Constantinople. Michael abdicated the throne after only two years of reign. Had Leo's treachery not won, Michael may have proved to be an effective leader.

## SECOND ICONOCLASTIC WAVE

Following his treachery to gain the throne from Michael (I) Rhangabe, in his decisive battle against the Bulgarians, Leo V[59] assumed the throne in 813, and with him came a return to iconoclasm. The reestablishment of iconoclasm was not immediate. It was not until 815 that the old iconoclastic polices were reintroduced. Likely the Armenian had some iconoclastic leanings prior to his advancement to the throne and saw the iconoclasts in the East as a strong branch of support. Furthermore, the military setbacks of the last decade helped to convince many of the iconoclasts in the military that God was unhappy with Irene's council. After the Bulgarian threat was mitigated, Leo turned his attention toward the scriptures and patristic writings in favor of iconoclasm. The key person behind this was fellow Armenian John the Grammarian.[60] Leo and John tried to win over Nicephorus, the Patriarch of Constantinople. Their arguments were practical, pointing to military defeat. Leo's objections to icons had the same basis as his namesake Leo III: military defeat must mean that icons are some sort of abuse. Following the Second Council of Nicaea in 787, Leo was not able to advance as strong theological language though. Instead, he saw the acts of veneration as the abuse. He proposed a middle ground, where all those icons that were hung low and could be kissed were removed, but those higher and useful for instruction could remain. This would demonstrate a difference between worshiping them and revering them. Patriarch Nicephorus rejected this proposal. As a result, in 815 he was driven from his office and Leo advocated for the elevation of

John the Grammarian. John would eventually become the Patriarch, but not until 837. Theodotus Melisseus Cassiteras,[61] a relative of Constantine V, was named the new Patriarch.

Leo's theological vision came to pass. With Nicephorus deposed, he ordered all the icons to be placed out of the reach of the faithful. In open defiance to the resurgence of iconoclasm, Theodore the Studite ordered a public procession with icons on Palm Sunday. For this, he was sent into exile. Leo, while an iconoclast, tried to temper his aggression against the images. He did not want to produce the surge of martyrs that existed in the first wave of iconoclasm, nor was his aim as universal in scope. Largely one could survive with icons easier outside of the city than in Constantinople itself. Leo could not stand for open rebellion that Theodore represented. He was thrown into prison three times and exiled, but Leo would not resort to the violence of Constantine V. There were no stringent measures against those who refused to submit.

On Easter, Leo called a general synod to speak on the matter. Unsurprisingly, many of the iconodule bishops were not invited. The iconoclast Patriarch Theodotus Melisseus Cassiteras, who replaced Nicephorus, was unable to manage the synod. Even with many iconodules omitted from the proceedings, the tempers flared up and many prelates were physically attacked, punched, kicked, and spat upon. The result was a watered-down proclamation that supported the new iconoclastic tendencies of the emperor.

Leo's earlier treachery against Michael I came back to haunt him with Michael II.[62] Michael was an uneducated soldier from Amorium in Phrygia. He had a speech impediment. He is referred to as the Stammerer. Michael was friends with Leo, as they served together, but like Leo he was also ambitious and cunning. He began plotting against Leo in the fall of 820. Eventually he was discovered and brought to Constantinople. Leo sentenced his old friend to death, but Leo's wife Theodosia, moved with compassion on the eve of the Nativity, urged leniency. After all, how could he receive the Eucharist with blood on his hands? Leo relented but made sure he had the key to Michael's cell to ensure no rebellion would spread. Possibly the words of Saint Theophylactus, the Bishop of Nicomedia,[63] rung in his ears. The saint, early in Leo's reign, told him to shun his iconoclasm and if he did not, then "great ruin will unexpectedly befall you, and you will find no one to deliver you from it."[64] The saint was exiled, but Leo was about to fall into unexpected ruin. Unable to sleep, Leo chose to check on Michael to ensure he was still in prison. He opened the cell and counted the bodies to ensure Michael had not somehow escaped. In his count, he missed Michael's servant, who hid under the bed. When Leo left, the servant woke Michael, who convinced the jailer that he was in danger if he did not side with him. Michael quickly moved upon Leo and killed him on Christmas. Michael ascended the imperial throne with the blood of Leo on his hands and in irons. It was only later that a blacksmith was called to remove them from his legs.

Upon Michael's[65] ascension on Christmas Day of 820, Saint Theodore the Studite was recalled from exile. He remarked early on in Michael's reign that, "The winter is past, but spring has not yet come."[66] Michael's ambition lay in having power more than advancing any ecclesial goal. He was an iconoclast but did not care to enforce this too much if it would cause him to lose the throne. Outside of Constantinople one could do what they would like, but he would leave the church as he found it. Iconoclasm would stay. Michael was not a theologian. His poor education matched his poor speech. He was not prepared to engage in theological disputations. He was however prepared to use force to ensure stability. Michael II, the Amorian or the Stammerer, would not falter on ensuring his rule.

Michael II's son, Theophilus,[67] ascended the throne upon his father's passing in 829. Michael's reign brought in great riches to the empire and a few growing military threats. Theophilus's reign was marked with opulence. His throne, which was adorned with a golden and bejeweled tree and mechanical birds, lions, and other animals that would tweet and roar when someone approached, became legendary. The throne was to resonate the power of the imperial office, and this he did. To maintain his lineage, he needed an heir. To this end, Theophilus chose the Paphlagonian Theodora. Like Irene, her beauty was unmatched, and like Irene she was an iconodule. This did not seem to bother Theophilus, especially after the birth of their son Michael,[68] later Michael III, also called Michael the Drunkard.

Theophilus was an iconoclast like his father. Similarly, he was not primarily interested in enforcing his iconoclasm. Theophilus was an admirer of Baghdad and the increased prestige of the growing Islamic Caliphate. While remaining a Christian, he sought to emulate many of the cultural activities in Baghdad, primarily the art and learning. He opened a new school, and also advanced a stricter iconoclasm, favoring the artistic representation found in Islamic nature scenes. Theophilus sought to persecute the monks who were the last major defenders of icons.[69] The leading icon painter of the day, Lazarus, was scourged and branded on the palms of his hands.

Theophilus died of dysentery at 38 on 20 January 842, and with him died the last gasp of Orthodox iconoclasm. There are some accounts of Theophilus repenting of his iconoclasm shortly before his death. The validity of these accounts is questioned by many historians. In any case, having Theophilus recant this belief would preserve his legacy and ensure a continuity with his two-year-old son Michael III,[70] the new Emperor, and his son's regent Theodora.

The effects of the second wave of iconoclasm were not nearly as intense as the first. With Leo III and especially Constantine V, violence and destruction were rampant. From 726, when Leo removed the Chalke icon of Christ, to 787 and the Seventh Ecumenical Council, death, banishment, prison, and the closing of monasteries were common. In the second wave from 813 to 842, the consequences were considerably minor. Icons that were hung low were removed, and the monastics still faced retribution for their iconophilia, but massive martyrdom did not occur.

The arguments of later iconoclasts were similar to the more advanced arguments of Constantine V. The iconoclasts questioned how an image could contain the essence of Christ, who is uncircumscribable and holy. After all, "What is depicted in an icon is not a nature in general, but a person with particular features, so in the icon of Christ it is the person that is depicted, the person in whom the two natures are united."[71] They were not capable of separating veneration and adoration form worship. Finally, they failed to understand the arguments about image versus the archetype or its prototype. These iconoclasts still maintained that an image must have the same essence as the original, despite the clarification by John of Damascus.

This second wave of iconoclasm also issued a similar pushback by Rome. The pope was already firmly in the camp of the Carolingians and felt free to criticize the second wave of iconoclasts without fear of retribution. Pope Pascal I[72] condemned iconoclasm with an encyclical. Rome also served as a refuge for the monks, who fled the second wave of iconoclastic persecution. This resulted in a great deal of learning for the Italians and hampered the intellectual growth of Constantinople that Theophilus desired.

Throughout the second wave of iconoclasm, Patriarch Nicephorus was sidelined. The primary theological voice against Leo was Theodore, the abbot of the Studite Monastery. Theodore built upon the arguments of John of Damascus. Unlike John, Theodore spent his life under constant imperial threat. He was born in 759 during the reign of Constantine V. His uncle, Plato of Symbola, urged him to become a monk, which Theodore did. Theodore endured three periods of exile, largely in connection to his position on icons and his insistence that the emperors live moral lives. He was opposed to the divorce and remarriage of Constantine VI. For this, he was exiled. This also resulted in a fractured front on icons as it divided him from the patriarch at the time. That relationship was eventually reconciled. So too was his first exile. Irene recalled him and Theodore transferred his monastery to the Studite Monastery.

Theodore faced a second brief two-year exile, still in connection with his opposition to the divorce. His third was for opposing the reimposition of icon-oclasm of Leo V. Recalled by Michael II, he continued his strong support for the holy images. Under Michael, Theodore lived in semi-exile until his death on 11 November 826. In addition to his support of icons, Theodore is known for his reformation and organization of monastic life. His theology focused on the concerns of the second wave iconoclasts as addressed in chapter 3.

Empress Theodora[73] was a long supporter of icons. Since Michael, at two years old, was still too young to reign, she served as regent when her husband Theophilus died in 842. By this time, the ill feelings that went along with the latter half of Irene's reign had vanished. Theodora was also a more patient woman than Irene. She steadily worked to rid the empire of the iconoclasm of the last thirty years. Her main opposition was John the Grammarian, now the Patriarch of Constantinople. The long iconoclast and friend of Leo was not willing to repent so quickly. She relied heavily upon some advisers, namely her uncle Sergius Nicetdates, her brother Bardas, and Theoctistus, Logothete of the Course. With their assistance, they forcibly deposed John and elevated a monk, Methodius, who in his defense of icons had spent seven years in prison.

Now in 843, with the iconoclasts out of power, Theodora called a local council to reaffirm the Second Nicene Council of 787. They anathematized the iconoclastic leaders, but just like with Nicaea they were not ill-treated or imprisoned. The return of the iconodules in both cases was accomplished through freedom and love of Christ, not cruelty and with the force of arms. The jubilant return of icons is known as the Triumph of Orthodoxy. The council concluded on the first Sunday of Great Lent, 11 March 843. What followed was a huge procession with icons and the firm establishment of icons in the Church. From that triumphant day until today icons are used in veneration in all Orthodox Churches. The day is commemorated as the triumph not of icons, but of Orthodoxy, because the icons affirm a Christological truth as was expressed by Saints Theodore the Studite, John of Damascus, and many others who suffered and died during the iconoclast periods. Icons are Orthodoxy. Thus, the proclamation:

> As the prophets beheld, as the Apostles have taught, . . . As the Church has received . . . as the teachers have dogmatized . . . as the Universe has agreed . . . as Grace has shown forth . . . as Truth has revealed . . . as falsehood has been dissolved . . . as Wisdom has presented . . . as Christ Awarded . . . thus we declare . . . thus we assert . . . thus we preach Christ our true God, and honor His Saints in words, in writings, in thoughts in sacrifices, in churches, in Holy Icons, on the one had worshiping and reverencing Christ as God and Lord; on the one hand honoring as true servants of the same Lord of all and accordingly offering them veneration. . . . This is the Faith of the Apostles, this is the Faith of the Fathers, this is the Faith of the Orthodox, this is the faith which has established the Universe.[74]

While icons were ultimately restored, the effects of the two iconoclastic periods had lasting repercussions. As Metropolitan Hilarion Alfeyev points out, iconoclasm was a "regressive movement turning Christian art back to conventional symbols and allegories."[75] It was an attempt to return the telos of Orthodoxy to *theoria* instead of the *theosis*. Iconoclasm rejected the material for the realm of ideas, thus severing the connection to the divine and failing to affirm the incarnation.

In Leo III's attempt at reform, we saw the first reformation in the Church. Much like the Protestant Reformation in the 1500s, the destruction of icons and the transformation of how we approach God was central. Thankfully for Orthodoxy, this reformation failed. The theology of the iconoclasts could not surmount John of Damascus or Theodore the Studite. Moreover, iconoclasm never resonated with the people. It was always something enforced, as it attempted to create a new trajectory for Christian life, one that was alien and foreign to the traditions of the church and writings of the Fathers.

This enforcement resulted in a great toll. Primarily in the first wave, everything that could be destroyed was. A contemporary account says that all icons "were destroyed by fire or thrown to the ground, or effaced with a coating."[76] Military officials and civil servants were sent to remote provinces to destroy icons. The loss of icons is uncountable. Many of the Church's earliest icons are simply lost as a result of this. Today many Protestant iconoclastic scholars like to argue for a lack of evidence of icons in the period before Constantine. While Saint Nektarios provides evidence to the contrary, their claims are largely contingent upon the fact that we simply do not know what icons were destroyed. Undoubtedly, the most revered and earliest icons would have been housed in Constantinople and would have been the first to be destroyed under Leo III and Constantine V. A similar argument could be made about icons that were held in churches that were destroyed or converted over to mosques as Islam militarily dominated the Patriarchal sees of Alexandria, Antioch, and Jerusalem.

The production of icons resumed in both 787 and 843 with the ending of iconoclasm. Many icons were still produced but not in the same numbers as before. Generations of icon production were lost, in addition to those icons of antiquity. The lasting effect was that sculptures and other three-dimensional objects were scarcely generated in the East. As we see the beauty of the icons that the Later Roman Empire produced, we can only imagine the loss to sculpture and other arts as a result of this period.

There were also numerous political repurcussions as a result of the iconoclasm of the Isaurians and the second wave iconoclasts Leo V, Michael II, and Theophilus. The most notable effect was the relationship between Rome and Constantinople. Rome properly condemned the iconoclasm of the Isaurian Emperors. They in turn simply did not respond; they also failed to protect the West from the advancing Lombards and lost territory. This resulted in Rome looking toward the upstart Franks. Ultimately, this allowed for Charlemagne to drive a further wedge between Rome and Constantinople. Furthermore, it also resulted in the pope assuming universal ecclesial status instead of the honorary title, first among equals. As the relationship between Rome and the Germanic nations grew, so too did their ambitious claims. If the iconoclastic controversies never occurred, that relationship could have been salvaged. As it was, the long slow march toward a final schism was launched with the removal of the Chalke icon.

The Photian schism, or properly the Nicholatian schism of the 860s, is also in effect a result of the iconoclastic controversy. The treatment of the Studite monastery during this period and the zeal to enforce strict morality resulted in the Moechian Controversy[77] concerning Constantine VI's second marriage. While Theodore was right to condemn the practice, the issue of *economia* was muted during the following years. Even with the Triumph of Orthodoxy, Patriarch Methodius found himself at odds with the rigor that the Studites desired. The schism that resulted led to the eventual conflict between not only the Methodians and the Ignatians, but those opposed to Photius upon his elevation as well. This opened the door to an overly ambitious Pope Nicholas to try to assume more power than was due his office and the resultant schism. While iconoclasm was not a central factor in these later disputes, the legacy of iconoclasm was something that directly impacted the monastic practice.

The early iconoclasts were favored by a shifting political landscape in the Middle East. When the Abbasid Empire arose and turned their attention east instead of west, a period of relative peace on the Later Roman Empire's borders strengthened the iconoclasts belief that the military setbacks were a judgment of God upon the Empire. This argument was used again by Leo V. Interestingly enough, following the restoration of icons in 843, we have the beginning of a century of military expansion for the Empire. Instead of a defensive war, territory was restored, and until the cataclysmic loss at the Battle of Manzikert and the Normans with papal support conquering southern Italy, both in 1071, the restoration of icons provided as much military success as the loss provoked Leos III and V to fear their presence.

The Iconoclastic controversy did provide a significant advantage to the Church in the realm of developed theology concerning images. Until Christians questioned icons, the criticisms of Jews and Muslims were of secondary importance. When Leo III launched his attack, it unleashed the brilliance of John of Damascus to expound on the theological concerns with icons. Like every heresy that comes against the Church, there appears a theologian with the specific skills to demonstrate why those claims are not only against tradition, but against the foundations of the Church. Once developed, the defense of icons could be reasonably demonstrated to those Jews and Muslims who earnestly sought to understand this process. Jaroslav Pelikan also demonstrates how dialogues on icons were commonplace throughout the subsequent centuries. Even when veneration of the cross drew ire, Christians can say, "I do not say, 'Glory be to thee, O wood.' God forbid! But I say, 'Glory be to thee, O cross, all-powerful sign of Christ.'"[78]

## NOTES

1. Hopko, Thomas. *The Orthodox Faith, Volume 1: Doctrine and Scripture.* Yonkers, NY: St. Vladimir's Press, 1981, 37.

2. Those who war against the Icons.

3. St. Nektarios Kefalas. *Collected Works, Volume 9: On The Holy Images.* Jerusalem: Virgin Mary of Austrialia and Oceania, 2022, 9.

4. Hussey, J. M. *The Orthodox Church in the Byzantine Empire.* Oxford: Oxford University Press, 2010, 31.

5. Primarily we see prohibitions of Christ being depicted as a lamb. Canon 82 states: In certain paintings of holy icons a lamb is represented, being pointed out by the figure of the Forerunner, a lamb which is the prefiguration of grace, prefiguring for us in the Law the true Lamb which is Christ our God. (J. M. Hussey. *The Orthodox Church in the Byzantine Empire*, 33.)

6. R. 685–695 and 705–711.

7. R. 695–698.

8. R. 698–705.

9. 685–741.

10. R. 717–741.

11. R. 720–724.

12. Hussey, *The Orthodox Church in the Byzantine Empire*, 36.

13. Louth, Andrew. *Greek East and Latin West: The Church AD 681–1071.* Crestwood, NY: St. Vladimir's Seminary Press, 2007, 49.

14. "If we accept only the divine nature of Christ we cannot logically approve of a two- or three-dimensional portrayal of him as a human being" (John Julius Norwich. *A Short History of Byzantium*, Vintage, 1999, 111).

15. Met Hilarion Alfeyev, *Orthodox Christianity, Volume I*, 55.

16. 2 Kings 18, 2 Chronicles 32

17. Runciman, *The Great Church in Captivity*, 61.

18. Norwich. *A Short History of Byzantium*, 112.

19. Morris, *The Historic Church*, 101.

20. Norwich, *A Short History of Byzantium*, 112.

21. Some refer to this dynasty as the Syrian rather than Isaurian dynasty.

22. 718–775.

23. All were blinded

24. R. 730–754.

25. Norwich, *A Short History of Byzantium*, 113.

26. R. 741–770.

27. Hussey, *The Orthodox Church in the Byzantine Empire*, 39.

28. Louth, *Greek East and Latin West*, 56.

29. Also known as iconophiles, the lover of icons

30. Florensky, *Iconostasis*, 71.

31. St. Nektarios Kefalas, *On the Holy Images*, 14.

32. Oman, Charles. *The Byzantine Empire.* Yardly: Westholme, 2008, 202.

33. 675–749.

34. 775–780.

35. 750–803.

36. 771–797/805.

37. D. 784.

38. 730–806.

39. Hopko, Thomas. *The Orthodox Faith, Volume 3: Church History.* Yonkers, NY: St. Vladimir's Press, 1981, 97.

40. Hopko, *The Orthodox Faith Volume 3*, 97.

41. Hussey, *The Orthodox Church in the Byzantine Empire*, 47.

42. R. 715–731.

43. R. 795–816.

44. 747–814.

45. R. 772–795.

46. Pelikan, *The Christian Tradition, Volume 2*, 167.

47. Some accounts have that he was transferred to a monastery where he outlived his mother by a few years.

48. R. 802–811.

49. Hussey, *The Orthodox Church in the Byzantine Empire*, 54.

50. D. 814.

51. R. 811.

52. 770–844.

53. R. 806–815.

54. R. 811–813.

55. 759–826.

56. Norwich, *A Short History of Byzantium*, 125.

57. 816.

58. 775–820.

59. R. 813–820.

60. 490–570.

61. R. 815–821.

62. 770–829.

63. D. 845.

64. St. Nikolai of Ohrid and Zhicha. *The Prologue of Ohrid, Volume 1.* Alhambra, CA: Sebastian Press, 2017, 279.

65. R. 820–829.

66. Hussey, *The Orthodox Church in the Byzantine Empire*, 61.

67. R. 829–842.

68. 840–867.

69. Louth, *Greek East and Latin West*, 126.

70. R. 842–867.

71. Louth, *Greek East and Latin West*, 130.
72. R. 817–824.
73. R. 842–856.
74. Morris, *The Historic Church*, 102–3.
75. Met Hilarion Alfeyev, *Orthodox Christianity, Volume III*, 139.
76. Met Hilarion Alfeyev, *Orthodox Christianity, Volume III*, 147.
77. 795–811.
78. Pelikan, *The Christian Tradition, Volume 2*, 205.

*Chapter 6*

# A Western Interlude

## *Protestant Iconoclasm*

Following the Triumph of Orthodoxy, Orthodox Christians forever confirmed their tie to icons, the place of icons in church, and their theological significance. The only challenges to icons in the church were stylistic in the case of Peter the Great's Western innovations in iconography, and from the outside with the destruction of icons by the Soviets and Islamic rule. There has never truly been another substantive challenge to the place of icons. Icons in the East do differ from images in the West, though both are used often to serve the same liturgical and devotional practice. Eastern icons remain two-dimensional, while Western art contains two-dimensional images, including stained glass, as well as three-dimensional representations, statues, reliefs, etc. Following the Italian Renaissance, Western art took on a very "realistic" dimension that stylistically differs from Orthodox icons. It was for this reason that Peter's attempt to bring Western style into Eastern piety eventually failed. The East has largely returned to more traditional modes of representation in icons, while the West would have to reevaluate the purpose of images on its own.

Unfortunately, the West did not undergo the same sort of transformation that affected the Later Roman Empire. The Seventh Ecumenical Council, while accepted by Rome, did not have the impact it did in the East in part due to Carolingian misrepresentation, whether intentionally or not. While the council was affirmed by Rome, it was really the *Libri Carolingi* that set the tone for the West going forward. This meant that the issue of religious images and their place in the Church and at home was delayed. In 843, Roman concerns were about the rising threats of the Lombards and other Germanic tribes, then with the ascension of the papacy they key issues were between church and state with different manifestations of this church's supremacy relating to the Crusades, Avignon Papacy, and the resultant Western Schism.

With the Council of Florence, the Papacies' trajectory toward universalism was halted. The failed unification council foreshadowed the effects of denying the conciliatory solution advanced in Pisa and Constance. German, Swiss, English, and others soon reacted against Roman hegemony. With the Protestant Reformations also came a reprisal of religious art in the West.

## PROTESTANT ICONOCLASM

Images containing religious themes dominated the late-medieval and early modern landscape. The use of the printing press allowed for woodcuts to be viewed by the populace, and as Robert Scribner and Tessa Watt point out, the circulation of these sheets advanced the cause of the Reformations. As the printed image grew in importance, the place of painted or sculpted images in late-medieval and early modern Europe became hotly debated. Outbursts of iconoclasm erupted and either took fire or vanished away leaving only the destruction as a result. In many cases what determined the future of these iconoclastic spasms was how satisfying people found their religious lives, and what revitalization of their religious life needed to look like to answer the challenges they faced. In other words, the treatment of images mirrored the challenges that people faced at the dawn of the Reformation and the subsequent few centuries. Images became a symbol not only of what was represented but the place for that symbol moving forward.

Protestantism is not a single church, and neither was there a single treatment of icons and other religious images by Protestants. As the confessionalization process developed different trends in theology, so too did their other liturgical expressions including images. We should keep in mind that a wall covered in religious art and one with none both convey a spiritual message to their parishioners. Who determined what should be on the walls was not always the people but the interplay between the masses and the political elites in the realm. As Eamon Duffy points out, in the case of England, we find that most of the people did not desire radical change. Yet as Erasmus's impact on the continent displays, there was a dissatisfaction with the status quo. While some wanted to rid the churches of abuse, or to move toward a more conciliatory ecclesial structure, what the Russians in the late nineteenth century called *sobornost* (ecumenicity), there were those who sought a transformation of society as a whole. Those who wanted to alter society the most were those who wanted to destroy the images as we see in the famous conflict between Andreas Bodenstein von Karlstadt and Martin Luther. Andrew Pettegree argues that, "Iconoclasm represented the most spectacular collision between the competing imperatives of reformation in the renovation of the church and the preservation of social order."[1]

In most cases, the issue of religious art was a pawn to be brokered between the princes and the firebrands. If the princes held enough control over their people, images were likely to stay. If the princes needed to radicalize the people toward greater action to advance the political or ecclesial goals, then the place of images was compromised. As Susan Karaant-Nunn points out, "Most works of art disappeared not as a result of violence, however, but of the determination of princes and Reformers to eliminate all depictions that could not withstand scriptural and historical scrutiny."[2] Ouspensky maintains that whatever the proximate cause for the rise of iconoclasm in the West, the ultimate reason was the "degeneration in the medieval West."[3] In other words, the religious landscape had moved too far from the East and the Fathers such as John of Damascus, Theodore the Studite, and Basil the Great, that the notion of honor paid to the image passing over to the prototype seemed foreign. Along with the silenced voices of these luminaries and saints, Protestants increasingly lost sight of the telos of an icon. The distance between the prototype, be it the saints, Mary, or even Christ, and the people resulted in a distance between the people and the image.

In recent years, another critique of Western iconoclasm has arisen. Less theological and more practical, this concern focuses on the Reformation's effect upon women. Sherrin Marshall has a great collection on women in Europe during the Reformation, where the various contributors address the gender ideology of the Protestants. This ideology stripped the advances that women had made in the West as a result of traditional religion. David Cressy addresses the ritualistic loss that affected women with the removal of adiaphora practices such as churching. This, along with eliminating any other sacraments or ritualistic prescriptions that people found meaningful, disconnected them from their previous religious mode of understanding, and disempowered women. Steven Ozment and Lyndal Roper both address the household in Germany and the effect that the Reformations had upon the people there. Karant-Nunn specifically addresses the impact that images had upon women's religious consciousness. "I am arguing that there were other effects, unconscious though they may have been. For one thing, holy women with all their levels of meaning nearly vanished."[4] This happened, because as she points out, the Reformation's iconoclasm resulted in the "near elimination of pictures of women."[5] Even in those images of Mary that survived in Protestant areas, her place was diminished, her gaze was usually downcast, and she no longer stood as the Queen of Heaven, but only as background figure.

The feminist critique is not only justified, but it provides a bridge of understanding back to Ouspensky's earlier critique and how iconoclasm is understood in the East. Removing images disincarnates the saints, men and women. Mary and even Christ's incarnation are lost. The Church and its members are alienated from one another as their representations of one another are hidden behind whitewashed walls or found in rubble. It also serves to confirm Florensky's hypothesis that the removal of the iconostasis would also result in the loss of the altar itself. The level of destruction and the image of men and women that remained was a product of the confessionalization process. Lutheranism, Reform, Anabaptist, Anglican, and Catholic each had a different treatment of images and model for their parishioners in how they approached the divine.

The Lutheran approach to reform in general and images specifically was far more cautious than that of other Protestants. The aim of all of the reformers was to clean the errors and abuses of the church that had accumulated throughout the centuries. Luther simply saw these abuses as less systemic than Zwingli, Calvin, and Simons. Still, Luther's church saw a radical reduction in the number of saints. While he once called out to Saint Anne to save him, it was now the saints whose images and place in the life of the church needed saving from Luther.

Luther fought to preserve statues and other works of art from Karlstadt who sought their destruction. Luther saw the wholesale removal of images as dangerous and it prompted his return to Wittenberg in 1521. Karlstadt called the images idols, while Luther saw that they had a place in pious worship. Eventually Karlstadt's position won out. Lutheranism, in the next few generations, rid the church of most saints. "Crucifixes were permitted to remain but not usually such scenes as the descent from the cross or the Pieta, which diverted attention from the act of atonement."[6] This was not the decision of the Lutheran people as much as it was the decision of the Lutheran princes and governors. As Calvin's ideas made headway into Lutheranism, so too did more radical iconoclasm. Few images remained, fought for by strident Gnesio-Lutherans who wanted to preserve illustrations of the life of Christ and major points of Lutheran theology.

The Reform approach did not have such concerns. Beginning with Zwingli, anything that did not "belong" to the New Testament was to be removed. The problem was that Zwingli vision of what belonged in the New Testament and therefore the Church was neither grounded in the tradition of the Church nor in the New Testament itself. As Zwingli's eucharistic theology eliminated the real presence of Christ, so too the archetype was removed from images. The spiritualization and Platonizing inherent in Zwingli's theology disenchanted the world. He complained about people's desire to "keep company with outward and visible ceremonies . . . than worry about the true, inward, and spiritual service of God."[7] Zwingli eliminated the material, thus disenchanting the world and de-incarnating the divine from it. *Theoriac* contemplation is all that is left instead of full participation that *theosis* advances.

Zwingli used the political apparatus of Zurich and Switzerland to remove not only images but also other practices that he disapproved of. George Williams looks to Zwingli as the archetype of the Radical Reformation as he "shared the radical evangelical view on the Mass, images, and coercion in religion."[8] It was Leo Jud, Zwingli's successor in Zurich, who demanded that statues and paintings should be removed from the churches. This resulted in the city's crucifix being removed and hacked into firewood. What followed was a disputation on images and the mass. They first turned their attention to the removal of images. Once that hurdle was removed, then the rest of the divine services would soon follow, having lost their pictorial representations. From Zurich iconoclasm spread uncurtailed throughout Europe. Antwerp lost thousands of images and Strasburg abolished the mass, closed down religious houses, and rid itself of all icons and statues.

Still the greatest systematic defamer of icons and their place came from Jean Calvin. Calvin dedicated three chapters of his *Institutes of Christian Religion*[9] to undermining icons. One could charitably say that Calvin's ideology blinded him to church history and the explicit statements of many of the Church Fathers when he erroneously claims that "for about five hundred years, during which religion was still flourishing, and a purer doctrine thriving, Christian churches were commonly empty of images."[10]

Calvin's theology developed from a radicalization of Anselm and Augustine, wherein God's sovereignty, not God's love, is the guiding principle behind Christianity and the incarnation. For Calvin, God is supreme, rational, and distant. Calvin's God is fundamentally different than the God of John of Damascus and so too is the image of God in the world and the images one can have about God in this world. Calvin openly refutes the Ecumenical councils[11] in chapter 11 of book 1 of his Institutes. In the same chapter, Calvin advances his view that all images are idols[12]and the works of men's hands, furthermore he asserts that "Scripture declares images to be teachers of vanity and lies."[13] Calvin never takes seriously the argument of John of Damascus that Christ's incarnation transforms our relation to the invisible world as the invisible God became visible to us.

Calvin's iconoclasm was primarily theological. He opposed any representation of his distant God. However, Calvin did not advocate for violent acts of iconoclasm. He believed that they should orderly be removed and destroyed. Calvin wanted to remake society in the image that he saw fit. While violence was sometimes necessary, as in the case of Michael Servetus, whom he burned at the stake in Geneva, it was supposed to be well-reasoned violence in service to the higher truth. Eventually, even crucifixes were removed. A plain cross was all that was allowed to ordain a meeting hall. For Calvin, all images have at their root abuse; they are the result of the flood, not present in the antediluvian world where God's intimacy with man could be better known.[14]

Without any images, the distance between Calvin's reformed parishioners and the saints grew. The symbols of the old church were gone. To ensure all vestiges of ancient Christianity was gone, even the vestments were removed on 10 January 1567.[15] By this time, communion napkins also vanished, along with the priest facing the elements during the words of institution, altars, exorcisms, some songs, and all images. Bodily worship, material worship, worship with the senses, was gone, minimalized, transformed. Liturgical rites were made new with new loyalties. The word grew dominant, as did a hyper-legalized relationship between God and Man.

Anthony Wallace would define what Calvin was doing as a revitalization movement. This culture change phenomena was not a gradual one, but was a "deliberate, organized, conscious effort by members of a society to construct a more satisfying culture."[16] For Calvin, this was a new earth, where God's favor upon man would shine forth because proper worship was accomplished. This was a world where the practitioners would know God in Spirit and in truth, but not materially. The removal of images and even the real presence[17] from the Eucharist eliminated not only images but the entire material world from the Reformed practitioner. Like the iconoclasm of the Leo the Isaurian, Calvin's vision was a tacit rejection of the material world in worship. For Calvin, Plato's *theoria* was the most anyone could expect to achieve.

This new spiritual world's material effect was found in the rise of Swiss nationalism. From here, nationalism and the destruction of the previous imperial system served as a driving force. Swiss, German, Dutch, and even English autonomy was held captive by Rome. Nationalistic fervor advanced the cause. One way people tangibly could take up arms against a distant Roman pontiff was by destroying the images of his Church. What previously brought piety and devotion now became the object of a newly fostered vehemence and wrath. As Pettegree argues, "At moments of decision or heightened political tension Protestants turned on the statues and pictures of the Catholic devotion with a previously unimaginable fury."[18]

Iconoclasm served a practical as well as ecclesial purpose for Calvinism and Reform traditions. Zwingli and Calvin's acolytes spread their iconoclasm throughout Western Europe. Theodore Beza saw the place of images as the clear demarcation between the "true" church and a false faith. Not only would Catholicism be rejected, but also Luther's more moderate stance. Beza urged those who would listen to "Flee from the false church, which is the kingdom of perdition! . . . They [adherents of other faiths] follow only a mute Jesus Christ—as these idols such as the crucifix are which are painted or carved by the hands of men and not by the Spirit of God."[19] Hearing Beza and others express the desire to rid themselves of holy images, which they perceived to be idols, forced some to take action. They no longer waited upon magistrates or princely authority but would destroy images. In Metz, Jean Leclerc took all of the icons and relics of the saints from the shrine and destroyed them on the night before their procession.[20] Bishop Brigonnet of Meaux fell under the sway of the reformers and tried to launch his own reformation beginning with outbreak of iconoclasm.[21] The religious wars of Scotland and France also began with calls denouncing images as idolatry. In one location they succeeded, in another they failed, but central to both was the place of religious art.

With the Lutheran and Reform models of transformation differing, it should come as no surprise that many Lutherans saw the iconoclastic fervor of the Reform as something dangerous that must be avoided. Beginning with Luther's conflict with Karlstadt, who we could identify as at times a Lutheran, Reform, or a member of the Radical Reformation, we see that images and their place served as a point of tension. R. Po-Hsia points out that when the Lutheran burghers in the university saw the Calvinist ministers coming, they went out to fight for the preservation of their beloved churches from "iconoclasts."[22] In 1614, when the Reform church came to Berlin a riot broke out. The Berliners too identified the Reform church as "iconoclasts." Johann Georg tried to settle things down and was shouted down. "You black Calvinist you give permission to smash our pictures and hack our crosses; we are going to smash you and your Calvinist priests in return."[23] Iconoclasm became such a hallmark for the Reform church that the Lutherans equated Reform not with deniers of the real presence in the Eucharist, as many scholars point out prevented the union at the Marburg Colloquy, but as iconoclasts.

Still further along the iconoclastic spectrum we find the Anabaptists. As a general rule, Anabaptists were far less organized than Lutherans or Reform. Their iconoclastic outbursts were less structured or integral in reforming a town. There are instances of iconoclastic riots being provoked by Bugenhagen and Knopken, who stole icons and threw them down a well in flight from the townspeople who opposed their sacrilege. Still there exists a more theologically grounded iconoclasm. For many early Anabaptists, the Eucharist itself was seen as the symbol that needed to be eliminated. Eucharistic theology and iconoclasm became one issue. In 1524, Ziegler argued that both iconographic and eucharistic idolatry[24] must be denounced. They accepted the flawed theology of Constantine V's iconoclasm, where the Eucharist was the symbol of Christ. Instead, the Orthodox Church rightly affirmed that the Eucharist is not a symbol like an icon, because Christ is truly present. Unlike the earlier Eastern iconoclasts, the Anabaptists thought even this symbol went too far.

Unfortunately for the Radical Reformation, acts of violence dominate historical memory of the early period of Anabaptists before Meno Simons. The bloodshed associated with Beggars and Muster have lasting effects when discussing the Radical Reformation and sacred images. The Beggars, who served as armed thugs advancing Protestant ideals in areas opposed to reformation, were known for forcibly invading churches. Once there, they overturned altars and destroyed all images in the church. When Jon Matthys and John Van Leiden set up their Kingdom in Munster, they quickly exiled the Catholic Bishop and moderate Protestants. Then they went to destroying all images.

The English approach to iconoclasm has elements of Lutheran, Reform, and the Anabaptists. As has been pointed out several times, England did not have one Reformation but several, one under each of the Tudor Monarchs and the Stuarts as well. With each new monarch came a different approach to religion and with it also came a new approach to images and the place they should hold in English society. Under the early reign of Henry VIII and that of his predecessors, the reputation for exporting heresy loomed large. The Lollards, following Wycliffe, put England on the defensive. As a result of the Lollard humiliation, they prized their traditional piety in all of its forms. As the Lollards attacked images, the English would defend them. Between this and the monarchs' desire to ever grow their titles, Henry wrote his tract against Luther in 1521, gaining the title Defender of the Faith from Pope Leo X.

Christopher Haigh points out that despite any Lollard residue in England in 1516, images and stories connected with them still moved the masses as well as the king.[25] Throughout the 1520s, the English commitment to their Catholicity was unwavering. Any iconoclasm took place under the cover of darkness and did not hope to sway the masses to act. Critics of the saints and images were denounced and treated as traitors not only to their faith but also to the crown. Duffy points out the images of Christ, Mary, and the saints resonated with the people. They were "embodiments of religion harnessed as much to the everyday material needs as to the spiritual longings of labouring and suffering men and women."[26] People sacrificed their time and money for images of the saints. In Morebath, the cult of Saint Sidwell elicited devotions and adornments of statues.

When Henry began his break with Rome, he did not have the privilege of Calvin in simply denouncing the entire system. He did not want to rebuild Christendom, only preserve his dynasty. J. J. Scarisbrick and others paint a picture of Henry VIII who was sincerely pious. Henry wanted to construct a middle way that preserved the structure and form of the Church but allowed him his royal prerogatives.

When Henry did close monasteries, destroy shrines, and loot churches, he did so not only for the financial windfall but under the belief that doing so could still preserve more of the Church as well as his lineage. The Lutherans and Calvinists were dismissed before the Act of Annates of 1532, the Act of Restraint of Appeals in 1533, and ultimately the Act of Supremacy in 1534. Once these legal acts broke London from Rome, we also see a rise in iconoclasm. Not surprisingly the iconoclasm took place nearly all in eastern England closer to London, and instead of being supported, those who performed such sacrilege were punished. In 1538, there were some who tried again to launch English iconoclasm by tearing down St. Paul's Cross from the open-air pulpit in London. Others in London smashed images. Still the English and Henry would not tolerate these acts. While the radicalization of English religious life increased during Henry's tenure, a balance was always attempted. Henry was a tentative supporter of reform and had to be convinced to launch any forms of iconoclasm.

This was not the case for the nine-year-old Edward or his regents. Early on Somerset was swayed by the minority who clamored for radicalization. Thomas Cramner and Nicholas Ridley also pushed for iconoclasm. In 1547, when Henry died, new royal injunctions were issued against icons. Under Edward iconoclasm, as well as other radical forms of religious persecution, erupted. Even though the radicals were few in number, they systematically went about destroying vestiges of Henry's moderate Protestantism. St. Paul's now lost its images inside the church. Edward's iconoclasm was painted in the light of King Hezekiah's removing the idols and Josiah's cleaning out the temple. The young king was inadvertently a reformer on a grand scale.

Somerset's iconoclasm extended beyond London in 1548 and was extended to the entire kingdom. There was resistance. While Edward and his regents wanted all images removed, many hid them away. Icons and other sacred images were preserved in the countryside as the people were not ready to abandon their traditional piety. Diarmaid MacCulloch points out that many of the evangelical English were not dissuaded by their resistance in England. Instead, they went abroad near the end of Edward's brief but destructive reign. There are accounts of English visitors to France in 1551 accused of image smashing, and in Portugal in 1552, William Gardiner desecrated the host during the mass.[27] While the traditional Englishman was not in favor of iconoclasm, those who were made the most of their Edwardian opportunity.

The clearest effect was the loss of rood screens. Duffy points out the centrality of these screens in devotion, which are the English equivalent of the iconostasis for the Orthodox. They were ornate with several levels of depictions of Christ, Mary, and the Saints. The sections with the saints were the first under attack, followed by the screens in their entirety. Resistance to this was high, and the total percentage of churches who abandoned their roods was fairly low.

The aim of Edward's regents was similar to those of Calvin, to rewrite history. England was to move beyond its past, not by remaining more faithful, but by eliminating all vestiges of traditional religion, which was understood as Catholic. Given enough time, Edward would have had to deal with the ramifications of his revolution, but his reign lasted only five years. Still the damage was done.

When Mary ascended the throne in 1553, she attempted to restore England to Catholicism. This included the restoration of the images of the English Church. The problem was that ornate rood screens, altars, icons, statues, and vestments take time and money. Mary, in her short five-year tenure, was unable to reconstruct the faith following the destruction wrought by Edward's five-year reign. Many images were restored because people had hidden them away, but most were simply demolished and not able to be replaced by more impoverished parishes.

England largely was happy to return to Catholicism and whatever saints and icons remained. When Mary died in 1558, many had hope that Elizabeth would continue her sister's piety. Haigh goes so far as to argue that, "When Elizabeth became publicly Protestant, it was not by popular demand."[28] Elizabeth's reign was marked by her temperance in instituting Protestantism. Much like her father, she tried to balance the demands upon her by traditional piety while maintaining her ecclesial independence. Furthermore, Elizabeth now inherited an England that had far more Protestants than Henry had, and whose sacred art had already been destroyed. In 1559, Elizabeth was concerned by the results of ecclesial visitation records. She was outraged by the iconoclasm of the radicals while simultaneously dismayed by the disobedience of the conservatives. The factions of English religious life were not easily swayed by one monarch or another. Images also provided the key to transformation.

When Elizabeth promoted more Protestants to the rank of bishop, they carried out a sustained assault of iconoclasm. Many English Protestants now took their theological training from Calvin. People like William Perkins, the architect of Elizabethan Puritanism, articulated the Calvinist theological positions that shaped English as well as continental Calvinism in the years to come, in his work *A Golden Chain*.[29] Elizabeth was not as radical as Perkins. She desired that a crucifix and candle were placed on the communion table, and, in 1559, she ordered that the roods should be restored. The order for the restoration of the roods was later abandoned as her bishops openly opposed the Elizabethan compromise. Elizabeth had come to the same view of icons as Leo the Armenian. She accepted them as long as they were up high and could not be venerated.[30]

Even this compromise was abandoned in 1561, when she ordered all rood lofts to be taken down to the level of the beam. Enforcement was difficult. If the church wardens did not want to enforce them and they had a sympathetic bishop, altars and roods would remain. With more visits, fewer images survived. By 1562, two-thirds of the lofts were destroyed.[31] One commission in

Lincolnshire stated that in 1566 only 13 percent of churches removed their holy images, contrary to reports from 1559 that stated 60 percent complied.[32]

England demonstrates that iconoclasm was not advanced by popular piety but was the systematic accomplishment of radical Calvinists and Protestant bishops who sought to remake England. Instead, the people were attached to the saints and the community of prayer associated with them. A few vandals, zealots, and looters destroyed the images, and little by little the connections that existed were lost. England illustrates what could have occurred if it were not for rulers like Irene or Theodora in Constantinople or theologians like John of Damascus or Theodore the Studite.

## THE CATHOLIC APPROACH

The traditional view of saints was even stronger in areas that remained Catholic than it was in England. Broadly speaking, the Catholic church allowed for a great degree of tolerance toward outer expression of faith. Religious images were permitted in nearly any form, two dimensional and three dimensional. The purpose of religious images was to persuade the Christian toward sanctity. Unlike Eastern Orthodox icons that minimize the emotional response of images, Karat-Nunn argues that "emotional involvement was an ingredient and means of persuasion"[33] for Catholics. Especially during the time of the Reformation, traditional images, whatever their form, equated to traditional religion.

Pettegree demonstrates the link in the mind of Catholics between iconoclasm and revolting against the Church. A tirade from an irate clergyman from the pulpit in 1566 stated,

> "You Flemings," he shouts while jumping up and down and bashing the pulpit, "are the most rebellious of all Dutchmen. It's a flaw in your character, you have always revolted against your princes. You were the first ones to turn against the Catholic religion and to preach all kinds of heresies. You are the initiators of iconoclasm. Therefore I advise you to keep quiet and to shut up. Shit all over yourselves! All misfortunes, miseries, plagues will befall you. In short, you will be slaves for ever, you are finished and so are all your laws and privileges. From now on I don't want to pay any attention to you anymore. I shit on your rights, I wipe my ass with your privileges!"[34]

While more crass than other deliveries, the connection of iconoclasm with heresy and curses is clear.

It goes without saying that in Catholic shrines and churches, images abounded. These images included those of women and allowed for female representation that was growing absent in Protestant areas. In Catholic areas, the icons and other images of the saints could be looked upon, sung to, venerated, and involved in their worship. Images of Christ's crucifixion and suffering were to move the Christian toward a spiritual reflection. Saint Bernard articulates that this interior grasping included a Neoplatonic understanding that one would move inward through reflection. Halfway between Plato's *theoria* and Orthodox *theosis*, the Catholic church retained the value of the material world in connection to spiritual truths.

## WESTERN TRENDS IN IMAGES

What we see in nearly all forms of Protestant iconoclasm is the denial of a traditional understanding of the spiritual and material world. The saints are lost. With the abandonment of their relics and their images, they become absent to the experience of the believer in the Church and in their home. There is a loss of a community of saints, and Christians find themselves more isolated. This isolation grows to include the loss of the material world. A sort of Manichean dualism arises, where the material world is effectively deemed evil or at the most neutral in their spiritual progress. Iconoclasm included a rejection of the real presence in the Eucharist for the Reform and Radical Reformation. Nothing is left in the material world that is holy. Behind Calvin and Cromwell's iconoclasm was the belief that images could serve in one's relationship with God, and that the material world could benefit them in any way toward their progress in the faith.

Surprisingly, some forms of art were preserved. Just like earlier forms of Eastern iconoclasm, some depictions were retained outside of the church. One could have a picture of scenes found in nature, but not of feasts of the church. One could have a picture of people, as long as they were not holy. The world of art became desacralized along with matter. Instead of art being used to vault one toward a holy and pleasing life, art became an amusement not fit for spiritual consumption. Even the place for secular art was appreciated less by Calvinists than it was by Lutherans. This only serves once again to bifurcate the Christian between their religious and spiritual obligations on the one side and their temporal and material obligations on the other.

The use of art in community formation has been a theme throughout this work. It should not surprise the reader that when it is removed from the sacred sphere, it desecrates humanity. When people are not revered, when a holy face is not looked upon, then the attempt to become holy is isolated from a community. Holy tradition is lost when we abandon the images of the saints. God's purpose of creating man in community is lost, and salvation becomes impossible from the Orthodox point of view. Images are destroyed and new ones are created when rewriting history because humans produce images, even in iconoclastic societies. In the Soviet era icons were destroyed, but new images were created of Lenin and Stalin. When Protestants destroyed images, new paintings were commissioned to beautify not churches but their homes. Beauty was found for individuals and not as a collective affair.

The desacralized space created by Protestant iconoclasm was first used for the rise of nationalism. With a revaluation of nationalism after the twentieth century, an emerging interest is taking place in reenchanting the world through use of symbols and religious art. During the last half of the twentieth century, as Orthodox Christianity moved into the West, we have a resurgence of icons in the West. Protestants who destroyed images at the dawn of the Reformation and have not experienced the beauty of an adorned church are seeking them out. Metropolitan Hilarion Alfeyev points out that the twentieth century witnessed a renewal of iconography not only in the East but also in the West. New schools have emerged that continue the work of Saint Luke, Theophan the Greek, and Andrei Rublev. Catholics are beginning to use Orthodox icons in their private devotion. Many Anglican and Lutheran Churches are also commissioning icons because of the beauty and meaning found therein. Even Evangelical churches that would have called all religious images idols a century ago are using icons as illustrations in their churches and periodicals. New "Emergent" churches have icons, including their veneration, as central to their communal church life. Pentiuch tells us that, "For a long period, the West, not only Protestant but also Roman Catholic, was deprived of the richness of Christian iconography."[35] This long period is coming to an end and with it we should anticipate that the deeper meaning behind the icon will follow.

## NOTES

1. Pettegree, Andrew. *Reformation and the Culture of Persuasion.* Cambridge, UK: Cambridge University Rress, 2005, 31.

2. Karant-Nunn, *Reformation of Feeling,* 67.

3. Ouspensky, *Theology of Icon,* 489.

4. Karant-Nunn, *Reformation of Feeling,* 68.

5. Karant-Nunn, *Reformation of Feeling,* 68.

6. Karant-Nunn, *Reformation of Feeling,* 67–68.

7. Karant-Nunn, *Reformation of Feeling,* 240.

8. Williams, George Huntston. *The Radical Reformation.* Kirksville, MO: Truman State University Press, 2000.

9. Book 1, chapters 10–12.

10. Damick,"What John Calvin Really Thought about Icons in the Church." Institutes 1.11.13.

11. Specifically, the second council of Nicaea 1.11.14.

12. Calvin, John. "Institutes of the Christian Religion." Bible Study Tools, n.d. https://www.biblestudytools.com/history/calvin-institutes-christianity/book1/chapter -11.html (accessed 2023). 1.11.4.

13. Calvin, *Institutes of the Christian Religion.* 1.11.5.

14. Calvin, *Institutes of the Christian Religion.* 1.11.8.

15. Karant-Nunn, Susan C. *The Reformation of Ritual: An Interpretation of Early Modern Germany.* New York: Routledge, 1997, 122.

16. Wallace, *Revitalizations and Mazeways*, 10.

17. Calvin's "Real Spiritual Presence" of the Eucharist notwithstanding.

18. Pettegree, *Reformation and the Culture of Persuasion*, 212.

19. Karant-Nunn, *Reformation of Feeling*, 116.

20. Damick, "What John Calvin Really Thought about Icons in the Church."

21. Van't Spijker, Willem. *Calvin: A Brief Guide to His Life and Thought.* Louisville, KY: Westminster John Knox Press, 2009, 7.

22. Hsia, R. Po-Chia. *Social Discipline in the Reformation Central Europe, 1550–1750.* New York: Routledge, 1989, 36.

23. Hsia, *Social Discipline*, 36–37.

24. Williams, *Radical Reformation*, 621.

25. Haigh, Christopher. *English Reformations: Religion, Politics, and Society under the Tudors.* Oxford: Oxford University Press, 1993, 69.

26. Duffy, Eamon. *Voices of Morebath: Reformation and Rebellion in an English Village.* New Haven, CT: Yale University Press, 2001, 72–73.

27. MacCulloch, *Tudor Church Militant*, 135–36.

28. Haigh, *English Reformations*, 238.

29. Davis, Justin. *Pietism and the Foundations of the Modern World.* Eugene, OR: Pickwick Publications, 2019.

30. Haigh, *English Reformations*, 244.

31. Haigh, *English Reformations*, 245.

32. Haigh, *English Reformations*, 246.

33. Karant-Nunn, *Reformation of Feeling*, 243.

34. Pettegree, *Reformation and the Culture of Persuasion*, 37.

35. Pentiuc, *Old Testament in Eastern Orthodox Tradition*, 266.

## Chapter 7

# A Christian Return to Plato?

In about 518, a writing of Dionysius the Areopagite emerged seemingly out of nowhere. The writing was used by Monophysite Syrians to try to make a philosophical point against Orthodox Christians. What it did was shake the philosophical landscape of the Later Roman Empire and transform the vocabulary for theology in both the East and the West. The writings soon became the possession of everyone, Monophysite and Orthodox, East and West. The theological and philosophical lessons from the Areopagite received the utmost attention and prestige.

From the first recorded use of Dionysius until the outbreak of iconoclasm, two centuries passed. In the interim, another Christological heresy emerged that bridges these two events. This heresy did not deal with how Christ should be depicted, instead it focused on what exactly became incarnate. The question had to do with Christ's will, and if he had a human will or only a divine will. This heresy, Monothelitism, advanced by Pope Honorius I[1] as a compromise position between Orthodox Christology and Monophysitism. Following Honorius, Monothelitism gained some initial support by several Patriarchs of Constantinople,[2] the Emperor, and one Patriarch of Alexandria.[3] Through the writings of Pope Martin of Rome and Maximus the Confessor, the heresy of Monothelitism, as well as Pope Honorius and the erring Eastern Patriarchs were condemned at the Sixth Ecumenical Council.[4] The council confirmed that Christ had a human will. Otherwise, Christ would not have assumed all of our humanity, and our will would not be assumed into Christ.

For our purposes, the standout from this council was the theological champion, Maximus the Confessor. Maximus had already died before the council began but the arguments presented at the council are easy to identify as his. Maximus built on the arguments of Dionysius. He clearly demonstrated that any Monophysite ideas in the Areopagite's writings were falsely interpreted. Maximus and Dionysius's theology ran contrary to not only Monothelitism, but also Origenism. With Maximus and Dionysius, we have a reassessment and a potential return, at least in part, to Plato. Specifically, we see how later

Christians engage with the philosophy of Neoplatonism, how they correct that system and how Platonism reemerges especially in the West as a result.

One of the most controversial characters in philosophy is Dionysius. Not that his ideas are controversial, or that his life was debauched, destructive, or devoid of reason. Instead, what is contentious is his very existence. The name indicates that Saint Dionysius was the person who Paul spoke to and converted in Athens, a judge of the Areopagus as recorded in Acts 17:34. The Areopagus or Ares Hill was a rock outcropping where early aristocrats met to discuss philosophical and other practical issues of the day. Whoever was an Areopagite was likely fairly wealthy, well educated, and knew Greek philosophy.

Tradition holds that this Dionysius later became a bishop in Athens, and the French claimed also became the first bishop of Paris. The French claim was never held by anyone but the French. In all likelihood, it was a different Denis that went to France. The Areopagite remained in Athens according to Greek records. The name was fairly common, and we have records of many different bishops by the name of Denis, including ones in Corinth and Alexandria during the first two centuries. Throughout the centuries, even the French accounts do not take the account that it was the same Denis seriously. It was likely in honor of Dionysius the bishop of Athens that the later Parisian bishop took his name. Dionysius, given his training, is accredited by many as one of the great bishops of the early church.[5]

Many of the writings of Dionysus identify him not only as a first-century bishop, but also familiar with events of the first century. We have letters addressed to Polycarp, the disciple of Saint John, and bishop of Smyrna. His work on the *Divine Names* is addressed to Timothy, the disciple of Paul, where he quotes Saint Ignatius's letters before his martyrdom. He also has several other letters, some to prominent people in the first century such as the Apostle John and Titus. There are also other, more obscure people mentioned in his works including philosophers and priests. It is uncertain which if any of the works of Dionysius are the works of Saint Dionysius the Areopagite. What is known was that until the eve of the Protestant Reformation the works were identified as genuine. Their impact is received as genuine work of Saint Dionysius. Lossky tells us that, "whatever the results of all this research maybe they can in no way diminish the theological value of the *Areopagitica*. From this point of view it matters little who their author was."[6] This attitude toward the authorship encapsulates the Orthodox position. The works are received into the church as belonging to Dionysius, thus they belong to him.

Since the Protestant Reformation, many refer to the writings as coming later, identifying the author as Pseudo-Denis or Dionysius the Pseudo-Areopagite. The bulk of scholarship in the West until fairly recently remained consistent and somewhat dismissive of late first-century or early second-century authorship. Even Lossky in his fairly lengthy treatment of the authorship of Dionysius in *Mystical Theology of the Eastern Church*, calls to attention the silence concerning the *Areopagitic* works. Yet recently some scholarship is revisiting what of the documents ascribed to Dionysius may properly belong to the Areopagite.

This recent scholarship demonstrates that at least some writings from the first-century bishop are clearly genuine. A key piece of evidence is the recent discovery of a letter that Dionysius of Alexandria wrote to Pope Sixtus II in about the year 250 discussing the writings of Dionysius the Areopagite. In the letter we read, "That no one can intelligently dispute their paternity—that no one penetrated more profoundly than Dionysius into the mysterious depths of Holy Scripture—that Dionysius was disciple of St. Paul, and piously governed the Church of Athens."[7] Yet what was penned by Dionysius and what is given in reference to Pope Sixtus II is not clearly identified. The description could apply to *Mystical Theology*, *Celestial Hierarchy*, or any number of works accredited to Dionysius. The writings we have may not be the same ones referenced. What is beyond dispute is that by 250 philosophical writings did exist and were credited to Dionysius the Areopagite.

Historically three main pieces of evidence are used to argue against first-century authorship. This begins with the relative silence from any works credited to Dionysius until their use in Syria around 528. This means that the latest the work could have been written is roughly 518, the date many modern scholars put the works of pseudo-Dionysius. While this is the common dating, it is a bit suspicious since traditionally specific works are not referenced so quickly after they were written, and then accepted universally as true. Generally, works are expected to circulate around for a long period of time with the authorship known for decades before casually referenced. Even longer is typical when the work is expected to drive home a polemical argument, and when the authorship helps to prove that point.

A further complicating factor in ascribing such a late date is that the writings of Dionysius are in Greek. They are not of Syrian origin. The Greek is also technical philosophical Greek, and not something that would be written by someone with only a passing familiarity with the language. This is key, since time to translate them is necessary, not only before the Syrian source would reference them, but also for it to prove to be an effective reference. With this said, a more realistic dating at this point would only need to shift the authorship back a bit more. A date in the mid-fifth century would be far more reasonable than the eve of the sixth.

Moving the authorship back even to the beginning of the fifth century instead of the sixth is still a way off from late first- or early second-century authorship. This brings us to a middle position where a Dionysian school emerged in Athens or elsewhere expounding on the writings of the first-centuy bishop. These writings then addressed the philosophical and pragmatic problems facing the church and were written in the name of their teacher, Dionysius the Areopagite. This is not an uncommon practice in the ancient world and would separate "legitimate" authorship but retain some degree of authority whereby the teachings are legitimately Dionysian, even though they were not written by Dionysius specifically. This compromise position is held by some who wish to argue against early authorship but demonstrate why the writings became universally adopted when they did. This would not be understood as a forgery but citing one's work. We see a corollary with other medieval works where the authors died and their students finished the work for them and published it posthumously.

The third piece of evidence against Dionysius's first-century authorship is internal to the texts themselves. Many point out that the references to key first-century saints are a little too perfect, possibly trying to artificially connect the work to an earlier period. This is an argument of motive rather than any clear evidence. If the works are genuinely first-century works, it would not be unreasonable for the author to speak about prominent members of the Church and the events of the day. Furthermore, the works also refer to people who are unfamiliar to a modern or even sixth-century audience. This shows that names were not universally used to assert authorship.

More important than the use of names is the use of concepts which are more familiar in the fifth century than the first. The writing appears very much in line with Neoplatonism rather than Middle Platonism. The discussion and use of triads and the cosmic progression is akin to Plotinus's writings and even of the later more mature Neoplatonic thought of Proclus[8] and his *Elements of Theology*. Hugo Koch, in 1900, largely based upon the use of triads, identified Dionysius as a student or at least a close reader of Proclus.[9] Koch's assertion became the key justification for placing authorship in the early sixth century. The use of triads is also found rather frequently in the writings of Justin and Irenaeus in the second century. While not as developed as with Proclus, the use of a triad is hardly definitive evidence of dating Dionysius in the Neoplatonic era instead of with Middle Platonists.

Neoplatonism begins with Plotinus in the third century and is matured in the fifth. Many believe that Pseudo-Dionysius used Proclus and reinterpreted his Neoplatonic theology into a Christian system. In many ways this argument is a bit odd given that Proclus's triads were a reworking of the Trinity to apply it to Neoplatonism against the monads of Pythagoras. Christian use of triads that correspond to the Trinity is an easier fit than Proclus's venture. Proclus saw everything in a series of threes, including people, ontological reality, and participation in reality. For Proclus, triads are products of existing triads and create others. For example, the triad between being, life, and intellect, when united, causes the triad of triads, immanence, procession, and reversion.[10] This explains the unfolding of the universe from the One and our ascent toward the One for Proclus. It also has many parallels with Dionysian cosmos. Dionysius has many triads as well in addition to the Trinity, including the celestial hierarchy consisting of three groups of three different ranks of angels, and the church hierarchy also arranged in a triad.

Lossky and others believe that Origen did much of the same work that Proclus and Dionysius did. He is one of the authors of Neoplatonic thought, though remaining a Christian. Seeing patterns of the Trinity in creation is not a difficult task if one desires to see it. This, in addition to the adage attributed to Aristotle, that "everything that comes in threes is perfection," provides a reasonable use of three instead of one for the construction of a common numerology. Since many of the writings of Origen are lost, it is difficult to tell which areas developed later by Proclus may have their beginnings with Origen and not with Plotinus. Lossky asserts that Pseudo-Dionysius was actually a student of Origen.[11]

A challenge to this final piece of evidence remains with the origins of Neoplatonism itself. As addressed in chapter 2, both Plotinus and Origen shared the same teacher, Ammonius Saccas. By all accounts he was a Christian Middle Platonist and the founder of Neoplatonism. Ammonius Saccas's teachings then took the forms of a heavily Platonized Christianity found in Origen and a pagan version with Plotinus.

There is another teacher we can look to as well to contextualize Origen's writings as it relates to Plato. John Parker points out that both Origen and Clement shared a common Christian Platonist teacher, Pantaenus. According to Parker, "Origen confessed that Pantaenus was his superior in the philosophy of the schools, and that he moulded his teaching upon the model of Pantaenus."[12] This is significant because the few surviving writings we have from Pantanus have similar phraseology and philosophy of Dionysius as found in the *Divine Names*, *Mystical Theology*, and elsewhere. Since Pantaneus was in Alexandria in the third century at the same time that Dionysius the Alexandrian wrote to Pope Sixtus about the Areopagite's works, it would be logical to assume that Pantaenus was familiar with whatever writings existed and are referenced by his fellow Alexandrian.

Since Pantaenus was one of the immediate philosophical predecessors to both Clement and Origen, his writings were undoubtedly known to Origen's teacher Ammonius and by extension Origen's fellow pupil Plotinus as well. There is considerable overlap between the writings of Clement and Origen with Dionysius as well to advance this point. It is as equally likely that Pantaenus and Ammonius were familiar with some Dionysian writings as it is that Dionysius came later and based his writings only in response to Proclus. Dionysius may in fact be the bridge between Middle Platonism and Neoplatonism rather than a response to it. The similarities in the text suggest a familiarity either of Dionysius with the writings of Clement and Origen, or the Alexandrians being acquainted with Dionysius likely through Pantaenus.

Since the Reformation, the overarching consensus was to put Dionysius later. The problem with this is some evidence exists that points to an earlier origin, to some of these philosophical speculations. Beyond an intriguing question about what of Dionysius contributed to Neoplatonism and what is a response to it, is the issue of reception history. Too many dismiss Dionysius as a concession to Neoplatonism and an immediate return to pagan Neoplatonism, instead of reading Dionysius as a Christianized philosophy following the lines of Justin or Clement, understanding the work was done by a Christian who is familiar with Platonic and other Athenian philosophy due to their studies before becoming a Christian. The refusal to see any of the writings of Dionysus as genuine or at least existing before Plotinus skews the reading of Christian reception of Plato, and our reception of Dionysius. For our purposes, it reverts to an earlier argument for the telos of man. Dionysius is read as affirming *theoria* and Platonic mysticism as the means to achieve this telos, instead of his arguments concerning telos resembling Justin, Clement, and Irenaeus's position.

The modern consensus position makes Dionysius primarily a Neoplatonist.[13] His Christianity is a veneer applied to make his voice palatable to the sixth-century Christians who were growing uneasy with Neoplatonism and Origenism. This included the radical interpretations of Origen that eventually led to Origen's condemnation at the Fifth Ecumenical Council in 553. It is clear that the landscape for speculation during the sixth century was contentious. Not only was the fall out of Chalcedon unresolved, but so too were many philosophical ideas that were identified as pagan. Justinian shut down the Athenian Academy in 529. It is plausible that if a mostly pagan philosopher wanted to advance their position, they would put it in Christian language and try to place the authorship of it before Origen. Someone with a philosophical background that is mentioned in scripture and revered as a saint would be helpful, since they would be beyond reproach. The use of Saint Dionysius would have been a logical choice.

Those who argue that the use of Dionysius was a convenient way of circumventing criticism also make mention of the many "lost writings" of Dionysius. In his letters and works, Dionysius makes mention of other works that fully address a concept, but we do not have copies of these works. The theory goes that whoever Pseudo-Dionysius was, he planned on writing these more complicated works and tried to lay the groundwork for their later discovery whenever they were written. They are lost because they simply were never written. Others have a more reasonable treatment of these referenced works and see them as a means of convincing the reader that the author has many more works that fill in the gaps in what is existent, thus making what they are reading more plausible. Both of these explanations do not account for the fact that many works from antiquity are lost, renamed, or combined with others to make a single volume of a multipart work.

The main fault with the prevailing scholarship is twofold. First is that not all works are accepted simply because they have the name of a saint attached to them. While the use of Dionysius is a convenient way of advancing a philosophical idea by removing it from the controversy, rarely are newly discovered texts accepted without any criticism. For example, the "donation of Constantine" since its fabrication in the late eighth century was always held as suspect by the church, especially by the church in the East. The document was convenient, as the Eastern Empire was losing its influence over Europe with the ascension of the Franks and Lombard threat. Its origins may also have been used as a pretext of Pope Adrian I in a letter to Charlemagne as a negotiating tool. Still, by the turn of the millennium, the French Pope Sylvester II[14] demonstrated it to be false. Documents have never been adopted simply because of a supposed authorship by a saint.

What is also rather striking is that Dionysius was used in translation by Syrians against the Greek-speaking people of the Later Roman Empire, and yet was then used by that same audience later. Likely the dating of a large number of Dionysius's works is significantly before the fifth century. More important is that the work was not read as a pagan Neoplatonic tract with a thin veneer of Christianity, but something that is consistently Christian. Dionysius never advances the notion of emanation as Plotinus and Proclus do, rather he consistently advanced the doctrine of creation ex nihilo as Middle Platonists and Second Temple Judaism and Christianity do. When emanation is mentioned, it pertains to illumination not being. This concept of illumination is also consistent with Christian language of the first and second century as we see with Justin and others.

Dionysius, whoever he may have been, and whenever he may have written, expresses a Christian position that is knowledgeable of Plato. Just like Basil, Clement, Justin, and others, knowledge of Plato should not be understood as a wholehearted endorsement, rather accepting what is consistent and expressing Christian ideas in the language of the culture. Given the content of Dionysius's corpus if it is written early, we see a use of Christian Middle Platonism by Neoplatonists. If a later date is affirmed, then oddly enough we see the apologetic use of Dionysius. As the apologist, he could be identified as the "Christian Proclus," as he has been called in more recent years. The Christian part is not incidental but central. The use of philosophy was used to express understanding of the sacraments, ecclesial, and celestial hierarchies. The subject and treatment of Dionysian philosophy remains fundamentally Christian, just like Philo's remained consistent with Judaism during the

Second Temple period. This debate is similar to those who question the Christian language of Saint Gregory of Nyssa.

Lossky, arguing against the notion that Dionysius was a Neoplatonist who tried to smuggle Platonism back into Christianity, asserts that, "After studying St. Dionysius it seems to me that just the opposite is true: here is a Christian thinker disguised as a neoplatonist, a theologian very much aware of his task, which was to conquer the ground held by neoplatonism by becoming a master of its philosophical method."[15] Louth says that despite similar language to Neoplatonists, Dionysius's meaning is fundamentally different, as is his conception of the divine; it remains Christian.[16]

Even if we accept a later Dionysius, the idea that he returns to the Platonic and abandons the philosophical distinction between Christianity and Plato should not be affirmed. Dionysius safeguards the doctrines of the Trinity from Proclus's triads, the incarnation, and creation from simple emanations. The freedom of the will is preserved, as is a God who is knowable and is the object of love. This becomes the theological interpretation of Dionysius and the reason for his version of Platonism to return to the Church, which began the process of abandonment of Plato following the Cappadocians.

Dionysius's theology follows the philosophical conceptions of Middle Platonists such as Philo. Apophatic theology, where we do not know God in God's essence, is central to any reading of Dionysius. God is unknowable since God is infinitely beyond people. God is beyond essence to the point that we cannot affirm that God is essence. God is beyond goodness to the point that we cannot properly say that God is good. While Plotinus and Proclus say similar things about the One, we must remember that they advanced a position affirmed by Philo in the first century, they did not invent it. Dionysius's use is in no way dependent upon Neoplatonism, as it was already established in the Middle Platonism of the first century. For Dionysius and Philo, cataphatic theology is in many ways limiting because our conceptions of God are based in our imperfect knowledge and understanding. Therefore, the only appropriate statements of God are apophatic, where we describe what God is not. Lossky asserts that, "Negative theology is thus a way toward mystical union with God, whose nature remains incomprehensible to us."[17] This separates Dionysius from Plotinus's One, who is not incomprehensible by nature. Essential to Plotinus is the concept of ecstasy reducing being to absolute simplicity.

For Dionysius, God is incomprehensible in who God is, in God's essence. God still remains approachable through God's uncreated energies. These energies allow for some positive statements to be made even with the knowledge that they are limited. One of the favored ways of addressing what can be known about God for Dionysius is through symbols. Symbolic theology makes use of the material and intellectual images to form a conception of

God. As Temple points out, this is rather similar to the use of icons and approaching God or the saints.[18]

The use of symbols is a perfect union of apophatic and cataphatic theology since symbols move beyond representation. They may be like the object they symbolize or unlike them, but they bring together the images and understanding that is beyond the object. God is never taken as a literal representation of the symbol but is always understood to be beyond the symbol. Dionysius points out that scripture itself uses symbols to affirm things about God. For example, Dionysius makes use of Psalm 78 where we are told that, "The Lord awoke, like a strong man, powerful but reeling with wine." Scripture affirms something about God, but Dionysius demonstrates that we should not believe that God slumbers, or dinks wine, let alone to excess. Rather the context of the Psalm and of tradition help to clarify what this Psalm symbolizes.

Dionysius's use of theology is precise and comfortable, using Platonic verbiage when helpful. Louth maintains that the different uses of cataphatic, symbolic, and apophatic theology are used at different times to express different things for Dionysius. "Cataphatic and symbolic theology are concerned with what we affirm about God: apophatic theology is concerned with our understanding of God, when, in the presence of God, speech and thought fail us and we are reduced to silence."[19]

Symbolic language and cataphatic language are used to express what has been revealed and how one positively can relate to God. The icon is one symbol, but so too is the architecture of the universe. The celestial and ecclesial hierarchies speak of degrees of understanding and participation in much the same way that Neoplatonic thought does. The image moves closer to the archetype depending on the level of grace or divine energy that is presented to it. Even the ascent is accomplished by and through the divine. One medium we have addressed in this ascent is the icon. The icon also differs from any other similar image in that it points toward its archetype and is the means of the archetype to communicate through the symbolic representation.

The hierarchy describes the soul's ascent beyond *theoria*, as the Platonists see the final resting point of man, but to *theosis*. *Theoria* resides in the end of cataphatic theology, knowledge can give rise to knowledge. The use of symbols and symbolic theology can aid in this process, but knowledge of the divine can only be achieved beyond the use of symbolic theology and the acceptance of apophatic theology. Fr Thomas Hopko, in a talk on Dionysius's apophatic theology, expressed that when language is used in scripture it is both apophatic and cataphatic; it is an approachable symbolic theology. For instance, when we are instructed to pray and speak of God as father, we recognize the term father. Father has limitations, as typically we envision our earthly father with all of their gifts and limitations. We deny that God is father because God is beyond father. That is our conception of it. Yet the symbol of

father allows one to approach God, even though we have denied the appro-
priateness of this term. Still, since Christ himself told us to speak of God as
father, God must actually be father. Therefore, we have an affirmation of not
only God, but also fathers. Human fathers become the symbol for God. They
are what is actually denied when we say father. God remains father, but our
father is not. Language pushes us beyond its conception and is the means of
abandoning our false conceptions for a reality that we do not yet know.

This reality is the basis of *theosis*. It is a reality beyond symbol, where what
is seen is abandoned for what is unknowable. Lossky adds, "Negative theology is not merely a theory of ecstasy. It is an expression of that fundamental
attitude which transforms the whole of theology into a contemplation of the
mysteries of revelation."[20] This is why the Eastern doctrines concerning the
essence of God and the energies of God are essential. This preserves God's
unknowability, and yet union with God's essence. *Theosis* is understood as
participation in the uncreated energy, but not a reduction of self into a divine
monad. *Theosis* is also not reduced to personal mysticism, but a process
mediated through the Church.

This mediation is a product of the divine will. This will is the λόγοι *logoi,*
or forms that exist in all creation. This Christian use of the forms provides the
philosophical basis for Maximus the Confessor. Maximus identifies the use of
λόγοι by Proclus as the beginning of a nihilism, since for the Neoplatonists
union is impossible. Instead, Maximus's use of Dionysius, and specifically
the λόγοι as the drive and activity in creation, leads to union through Christ.

Saint Maximus[21] the Confessor lived at the zenith of the Later Roman
Empire. He was born fifteen years after the repose of Justinian, when the
empire was its largest since the Germanic invasions of Gaul and Italy.
Maximus had a privileged childhood. His parents were nobles and provided
him with the best education. In his thirties, Maximus was the head of the
Imperial Chancellery to Emperor Heraclius. During Maximus's life he saw the
loss of three of the seats of Christianity, Alexandria, Antioch, and Jerusalem
to the advancing Islamic forces. This undoubtedly led Maximus to the conclusion that security cannot be found in this life. Turning his back on courtly
life, Maximus decided to become a monk and to live a life of quiet prayer.
In 630, he moved to North Africa to further develop his monasticism under
Sophronius before Sophronius was elected Patriarch of Jerusalem in 634.

Seeking refuge from Arab invasions, Maximus moved again, this time to
Carthage and took up residence in the Eukrates monastery. It was around this
time that Maximus began to utilize the teachings of Dionysius and develop
what is later called his symphonic theology. Maximus uses analogy along
the lines of Dionysius's symbolism combined with logic and syllogism to
address nuance in theological issues. Central to Maximus's theology is the
notion of the three births all of us face. These include our coming into being,

our baptism, and ultimately our resurrection. This triad of births moves from natural through Platonic notions of *theoria* in baptism, and ultimately toward *theosis* in the resurrection. These three births unite the *logoi* of creation with its telos, both of which are opened up in Christ through the incarnation. The goal for Maximus is similar to earlier Christian philosophers, moving beyond contemplation of God toward rest in God. Central to this is the incarnation of Christ the divine Logos.

Maximus's theology is both singular and universal. The arc for the cosmos follows the same trajectory of becoming that people do in particular. In this way, Maximus identifies people as a microcosm of the universe in a similar way as the Cappadocians, the Neoplatonists, and the Middle Platonists. Of course, what separates the Christians from the Platonist position is the goal not the act of becoming. Also, given the use of triads by later Neoplatonists, the triadic composition of Unparticipated-Participated-Participating, as found in Proclus's *Elements of Theology*, is not surprising. Like Plotinus,[22] Maximus holds that the soul is this moving power in participation and becoming. Following Dionysius, the source is not the One, but is the Trinitarian God of Christianity.

Specifically for Maximus, Christ as the *logos* gives the *logoi* to creation and each part of that creation. From Christ who is the *logos* λόγος there are many *logoi* λόγοι. These purposes or definitions exist in God, but not the being. In Ambiguum 7, Maximus states all the λόγοι preexist in God,[23] since in Christ there exists the substance of virtue in each person. Maximus maintains, "For our Lord Jesus Christ himself is the substance of all the virtues."[24]

In many ways, Maximus's philosophy resembles Origen. The movement is similar since the cosmos resembles the philosophical and Platonic structure advanced by Neoplatonists and Origen alike. The key difference is that for Maximus, the directional cast of this cosmic arc is different. Maximus's cosmic theology serves as the corrective to Origen. For Origen, the preexistence of the soul was the starting place, as it is for Platonists. Similar to Plato, Origen held that rational beings fell way from pure *theoria* and eventually cooled off into a state of matter, only to eventually return again at some point, as addressed in chapter 2. Maximus thought this act of rest, movement away from God, and then becoming, did not make sense. First, nothing would stop this cycle from repeating even after rest in God is received. Maximus questioned how someone after resting in God's truth and beauty would ever leave it. A charitable read of Origen is that the initial pre-eternal rest in God was in a state of immaturity, and only *theoria*, not *theosis*. The process of becoming, then movement toward God and ultimately restoration is one of completion, moving beyond *theoria* toward *thesosis*. Though this argument may work, it is not explicit in any of Origen's texts that have survived. This argument is also not one held by Neoplatonists, who still understand contemplation as the end rather than a middle point toward *theosis*.

Maximus therefore argues for an inverse of Origen and a cycle that does not open itself for eternal repetition. For Maximus, the state of becoming is the first step. This corresponds to the first birth, and the first of Proclus's triad of unparticipated, the state of being that is existence. The second birth is baptism. This marks our second step for Maximus and Proclus's step of participated, a state of becoming akin to *theoria*. The final step is an act of participating, ultimate being beyond simple existence, as this is found in the resurrection. This is *theosis*, ultimate rest in God. God

> has created us in order that we may become partakers of the divine nature, in order that we may enter into eternity, and that we may appear like unto Him, being deified by that grace out of which all things that exist have come, and which brings into existence everything that before had no existence.[25]

The end is found in the beginning for both Origen and Maximus. For Maximus, the beginning only exists, as the *logoi* is found in God, not our being. As Patitsas articulates, Maximus's cosmology in *Ethics of Beauty*, "Since things are created for a purpose, their end is actually the trigger for their very existence. Or, what first got creation going was the primordial appearing of that perfect Beauty that creation was destined to embrace—the anointed Son of God, the triumph of self-sacrificial love."[26]

Key to Maximus's cosmology is also the freedom to participate in Christ, our source and our personal God. To this end, Maximus developed his philosophy of the will and activity. In combating Monothelitism, Maximus advanced and surpassed the ideas of Pope Martin in challenging the heresy of Pope Honorius. Maximus maintained that for Christ to be consubstantial with both God and humanity, as Chalcedon proclaims, Christ must have both a human and divine will.[27] Christ's human will resembles ours, but Christ did not possesses a *gnomic* (deliberative) will. As Louth explains, "The result of the Fall is not that natures are distorted in themselves, but rather that natures are misused: The Fall exists at the level not of logos, but of tropos."[28]

Virtue is therefore the outgrowth of the common will of mankind and brings us closer to God. As Maximus states, "It is evident that every person who participates in virtue as a matter of habit unquestionably participates in God, the substance of the virtues."[29] Virtue here is understood closer to Aristotle and Antisthenes than Plato, as something that can be developed and nurtured through habit.

Triads exist in abundance, but they increasingly take the form of being, *theoria*, and *theosis*. This exists with the three laws as Maximus identifies them, the natural law, scriptural law, and the law of grace, in addition to our personal existence and that of the cosmos. For Maximus, it is ultimately through this Christian triad that "he places himself wholly in God alone, wholly imprinting and forming God alone in himself, so that by grace he himself 'is God and is called God.'"[30]

For Maximus, *theosis* has its basis not only in the telos of man, but consistently in the incarnation. "By his gracious condescension God became man and is called man for the sake of man and by exchanging his condition for ours revealed the power that elevates man to God through his love for God and brings God down to man because of his love for man."[31] Building on Dionysius and the tradition of apophatic theology, Maximus expresses the essence energies distinction when he states, "God is communicable in what He imparts to us; but He is not communicable in the incommunicability of his essence."[32] Maximus defines *theosis* as being "by grace (that is to say, in the divine energies), all that God is by nature, save only identity of nature."[33]

Maximus finds a balance between the Platonic conception of the universe and other dominant philosophical conceptions, while remaining decidedly a Christian. The will is free and directed toward virtue because the source and telos of the will resides in Christ. The Neoplatonic cosmology is understood and reworked in a way that is consistent not only with the Cappadocian Fathers but within Christian tradition.

Under both Maximus and Dionysius, Platonism is reintroduced into Christianity. Plato once again becomes conversant but not embraced. Maximus and Dionysius address the cosmic direction of Neoplatonism and correct it. Christianity is not a facade but the substance behind the cosmic theology and directional cast inherent in it. Plato, Plotinus, and Proclus provide some language but not the ultimate content. Again, the distinction remains one of ultimate telos under each of the systems. *Theoria* is incomplete, but not incompatible with the telos of man under Christianity.

## THE WEST

In the West, the writings of Dionysius and Maximus had a later significance. Their impact was also understood not on their own, but like all Western theology and philosophy in conjunction with Saint Augustine of Hippo.[34] Augustine, a dominant influence in the West, is not a continuation of ancient Christian thought as it is expressed in the East. Not only did he write in Latin instead of Greek, but his knowledge of the Greek Fathers was fairly minimal. Augustine's impact in the East is equally sparse. Between linguistic and cultural differences, the main theologians in the West were less conversant with those in the East. One notable exception was Saint John Cassian. Cassian came from the East; he spoke Greek and understood the

Eastern mindset. He was instrumental in founding monasteries in the West and in the Third and Fourth Ecumenical Councils assisting Celestine I and later Leo in their interpretation of Greek terms and ideas. Similarly, Ambrose of Milan can serve as a bridge, even though for many Western thinkers his influence is reduced to hymnology and his role in converting Augustine. Unfortunately, these other voices conversant with Eastern Christian thought were muted by later developments in the West. This was in part due to the ascendency of Augustine. More than anyone else, Augustine is the source of Western Christian interpretation and theology. Augustine was indebted to Ambrose of Milan and lived at the same time as Saint John Cassian. He had access through them at least to the writings of the Greek Church Fathers. Unfortunately, Augustine does not cite Greek saints in his works. This has led some to call Augustine "the first Protestant." Instead of building on the tradition of the Church, he builds on his own brilliance.

Given what Augustine tells us about himself in the *Confessions*, it is also reasonable to take his lack of engagement with the Greek Fathers to be a result of his poor knowledge of Greek. Augustine tells us, "I dislike Greek learning."[35] "For not a single word of it did I understand."[36] Augustine did understand rhetoric and the philosophical landscape of northern Africa and southern Italy. This philosophy was dominated by Latin and by theological disputes that are particular to Latin Christianity. Latin concerns were with ecclesiology more than the Christology, which dominated the East.

Augustine uses polemic and experience to draw out his theological points. His *Confessions*, the *City of God*, and the breadth of writings that Augustine produced throughout his life demonstrate this over and over again. When reading Augustine, one must remember that even though he was a bishop, he was a trained rhetorician and would use whatever evidence was necessary to drive a point home. His developed theology is livelier, more personal, and less objective than that of any other theologian of the period. As a rhetorician, sometimes Augustine may advance one claim and at another time dismiss that same notion.

Augustine's treatment of Plato follows this tract. In the *Confessions*, he says that Plato and the Platonists he read in translation are "inflated with most monstrous pride."[37] In the *City of God*, Augustine tells us, "To Plato is given the praise of having perfected philosophy."[38] Similar to Justin, Augustine dislikes the Greek mythos and the gods as presented by Homer. They are too immoral. Like Justin, Augustine in his *Confessions* also views Greek philosophy as a halfway philosophy. "But having then read those books of the Platonists, and being admonished by them to search for incorporeal truth, I saw Thy invisible things, understood by those things that are made."[39] In the *City of God*, reading Plato is encouraged since "It is evident that none come nearer to us than the Platonists."[40]

Augustine's position regarding Plato is nuanced to say the least. He does not read Plato in Greek and therefore some of the subtleties are lost, as any work in translation loses something. Yet he compares the Platonist doctrine of the Logos with Christianity and approaches some ideas of *theoria* but encourages his readers to look toward scripture to find more than what is in Plato. Augustine was deeply indebted to Plotinus and his discussion of movement of the soul, and its ascent toward God.[41] Similar to Maximus's use of the *logoi* to explain the soul's ascent, Augustine speaks of the soul's desire to return to God. This is similar to the exchange formula advanced by Irenaeus, Athanasius, and others. In his Mainz sermons 13.1, Augustine states, "The son of God became the Son of Man that he might make the sons of men sons of God."[42] In this quest, Augustine speaks on God's grace and dependence in a similar way to Plotinus's argument, that the soul is dependent upon the One. Yet for Augustine, this remains a personal God, not an isolated monad as we find among the Neoplatonists.

At the same time, Augustine distances himself from the cosmological structure of the Neoplatonists in other ways. Porphyry tells us that Plotinus was ashamed of being embodied to the point that he would not allow his portrait to be painted.[43] Augustine's relationship with the material world and its impulses is a bit more nuanced. Augustine's interpretation of Platonic cosmology is complicated because of the influence of Gnosticism and Manicheanism. Notions of cosmic dualism alter the Neoplatonic emanations, distancing oneself to form a material body. If interpreted as the Gnostics and Manicheans, this results in fallen angels or an evil god creating matter. Matter is a curse rather than the effect of cooling due to distance from the source. Augustine vehemently opposes any Platonic theory of matter, as he rejected his Manichean past.

Still, Augustine values Plato. "Among the disciples of Socrates, Plato is the one who shone with a glory which far excelled that of the others, and who not unjustly eclipsed them all."[44] The reason for Plato surpassing other Greek philosophy was due to his time in Egypt, where Augustine posits, he read the Old Testament Prophets, likely Jeremiah. This revelation helped to shape Plato's philosophy in a similar way as Clement and Justin theorized. Plato, Plotinus, and the Platonists provide the longing to escape the cave and return to their source. For the Platonists, this was the journey associated with *theoria*. For Augustine, this is the work of the Holy Spirit.

The return to the source for Augustine is connected to the notion of icon. As discussed in chapter 3, mankind is made in the image of God. Augustine, in *De Trinitate*, argues that mankind approaches God by a sort of likeness. "For approach to God is not by intervals of place, but by likeness, and withdrawal from Him is by unlikeness."[45] The likeness of man to God is similar to the icon and the prototype. One stands for the other and draws the image to the source. Augustine's conception is closer to Plotinus than it is to St Irenaeus or the Cappadocians. While the epistemological distance between God and man was used to allow for the Christian to mature into *theosis* for Irenaeus and the Cappadocians, Augustine sees the relationship between image and archetype closer to *theoria*. Louth maintains that for Augustine, "the act of contemplation is the act of return."[46]

This cannot be overstated. Since the telos of mankind for Augustine is more akin to *theoria* than *theosis*, it should not surprise us that the concept of *theosis* is not developed as much in the West. It was only with the integration of Dionysius briefly in the ninth and to a greater extent later in the thirteenth century that this concept began to emerge. In the East, Dionysius pushed past Platonism, showing it to be incomplete, but in the West, Dionysius became the vehicle of reintroducing Neoplatonism. For this reason, Western scholars often retort that Dionysius's writings had a greater influence in the West than the East until the time of the Reformation. Lossky says this conclusion "is only superficially true."[47] Dionysius was consistent within Eastern thought as mentioned earlier. Only when brought to the West and read through an Augustinian lens do Dionysius's writings appear to support a Platonist position and provide this counterpoint to Western thought.

Following Augustine, John Scotus Eriugena,[48] the great Irish philosopher, was the only one in the Carolingian period to really engage with Greek thought to any extent. He read the Cappadocian Fathers, primarily Gregory of Nyssa, as well as Origen, and he translated Dionysius and Maximus the Confessor's *Ambigua ad Iohannem* into Latin. Eriugena cosmology centered around "the immovable self-identical one,"[49] akin to Neoplatonism. The cosmic movement is similar to Neoplatonism, that things move from the One and return to the One, that is God. Similar to Augustine, Eriugena describes this movement akin to Platonic *theoria*. Parallel to Maximus, Eriugena interprets the incarnation as central in this cosmic movement and final rest in God as the goal. Furthermore, like Dionysius, Philo, and other Middle Platonists, Erigenia utilized aspects of apophatic theology. God was both unknowable and knowable. "Thus, [God] is called Essence, but strictly speaking He is not essence: for to being is opposed not-being."[50]

Eriugena's use of the Greek Fathers, Dionysius, and Maximus amounted to little for the next three hundred years after his death and the death of Charles the Fat. Eriugena's works were accused of being too Platonist and potentially pantheistic. With the dissolution of the Carolingian dynasty, the legacy and works of the Irish scholar were pushed aside for a more Augustinian reading of Plato under the influence of Lanfranc and Anselm. Anselm wholly embraced the Christianized Platonic cosmology. His famed ontological argument rests on the presupposition that things truly exist in the realm of thought. Much of his theological outlook is also deeply indebted to Augustine more than anyone else. Anselm advanced and reinterpreted Augustine for the medieval mind in the West, and until the thirteenth century it was his interpretation of Augustine that became normative.

At the beginning of the thirteenth century, Western philosophy once again looked to voices outside of Augustine, though always interpreted alongside Augustine. This included the Latin translations of Dionysius and Maximus that were read by Bonaventure and Albert the Great. Even a cursory reading of Bonaventure's *Journey of the Mind to God* reveals the use of Plato's Cosmology. The central position of the microcosm interacting with the macrocosm influences Bonaventure's notion of apprehension. This concept builds rather heavily upon notions of *logoi*, as discussed by Maximus, though Maximus is not referenced directly in the work. Dionysius is one of the major influences in Bonaventure's work. Dionysius's *Mystical Theology* is the first work referenced by Bonaventure and provides the basis for this treatise.[51] Dionysius is further addressed in the sixth step where the Good is used as a name for God. This usage and its interpretation comes directly from Dionysius's *Divine Names*. At the end of the work Bonaventure encourages his reader with Dionysius. "We can say with Dionysius: And you, my friend, in this matter of mystical visions, renew your journey."[52] It is Dionysius's corrective to Platonic ascent that serves as the foundation for Bonaventure's major philosophical work. Bonaventure interprets Dionysius through his reading of Augustine.

Albert moved away from a strict Augustinian philosophy and added the voices of Dionysius as well as Aristotle. This produced a more nuanced philosophy that opened the door to speculation and mysticism. Albert wrote several commentaries on Dionysius and provided the University of Cologne with a distinct philosophical and theological lens. In the opening to his commentary of Dionysius's *Mystical Theology*, Albert tells Odo and his readers "it is clearly called 'mystical' because it is hidden and closed; in this kind of theology we rise to the knowledge of God by way of abstraction and at the end it remains a closed and hidden secret what God is."[53] For Albert, the archetype of the theologian was Dionysius and the experience of the divine through meditation.

In his commentary on Dionysius, Albert also criticized some of his Dominican brothers because they fought against philosophy. There are different ways of knowing, following Dionysius.

Knowing can be of two kinds. One form refers to all that is accessible to the knowledge of reason, and that kind is cultivated adequately through research and teaching. Another kind concerns knowledge which our reason does not reach. Knowledge of this sort, of a high nature, needs participation in the fullness of light.[54]

More than anyone else, Albert's use of Dionysius brought Western philosophy and theology closer to the understanding of *theosis* of the East.

Albert's most famous student is Thomas Aquinas. Aquinas, in the first part of the second part of his *Summa Theologica*, speaks of the telos of man. He separates the end of man from those pertaining to irrational creatures. He then speaks of our motivations and the end of our actions to be happiness. In both of these accounts, he frequently quotes Aristotle and Augustine. In 2:1 Q1A8, he reiterates that, "God is the last end of man."[55] This advances the concept of divine beatitude that Aquinas speaks about in Question 26 of the first part of the Summa. In article three, we read, "God is the only beatitude; for everyone is blessed from this sole fact, that he understands God."[56] For Aquinas, beatitude is a uniquely human aspiration that is very much akin to Platonic contemplation. In article four, Aquinas adds to this by stating, "divine perfection embraces all other perfection," and "As to contemplative happiness, God possesses a continual and most certain contemplation of Himself and of all things else."[57] Aquinas moves beyond Platonic *theoria* as the telos of man, and speaks of participation in divine perfection, but this participation is still not the same as *theosis*.

Aquinas's reading of Dionysius is also not wholly consistent with Albert's. Aquinas's use of apophatic theology is primarily understood as a corrective to cataphatic statements. Aquinas preferred cataphatic statements, except for when our human reason is limited. This is a break from Dionysius, who understood apophatic theology as surpassing cataphatic. For Dionysius, negative theology was a way toward mystical union with God. One ultimately cannot know God through contemplation, but only in surrendering the confidence of our intellect and accepting that God is beyond comprehension. Thankfully for Dionysius, Middle Platonists, and Eastern Christians, God still reveals Himself through His uncreated energies. This distinction between man's participation in created and uncreated grace serves to highlight the distinction between the Western position, where Aquinas states, "beatitude is a created thing in beatified creatures."[58] Saint Gregory Palamas proclaims, "all the energies of God are uncreated."[59]

In the East, the reading of Dionysius's apophatic theology is essential. God in God's essence remains unknowable; one can only approach God through the divine energy. If this was a created grace then God remains unapproachable and union would be impossible. Lossky maintains that as interpreted in the East, "the way of the knowledge of God is necessarily the way of deification."[60] Following the apophatic theology of Dionysius, one must participate in the uncreated grace to approach God. That is why Lossky also states elsewhere, "while intimately united with God he knows Him only as Unknowable, in other words as infinity set apart by His nature, remaining even in union, inaccessible in that which He is in His essential being."[61] Knowledge requires union, and this union requires *theosis*. Gregory of Sinai, in his hymn on the Transfiguration, proclaims, "because he dwells in you in this world, . . . you will be divinized in the next."[62] It is the uncreated energies that transform contemplation into knowledge, and this knowledge is experienced not as an act of will or contemplation. It is partaking of the divine light, as affirmed by the Hesychasts; this is *theosis*.

Albert was the teacher not only of Thomas Aquinas but also Meister Eckhart. Aquinas is usually interpreted as the rational Aristotelian; Eckhart is read as the Dionysian mystic. In reality, both students incorporated Aristotle and Dionysius to some degree into the set Augustinian mold. Aquinas's mysticism is evident by his eventual renunciation of writing following an ecstatic experience during the Eucharist. Eckhart's mysticism is evident through the Rheinish mystics who followed him, as well as his heresy show trial. Eckhart's debt to Dionysian apophatic theology is demonstrated when he declares that God is beyond being and as such is not being.

Eckhart's intellectual heir was his student is Johan Tauler. Tauler's philosophy is primarily concerned with the relation of the inner man with the outer man. His conception of the inner man expands on Aquinas's doctrine of divine contemplation and relies heavily upon the notion of eternal return and rest in God, similar to what Maximus advanced and was likely a product of Eckhart's teaching regarding Dionysius. When discussing Christ as the architect of human ascent to God, Tauler proclaims, "This interior God-man, formed in the Image of God, flies back to His Divine Source and to His first condition before the Creation."[63] This ascent not only connects Christ as the interior man, which is central to Tauler's mysticism, but also Christ as the image connecting to its source, akin to Augustine and Plotinus speaking of the image returning to its source.

Tauler comes close to the concept of *theosis*, since he is identifying in Christ the characteristics that are consubstantial with humanity. Tauler, Eckhart, Albert, and Bonaventure all move closer to the Eastern conception of mystical ascent. Since their theological and philosophical foundation is Augustine, his conception of Platonism rather than the conception of Gregory of Nyssa or the other Greek Fathers limits the telos of man. Augustine and those in the West following him have a beatific *theoria*, not *theosis*. Their telos is not Plato's, nor does it belong entirely to the Neoplatonists as it retains a larger degree of union with the divine than could be said about the One.

In the dominant voices of the West, we do not have any proclamations akin to Athanasius, Dionysius, or Maximus, let alone the development of *theosis* through Hesychasm. While some Western thinkers hint at the distinction between God's unknowable essence verses God's knowable energies, there is no development of this doctrine like what is accomplished by Symeon the

New Theologian or Gregory of Palamas. Instead of moving beyond Plato, the West even when prima face rejecting Plato in favor of Aristotle, Nominalism, or any other philosophical trajectory, do not end up in the same place as Eastern Christian philosophy. For the West, Plato's goal of *theoria* remains central when describing the telos of man.

This centrality is also manifest in the distinction between Eastern and Western religious art. In the West, especially following the Italian Renaissance, realism rather than symbolism dominates. This realism is beautiful but does not have the same depth of meaning as icons do in the East. Western iconoclasm also demonstrated that while the images were popular sources of and expressions of piety, the defense of images did not resemble the theological and philosophical arguments of John of Damascus or Theodore the Studite.


## EASTERN CRITIQUES

As evidenced by both Dionysius and Maximus, the philosophy of Neoplatonists has a degree of overlap with eastern Christian thought. Unlike claims that believe that Christianity was a veil placed upon Plato, we have demonstrated that Plato's cosmology was discussed and rejected as inadequate in the East. As Lossky clearly states,

> All that can be said in regard to the platonism of the Fathers, and especially in regard to the dependence of the author of the *Areopagitica* on the neo-platonist philosophers, is limited to outward resemblances which do not go to the root of their teaching, and relate only to a vocabulary which was common to the age.[64]

Neoplatonism and its limitations were addressed by a number of other Orthodox authors following Maximus. The clearest voice against the Platonic telos in favor of Orthodox *theoria* is John of Damascus. As discussed in chapter 3, his defense of icons incorporated preceding generations of Christian thinkers as well as philosophical concepts from Plato and other Greeks. The Damascene, like Dionysius, Justin, Clement, Basil, and others believed that what was good from the Greeks could be used. "First of all I shall set forth the best contributions of the philosophers of the Greeks, because whatever there is of good has been given to men from above by God."[65]

John of Damascus understood philosophy as the study of knowledge. "Philosophy is knowledge of things which are in so far as they are, that is, a knowledge of the nature of things which have being. And again, philosophy is knowledge of both divine and human things, that is to say, of things both visible and invisible."[66] Since the world, both the sensible world and the intelligible world, are the domains of philosophy, John maintains that the real aim of philosophy is not simply knowledge but *theosis*. "Philosophy is the making of one's self like God,"[67] or as he says later, "Philosophy is a becoming like God, in so far as this is possible for man."[68]

John of Damascus demonstrates the essential difference between Eastern and Western conceptions of philosophy; it is not simply to know but to be transformed. It is not *theoria* but *theosis*. Plato and Neoplatonic cosmic construction are only half philosophies that remain stagnate at the very moment when they should excel, uniting contemplation with the material and spiritual being that contemplates with the divine source.

For the Damascene, Greek philosophy anticipates the divine revelation and can be useful since philosophy is love of wisdom and "true wisdom is God. Therefore, the love of God, this is the true philosophy."[69] Pythagoras anticipated God as monad and held notions of providence. This and his moral applications were closer to approaching God than the broader culture but were still contaminated with error. Worse still was his doctrine of transmigration of souls, and as John tells us, that "finally he called himself God."[70]

John's treatment of the Platonists is not terribly different. They were correct in recognizing God, matter, and form, but the notions of an uncreated, immortal, and divine soul are not Christian. John also did not approve of the Platonists' treatment of women as common property, and was also opposed to the inherited notion of transmigration from the Pythagoreans. Finally, John criticizes the idea that "there were several gods produced from the One."[71]

John also spoke on the Stoics and the Epicureans. He demonstrates the limitations of speculation since both philosophies have a similar aim, yet disagree with one another on cosmology and the telos of man. John of Damascus expresses that later forms of Greek philosophy can be useful when consistent with matters of faith and guided by logic based upon metaphysical truths. It is of no benefit when it is excluded from this foundation.

Later Orthodox thinkers approach Plato and Greek philosophy in a similar way to John of Damascus. Saint Paisius Velichkovsky, in the eighteenth century, fled from one of Peter the Great's academies, saying,

> I hear only the names of pagan gods and wise men—Cicero, Aristotle, and Plato. By learning their wisdom people of today have become blinded to the end and have digressed from the true way. Intellectuals utter words, but internally, they are filled with darkness and gloom, for their wisdom is of the world only. Not seeing any purpose to such learning and fearing how I myself cannot but be corrupted by it, I have left it.[72]

He then went to Mount Athos and dedicated himself to prayer over learning.

For Saint Paisius Velichkovsky and others, Plato has some redeeming characteristics, but worldly speculative wisdom is doomed toward error. Many eastern Christian philosophers rejected Plato's cosmology as well, if it was understood as limiting God. Some later Neoplatonists were open to the idea of the One as creator. The Platonic conception that God ordered rather than created the world is understood as inherently incompatible with Christianity. When trying to unite Plato with Christianity, there remains the danger of falling into the errors of Origen. It should not surprise us that many of the critiques of Plato and Neoplatonism are the same critiques against Origen. Origen, according to Maximus the Confessor, "borrowed too much from Greek teachings."[73]

Maximus, John of Damascus, and many others quickly reject the notion of preexistence of souls. Maximus proclaims, "Away then with the foolish view that souls exist before bodies."[74] Meyendorff also points out that, "Against Origen, the Fathers unanimously affirmed that man is a unity of soul and body. On this point, the Biblical view decidedly overcame Platonic spiritualism."[75] Central to the issues concerning body and soul was the Platonic supposition that ontology dictates teleology, that what we are dictates our ends. This Platonic concept once accepted forces the rejection of other Platonic suppositions.

Maximus has clearly demonstrated that the *logoi* of beings provide their context and must have their source in the divine, but the *logoi* is not the same as the soul. It is the conception held by God, not the animating spirit of man. "He will also know that the many logoi are the one Logos to whom all things are related and who exists in himself without confusion, the essential and individually distinctive God, the Logos of God the Father."[76] Therefore, the telos of man is toward God and man was created out of nothing except the free will of God. Maximus leans more on Aristotle than Plato and declares, "For the maker is always existent Being, but they exist in potentiality before they exist in actuality."[77]

While dominant, Plato was not essential for Eastern Christians' conception of the cosmos as it develops past the fifth century. Any philosophy could be applied when beneficial and appropriate. Maximus can build on potentiality and actuality that is central to Aristotle's cosmology without accepting it entirely, just as he could borrow some of Plato. In both cases, Maximus and others are applying those philosophies into Christianity not conforming Christianity to those systems. Debates continue to exist in the east after Maximus. During the ninth century, a preference toward Aristotle arose, similar to what takes place in the West during the thirteenth and fourteenth centuries. One of the greatest Eastern Christian philosophers of the ninth century, Saint Photios the Great, belonged to the Aristotle coalition.[78] Many of the Antiochian fathers are also understood as being closer to Aristotle than Plato.[79]

A preference for Aristotle or Plato is inconsequential. Rather the language of telos and return can be useful, just as act and potential. In any case, these notions are used for the same conclusion, *theosis*. *Theosis* is relational and communal as mentioned in chapters 3 and 4. It can also only be understood within the Christian symbolic world. Here Florensky tells us in the symbolic world we have a "meeting of the lowest experiences of the highest world with the highest experiences of the lowest world."[80] The icon is therefore indispensable in this process of understanding. It is not a philosophical concept, but a tool that helps bridge potentiality with its telos of actuality; it brings the image and likeness together and transforms the person.

## NOTES

1. Pope between 625 and 638. Honorius was asked by Patriarch Sergius I about Monophysitism, and Honorius advanced the compromise position that Christ had the nature of a man but not the will.

2. Sergius I, Pyrrhus I, Paul II, and Peter I.

3. Cyrus.

4. The Third Council of Constantinople, 680–681.

5. Temple, *Icons and the Mystical Origins of Christianity*, 78.

6. Lossky, *Mystical Theology*, 25.

7. Parker, John. "In Defense of the Dionysian Authorship." Orthochristian.com, n.d. https://orthochristian.com/86817.html (accessed 2023).

8. 412–485.

9. Lossky, *Vision of God*, 121.

10. Elem. Theol. § 35

11. Lossky, *Vision of God*, 45.

12. Parker, "In Defense of the Dionysian Authorship."

13. Lossky, *Vision of God*, 122.

14. 999–1003.

15. Lossky, *Vision of God*, 122.

16. Louth, *Origins of the Christian Mystical Tradition*, 164.

17. Lossky, *Mystical Theology*, 28.

18. Temple, *Icons and the Mystical Origins of Christianity*, 79.

19. Louth, *Origins of the Christian Mystical Tradition*, 165.

20. Lossky, *Mystical Theology*, 42.

21. 580–662.

22. Second Tractate of the Second Enade.

23. Mitralexis, Sotiris, Georgios Steiris, Marcin Podbielski, and Sebastian Lalla. *Maximus the Confessor as a European Philosopher.* Eugene, OR: Cascade Books, 2017, 157.

24. Maximus the Confessor. *On the Cosmic Mystery of Jesus Christ.* Crestwood, NY: St. Vladimir's Seminary Press, 2003, 58.

25. Lossky, *Mystical Theology*, 90, quoting "Epist 43, Ad Joannem cubicularium" P.G., XCI, 640 BC.

26. Patitsas, Timothy G. *The Ethics of Beauty.* Maysville, MO: Road to Emmaus Foundation, 2020, 525.

27. Maximus the Confessor. *Classics of Western Spirituality: Maximus Confessor, Selected Writings.* New York: Paulist Press, 1985, 4.

28. Louth, Andrew. *Maximus the Confessor.* London: Routledge, 1996, 57.

29. Maximus the Confessor, *On the Cosmic Mystery of Christ*, 58.

30. Maximus the Confessor, *On the Cosmic Mystery of Christ*, 60.

31. Maximus the Confessor, *On the Cosmic Mystery of Christ*, 60.

32. Lossky, *Mystical Theology*, 73

33. Lossky, *Mystical Theology*, 87, quoting "De Ambiguis" P.G., XCI, 1308 B.

34. 354–430.

35. Augustine, *The Confessions of St. Augustine.* Translated by J. G. Pilkington. New York: Liveright Publishing, 1943, 18. Book 1, chapter 14.

36. Augustine, *Confessions*, 18–19. Book 1, chapter 14.

37. Augustine, *Confessions*, 146. Book 7, chapter 13.

38. Augustine, *City of God*, 247. Book 8, chapter 4.

39. Augustine, *Confessions*, 158. Book 7, chapter 20.

40. Augustine. *The City of God.* Translated by Marcus Dods. New York: Random House, 1993, 248. Book 8, chapter 5.

41. Louth, *Origins of the Christian Mystical Tradition*, 140.

42. Russell, *Fellow Workers with God*, 39.

43. Life of Plotinus I.

44. Augustine, *City of God*, 247. Book 8, chapter 4.

45. Augustine, "On the Trinity." In *Nicene and Post-Nicene Fathers, First Series, Volume 3*, by Augustine. Edited by Philip Schaff. Translated by Arthur West Haddan. Buffalo, NY: Christian Literature Publishing, 1887. Book 7, chapter 7.12.

46. Louth, *Origins of the Christian Mystical Tradition*, 147.

47. Lossky, *Vision of God*, 127.

48. 800–877.

49. Patrologia Latina 122: 476b.

50. Eriugena, John Scotus. *Periphyseon (The Division of Nature).* Washington, DC: Dumbarton Oaks and Editions Bellarmin, 1987.

51. Bonaventure. *The Journey of the Mind to God.* Indianapolis: Hackett, 1990, 5.

52. Bonaventure, *Journey of the Mind to God*, 39.

53. Albert the Great. *Classics of Western Spirituality: Albert and Thomas, Selected Writings.* New York: Paulist Press, 1988, 134.

54. O'Meara, Thomas. *Albert the Great: Theologian and Scientist.* Chicago: New Priory Press, 2013, 32.

55. Aquinas, Thomas. "The Summa Theologiæ of St. Thomas Aquinas." *New Advent*, 1920. https://www.newadvent.org/summa/ (accessed 2023), 2:1 Q1 A4.

56. Aquinas, *Summa Theologiae*, 1 Q26 A3.

57. Aquinas, *Summa Theologiae*, 1 Q26 A4.

58. Aquinas, *Summa Theologiae*, 1 Q26 A3.

59. Palamas, Gregory. *The Triads.* Mahwah, NJ: Paulist Press, 1983, 96. III.ii.8.

60. Lossky, *Mystical Theology*, 39.

61. Lossky, *Mystical Theology*, 38.

62. Gregory the Sinaite. "Discourse on the Feast of the Holy Transfiguration of the Lord." In *Light on the Mountain: Greek Patristic and Byzantine Homilies on the Transfiguration of the Lord.* Translated by Brian E. Daley, 325–50. Yonkers, NY: St. Vladimir's Seminary Press, 2013, 339.

63. Tauler, John. *The Inner Way.* London: Aeterna Press, 2015, 200.

64. Lossky, *Mystical Theology*, 32.

65. St. John of Damascus. *Fathers of the Church, Volume XXXVII: Saint John of Damascus.* Jackson, MI: Ex Fontibus Company, 2015, 5.

66. St. John of Damascus, *Fathers of the Church*, 11.

67. St. John of Damascus, *Fathers of the Church*, 11.

68. St. John of Damascus, *Fathers of the Church*, 106.

69. St. John of Damascus, *Fathers of the Church*, 11.

70. St. John of Damascus, *Fathers of the Church*, 113.

71. St. John of Damascus, *Fathers of the Church*, 113.

72. Hopko, *Orthodox Faith, Volume 3: Church History*, 207.

73. Maximus the Confessor, *On the Cosmic Mystery of Christ*, 45–46.

74. Maximus the Confessor, *On the Cosmic Mystery of Christ*, 72.

75. Meyendorff, *Byzantine Theology*, 140.

76. Maximus the Confessor, *On the Cosmic Mystery of Christ*, 54.

77. Maximus the Confessor, *On the Cosmic Mystery of Christ*, 57.

78. Gerostergios, Asterios. *St. Photios The Great.* Belmont, MA: Institute for Byzantine and Modern Greek Studies, 1980, 20.

79. Hill, *Reading the Old Testament in Antioch*, 8.

80. Florensky, *Iconostasis*, 43.

## Chapter 8

# Treatment of Selected Icons

Plato and his goal of *theoria* calls the student of philosophy to look past perception to the idea that lays beyond. For Plato, the material world gave some signs of the ideas that lay behind them. Therefore, we can see a beautiful tree and recognize the pure idea of beauty and tree-ness from this observation. For the Neoplatonists, this was accompanied by the desire to return to the source. The material world moves one toward the realm of ideas and ultimately toward the One. For Christianity, the language of Plato allowed for more than contemplation. *Theoria* was replaced by *theosis*. Both *theoria* and *theosis* begin with the material and move beyond that as an act of ascent toward the source. One key difference is that *theosis* sanctifies the material realm while moving beyond contemplation and toward participation with God. The image not only signifies the prototype, providing signs toward its source, but also provides a union with the prototype transforming the signifier.

This is the symbolic explanation of icons. In chapter 3, we discuss the nature of an icon and its role as symbol, as a depiction of reality where two things are brought together; in this case it is the material object and the spirit behind it. Here it is important to shift our attention toward some specific icons and the symbols contained in those to deepen our understanding of Orthodox use of icons as one means of differentiating the telos of man from the Platonic. Like any symbol and piece of art, there can be multiple layers of analysis to understand what the iconographer intended on conveying and what is understood by the community when they encounter the object. The treatment of specific icons in this chapter is not intended to be an exhaustive explanation of every aspect of the icon, nor the construction of icons. Instead the goal is that by touching on some of the more significant aspects of important icons one can walk away with a greater understanding of that encounter.

Orthodox Christians read icons much as they do scripture. The text and icon both possess a plain meaning: the story of an event or a description of a person. In reading Saint Luke's account of John the Baptist and seeing an icon of the Forerunner, John can be understood through any cursory encounter. Yet this encounter is not intended to fully explain the significance of the person, their mission, and who they are for the Orthodox Christian. Like scriptural analysis, icons are analyzed through different schools of thought. They possess different histories and interact with the community in different ways. The allegorical approach to the reading of scripture found in Alexandria that incorporated the language of Plato in the development of Middle and Neoplatonism applies to the reading of icons as well. But unlike scripture, icons do not need to be translated into a different language. Still, to fully encounter an icon with its symbolic importance, some rules of interpretation need to be identified.

One foundational rule is that icons, as conveyors of theology, must be consistent with the theological and liturgical life of the Church. Jonathan Pageau points out that this theological understanding of an icon does develop an iconology. This theory of terms used in the icon is applied when internalizing the icon. "Understanding everything you see in icons, also understanding the theology of icons and its role in the liturgical life of the Church—that's what iconology is, whereas iconography is the practice of painting icons."[1]

Countless canons regulating the life of the Christian and community have been developed over the last two thousand years, from local jurisdictions to national, and even ecumenical councils. Yet relatively few canons are formed about icons specifically. There is not a defined iconology. While Orthodox Christians around the world affirm the same faith, there are different ways that this faith is expressed. There are different techniques incorporated into worship. Icon symbolism and style are not uniform. There are very few dogmas concerning the symbolism of icons. The majority of "rules" that exist have exceptions for them. Unfortunately, what is often declared to be universal by many scholars is not so. Reputable sources get things wrong, even when credibly researched. Some incorrectly believe that what happens in one location is universal. Unfortunately, things do not work that way within the Orthodox Church by and large. For example, many books and articles state that the first icon an iconographer paints once they have completed their apprenticeship is an icon of the Transfiguration. Largely, this is a practice that has grown out of a specific Greek school of iconography and is not in any way universal.

With the exception of "basic" Christological and Trinitarian dogmas, there are exceptions, local customs, and pious traditions that vary from one jurisdiction to another and sometimes from one church to another. Just as veneration of icons varies in how it is performed from church to church and even person to person, the same principle exists when creating icons. Orthodoxy follows the teachings of their local bishop, who as long as they are in communion with others permits a sense of ambiguity. This does not rest easy for many Western Christians or scholars in the West, but it is indeed the case.

It is best to follow the spirit of what Dostoevsky proclaimed in his author's introduction to the *Brothers Karamazov*: "Being at a loss to resolve these questions, I am resolved to leave them without any resolution."[2]

The first rule is simply to understand that exceptions are not only common but taken for granted. There is not one universally consistent way of "properly" interpreting an icon or in how to construct one. As long as the image is received as an icon by the people and not censured by a bishop, it is an icon. The issue of reception is key to every aspect of the icon. The development of an iconology is similar to the development of the Creed and Canons of the Church. They come later and are used to define the limits of belief. When Saint Luke painted his first icons, there were no rules in place. In constructing later icons based upon Luke or the original Mandylion, iconographers remained faithful to what they understood was important, but this does not mean that they followed a consistent rule that remains today. Iconographer and Priest Fr Matthew Garrett points out in his thesis on the theological layers in icons that, "Modern beliefs about the theological meaning of icons are often greatly influenced by writers of the last century who focused on the stylistic conventions of iconography."[3]

The second rule is that local customs are not unfaithful to conventions or exceptions to rules but are faithful renderings of tradition. In Sister Gabriela's monograph on the iconographic legacy of the twentieth-century Saint Elder Sophrony, she points out that, "The work had to be specifically tailored to a location and its epoch."[4] In England, the light is softer than in Greece. Thus, the palette used for the Chapel of Saint Silouan in Essex is muted and has more earthen tones than one would find in the Mediterranean. St Sophrony reminds us that when approaching an icon, we should remember that, "Each work of art is created for a specific place, at a specific time."[5]

The next rule in approaching icons is to recognize that each icon is not a nature scene. The place of a person is central to the icon. Met Hilarion Alfeyev states that, "Every icon is anthropological in its content. There is not a single icon on which a person is not depicted, whether the God-Man Jesus Christ, the Most Holy Theotokos, or one of the saints."[6] Icons affirm the incarnation, the transformation of people into living icons of Christ and the sanctity of matter. Therefore, icons must possess a sanctified person to be an icon. A possible exception to this rule is with an icon of the cross. A cross can be understood as an icon, but that is because the cross always points one back to Christ. Even a simple cross that does not contain any corpus or people around it directs one to Christ and affirms Christ's humanity. Even while there are exceptions, icons remain anthropological.

Icons must be anthropological because there must be a prototype to which the image is mediating. There must be a spiritual ascent toward an ontological reality presented to the viewer. As Florensky states,

Iconic art accords to its essential symbolism and thereby reveals its spiritual essence in nothing other than our (the viewers') spiritual ascent "from image to prototype," i.e., in our attaining ontological contiguity with the prototype itself . . . the sign (always inseparable from its prototype) is no longer merely "art" but is rather the first wave called forth—evoked—by essential reality.[7]

If this reality is absent, then the veneration of icons is reduced to idolatry.

Fear of idolatry is also the reason why no icons are made of God the Father. The Great Council of Moscow of 1666/1667 decreed that,

It is most absurd and improper to depict in icons the Lord Sabaoth (that is, the Father) with a grey beard and the Only-Begotten Son in His bosom with a dove between them, because no-one has seen the Father according to His Divinity, and the Father has no flesh, nor was the Son born in the flesh from the Father before the ages.[8]

Yet there is at least one icon where the Father is depicted along these lines. The icon of the Ancient of Days from Daniel depicts the Father as an old man with a triangle in His halo. This icon is an exception and one that developed by synthesizing different iconographic images. First was the Ancient of Days icon of where Christ is represented as the older figure revealed to Daniel. Next was an icon that existed representing the love of God the Father for His Son Christ through Abraham holding Isaac in a similar depiction to the Theotokos holding Christ. This elderly depiction of Abraham and the elderly Christ from the Ancient of Days were placed together, and a dove was placed between them to become an icon of the Trinity. It should be noted that the council of Moscow rejects this image, and it is not one that has wide support throughout the Church. Still, the icon remains.

Not surprisingly, Russia develops the most statutes concerning icons. The Council of a Hundred Chapters convened by Ivan IV in 1551 provides the most extensive rules regarding icons and their construction. The council forbids iconographers from using their own imagination when painting icons, instead telling them to remain within tradition. This regulation has a variety of interpretations, but was essentially an attempt to remind iconographers that icons differ from profane art.

In the last few centuries, a few other conventions have become normalized and are often taken as rules by many today. These conventions include painting from dark to light, not having any shadows, and that all saints have halos. People are not to be represented in profile, at least three quarters of their faces must be shown, otherwise they are understood as evil or lacking faith because they are "absent." Yet not all saints have halos, and not all faces are shown to the degree that is mandated. Oftentimes this is not because of an editorial concerning the person's sanctity but because of need. Some icons, such as the forty martyrs of Sebaste, for instance, do not have halos on each of the martyrs because doing so would prevent the faces of others from being shown. Similar decisions are made by iconographers in other icons where providing a halo would otherwise distort or hide the image of another person. Similarly, some faces are turned toward profile more because not doing so would distort the figure to a degree that is uncharitable. While the modern conventions are enshrined in many modern interpretations of icons, they are not universally held to be the case. This is true not only in the two-thousand-year history of icons but even by iconographers today. Other conventions exist as well, including the three stars upon the Theotokos, the use of colors, the letters in Christ's halo, and naming of icons which will be discussed later in this chapter.

The more recent norms concerning icons also apply to the iconographer. There are many rules which have grown concerning who the iconographer should be. The task of the iconographer is to open the eyes of the observer to the veiled reality behind the icon. The most important rule for any iconographer is that they are a man or woman of prayer. It has been said that the iconographer says the Jesus Prayer with every brushstroke. This is not the case. The spirit behind this saying should be true though, that every action connected with the icon should be dedicated to God and consecrated in prayer. The iconographer must try to rid themselves of ego and pride. Typically, icons are not signed. Jim Forest, in *Praying with Icons*, adds that, "The iconographer avoids stylistic innovations intended to take the place of a signature."[9] There should not be a signature mark, because the icon, while done through the labor of the iconographer, does not properly belong to them. If done correctly, it belongs to the Church and to Christ. Ouspensky states that, "The painter's personality is actualized in this catholicity not when he affirms his individuality, but when he surrenders the self; its highest manifestation consists in moving beyond what separates him in relation to others."[10]

Icons are revelations given by God to the iconographer in prayer. Florensky states that, "All icons are therefore revealed icons. And even when the icon is a portrait icon, it is clear that for it to be an icon, it must in the iconpainter be based in a vision."[11] To receive this vision, the iconographer must be "humble, gentle and pious, avoiding immoral conversations and mundane scurrility; he must be neither quarrelsome nor envious of others, neither a drunkard nor a thief; he must practise both spiritual and corporal purity,"[12] according to the 1551 Moscow Council of a Hundred Chapters. Florensky reiterates that iconographers are "holders of a unique Church office."[13] Just as there are rules concerning who can be ordained, similar guidelines exist for those who convey the Epistle, Gospel, and sacraments, and so too are those who present Christ in icons. The council forbade murderers and thieves but said nothing about artistic ability. Naturally, those who possess no natural or God-given

talent would likely not pursue the task, but the regulations are more concerned with the quality of the person than with the quality of their art.

With this said, there are many lay iconographers. Not all iconographers are
monastics or clergy. There are married and celibate iconographers, though
there are some prescribed periods of abstinence called for before undertak-
ing a task. There are men and women who undergo this task, and while the
rules and regulations connected with becoming an iconographer resemble
orders in the church, there are no vows taken or any ordination performed.
The iconographer produces a work for the community, and it must be done
through prayer, repentance, and love. The Church does not require that the
iconographer is perfect, but that they are capable of producing a work done in
this spirit. They must be a person who can see the world as sacred, and their
endeavors as belonging to the Church. It should be no surprise that Florensky
declares that, "In the most precise sense of the word, only the saints can be
iconpainters."[14] It was for this reason too that Ouspensky, before his conversion, painted an icon to prove that no developed religious skill or training was
necessary to paint one. He subsequently destroyed it because he felt that he
had sinned in making an icon as an atheist.

As an affirmation of matter that is transformed by prayer, icons can be
made of a variety of materials. Typically, the vast majority of icons were
painted with egg tempera, though this practice is not canonized. Egg tempera
has a certain mystique for some because it is time consuming as the painter
mixes the pigment with egg yolks and a little water. The artist then applies
many different layers of paint to build up the image, which then is more
luminous than oil and other paintings and typically more durable as well. Egg
tempera necessitates small, detailed strokes instead of large ones as it dries
rather quickly. It is relatively thin and holds only a small amount of pigment
so multiple layers are needed to produce any image. This is what allows for
its durability and for its luminosity as well as the attention to detail.

While egg tempera was selected by many iconographers over the centuries,
it is by no means the only medium used. The very first painted icons were
done with beeswax. Encaustic painting was the norm for the first three to
eight centuries when painting icons, depending on location. Like egg tempera, encaustic painting requires slowly mixing the medium with pigment and
detailed application in multiple layers. The practice of painting from dark to
light that is characteristic among iconographers and less so with conventional
art allows for light to permeate the layers and produce an image that can
appear luminescent. Encaustic painting may also be more transparent and can
have more depth in each layer than tempera.

Traditionally both egg tempera and encaustic icons are made on a wooden
board and then hung in a home or a church. The preparation of a board
became an industry in itself in medieval Russia. The wooden boards are

selected, having no knots in them and a clean surface. Sometimes the surface is prepared by recessing the center or trimming the edges. Slats are then placed in the back of the board to prevent the board from warping and cracking. The boards are then cleaned and prepared, adding a layer of cloth to the board that will allow for the paint to apply to the board evenly. Then several layers of a base material are applied before the icon is painted. Icons are painted from the background to the foreground, from dark to light, and may include application of gold leaf or other mediums, and some are even gilded, being covered in metalwork or jewels.

Many modern observers are awed by the technique of both egg tempera and encaustic, as well as the construction of the icon. Today it is common to hear that traditional icons are "written" instead of "painted," that constructing an icon is akin to writing a text, layer by layer, word by word. Elizabeth Zelinsky and Lela Gilbert point out that, "In the Russian language, the verbs to paint or to draw are used only in connection with secular painting, including the painting of religious subject matter. Therefore, iconographers do not paint icons; they write them."[15] Contrary to this fairly late linguistic practice, Florensky calls iconographers icon painters throughout his works, and many iconographers prefer to speak of prayerfully painting to writing, especially in areas that do not have the theological vocabulary to understand what "writing an icon" would mean. Describing the task as writing an icon or painting an icon are both acceptable.

Icons are not universally painted images on wooden boards. Sometimes icons are painted on canvas and then transferred to a wall of a church. Other times, icons are painted directly on the walls of a church. Still other mediums are used. Beginning around the fourth century, when Christianity became licit in the Roman empire and permanent structures could serve as churches, we have the use of mosaic in iconography. Small cubes of tile are placed, making the image and being positioned on the walls or the ceilings of churches. The high point of mosaic came during the reign of Justinian I.[16] Mosaics of other scenes may be found on the ground, but not icons so as to keep them from being stepped on or otherwise disrespected.

Jonathan Pageau shares that his entry into iconography came while still a catechumen when his parents cut down a linden tree in their yard. "Right away, I was like: I'm going to make a blessing cross. But I had no tools. I basically had X-Acto knives."[17] Pageau and others today carve icons instead of painting them or creating mosaics. These images are still largely two-dimensional carvings that resemble icons, but without being painted. They serve the same function and use in homes and churches where they are used.

Respect is more important than the medium. Today many iconographers use acrylic or other paints. Modern paints are used because they are able to accomplish much of the same effect and durability as traditional mediums.

Saint Theodore the Studite, in his defense of icons, shows no preference for materials used. He speaks of stones, precious metals, pigments, and even sculpture as acceptable. The Council of a Hundred Chapters requires that the medium is appropriate but is otherwise left vague. The theology of the icon is not dependent upon what materials are used, but in what they are used for. Inappropriate mediums are simply those that detract from the respect and veneration due to the subject matter and not in affirming one technique or medium over another. As Fr Garrett reminds us, "at one time egg tempera was a new, untested material."[18]

Today many icons are mass produced or reproductions. There are many icon sites that print an image on paper or canvas and then mount them to boards. Much of the prayerful attention that was necessary in earlier construction of icons is still done with these much more affordable mounted icons. Many of these productions are done in monasteries or connected with a local church community, though others are business ventures to make icons more accessible to the Western audience where the desire for icons outpaces the number of skilled and trained iconographers. Still, many of these mounted icons are more expensive than some can afford, and icon cards are sold as well.

One may be inclined to say that a painted icon with traditional mediums is "more" of an icon than one painted with modern paints, or that a painted icon is more of an icon than one printed, or that a mounted print is more of an icon than a postcard, yet this is not the case. Just as the relative skill of the iconographer does not make the image more or less an icon, the medium does not limit the reception or use of an icon. There are even some wonder-working icons, as discussed in chapter 4, that are postcards. What makes the image an icon is how it is received and used in prayer. There are many beautifully hand-painted icons that are only art pieces and not icons because they are not instruments of prayer.

Icons as observed by Western audiences seem to have a traditional look, yet there is no distinctive rule concerning style, just as there is no rule concerning the medium. Ouspensky reminds us that, "There is no 'religious,' no 'church' style."[19] Many similarities do exist in what is understood to be an icon. Variations from those styles have been rejected or dismissed. Some icons have a distinctive ethnic feel. For instance, icons from Ethiopia, Persia, and India are easily identifiable as distinct from Greek icons. Greek and Russian icons have a greater degree of similarity. The images, while having an ethnic stylistic expression, are still universally accepted as icons.

The only style that was largely rejected by the Church was the overly realistic style of icons that came into use following Peter the Great in Russia. Peter instituted rules that icons should emulate Western art. For about two centuries Russian icons fell under the sway of Western realism and lost some of what made the icons distinctive. By becoming more realistic, the symbolic realism of the icon was obfuscated. Ouspensky states that "this 'distortion' is natural, or rather indispensable to express the content of the icon."[20] Fr Silouan Justiniano argues that "the current notions of 'realism' as pictorial ideology ignore, if not completely deny, that art is in fact ultimately symbolic and communicative, an interpretation of reality that carries a worldview, and not merely a neutral mirror of the world."[21]

The indispensable distortion of icons is usually dismissed by a Western audience. They appear to many as unsophisticated. The formalized positions and absence of emotion on the face does not elicit the same sort of response that one finds in Western religious art. Yet the mysterious and peaceful quality found in the faces does have a trait that when meditated upon reveals something else. The faces are typically much larger than you would expect, with the eyes larger still, expressing watchful attentiveness. The mouth is nearly always closed, even when someone is giving a message. The lips are drawn straight not presenting a smile yet conveying peace. The faces are not exaggerated to the point of cartoonish-ness but are a step beyond what is realistic and typical in Western art. Pentiuc maintains that these distortions "discourage the beholder from finding delight in the aesthetic beauty of the icon, while reminding one of a 'hidden' beauty to be fully revealed at the eschaton and now given only as a foretaste within the liturgical setting."[22] The body is refined in the icon. Icons reflect the transfigured state, not the natural one.

Icons affirm the goodness of matter while also directing the observer to an ultimate reality beyond that matter. Beyond Platonic *theoria*, the icon calls for participation through *theosis*. The icon is not simply intended to be observed but engaged with. As an object of engagement, icons are often called windows to heaven. The saint is glorified and asking for engagement. As iconographer Aidan Hart says, "Icon painters' perspective systems slap our rational minds out of their complacency."[23] This calls for greater engagement. Realism is limited compared to revelation.

This call for greater engagement is also present in icons through the use of reverse perspective, unlike traditional art where the vanishing point is placed in the background of the piece. From this perspective, items get smaller the farther away they are in the icon, as they do with any photograph. Some pieces of art have a linear perspective where there is no vanishing point. In these pieces of art nothing diminishes and typically there is either no background or a flat static background. Characteristic of icons, the vanishing point is the observer and icons seem to grow the deeper one goes into the background. This is known as reverse perspective. Since icons do not usually have many objects in the background, this perspective is most obvious when looking at books, chairs, footstools, and pedestals under a chair. One notices that the back is wider than the front. This technique is employed to invite the observer into participation, arguing that real life exists in the icon and that the icon is observing the person instead of the other way around. The use of reverse perspective is incorporated to personalize the encounter.

Reverse perspective is not universal in all icons but is a common feature of icons that have multiple people and some way of designating depth. This perspective also adds to the notion that icons are doors or windows to a world beyond the icon. Looking through a window, one would expect the world to grow beyond the frame of the window itself, and the same is true of the icon. Met Hilarion Alfeyev reminds us that reverse perspective can be found as early as the fourth century in the catacombs.[24]

One other fairly common but not universal trait among icons is the lack of shadow. Like the reverse perspective, the lack of shadow is employed to convey a deeper message. The message is that of light. Icons depict scenes that are awash with light. God becomes the source of light and covers all things as described in Revelation and Isaiah. Because God is the source of light, there is no need for a source of illumination, or for gradation of light as one moves further from this source. Light is therefore independent and often expressed by a golden color, and when possible, goldleaf is often applied. This allows for reflection and the light to shine from all around the object.

The perspective and lack of shadow are not universal but are both used to convey something extraordinary into the scene. Similar treatments are found with other objects placed into the icon. While many icons only have a single person, the objects that accompany the person are chosen deliberately because of the symbolic value that their inclusion signifies. Buildings are often limited in the background but are used to set the scene as belonging to a city. Trees point to the Tree of Life mentioned in Genesis and Revelation. Mountains signify revelation, standing for Sinai, Horeb, Zion, Tabor, or other significant mountains where one encounters God. Following Eliade, the use of a mountain "constitute[s] the pre-eminent 'link' between earth and heaven."[25]

The purpose of all things in icons is to convey a divine reality that exists beyond the mundane. Icons are less interested in mere representation and are focused more on this transformative cosmic connection. Fr Justiniano points out the icon "is a symbolic realism that speaks the truth by bypassing the tendency to fixate solely on sense perception."[26] Icons, to fulfill this functional aim, must also possess an aesthetic quality to them that continues to draw the observer into prolonged engagement. Icons must therefore be beautiful. As Pentuic says, "the aesthetic aim is functional."[27] The face shown must be attractive as well as dispassionate. The objects must be familiar yet somehow removed. Icons are simple yet elegant.

There is no noise or confusion in an icon, even when depicting scenes of chaos. The message of a saint is reduced to a beautiful expression of their life. They may hold a scroll, a book, a cross, or a church. The size of the object is not realistic. For example, icons of Saint Justinian may include him holding the Hagia Sophia. The great church of Constantinople is reduced to something carried by the saint. It is recognizable, and it is understood as his offering. The saint offered his life and brought this church as his gift back to God. Similar objects are found in Western saints, including icons of Saint Matilda, who holds a church, signifying her building many churches throughout the German lands. Other icons may possess objects that designate rank or position. Soldier saints such as George, Demetrios, and the Theodores (the General and the Recruit) show them holding a sword or spear, even though they laid down a sword and embraced martyrdom. Others have objects in the background demonstrating events of their life. A Western saint, Saint Gwen, is often depicted with a boat in the background, recalling her abduction by pirates and her journeys across the English Channel. Traditionally monastic saints including Basil the Great, Saint Sergius of Radonezh, and his disciple Saint Sylvester of Obnora are depicted holding scrolls instead of a monastery. These items as well as others are elegantly placed as signifiers about who the saint is. They are minimized in size and used to convey something about who the saint is and how one can relate to them. The objects are reduced, as they are not the important feature and do not want to diminish the beauty found in the icon.

The purpose of identifying the saint in icons was intensified after the iconoclastic controversy. Since the purpose of the icon was to transfer the veneration from the image to the prototype, clearly identifying the prototype is essential. A practice of inscribing the name of the saint upon the icon became normative. Typically, this is flanking the halo. The naming of the saint through writing the name grew to be the last act done on an icon after it was approved of. If the icon conveys a scene where multiple people are present or a great feast, the name of the feast was written on the icon. While this practice has obvious benefits, it is also not universally done. Many icons have no name attached to them. Earlier icons typically did not have any writing other than signifying Christ and the Theotokos. Christ can be identified through the IC XC outside the halo, or the letters O ΩN inside, these letters signifying Jesus Christ and the existing one.

## ARCHETYPICAL ICONS

There are many icons that we could discuss to help illustrate the symbolism inherent to icons. The first two I would like to discuss are archetypical icons from different eras. The first is possibly the oldest icon ever painted, and the second is identified as the pinnacle of Russian iconography. Both are famous works that are treated in great detail by numerous authors, and both reveal to us the nature of Orthodox icons.

## The Vladimir Theotokos

The first icon that we should consider is the oldest surviving icon of the Church. While the first icon is the Mandylion or the "image made without hands," the first icon made with hands was created by Saint Luke. Luke, who wrote the Gospel of Luke and the book of Acts also, is regarded as the first person to paint an icon in the Church. As a physician, Luke's understanding of the body was used in the creation of three icons of the Theotokos. According to tradition, Mary was present during the construction of these icons and when gazing upon them exclaimed, "May the grace, of him whom I bore and of myself be forever with these holy icons."[28] The three icons that Luke produced are the Smolensk-Hodigitria, the Virgin of the Sign, and the Protection of the Veil. Some hold that the Vladimir Theotokos, which is similar to the Smolensk icon, both being tenderness or mercy icons, was painted by Luke himself.[29] Others believe that it was a copy of Luke's icon. The icon is clearly done in an older Byzantine or Roman style. It made its way to Kiev, but in 1169, the icon was taken to the city of Vladimir, thus the name Vladimir Theotokos. It has served as a central icon in coronations of both tsars and patriarchs. It has also been copied several times, including a copy in the nave of St. Paul's Anglican Cathedral in London.

Besides possibly being the oldest surviving icon, the Vladmir Theotokos reveals a lot about the nature of icons for Orthodox Christians. The icon, like nearly every icon of Mary, is also an icon of Christ. Here Mary holds the Christ child on her lap, embracing him and gesturing toward him with her head and her hand. The focus of the icon moves from the Theotokos to Christ. Christ is robed in gold and presses his face upon Mary's, reciprocating the embrace.

The tenderness of the icon is complemented by a look of compassion, sorrow, and grief. Her face is peaceful, but also conveys the understanding of what will transpire for her son. She models love but also an awareness of the cost of that love. In the icon, Luke connects the joy and sorrow of Christ's entrance into the world in a similar way as he did with the presentation of Christ into the Temple as recorded in Luke 2. Here Luke records the prophecies given by the Righteous Simeon, prophecies that Christ is the salvation of the world, and a light to the Gentiles. Also, that Christ is destined for the fall and rising of many, and a sword will pierce Mary's own soul. Mary, while full of tenderness and love for her son, is also aware of what it costs and the sins of the world.

In the icon, Christ's eyes look toward Mary. He embraces and loves his mother, seeking to honor her. Her eyes look out to the person who is engaged with the icon. As the Theotokos, she is the bridge linking Christ to the world. Her glance is inviting and penetrating. Her eyes invite the spectator to engage with the icon and penetrate, urging them toward eternal life found in her son.

We also observe three stars upon Mary in the icon, one on the forehead and two on the shoulder, though one is obscured by Christ. These three stars are a common signifier of Mary in the icon and reveal her as ever-virgin. The stars stand for her virginity before the incarnation, during the incarnation, and afterward. Orthodox Christians speak of Joseph as betrothed to Mary, and not married. The union was not consummated nor was the second half of the wedding ceremony, as it is done today, concluded. Orthodox tradition holds that Joseph was already an old man when he agreed to be the husband of Mary, a widower with adult children. Joseph accepted the calling to marry Mary, who coming of age was too old to be in the temple, and to care for her. Joseph's sacrifice was caring for a young woman during a time where there was no honorable way of making a livelihood for single women.

Ever Virgin is one of many titles given to Mary by Orthodox Christians. Commonly she is referred to as the Panagia, all holy one. She is called the Queen of Heaven. She is also called the More Spacious One, in connection with Christ, who is uncontainable by the heavens but condescended to be carried by Mary, making her womb more spacious than the heavens. Stars were placed upon her garment not simply because they are an easy identifier but in connection to Mary's role as the chief intercessor to her son. Stars are often connected with the heavens, and Mary's place there is manifested through the symbolism of the stars. As the Panagia, the Theotokos, Mary reveals her compassion and intercession for those who approach her icon. The Vladimir Theotokos reveals all of this because the image unites the observer to her.

## Andrei Rublev's Icon of the Trinity

The icon that is often most discussed in and outside the Church is Andrei Rublev's icon of the Hospitality of Abraham or it is sometimes referred to as Rublev's Trinity. Andrei Rublev is Russia's greatest iconographer. Dennis Sardella, docent at the Museum of Russian Icons in Clinton, Massachusetts, considers Rublev to be "the greatest iconographer of the medieval era."[30] Fairly little is known about the life of Rublev, other than at a young age he sought out Sergius of Radonezh and entered the Holy Trinity Monastery founded by Saint Sergius.

Saint Sergius was the exemplar of Russian monasticism. In the fourteenth century, Sergius removed himself from Moscow and set up a small chapel dedicated to the Holy Trinity. As others attached themselves to Sergius, his cell and chapel grew into the monastery. Even though he preferred isolation, Sergius's fame grew, and his monastic rule spurred on other monasteries all over Russia. Saint Sergius also advised Prince Dimitri in his struggle against the Tatar oppression, and his prayers before the battle of Kulikovo are credited for the first decisive victory of the Russians over the Tartars in 1380. Sergius reposed in 1392. It was in honor of Saint Sergius that Rublev began his most famous icon.

Andrei Rublev left Saint Sergius and was tonsured a monk by Saint Andronik. Shortly thereafter, he began to study iconography. The formative training for Rublev came in 1405, when he assisted the master Constantinopolitan iconographer Theophanes the Greek while working with him on the Annunciation Cathedral in the Kremlin. From here, Rublev painted frescoes in the Dormition Cathedral in Vladimir and elsewhere. Eventually, somewhere around 1425, he returned to Saint Sergius's Holy Trinity monastery to restore the chapel that was destroyed by Tartars in 1408.

In reconstructing the iconostasis, Rublev painted the Old Testament epiphany of Christ at the Oak of Mamre as recorded in Genesis 18. This was interpreted through Saint Sergius's vision of the event. The icon is not a new innovation in the Church. Bogdan Bucur points out that commentaries surrounding this encounter go back to Philo, who "sees in the mysterious guests 'the Father of the universe' and his accompanying two powers, the creative power and the royal one."[31] For Philo, these are not three distinct entities but one ineffable God, consistent with both Philo's Judaism and his Middle Platonism. Early Christianity took from Philo an interpretation of this event as an epiphany of Christ accompanied by two angels. Early iconographic representation of the event has the middle figure illumined and therefore clearly identified as Christ.

It was only under Origen that we begin to see a reorientation of the event to illustrate the Trinity. Origen's phrase "Abraham saw three, but worshiped only one,"[32] was used to transform the interpretation of the event. The reorientation of Genesis 18 from Christological to Trinitarian was not complete by the time that Rublev painted his icon. As such, it is important to note that the placement of the icon upon the iconostasis is not in the location of the feast of the church (outside of the icon of the Theotokos); instead, it is placed in the position of the icon of Christ. Rublev masterfully unites the earlier interpretive traditions concerning who exactly was present with Abraham at the Oak of Mamre. There is no clear identification of any figure as Christ by placing a cross in the halo. All three are made equal, allowing for both understandings. The three divine figures are then located positionally on the iconostasis as Christ instead of the festal icon. Theologically this confirms that all we know about the divine is through our experiences of Christ.

The icon is rather simple yet profound. Rublev speaks volumes by what he chooses to omit in the icon. Unlike other icons of the event, Abraham, Sarah, and a servant are absent. Instead, only three figures are present. Each of the three-winged figures have the same face and is holding a staff. Each of the three have identical halos. The similarity between the figures helps advance the notion of equality, and that they are different persons of the same singular God. If one were to draw a circle around the backs of the figures, there is a circle that moves in a counterclockwise direction. This circle, we are told by Ousepensky, echoes the words of Saint Dionysius:

> According to whose interpretation circular movement signifies that God remains identical with Himself that He envelops in synthesis the intermediate parts and the extremities, which are at the same time containers and contained, and that He recalls to Himself all that has gone forth from Him.[33]

This circle is formed around one central object. This is the only object left upon the table, a chalice containing the head of a calf. Knives and bread that are found in earlier icons of this event are removed. Rublev maintains the killing of the fatted calf but removes the separate measures of bread. Unity is affirmed around the chalice, demonstrating unity and the centrality of the Eucharist in the communal life of the Church.

The garments and positions of the three angelic figures, along with what is behind them, separate them from one another. The central figure has a red robe covered with a blue cloak which is typical of icons of Christ. The red and blue signify Christ's humanity and divinity. This figure is also reaching its hand toward the chalice on the table, extending a blessing. Since this chalice is to remind one of the Eucharist, this blessing would affirm Christ's presence in the Eucharist. Behind the central figure is a tree. This tree connects the story of the Oak of Mamre to Christ as the tree of life.

The figure to the right is blue and green. Green is often the color associated with the Holy Spirit. This figure reaches its hand out toward the chalice, but not in the blessing as the central figure. This signifies that the Holy Spirit is what moves one toward receiving the Eucharist. Above this figure is a mountain. This mountain, like all holy mountains, stands for Sinai and Tabor, the giving of the law as well as the Transfiguration.

On the opposite side is a figure wearing blue and covered in gold. This figure would be God the Father, the most radiant of the three. It is to this figure as well that the other two incline their heads, signifying that they are giving this figure, not the central one, honor. This is a key indication that this is not an icon of Christ and two angels, but of the Trinity. Behind this figure is a building with an open door. This signifies not a city or even Abraham's domicile, but the Church. The open door demonstrates that any and all can approach God.

If one looks inside the body of the outside figures, another chalice is formed, placing the head of the central figure in the chalice. This again is a reference to the Eucharist and the partaking of Christ. The icon is as much an icon of Christ as it is of the Trinity, and as it is of the Eucharist. The Eucharist is in the center of the icon, and the Christ figure is made the Eucharist in the icon as well. Temple and others point out that this icon is indicative of the Hesychasm that was developing in Russia under Sergius and that was central to the religious life of Rublev. Temple states that in this piece and other hesychastic icons we see "the outward expression in physical matter of an inner spiritual state of union with the divine. Its characteristics in icons are silence and stillness, presence, natural unagitated rhythms and interior luminosity."[34]

Florensky, who died a martyr's death under the Soviets, expresses his understanding of this icon with great admiration. "The most persuasive philosophic proof of God's existence is the one the textbooks never mention, the conclusion to which can perhaps best express the whole meaning: There exists the icon of the Holy Trinity by St. Andrei Rublev; therefore, God exists."[35] The beauty of the icon is itself an epiphany of Christ and points one toward a life beyond contemplation and toward *theosis*.

## MODERN ICONS

While Saint Luke's Vladimir Theotokos and Rublev's Trinity are archetypical icons, many more icons exist that can further demonstrate the interpretation and use of icons for Orthodox Christians today. The following selections are all icons produced by the same modern iconographer, Fr Matthew Garrett. They each demonstrate some additional understanding of icons that will elucidate different aspects of an icon. I have selected seven icons that high-light something unique to that particular icon and yet something common to icons in general. These are the Annunciation, Christ's Nativity, Saint John the Forerunner, Theophany, Transfiguration paired with a discussion of the Bridegroom, and an icon of the Resurrection.

### The Annunciation

One icon that is found in every Orthodox Church is of the Annunciation. Like the other major feasts, this icon will typically be displayed somewhere and brought out on the feast. Unlike the other major feasts, this icon is also found on the royal doors of the iconostasis. Its location on the doors sets this feast

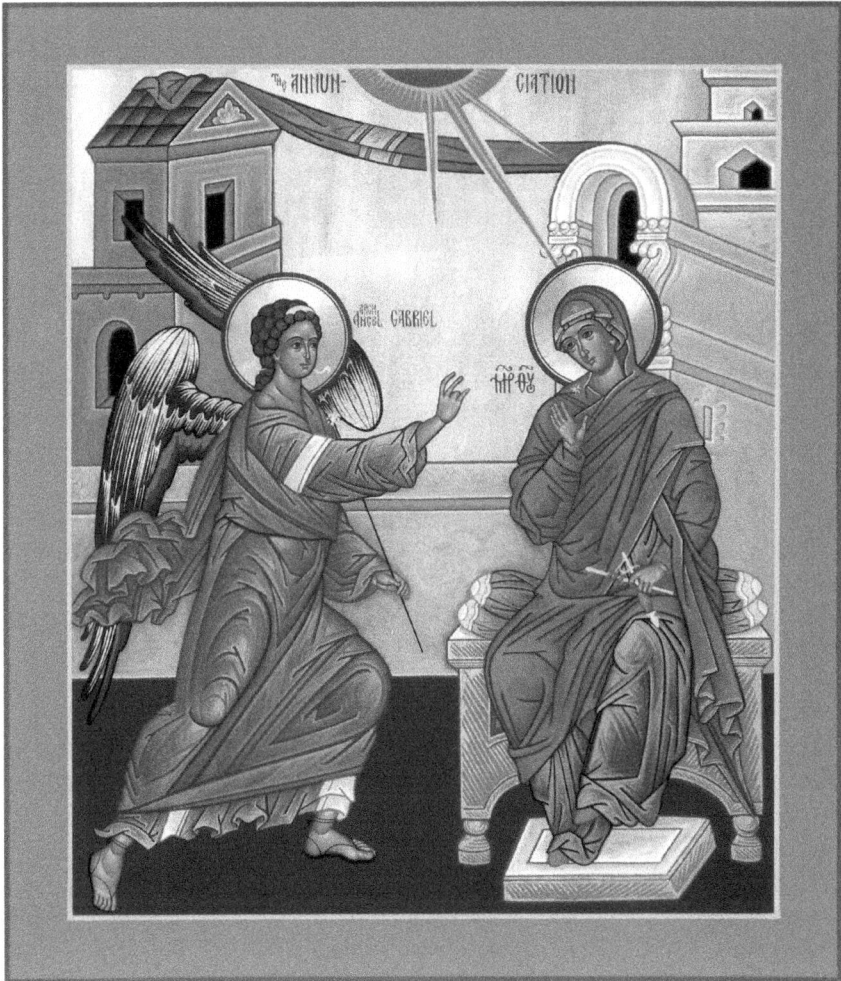

**Figure 8.1.  Icon of the Annunciation.** *By Fr Matthew Garrett*

apart from the others, as it serves a liturgical function as well as one commemorating an event.

The icon and feast commemorate when the archangel Gabriel announced to Mary that she was to give birth to Christ, the long-awaited Messiah, and her God. For the Orthodox Church, the feast is rather significant. As Saint Proclus, Patriarch of Constantinople, remarks, "He Who, in His essence did not have a mother chose His servant as Mother."[36] He adds that the feast is also "a praise of women."[37] God, who cannot be contained by the universe was contained in the womb of Mary, who as Mother of God, Theotokos, became "more spacious than the heavens."

The feast takes place on 25 March. The date for the Annunciation was picked because it was likely the day in which Christ was crucified and there was an ancient belief that important people were born on or conceived on the day on which they died. The date 25 March corresponds with the 14th of Nisan, the day before the feast of Passover, also commemorated by Christians as Good Friday. The event of the Annunciation is primarily recorded in the Gospel of Luke, with slight mention in Matthew and not in the other two Gospels, in keeping with their nativity narratives.

The placement of the icon on the Royal Doors of the iconostasis serves the purpose of signifying the coming of Christ. Furthermore, its location signifies that the doors of paradise, as the altar signifies heaven, were opened by Mary's acceptance. The doors are closed before the Liturgy and depending on jurisdiction they are closed during certain times of the liturgy as well. The opening and closing of the doors symbolize the activity of heaven making its way into earth, and this is all done through participation in this event. These doors always contain an icon of this event but may include other icons as well. The most common icons that will be found on the doors in addition to the Annunciation are the four Evangelists.

In the icon, we see two prominent figures, Mary and the Archangel Gabriel. The positions and postures of these two are rather striking. Gabriel the Archangel is depicted with his legs in stride as if he is running toward the Theotokos. He holds a staff signifying that he is a messenger, typically held by angels in icons. His hand is lifted up giving a blessing to Mary. Mary on the other hand is typically depicted seated. When seated, Mary's pedestal is clearly illustrated with the reverse perspective; it grows the farther in it goes. Her hands show both confusion and acceptance. The one in the air calls to mind the question of "how can this be since I do not know a man," while the one on her breast signifies her acceptance. Her head may also be inclined toward the Angel signifying acceptance as well.

In one or both of Mary's hands is a scarlet cord. This recalls her earlier life as recorded in the Protoevangelium of James where she served in the temple by knitting the temple veil. The contrast between making a veil which separated the Holy of Holies from the rest of the sanctuary and herself becoming the instrument where that veil was finally rent is intentional. Often icons will include with the yarn a spindle and needles to help drive this connection even more, though sometimes only the cord is present.

The eyes of Mary and Gabriel are typically not looking toward each other, nor directly to the spectator, but upward. Their eyes are toward a blue sphere at the top center of the icon. This sphere is symbolic for the high heavens, the dwelling place of God. From this, a ray shines forth upon Mary. This calls to mind the descent of the Holy Spirit upon Mary at this moment and the incarnation. Some icons depict an infant Christ already in the womb of Mary to further illustrate this point, though the rays and a cursory understanding of the Annunciation are sufficient to alert the observer that Christ is present in this icon as well. The ray that emits from the sphere is typically represented with three lines signifying the Trinity, though not always. Often there is a dove present in the ray, also demonstrating that this is the activity of the Holy Spirit, but not always. The Holy Spirit is described as descending like a dove in scripture, but doves are not universally connected with the Holy Spirit. Many also point out that a dove should not be present since the Holy Spirit is not a dove.

Even with the attention toward the orb, we have the full faces of both Gabriel and Mary present to us in the icon. We are spectators but also the audience of the icon. Halos surround both faces. In the icon, Mary's robe is blue and her outer cloak is red. This is reverse of what is common for icons of Christ. On Mary's cloak, we have the three stars signifying her ever virginity. The color signification is largely a later development and has no single statement corresponding to how they should be interpreted. Blue, as the color of the sky, is used by many to signify divinity as we already saw in Rublev's Trinity. Signifying the heavens, blue is connected to Mary, who is more spacious than the heavens. As Mary is where Christ takes his humanity from, blue can also be used to signify humanity in general. Often red signifies blood and therefore life. This life has its source in God. Red can signify both biological and divine life, humanity and divinity. The two primary colors can mean both humanity and divinity depending on usage. The important connection is made that upon the iconostasis Mary is blue covered in red, while Christ is red covered in blue. In this setting, blue signifies humanity and Mary is covered in red, in divinity. Christ is divine and is incarnate or robed in humanity. While colors are not universally applied to one specific meaning, their relationship is often used to signify a connection or deeper import.

Other colors that are often found in icons also have some typical usages. Gold is used to demonstrate divinity and radiant light. Purple maintains the connection to the ancient usage of royalty. White is used for purity and the robes of martyrs. White can also be used to signify the divine light, thus in many resurrection and post-resurrection icons of Christ He is also clothed in white. Green is often connected with the Holy Spirit as mentioned earlier, as it signifies life and growth. Many icons in the Middle East do not use green as often because of its association with Islam. Brown conversely signifies the earth and the perishable nature of things. Black is used to denote darkness, often death, both physical and spiritual. Gray is rarely ever used in large measure because it is rather vague. The color classification that modern iconographers incorporate is a fairly new innovation. Largely it is a result of icons migrating into countries that were not traditionally Orthodox. Color classifications held greater meaning in Western art and in an attempt to communicate to this new audience, that language was incorporated into the icon. It is as a result of Western usage that we have a standard meaning connected with the colors in icons. The earliest icons of the church did not subscribe to any formal conception of color.

## Christ's Nativity

Exactly nine months after the Annunciation is the celebration of Christ's Nativity. There are many different types of Nativity icons, some of which are rather simple. They focus in on the cave where Christ is born and have only Christ, Mary, Joseph, and rarely anyone or anything else. Typically, icons of the Nativity are more complex than this. There are many different events taking place, each adding to the occasion of Christ's birth, and drawing us into deeper understanding of how the Church interprets the coming of Christ.

In the broader icon of the Nativity, we can begin at the top. Like the icon of the Annunciation, we have a blue sphere shining down a ray of light toward the center of the icon. This symbolizes heaven and the presence of God the Father sending the Holy Spirit. This icon is also an icon that signifies the Trinity, the corporate act of God the Father and the Spirit in the sending of the Son. In the center of the icon, the ray rests upon the infant Christ. We can recognize this is Christ because of the cross in his halo even as a newborn. Christ radiates His divinity, which he had from birth, contrary to Nestorius.

Christ has a unique halo. Inside the halo is the shape of a cross and the letters O ΩN. These letters signify the name of God as revealed to Moses, the Existing One. The cross connects Christ's entire life, even in His Nativity, with the salvation that comes from his suffering of the cross. Christ's halo is the only one that ever has anything inside of it. Everyone else's halo is empty. This is done to signify that Christ is the source of His own illumination, while everyone else shines as a reflection of their closeness to God. Stylistically there are some exceptions, where stars or filigree may be added into some halos as an artistic expression and to add beauty to the icon. Yet these images are not seen as something that radiates from the saint or angel in the same way as Christ's cross in His halo does.

Christ is wrapped in swaddling clothes as an infant, laying in a manger inside a cave. This not only records the event but also demonstrates that Christ came covered in humanity and all the frailty of a newborn. Christ, while remaining divine, is also entirely made man. This central image affirms Chalcedonian Christology. Next to Christ are two animals, the ox and ass. These animals are not mentioned in the Gospels but are mentioned in Isaiah. Their presence signifies that Christ came to fulfill the prophecies of the Old Testament. He was born on this divine mission and not somehow later selected to become the Messiah as the heresies of Apollinaris and others

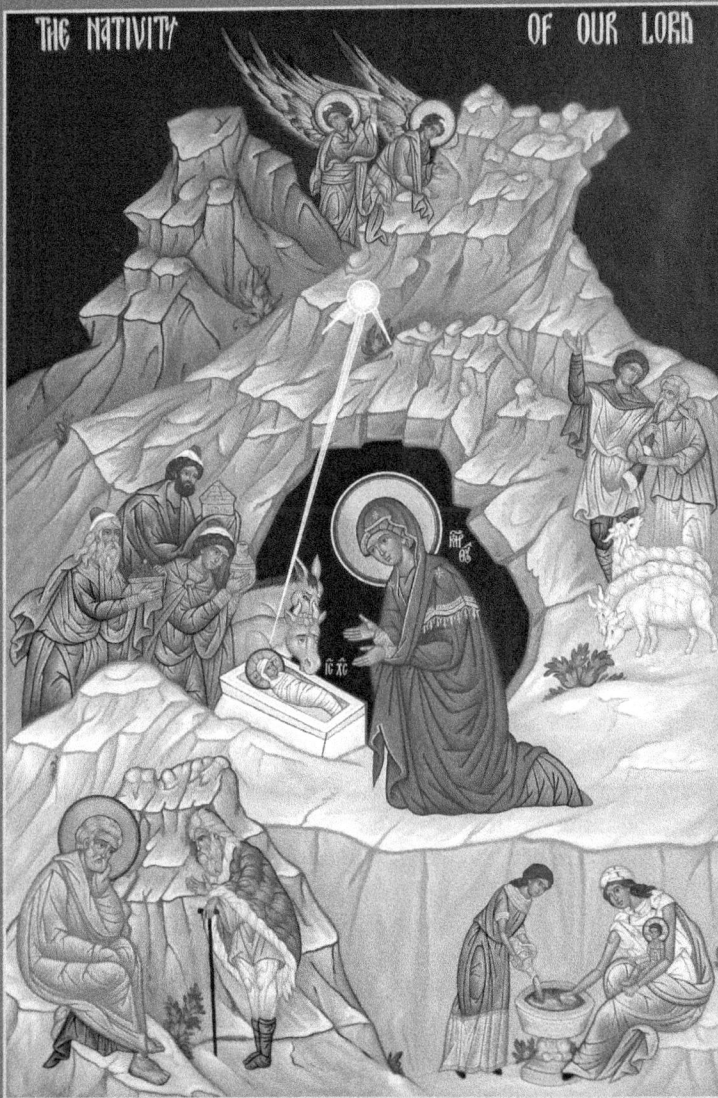

**Figure 8.2.   Icon of the Nativity of Christ.** *By Fr Matthew Garrett*

supposed. They also signify that just as man's fall had consequences for the animals and the totality of creation, so too does Christ's redemption.

Christ and the animals are found resting inside a cave. The cave has multiple meanings. Ouspensky, drawing upon Gregory of Nyssa, sees the black
mouth of the cave as symbolic of this world "stricken with sin through man's
fault, in which 'the Sun of truth' shone forth."[38] The darkness of the cave
is symbolic of a world given over to sin and death. This demonstrates that
Christ is found in the fallen world and is truly present in it. Christ in the cave
wrapped in swaddling clothes also prefigures Christ's burial in a cave. The
beginning and end of Christ's earthly ministry share him wrapped and placed
in a cave.

Jonathan Pageau interprets the cave in a slightly different light. For
Pageau, "The cave is the ultimate protection, a hidden place within the earth
in which people can find refuge against extreme hostility."[39] Pageau looks at
the prophets in the Old Testament that were hidden from opposition in the
caves including Obadiah, Elijah, and David. In the cave, we not only have the
threat of death but also a source of protection. Christ and the animals come in
death but are shielded in part.

From a Platonic view, we have addressed the significance of the cave holding both interpretations; one is bound in the cave, and yet is protected from
the rays of light. It is only by emerging from the cave that one encounters the
truth and can truly live. This is the case for a Christian reading of the icon as
well. One must emerge from the cave to truly abide in Christ.

Next to Christ immediately outside of the cave is the Theotokos. She is
reclining next to the newborn Christ, affirming her dependence upon Him
and that one rests in Christ. This also signifies that Christ was born of Mary
and not somehow appearing outside of this process. Mary being outside the
cave, or more accurately on the threshold of the cave, demonstrates that she
is already undergoing the transformative effects of the incarnation. She abides
in Christ and is redeemed through her participation with Him. Christ, Mary,
and the animals and their relation to the cave, symbolize the redemption of
Christ as central to the activity that surrounds the center of the icon.

As one moves from the cave outward, different scenes are present, each
adding something to the Nativity account. Met Hilarion Alfeyev tells us
that "Icons reflect the liturgical life and experience of the Church. As in
the liturgy, the boundary between past, present, and future is wiped away in
icons."[40] Events that took place over months or even centuries could all be
made present in a single icon. In the Nativity icon, we have four or five different periods of time present. In the center and above we have Christ's birth
and the angels celebrating His birth. The angels are directing their attention
toward Christ, though some also direct their attention toward the sphere,
showing that all of heaven rejoices over this event.

Flanking Christ on the outside of the icon, we have the shepherds marvel-
ing over Christ's birth. Usually this is signified by one or many shepherds

who may have musical instruments, demonstrating an act of praise and one or many sheep to signify their earthly vocation. Opposite the shepherds are the wise men who came bearing gifts from afar. The shepherds and the wise men were not both present at the same time, and likely by the time the wise men approached, Christ was also not still in the manger in Bethlehem. Despite this historical fact, they are made present at the birth in the icon. The presence of both shepherds and wise men holds another layer of significance. The Jewish shepherds and the Gentile wise men demonstrate that Christ's Nativity was for all people. Christ's salvation came first to the Jews and then to the Gentiles. Christ came to save the poor and the rich; those who have trained and studied and those who have not. They are also of different ages, demonstrating that Christ came to save people from every generation, each bringing a gift from their talents, and each able to approach God.

Below these, two more scenes are made present that happened before and after Christ's Nativity. To one side is a scene where we see a woman holding a baby and a bath. If one looks closely at this baby, they can identify that inside the halo is the cross. This baby is Christ. Christ receiving a bath by a midwife after birth signifies that his birth was natural. Just like all other newborns, he needed to be cleansed.

On the opposite side, we have an image of two old men. One of these old men has a halo and the other does not. The one with the halo is Saint Joseph the betrothed, and the other is the devil. This marks Joseph's doubt concerning Mary's divine conception. His halo signifies that Joseph is righteous and overcame this doubt. Joseph wrestles with the natural understanding that a virgin cannot give birth, that what is taking place is not possible. The halo shows that with God all things are possible. Joseph is also not present with Mary at the threshold of the cave. This is done to signify that he is not the father of the child. Mary's gaze in most Nativity icons is also directed toward Joseph, not to the newborn Christ. She abides in Christ but is praying for Joseph.

Joseph's engagement with the devil and his overcoming the devil recalls the temptation of Adam and Eve in the Garden. While Adam and Eve failed, Joseph and Mary overcame their temptations of doubt and fear. In the Garden, Eve led to the temptation of Adam. In the icon of the Nativity, we have Mary interceding for Joseph. Mary as the new Eve helps to bring salvation, not sin. This event took place well before the birth but is brought into this icon to demonstrate the supernatural occurrence of the Nativity of Christ.

It is also important to note the Joseph is an old man. Until the Middle Ages, Joseph was universally depicted as an old man. Fr David Moser points out that "he was already eighty years old, and according to the Great Menaion of St Dimitri of Rostov he lived to be 110."[41] This put his death right before Jesus's public ministry and would explain why he is then absent from any biblical accounts at this time. According to Metropolitan Isaiah of Denver, around the time of the Southern Renaissance the West began to depict Joseph as a younger man and place him with Mary, creating the image of the holy family. This served a pedagogical purpose to unite families in the West but was an abandonment of the traditional understanding of Joseph's role as protector of Mary's virginity and Christ as a youth. The East maintained the understanding that Joseph the Betrothed was a widower who had already had several children, all of whom were older than Mary. Joseph had tremendous trust in God and is a model of faithfulness.

The Nativity icon demonstrates that icons can serve more than one story. The depth of meaning found is not just based upon the use of color or motions but also in arrangement. This arrangement can include events that are not contemporary but are connected. The symbolic understanding from these connections serves as a better guide than any narrative can. The focus of the image can shift from one account to another while returning back to the central focus that is Christ. Icons exhibit a revelation beyond appearance and toward an ultimate reality. Unlike Plato, this is toward ultimate union and participation, not mere contemplation.

## Saint John the Forerunner and Baptist

This transformation to ultimate union with God is found in icons of Saint John the Forerunner, as he is known primarily in the East. In the West, John is called the Baptist. While both titles are appropriate, the connection of John as the forerunner of Christ speaks about the purpose behind his actions of baptizing people in the Jordan. John was called to prepare the way and to testify to Christ. Icons of Saint John depict a perfected image of a saint doing just that.

When icons depict saints, they present them in a glorified state. This does not always directly correspond to how they would have appeared while alive. Bodies are typically trimmed down, demonstrating the value of asceticism over complacency. Features that may elicit the passions are muted or disappear entirely. Clothes are added, modesty is encouraged. This is clearly seen in icons of Saint Mary of Egypt, who is robed, even though the story of Zosimas encountering her accentuates the fact that her clothing had disintegrated due to her life in the harsh desert. Clothing covers the body and does not accentuate the contours of the body; rather, the clothing marks the body symbolically. Icons show the destination of the saint. Eyes are larger and the mouths are smaller. The face appears to be peaceful even when what is depicted may have been a moment of extreme torment or pleasure. This is also why the main figure is depicted in a posture of stillness rather than motion. This is all done to demonstrate that they are free from sin. In the icon,

Figure 8.3. Icon of John the Forerunner. *Fr Matthew Garrett*

the saint who is made in the image of God returns to their prototype which is Christ.

In the icon of John the Forerunner, we have extremely thin limbs and a gaunt neck. His body is covered with a robe made of hair. His own hair is spiky, erratic, and disheveled. John's appearance is one of an extreme ascetic, showing him as both a wild man and as a man with extreme dignity. John is positioned in a wild place to accentuate his life outside of society, often in a desert or on mountains. Yet even outside of society, John remains dignified. This dignity often includes John possessing a pair of wings. Lossky tells us that the pair of wings lend to the motif that he is a messenger akin to the angels. John is a "terrestrial angel and a celestial man."[42]

John stands facing the blue sphere, or a cloud in this icon, found in the upper corner. In the sphere or on the clouds is Christ extending a blessing to John, who is gesturing toward Christ. John as the Forerunner points toward Christ in all that he does. Christ also called John the greatest of all men. The Church honors John as the greatest of the Old Testament prophets and places an icon of him on the iconostasis next to Christ. John is a symbol of repentance and new life; consequently, the outer cloak of John is typically green in recent icons.

In the icon, John holds a scroll that is unraveled. The scroll signifies the prophetic message that the saint possesses. Since John is not speaking, the scroll may be opened to spell out the message that encompasses the saint. For John, it is the call for repentance. This call is amplified by an ax in a tree or bush found in nearly all icons of John. The ax at the root of the tree signifies that every tree that does not bring forth fruit will be chopped down. It is fairly common that martyrs have the instrument of their martyrdom incorporated into their icon. For example, icons of Saint Katherine regularly have a torture wheel in the background. While John was beheaded, the ax here is not symbolic of his death but his message. John's death is shown with his head placed on a platter near his feet in the icon. With one head resting in a platter, we see the earthly fate of John. With the other head, we have his life both on the earth and in heaven, as one approaching Christ.

## Theophany

John the Forerunner is also present at icons of Christ's baptism. Icons of Epiphany or Theophany demonstrate Christ's transformation of the world. Theophany is one of the oldest feasts of the Church and it culminates the twelve days of Christmas. This feast highlights that not only did Christ come into the world but that He came into the world for the purpose of transforming it. In the feast, the worship of the Trinity is made manifest, as the center of the icon demonstrates. At the top is the blue sphere representing the Father.

**Figure 8.4. Icon of Theophany.** *By Fr Matthew Garrett*

Halfway down is the dove representing the Holy Spirit and in the center is Christ.

Christ, during His baptism, is not shown under the water; rather, Christ is above the water. This signifies that unlike other baptisms where water covers a person to cleanse the person, at Theophany it is the water that is cleansed by Christ. All of creation is made clean by Christ's incarnation and ministry; creation is set in order. The water is flanked by mountains, presenting an image of Christ in a cave. This cave signifies his death and burial, connecting baptism with death. Christ above the waters also shows that He is risen, and that baptism is also a new birth, connecting this cave with the cave at Christ's Nativity. Just as with icons of Christ upon the cross, He is mostly naked. This demonstrates that He was a man, thereby affirming the incarnation.

Christ is also the only person in the water. John stands on one shore and angels on the other. John reaches out toward Christ, demonstrating that he is baptizing Christ, but with a posture of humility. It is Christ who with his right hand blesses the water, not John. The angels hold clothes and are attendants serving Christ.

Depending on the icon, the scene may contain many different elements in addition to those already mentioned. The ax at the root of a tree is often found near John's feat, confirming his message. Sometimes apostles are also present at the event. In some icons, animals are also present in and around the water. Often, two small water creatures are seen fleeing from Christ. Sometimes they resemble fish or dragons. Other times, they are ridden upon by diminutive figures. These represent the demonic powers of the water that flee in the presence of Christ and recall that the Jordan itself turned back at Christ's baptism, a reference to Psalm 113.

### The Transfiguration and the Bridegroom

Two icons depict the different aspects of who Christ is for Orthodox Christians. They demonstrate His powerful divinity and His humanity. These icons are the Transfiguration and the Bridegroom. The first shows Christ coming in glory. The second demonstrates His humility. Both demonstrate different aspects of His earthly mission.

The feast of the Transfiguration is one of the most important feasts of the Church and one of the oldest. The event is the highpoint of Christ's ministry prior to Holy Week in the Synoptic Gospels. It is the event which allowed the disciples even in fear to still gather and allowed them ultimately to interpret and accept the resurrection. According to Bunge in his work on this icon,

> This metamorphosis of our Lord on Mount Thabor encompasses and explicates core Christian beliefs; early Christian sources viewed it as the event that solved doctrinal disputes, explained the continuity of the Scriptures, and clarified how human beings united with God, both here on earth an in the hereafter.[43]

The Transfiguration is the event recorded in Matthew, Mark, and Luke when Christ takes Peter, James, and John to Mount Tabor. While on Tabor, Christ reveals His glory in proportion as the disciples can bear it. Alongside Christ, Moses and Elijah are present.

Figure 8.5. Icon of Transfiguration of Christ. *By Fr Matthew Garrett*

The icon focuses our attention on Christ who fulfills the Law and the Prophets, as well as being the God of the living and the dead. As Saint John of Damascus states, "On this mountain the resurrection of the dead is confirmed, and Christ is revealed as Lord of dead and living: summoning Moses from the dead, bringing down Elijah, still alive as witness."[44] Additionally, Moses represents the law, while Elijah embodies the prophets. The icon displays the three disciples falling back away from the transfigured Christ, with only Peter reaching toward Christ asking Him if they should build a tabernacle. In the words of Gregory Palamas, "Christ assumes nothing foreign, nor does he take on a new state, but he simply reveals to his disciples what he is."[45]

Unlike other icons where God is revealed with a sphere on the top of the icon with rays shining from it, in this icon we have the mandorla behind Christ. There are three main types of mandorlas that are represented in icons of the Transfiguration. The round mandorla is found as early as the sixth century in the Rabbula Gospel. The circular mandorla connects with the symbolism of the Hellenic world at the time, that the universe was round. We have a similar connection with the use of the dome in church architecture. The metaphoric use of the circle behind Christ places Him at the focal point of heaven itself. Christ opens the door to paradise. Bunge maintains that this round mandorla provides a solution of representing the Jewish concept of *Kabod*, or glory, to a Hellenic audience. It combines some Greek concepts as well. It resembles the sun, a sign of divinity. The typical use of eight rays emanating from the body of Christ further connected Christ to this theme, identifying Christ as the Sun of Justice. In this style of mandorla, Moses and Elijah are also at least partially enveloped by the mandorla. This was the dominant mandorla between the ninth and eleventh century.

The oval mandorla was preferred between the eleventh and the fourteenth centuries. The oval, or potentially almond shaped, mandorla is present in the sixth century as well. We have an example of its use at Saint Catherine's Monastery of Mount Sinai. This mandorla narrows the focus onto Christ instead of including Moses and Elijah. This helps to explain that Christ is the source of the light instead of being a part of the light, signifying that He is the glory of God. Often it is painted with a pale blue or golden color to try to demonstrate the radiance of the white light that shone. This mandorla surrounds Christ and comes from every part of Him. The preference of the oval mandorla instead of the round mandorla was likely due to concerns raised by the iconoclasts. By limiting the mandorla to Christ specifically, the focus on representing Christ's divinity could be asserted.

Following the Hesychastic controversy between Gregory Palamas and Barlaam of Calabria, a new mandorla was preferred. The Hesychastic Mandorla was first used between 1370 and 1375, in an illumination from the manuscript of former Emperor and then monk John VI Kantakouzenos. John was a supporter of Palamas and took up the cause of Hesychasm by renouncing his throne and dedicating his life to prayer. The mandorla has two superimposed concave squares inside of a circle. In many ways, this mandorla uses the symbolism of both the oval and the circle. The circle maintains its symbolic depiction of the heavenly realm, and the two squares show Christ as the source of the light, in a similar way that the oval mandorla did. The eight points connects with the earlier symbolism that Christ is the Sun of Justice. The eight points also speak to the resurrection and the life on the eighth day, the Lord's day.

Recently, the Hesychast mandorla is depicted with slight variations. Instead of two squares over a circle, triangles or others similar shapes may be present. In whatever depiction the three overlapping shapes possess a round or oval background, bringing with them the earlier understanding of the cosmos. Additionally, the two identical but offsetting geometric shapes help advance a trinitarian understanding of the divine light. They also focus the source of light to Christ like the oval mandorla does. As such, the Hesychast mandorla in the earlier or more modern form incorporates the symbolism of both earlier mandorlas and adds to it a trinitarian source.

For both the oval mandorla and the Hesychast Mandorla, the use of light is a reference to the uncreated light of God. As Arch. Vasileios states, "The light in an icon is not of the present age. It does not come from outside to give light in passing. An uncreated light that knows no evening, like the grace and the gift of the Holy Spirit is shed from within the icon itself, from the faces of the saints and transfigured creation."[46] This light, which is attested to by hesychastic mystics, is the aim of *theosis*. Bunge states,

> This glow of the transfigured body eventually came to signify the negation of dualism and monism at the same time Christ's and ours. The resurrected body has its place in our postmortem future, but as the Transfiguration of Christ and the transfigurations of the saints show clearly, it is a body of glory in harmony with the spirit.[47]

The event of Christ's Transfiguration is a prototype for others and affirms the Palamite position that expands upon Dionysius and others, that we know God not through God's essence but through God's uncreated energy. Symeon the New Theologian describes his own experience of this divine illumination when he says, "The man whose soul is all on fire also transmits the glory attained internally to his body, just as a fire transfers its heat to iron."[48] John of Damascus, in his Oration on the Transfiguration, also connects the telos of man, *theosis*, with the symbolism found in this feast. John concludes his sermon declaring that, "If Adam had not sought after divinization before the right moment he would have gained what he yearned for."[49] The feast and the

Figure 8.6. Icon of Christ the Bridegroom. *By Fr Matthew Garrett*

icon of the Transfiguration serve as a pledge of future transformation. It demonstrates the uncreated light of Christ and union with God through this light.

While the icon of the Transfiguration models the telos for the Christian life, and Christ in His glory, the icon of the bridegroom demonstrates Christ's humility. The bridegroom services, held on the first three days of Holy Week during Matins, center around this icon. In the icon, we see Christ with a crown of thorns upon His head, holding a reed in His bound hands, and wearing a purple or scarlet robe. This icon is the only icon that shows Christ suffering. Other icons, including those of Christ on the cross, show Him downcast or already dead, but little or no emotion is present upon His face. Several bridegroom icons also show Christ with a serene look instead of one of a man who just underwent torture. Icons avoid depictions of suffering as they do not seek to provoke only an emotional response from the viewer but one that draws deeper levels of engagement.

Christ is shown here to be a man about to go to His death. Christ in this icon is a man of sorrow. Yet on Christ's face we can still see that this is done willingly, that the ropes binding His hands, hold Him only voluntarily. The reed, robe, and crown that were placed upon Christ were done out of mockery and are truly symbols of His love for mankind and His coronation as king. In the ancient world, the bridegroom would clothe his guests for the wedding feast. The garments that Christ provides his guests are the garments of light as mentioned on Tabor. The bridegroom icon reveals that while the garments that we provide are an instrument of scorn, Christ retains His kingly visage. It is through this act that Christ gains His bride the Church. In taking the Church as His bride, we see not Christ's glory but His humility.

## Resurrection

The icon typically used by Orthodox Christians of Christ's resurrection does not show Christ emerging from His tomb. Ouspensky tells us that this event is never iconographically depicted.[50] Occasionally the icon of the angel telling the myrrh bearing women that Christ is risen has been used to convey the resurrection. For the first few centuries, Christians used the image of Jonah emerging from the whale as a sign of Christ's resurrection. By the sixth century, the depiction of Christ's descent into Hades (or Hell) became the typical icon used to express the resurrection. For Eastern Christians, the resurrection icon, instead of focusing on the event, looks instead to the effect of Christ's death and resurrection. Showing the effect is far more powerful than simply one emerging from a cave. The icon of someone emerging from a cave may also be confused with the raising of Lazarus.

In the Descent into Hades, we have Christ defeating death by death. For Orthodox Christians this was the purpose of Christ's atoning work on the

**Figure 8.7.    Icon of the Harrowing of Hades (the Resurrection of Christ).** *By Fr Matthew Garrett*

cross. It is the defeat of the final enemy, death itself, that Christ came to conquer. Scripturally, the story follows what is mentioned in 2 Peter 3:19 and Acts 2:31. The icon also follows the apocryphal Gospel of Nicodemus. Christ is surrounded by mountains or caves, signifying this descent. It is in this account that Christ enters hell and destroys the gates. In the bottom of the icon, one can see the doors are broken with Christ standing triumphantly on them. These doors are often placed in a shape of a cross, thereby showing that through the cross death was defeated. Around the shattered doors are parts of gates, hinges, keys, locks, chains, and other items associated with holding one captive. As a result of Christ's death, Death cannot hold anyone. Regularly below the doors is a small person. This man is death himself, bound and impotent.

Above the broken doors is Christ. Traditionally, Christ is wearing all white and behind him is a mandorla. In this depiction, Christ is shown in His divine glory much like He was in the Transfiguration icon. One key difference between this image of Christ and that of the Transfiguration is that Christ's wounds from the cross are present. One can see on His hands and His feet the nail marks. Christ is glorified but this glorification includes the scars from His death.

Out of caskets Christ is lifting two figures. On Christ's right is Adam, and on his left is Eve. These two represent all of humanity, and by raising them Christ raises all people. When looking at Adam and Eve, we recognize that both are being lifted by Christ. Christ's hand is upon their wrists and pulling them out of the grave. The effort and sanctifying work is done entirely by Christ. The response by Adam and Eve is that they look upon Christ and accept His divine work. They each have a halo, demonstrating that even though they have sinned, they are redeemed. The garments of both Adam and Eve are also transforming. Artistically this is different depending on which iconographer is representing them, but the sleeves of the arms that Christ is lifting are a different color than the rest of the garment. Sometimes Adam and Eve are depicted as wearing drab gray looking clothing and the sleeves reveal the return of color and life to them. In other icons, they are transformed into pure white sleeves over and against a colorful cloak, connecting them with the martyrs, and the purification that is taking place. Still other icons depict a different color from the rest of their garment. The point is that Christ is transforming them while He raises them. This transformation affects the material world just as their sin did.

Above Adam, three or more figures generally stand. The one closest to Christ is John the Baptist who prepared the way in Hades for Christ's message even there. Next to John are two or sometimes three men with crowns upon their heads. These are the righteous kings of Israel. Closest to John is David and next to him is either Hezekiah, Josiah, or Solomon depending on the specific icon.

Above Eve are her children. Depending on the iconographer, there may only be two children represented, a young Abel, often holding a shepherd's crook, and an older Seth. Cain is often absent from this image, though some icons will have Cain represented as well. There are theological arguments for both the inclusion or exclusion of Cain, and his presence or absence maybe a commentary by the iconographer or church where the icon is found. Some icons will have a host of other people above Eve's children, and they would include Old Testament prophets and saints. Generally, they are not clearly identifiable. Instead, the argument that from Eve all humanity will be raised is the prevailing motif of the icon.

For Orthodox Christians, as Saint Symeon the New Theologian states, Christ's resurrection becomes our own personal resurrection. Christ's Pascha is ours. We participate in the Passover from death to life. For Orthodox Christians, this life is not where one simply continues to live, or even a life of contemplation that Plato speaks about, but a life where one participates with God and can know God through God's uncreated energy. Once again, this icon points us to the telos of man, toward *theosis*.

Icons become one of the avenues for *theosis*. Icons of Christ reveal who Christ is to people. Icons of saints reveal who we may become. Providing an image allows for access to the prototype and for personal transformation along the lines of that image. Icons are not simply models of reality but models for reality. They present the telos of mankind and a means to get there. Through icons the material world is transformed into a symbolic reality where the divine is present. Matter is not abandoned but used. Beauty is discovered as well as joy amid suffering. Icons are truly icons when they are received as such. There are countless icons and each one is an avenue of prayer. Each one belongs to the Church and is used for community formation.

## NOTES

1. Pageau, "The Inevitability of Re-enchantment."

2. Dostoevsky, Fyodor. *The Brothers Karamazov.* New York: Everyman's Library, 1990, 4.

3. Garrett, Matthew. "Theological Layers in Iconography." Des Plaines, IL: Pastoral School of Chicago and Mid-America, 2018, 1.

4. Anderson, Christabel Helena. "Seeking Perfection in the World of Art: The Artistic Path of Father Sophrony." *Orthodox Arts Journal*, 2019.

5. Anderson, "Seeking Perfection in the World of Art."

6. Met Hilarion Alfeyev, *Orthodox Christianity, Volume III*, 215.

7. Florensky, *Iconostasis*, 69.

8. Sardella, *Visible Image of the Invisible God*, 120.

9. Forest, *Praying with Icons*, 21.

10. Ouspensky, *Theology of Icon*, 502.

11. Florensky, *Iconostasis*, 76.

12. Hart, Aidan. *Beauty Spirit Matter: Icons in the Modern World.* Wales: Gracewing, 2014, 156.

13. Florensky, *Iconostasis*, 89.

14. Florensky, *Iconostasis*, 88.

15. Zelinsky and Gilbert, *Windows to Heaven*, 24.

16. R. 527–565.

17. Pageau, "The Inevitability of Re-enchantment."

18. Garrett, *Theological Layers in Iconography*, 52.

19. Ouspensky, *Theology of Icon*, 489.

20. Ouspensky, *Theology of Icon*, 492.

21. Justiniano, Silouan. "The Pictorial Metaphysics of the Icon: Part II." *Orthodox Arts Journal*, January 2016.

22. Pentiuc, *Old Testament in Eastern Orthodox Tradition*, 275.

23. Hart, *Beauty Spirit, Matter*, 163.

24. Met Hilarion Alfeyev, *Orthodox Christianity, Volume III*, 114.

25. Eliade, *Sacred and Profane*, 39.

26. Justiniano, "The Pictorial Metaphysics of the Icon."

27. Pentiuc, *Old Testament in Eastern Orthodox Tradition*, 273.

28. Zelinsky and Gilbert, *Windows to Heaven*, 61.

29. Ouspensky and Lossky, *Meaning of Icons*, 96.

30. Sardella, *Visible Image of the Invisible God*, 126.

31. Bucur, *Scripture Re-Envisioned*, 44.

32. Bucur, *Scripture Re-Envisioned*, 52.

33. Ouspensky and Lossky, *Meaning of Icons*, 202.

34. Temple, *Sacred Art*, 53.

35. Florensky, *Iconostasis*, 68.

36. St. Proclus of Constantinople. "Sermon on the Annunciation." Oca.org, n.d. https://www.oca.org/fs/sermons/sermon-on-the-annunciation (accessed 2023).

37. St. Proclus of Constantinople, "Sermon on the Annunciation."

38. Ouspensky and Lossky, *Meaning of Icons*, 157.

39. Pageau, Jonathan. "The Cave in the Nativity Icon." *Orthodox Arts Journal*, 2013.

40. Met Hilarion Alfeyev, *Orthodox Christianity, Volume III*, 229–30.

41. Moser, "Sunday after Nativity. Joseph the Betrothed." Orthodox Christianity.

42. Ouspensky and Lossky, *Meaning of Icons*, 106.

43. Bunge, *Metamophosis*, 15.

44. John of Damascus, "Oration on the Transfiguraiton of Our Lord and Savior Jesus Christ." In *Light on the Mountain: Greek Patristic and Byzantine Homilies on the Transfiguration of the Lord.* Edited by Brian Daley, S.J., 203–32. Yonkers, NY: St. Vladimir's Seminary Press, 2013, 209.

45. Clendenin, *Eastern Orthodox Theology*, 41.

46. Archimandrite Vasileios, *Hymn of Entry*, 85.

47. Bunge, *Metamophosis*, 22.

48. Clendenin, *Eastern Orthodox Theology*, 41.

49. John of Damascus, *Oration on the Transfiguration*, 226.

50. Ouspensky and Lossky, *Meaning of Icons*, 185.

## Chapter 9

# Icons and Community

For Orthodox Christians, icons are not pieces of art but agents for action. Icons are emblematic of not only the saint depicted, but also Christianity as a whole. Bunge states, "the icon shows a transfigured, spiritually perfected world, where salvation, the end of time, and the foundation of the Second Jerusalem have already taken place."[1] This is why the restoration of icons is known as the Triumph of Orthodoxy, not the Triumph of icons. Icons are Orthodoxy; the image is the prototype. The living faith of the people is assumed into that image. Schmemann states, "The Christian concept of faith and religion is not static but dynamic."[2] As we saw in chapter 4, the same applies to the Christian's relation with the icon.

The veneration of icons is one way that faith is dynamic. The acts of bowing, kissing, and crossing oneself are kinetic worship. Faith is not an intellectual pursuit but is a way of life. Since icons are central to this life, respect must be shown. This respect begins by actively demonstrating that Orthodox faith does not exist for an individual alone. As icons are objects that are seen and interacted with, they are objects that are separate from the practitioner. They force the Christian to look outside of themselves for salvation and to alter the way that the world is seen. Veneration of icons necessitates the respect for others, as all people are understood as icons of Christ who took on humanity. The egocentric worldview has to be abandoned for any encounter with an icon. One's encounter with the divine is not isolated but found in a living community.

This is one key difference between Platonic *theoria* and the Orthodox concept of *theosis*. *Theoria* is an individual pursuit. Plato did not expect the average person to be able to achieve this state. If it is accomplished, it is in isolation and only through self-mastery and self-effort. The concept of an *ecclesia* or community is absent. For Plato, there is no grace from the divine, let alone another person. Other people are as much an obstacle in achieving *theoria* as material existence is. Both hinder and entice away from the telos. There remains for Plato a potential benefit of the community and material existence. There are those people and some material objects where the ideas of truth and beauty are found. There are those philosopher kings that could properly rule and make it easier for the polis to seek the good and potentially aid them through proper governance to *theoria*. This is why in the Allegory of the Cave one must return. It is not out of love, but out of duty. It demonstrates that one has become dispassionate and can seek the good, which while achieved in isolation, is something greater than the individual. For Plato, following Pythagoras, perfection is a monad. Akin to the goals of the Stoics, it is self-sufficient.

The Orthodox concept of *theosis* is radically different. To begin with, *theosis* presupposes another; it can never be achieved in isolation. *Theosis* is dependent upon the grace of God and the grace of others. Icons serve as an instrument in achieving *theosis*. Just as discussed with the icon of the Vladimir Theotokos and other icons of the Mother of God, she points to Christ. All icons point to Christ, even those where Christ is not visibly present. Hands may not gesture to the infant *Theanthropos*, but the saint reflects Christ. This is the point of the halo in an icon. It demonstrates reflection and radiance from being in the presence of God. The holiness of a saint invites one into community, to share in the grace that they have partaken from. Matter is affirmed not only through the incarnation but in the material object of the icon. Other people are affirmed as instruments for one's salvation. As Met. Nafpaktos Hierotheos states, the church is "the Body of Christ and a communion of deification" borrowing from Gregory Palamas's phrase "communion of deification."[3] In this light, even the most challenging among us are not obstacles. They highlight our own weaknesses and need, even when that need is simply to pray for another. To see them as someone who needs mercy, solidifies that we all need mercy. The recognition of God as merciful and our need for mercy creates a community who share forgiveness and demonstrate mercy to one another. This is why the repetition of the Jesus Prayer is so central to Hesychasts and Orthodox Christians in general. By stating, "Lord Jesus Christ, Son of God, have mercy upon me the sinner," one demonstrates the need for another for salvation, and that this need is ultimately dependent upon the mercy of God. Our ability to give mercy comes from the fact that we have been given mercy. *Theosis* is demonstrated in mercy, received, and given. Other people are now essential, not accidental, or inconsequential, to achieving the telos of man as seen in an icon.

This abandonment of the self that is expressed in community formation is treated by scholars of religion. For many, this is one of the main purposes of religion. Durkheim's notion of the totem was that it is emblematic of the clan. One must respect the totem because it stands for the people. Worship of the totem was worship of the clan. Isolation from the totem would result in isolation from the community and loss of identity. Malinowsky says rather succinctly, "religion is a tribal affair."[4] Eliade expands upon this notion, arguing, "Human existence therefore takes place simultaneously upon two parallel planes: that of the temporal, of change and of illusion, and that of eternity, of substance and of reality."[5] The tribal affair, that is religion, is the expression of the transitory to the eternal. Like the Platonic forms, reality exists in the eternal. We only have shadows of that reality in the temporal. The purpose of religion is to connect to the eternal.

A totem for Durkheim, a rock for Eliade, and shamanism for Malinowski are all expressions of this eternal reality. One's actions are bound by this reality. As Marshall Sahlins points out, sometimes these actions are scandalous to an outsider who is not a part of that community. When Sahlins expressed the motivations for actions when the native Hawaiians first encountered Cook's sailors, that "the women offered themselves because they thought there was a god, and the sailors took them because they had forgotten it."[6] Faith is always something manifest by the actions that it produces. These actions are always understood through the framework established by this faith. Sahlins continues, "For the people of Hawaii Cook had been a myth before he was an event, since the myth was the frame by which his appearance was interpreted."[7]

Icons are the frame by which religion is expressed in Orthodoxy. Without knowing what an icon is of, the Orthodox Christian approaches it in reverence and in prayer. Once internalized, icons are not only prayer but also the means of community formation. They are an expression not only of the saint or the shared faith but of unity of its members. As Hart says, "The unity between humans in the Church is a manifestation of this eternal, divine community."[8] This unity is a participation in the mythic reality that exists beyond the structure.

## EASTERN ECCLESIOLOGY

Ecclesiology is the structure that exists for unity and participation with the divine. Worship is a common act. Unlike churches in the West, there can be no liturgy for one or private Mass for Orthodox Christians. The clergy must have at least one other person present; the laity must participate and have some representative. This basic structure demonstrates the reciprocal relationship that exists between the clergy and the laity. The priest leads a congregation in prayer. If there is no congregation present, then there can be no corporate worship, and the liturgy cannot be performed. From the point of view of religious studies, this corporate aspect of religious life makes more sense than any notion of private religion. Malinowski maintains that, "The community whole-heartedly engaged in performing the forms of the ritual creates the atmosphere of homogeneous belief."[9] Apart from a community engaging with a shared ritual, there will be no homogeneous belief.

Icons are this symbolic form that helps this shared faith. Eliade posits, "It is rare for a magico-religious phenomenon not to involve symbolism in some form or other."[10] It is fitting and right that in the liturgy icons have their true home. It is in the setting of the Church and its corporate worship of God that icons find their true expression. Icons are shared with the people. They are illuminated by candles deposited in front of them by many parishioners. Icons are approached at different times during the service when people arrive and depart. They demonstrate the corporate nature of Orthodox worship. When icons are taken home or given as gifts, they retain this corporate identity. Icons point to a shared worship of God. Home icon corners are a common feature of the Orthodox. The icon corner is not hidden away; typically, they are in public places. Guests and visitors approach icons in another person's home just as they would at their home or in their church. There is not the notion of private ownership of the icon. Instead, icons are an expression of a shared faith and a shared expression of that faith.

This common belief that produces a common action solidifies the community. As Malinowski declares, "Religion needs the community as a whole so that its members may worship in common its sacred things and its divinities, and society needs religion for the maintenance of moral law and order."[11] Icons provide this basis for the religion. Veneration of icons rises out of the self and reproduces the norms of the Church. Guroian, in *The Orthodox Reality*, maintains that culture "is among humanity's highest expression of freedom, for genuine worship is not compelled; it is 'done' voluntarily. The human person, made in the image of God, 'creates' culture."[12] This culture is created in freedom. Jonathan Pageau declares that religious people create a systematic pattern of belief that is not itself the mechanism of a system. "The pattern is coherent and that the pattern lays itself through Scripture, lays itself through tradition, finds itself in sacred architecture, finds itself in the icons and the liturgy—all of this is like a giant dance in which we engage and which holds our reality together."[13] Pageau echoes Bordeaux's notion of habitus, icons become a structuring structure that uphold and maintain the community. Pageau continues, that following the iconoclasm of the West it should be of little surprise that within a few hundred years without a suitable symbolic substitute, cohesion is being lost. Nationalism and civil religion lack the clear symbolic nature of reality that icons possess. A flag cannot substitute for regular shared expressed belief.

Pageau and other Orthodox Christians agree with Lossky's statement that "the final gift of the Father, and the only raison d'être of the Church, is personal holiness, in the communion of all."[14] Personal holiness is expressed in communion with others. These are not separate categories, but notions that are mutually dependent upon one another. If one tries to separate communion of all out of their personal piety, their object of veneration becomes themselves. Conversely if one only loves community, and does not see themselves as personally engaged, they become nihilistic, as Fr Seraphim Rose points out.[15] This results in abandonment of all expressions of piety as well.

Eastern Christianity affirms that being made in God's image means that we are made for community. According to Hart, "This means that we are persons fulfilled in relationship. God is love not only because He loves His creation, but also because before all eternity the persons of the Trinity love one another. It follows that to be a full person is not to be individualistic but to love, to live in community."[16] Living in a loving community that includes one's neighbors and the saints is necessary for one's salvation. Louth declares rather simply that, "We are saved in the Church, in unity with all her members."[17] Ouspensky adds that the icon is the representation of the totality of the Church. "The icon is an expression of Orthodoxy with its moral and dogmatic teaching . . . a revelation of the life in Christ and of the mysteries of the divine economy for the salvation of man."[18]

Icons express this corporate reality of the Church and its mission of personal sanctification and ultimately *theosis*. For Orthodox Christians, *theosis* is salvation. Salvation is not simply avoiding the consequences of sin, or not going to hell. Salvation is living in the image and likeness of God. It is more than Plato's contemplation, a task that can be accomplished in isolation. *Theosis* necessitates community, as love requires another. It is this love that is the agent for transformation and moves from *theoria* to *theosis*. Louth, quoting the sobornost Alexei Khomiakov, states, "We know that those among us who fall, fall by themselves, but that no one is saved alone. Those who are saved are saved in the Church as her members and in unity with all her other members."[19] Salvation is a corporate act. Love is expressed in a community, a community that shares faith and prays with one another. The desert monk Saint Dorotheos of Gaza taught that "whoever comes closer to his neighbor comes closer to God, while whoever is distant from his neighbor is distant from God."[20] Prayer brings people together. Otherwise, it is not prayer but solipsism.

Lossky posits that in the Church there is unity and diversity. These are linked to Christ and the Holy Spirit. One cannot be isolated from the other, just as these two persons of the Trinity cannot be separated. Since the Son took on humanity, the presence of God is made manifest in humanity. The Holy Spirit is the life of the Church. It is only in the Church that individual humans can find their purpose. Lossky maintains that "the Spirit is the instrument of Christ to create a unity of nature in the Church, to bind and sanctify the latter objectively."[21] Once bound to God man is made new and participates in this new creation. Here man "becomes perfectly unique and transmits an incomparable beauty to his liberated nature."[22] Therefore, Orthodox Christianity affirms that we are made truly ourselves and individuals when we are together, not apart.

Icons aid in unity because it is in the icon that we participate with others. This is one reason why icons always depict a face. It has been pointed out by several people that the word person originally meant face. When the term was initially coined, mirrors were a rarity and nowhere as clear as they are today. As such, a face did not mean one's own face but the face of another. We could never truly see our own face. The term person presupposed another. It presupposes relationship. To be ourselves means that we are seen by others, that they interact with our face, with who we are as a person. Icons not only provide us a person to interact with, but by looking at us they provide us with the opportunity to be a person.

Hell, then, is *not* other people, as Sartre quipped in *No Exit*, but it is isolation. The quickest way to believe you do not exist is to live in isolation, to live a life where no one sees your face. Others are needed to see you and you are needed by others to see them. Iconoclasm eliminates not only the opportunity to approach another but the ability to be seen. Therefore, one loses the means of existing. Iconoclasm denies the nature of what people are, objects to see and to be seen. Iconoclasm denies interaction with others. It further denies Christology as expressed in chapters 5 and 6. Iconoclasm is more than a Christological heresy. By denying this opportunity to interact and breaking communion, it is also an ecclesial heresy.

Lossky identifies the Christological heresies of Monophysitism and Nestorianism as ecclesial heresies as well. The Monophysites sacrifice "the ecclesial economy that involves a multiform action, a behavior always changing according to time and place, allowing the Church to feed the world with her salutary truth."[23] The Nestorians close themselves to the truth and are reduced to searching for values outside the Church. Lossky states that Chalcedonian ecclesiology affirms the concrete character of the Church, while also understanding that the Church is independent from the laws that govern the rest of history. It is only with Chalcedon that the Church as the body of Christ remains immanent and transcendent, that the Church makes individuals people, while living as a community.

Icons are therefore something that is contrary to modern Western culture. Modernity has resulted in notions of hyper-individualism that result in fragmentation. This is opposed to what Robertson Smith argued was the aim of primitive religion: "the concern of the community rather than of the individual."[24] While Smith identified this concern with primitive religion, concern for the community has shown itself to be concern for the individual. Corporate solidarity results in individual flourishing. Relations with others result in affirmation of self. Icons, as others, affirm the person by incorporating the individual into a community, producing a holistic living faith, not fragmented and broken people.

Within Orthodox Christianity, there is no single head of the Church apart from Christ. There is no individual who reigns supreme. Instead of producing a fragmented community, this has served to bring resolution to communities. The Orthodox Church recognizes that the Holy Spirit was not given to only one apostle. Neither did the apostles receive the Holy Spirit one at a time. Rather, on the day of Pentecost, they all received the Holy Spirit collectively. Collectively, they are overseers of the Church. The episcopacy is plural, with each bishop being able to trace their linage back to one of the twelve apostles. Eliade states, "There is no religious form that does not try to get as close as possible to its true archetype."[25] This archetype for the Church is having a multitude of bishops whose authority is derived from apostolic succession.

The apostles ministering to Christ are themselves an expression of the divine council found throughout the Old and New Testaments. This council is a prototype of community formation made manifest in the reality of the incarnation. Fr Stephen De Young asserts that "the coming of Christ transformed iconography in one major way: angelic beings in the divine council were accompanied by the saints in glory, depicted in the heavens with Christ Himself as they rule and reign with him, serving as priestly intercessors in His presence."[26]

Icons represent this council as a picture of corporate engagement with God. This is a council that emphasizes humility. It is not a bureaucratic or authoritarian system, but a family engaged in love. Love pushes one beyond their current state toward unity. This may include at times the need to grind down some rough parts or to build up where there is a deficit. Saint Sophrony maintains that, "Christ's image should be inspiring and comforting, especially in these troubled modern times. The strict, judgmental icons of earlier centuries are not suitable for our era."[27]

Icons are opportunities for this transformation. Within the Church, this transformation goes by the term repentance or *metania*, as expressed in chapter 4. Repentance means to change the way we see things and therefore how we act. Seeing always necessitates action. Icons, when seen, affirm the unity of the Church and necessitate action on the part of the individual to be one in this Church. The Church calls for holiness, something that the world apart from the Church cannot offer. As Lossky affirms, the "Church is in the world, she is not a constituent part of it, for she contains what the world cannot contain: the fullness of uncreated grace."[28]

As Boosilas points out, the result of this uncreated grace is love. Love is the "attribute of human nature reflecting the image of God."[29] Images proved the means and mechanism for repentance and community formation, creating a community of saints through love. Love looks for others.

As Pentiuc states, "In the Orthodox understanding, spiritual life is to be pursued within the ecclesial community, interacting with one another for the salvation of all."[30] This is done through the eucharistic assembly according to Schmemann.[31] Russell adds that, "we cannot achieve theosis on our own. We need the ecclesial community in which we are re-created in the image of God through baptism and the Eucharist. . . . Deification is a state of profound communion with God and with each other."[32]

In this eucharistic assembly, the people gather together in unity and become living icons for others. They recognize others are living icons as well. During the liturgy itself, the people sing a hymn where they affirm the representational character of themselves in this divine assembly taking the place of the cherubim. The cherubic hymn is sung during the great entrance when the gifts are brought forth before being placed on the altar and consecrated. Both action and song are used to affirm that transition where the gifts of the people are brought outside of the sanctuary through the deacon doors of the iconostasis by the priest and processed through the congregation and then set upon the altar.

This hymn and procession are sung shortly before the Eucharist is consecrated. The consecration in effect fulfills the transformation of the people in this divine council present in the Church. It is the promise of personal transformation and *theosis*. This is only capable of being accomplished because people recognize one another as living icons.

Once a year another service is done within the Orthodox Church that affirms the idea that people are living icons of Christ. This service is known as Forgiveness Vespers. It takes place on Sunday beginning the fast of Great Lent. At the conclusion of the vespers service begins the Rite of Forgiveness. During this rite, each parishioner asks everyone else there for forgiveness with a phrase "please forgive me a sinner," or some other expression that is fitting for their congregation or relationship. Traditionally, lines are formed so as to ensure that everyone is asked. In some parishes, people will bow in front of one another or even do a full prostration. Forgiveness is given with a customary rejoinder akin to "God forgives, and I forgive." Following that, the person who was asked for forgiveness requests the other person for forgiveness and both typically embrace. Depending on the size of the congregation, the exchanging of forgiveness may take several hours. Each congregation may vary its phraseology or the level of prostrations to one degree or another, but the purpose remains the same. All people seek repentance by asking everyone for forgiveness and offering forgiveness. People approach one another and ask for forgiveness even if they are not familiar with the other person or do not know if they have wronged them in any way. The exchange of forgiveness sets the tone for Lent. Observing it from the outside, one would notice that each person goes through a similar action that they do while approaching an icon of Christ. They may cross themselves, bow and ask for forgiveness, and then embrace. Forgiveness is granted. Pageau points out that we relate with one another through a pattern of belief and actions. "There's a pattern by which reality manifests itself. So every event in the world, every experience we have, is patterned. It's not arbitrary."[33] For Orthodox Christians, asking forgiveness and granting forgiveness is a pattern lived out during this vespers service and every time one approaches an icon in the church. It also transforms the relationships that exist in a community. Each person is elevated in love.

Mary Alice Cook, in her work *Community of Grace*, explains her experience of Forgiveness Vespers. She tells us that, "Real community, . . . is made up of real people, and it is sometimes messier than these pictures suggest."[34] The Rite of Forgiveness is not just a formal act but is one that consists in self-examination. There are people that have inflicted harm and one may not wish to ask them for forgiveness. Sometimes people do not approach them, but often they are compelled to seek them out more than any other on this day. It provides an opportunity to resolve problems without many words because people have put aside issues and approach everyone as a living icon. They approach one another as an icon of Christ. Eliade says, "The more religious a man is, the more real he is."[35] Forgiveness Vespers provides for a greater sense of reality to be manifest in the Church. This is why Schmemann affirms that "the concept of the person can be grounded only in a religious worldview."[36]

## ICON AS SYMBOL AND SYMBOLISM AS UNITY

Icons are therefore a symbol of this religious worldview. For Orthodox Christians, this worldview is one that affirms the incarnation of Christ and the transformation of the world as a result of the incarnation. Mankind is made in the image and likeness of God and a new telos is assigned. Icons are symbols, because as Pageau reminds us, "Symbolism means two things that are thrown together."[37] Icons throw together the material object and the idea behind it. They throw together the image and the prototype. Like two rivers joining to become one, the image *is* the prototype. Icons further join the individual with this object, incorporating the observer with what is made present to them.

As Florensky affirms, "If a symbol as carrier attains its end, then it is inseparable from the super reality it reveals, hence it is more than self-referential."[38] Florensky continues that if the symbol does not manifest reality, if it fails to achieve the synthesis that the symbol is called to achieve, then it is not a symbol. It becomes nothing more than an isolated image and an object of empirical study. For icons to be truly an icon, they must unite themselves with the broader reality understood to be present by the community.

Icons are made for people, for the acquisition of grace. Saint Dionysius says that icons are "visible images of mysterious and supernatural visions."[39] Therefore they are always more. This is why icons accompany the sacramental life in the Church. The use of icons not only aids in the sacramental life, but can be understood as sacrament in themselves. The fluid concept of sacrament in the East has always allowed for some items to be understood as sacrament. Lossky points out that for many Church Fathers the reading of the Gospel was considered a sacrament. Dionysius's list of sacraments only came to six, one of which was the funeral rite, which the West does not consider a sacrament.

These examples are easier to understand when the term sacrament is replaced with the Greek term mystery, instead of the Latin. Mystery denotes a lack of perfect understanding; it allows for the operation of God in the world to contain some degree of ambiguity. Some things clearly are mysteries. The Eucharist, for example, is a miracle whereby bread and wine are mysteriously changed into the Body and Blood of Christ. This is a symbolic act, but symbolic as understood as something that brings two things together. In this case, it is the presence of God and the material substances. The Orthodox Church affirms the Real Presence, but without holding to any conception of how this happens. That remains a mystery.

Sacraments in the East are an expression of God's actions in the world. Where God chooses to act and how is independent of our notion of understanding. Lossky states, "The Church is a perpetual sacrament. To speak clearly, there only is one sacrament, the Church, of which the sacraments are only aspects."[40] Sacraments are actions of the Church, the Body of Christ manifest in the world. Icons help to reveal the sacrament as they facilitate an understanding of a world which exists beyond mere perception.

When one approaches an icon with the symbolic understanding that the honor passes onto the prototype and that they are therefore engaged with the prototype, the mysteries of the Church are accepted as normative. Schmemann says that the proper function of the liturgy is "to bring together, within one symbol, the three levels of the Christian faith and life: the Church, the world, and the Kingdom."[41] Life is understood symbolically. Elsewhere Schmemann contends that "nowhere is this symbolic realism more evident than in the application by Maximus of the term 'symbol' to the Body and Blood of Christ offered in the Eucharist, an application which, in the context of today's opposition between the symbolic and the real, would be plain heresy."[42] This world is symbolically united to the world that is to come. The telos of the universe is accomplished, while still unfolding in the liturgy. Similarly, when receiving the Eucharist, the telos of man is accomplished while also unfolding. Man receives the divine within himself, is nourished by the divine and transformed by the divine into an icon of Christ, even while they still live and need repentance.

Sacramental theology is nuanced and difficult to express to the laity. The acceptance of sacrament as mystery allows for wonder to persist. This space allows for growth and anticipation. It allows for the sacrament to remain larger than the individual but instead to belong to every parishioner equally. Lossky states, "The faith allows the simplest folk to grasp it, for it is not the affective sketch of a *gnosis*, but the adhering of a person to a person. And the *gnosis* of the saint confirms it, for it does not cease to open and enclose the distance from the one to the Other in the movement of love."[43]

Icons too allow for one to approach another in love and to see them for who they are in Christ. They allow for people to see around them the apokatastasis, the restoration of all things. Icons sanctify the space that they are in, transforming them into lights pointing everyone to see the divine light of Tabor. Saint Symeon the New Theologian declares, "The one who has not seen the divine light here below, will not see it in eternity."[44] Icons allow for a glimpse of this light here below so they can recognize it in eternity.

## NOTES

1. Bunge, *Metamophosis*, 26.
2. Schmemann, *A Voice for Our Times*, 29.
3. Met Nafpaktos Hierotheos, *The Mind of the Orthodox Church*, 46–47.
4. Malinowski, *Magic, Science, and Religion*, 55.
5. Eliade, *Patterns in Comparative Religion*, 460.
6. Sahlins, *Islands of History*, 5.
7. Sahlins, *Islands of History*, 73.
8. Hart, *Beauty Spirit, Matter*, 154.
9. Malinowski, *Magic, Science, and Religion*, 67.
10. Eliade, *Patterns in Comparative Religion*, 437.
11. Malinowski, *Magic, Science, and Religion*, 54.
12. Guroian, Vigen. *The Orthodox Reality: Culture, Theology, and Ethics in the Modern World.* Grand Rapids, MI: Baker Academic, 2018, 15.
13. Pageau, "The Inevitability of Re-enchantment."
14. Lossky, *Dogmatic Theology*, 147.
15. Rose, Seraphim, Fr. *Nihilism: The Root of the Revolution of the Modern Age.* Platina, CA: St. Herman of Alaska Brotherhood, 2020.
16. Hart, *Beauty Spirit, Matter*, 46.
17. Louth, *Introducing Eastern Orthodox Theology*, 95.
18. Ouspensky, *Theology of Icon*, 472.
19. Louth, *Introducing Eastern Orthodox Theology*, 95.

20. Forest, *Praying with Icons*, 57.

21. Lossky, *Dogmatic Theology*, 146.

22. Lossky, *Dogmatic Theology*, 148.

23. Lossky, *Dogmatic Theology*, 149.

24. Malinowski, *Magic, Science, and Religion*, 55.

25. Eliade, *Patterns in Comparative Religion*, 462.

26. De Young, *Religion of the Apostles*, 254–55.

27. Anderson, "Seeking Perfection in the World of Art."

28. Lossky, *Dogmatic Theology*, 150.

29. Boosalis, *Person to Person*, 113.

30. Pentiuc, *Old Testament in Eastern Orthodox Tradition*, 275.

31. Schmemann, Alexander. *Introduction to Liturgical Theology.* Yonkers, NY: St. Vladimir's Seminary Press, 1966, 114.

32. Russell, *Fellow Workers with God*, 41.

33. Pageau, "The Inevitability of Re-enchantment."

34. Cook, Mary Alice. *Community of Grace: An Orthodox Christian Year in Alaska.* Chesterton, IN: Conciliar Press, 2010, 39.

35. Eliade, *Patterns in Comparative Religion*, 459.

36. Schmemann *A Voice for Our Times*, 247.

37. Pageau, "The Inevitability of Re-enchantment."

38. Florensky, *Iconostasis*, 65.

39. Florensky, *Iconostasis*, 65.

40. Lossky, *Dogmatic Theology*, 159.

41. Schmemann, *For the Life of the World*, 179.

42. Schmemann, *Liturgy and Tradition*, 123.

43. Lossky, *Dogmatic Theology*, 158.

44. Lossky, *Dogmatic Theology*, 162.

# Conclusion

In the *Republic*, Plato provided us with his Allegory of the Cave. The cave symbolized a world where all that was known is shadow, a vague imitation of a reality unknown to those bound and restricted. For Plato, some could escape the cave and see a world full of color and texture. This broader world is frightening and initially offensive. It was harsh, as man had grown accustomed to the dim reality of the cave. Plato believed it was the duty of the one who escaped to return to the cave and offer freedom. This offering was his argument for the rule of philosopher kings, those men who had been enlightened and could properly rule.

Plato and his philosophical ideals loved wisdom and tried to preserve an essence of truth and ethical reality from the Sophists. Pythagoras's cosmology was used to point out that a reality existed beyond this material world, that this world points us toward that reality. The goal for those who are capable is contemplation of this world of the forms. *Theoria* became the highest aim, escape and liberation from the material toward the immaterial ideas that lay beyond our perception. Middle Platonism, under Philo and others, incorporated a unity to this framework and a God. Neoplatonism advanced this system more and placed it under the One. Still for Platonism in all of its forms, the material world only gave a sign and a pointer to the world beyond this one. The goal is contemplation.

Christianity emerged during the context of Middle Platonism. Plato's cosmology dominated the Roman world and Christianity spoke in that language, but Christianity was not subject to it. Justin, Clement, and others saw some good in Plato. For them, Plato and his language were incomplete. They began the work of explaining the different telos that exists between Platonism and Christianity. Plato pointed to a world that existed beyond the material, that gave life and expression to this material world. Christianity agreed. Plato argued that one must move beyond this material world. Christianity also agreed in part. Plato said that the end, the telos of man was *theoria*. It was at

245

this point that Christians and Plato began to part ways. As Lossky states, "The God of the Christians is more transcendent than that of the philosophers."[1]

For Christianity, *theoria* was incomplete. For the first few centuries, Christians tried to expand the definition of *theoria*, to unmoor it from its Platonic deficiencies. Before too long, the term was sidelined for another. *Theoria* was understood as the telos for Neoplatonists, not for Christians. Lossky maintains that, "This mystery of faith as personal encounter and ontological participation is the unique foundation of theological language, a language that apophasis opens to the silence of deification."[2] Neoplatonic *theoria* abandoned the material and moved man toward isolation, not the silence of deification. The dignity of personhood and the reality that all people are made in the image of God is not found in Plato. Christianity affirmed that one cannot stay in the material world but was not willing to abandon it either. God formed man out of the earth and the material world is not evil, just fallen. The telos of the Church was not simply restoration to a pre-fallen state, but a return to the telos that God had planned before the fall. This telos was participation with God in love. This was becoming what God is by nature, by God's grace, *theosis*. *Theosis*, not *theoria*, was the aim, and *theosis* moves beyond contemplation of the forms into participation with the uncreated energies of God. This participation includes a return to the material as it affirms that we are both spiritual and material. The hope of the resurrection is essential to this participation with God. This participation is a participation in love. Love requires another. Love is extended to God, but also to our neighbor. Love forms the ecclesia and is formed by it. *Theosis* is not something done in isolation but with others, with grace and mercy.

This affirmation of the material, while recognizing a world beyond, and the necessity of others, gave rise to the use of icons and their theological expression in the Church. Icons give us a peek into eternity where the saints reside. We can encounter the holy things and holy ones through approaching their holy images. Met Hilarion Alfeyev affirms that, "Ultimately, icons fight for human souls, because the salvation of souls is the objective and meaning of the Church's existence."[3] The Fathers of the Seventh Ecumenical Council distinguished between an icon and a portrait. Portraits represent only ordinary life. The symbolic value that a portrait has is limited. It ends with the prototype, the object of the photograph. Since icons are images of saints, their object is not the person but who that person has become. Icons reveal unity in Christ. Icons reveal the true telos of man, *theosis*.

The destruction of icons is a denial of the telos of man. It denies transformation. It forces one to return to themselves. The face is absent, the person is gone. Iconoclasm asserts that the highest aspiration is Platonic *theoria*. Florensky concludes that iconoclasm results in a "vast obliteration which will destroy the whole image of this world."[4] He continues that iconoclasm is the destruction of faith. It is the loss of hope of the world to come, and ultimately it is the loss of love. For Ouspensky, icons survive in the modern world because they are expressions of hope and of love "it has survived as an expression of faith."[5] They are a "sacred inheritance, arising out of the depths of the catholic consciousness of the Church."[6]

Icons reveal beauty in the world. They reveal sanctification, the possibility of being transfigured and seeing the divine light. This is done by engaging with a beautiful image in community with others. People gather around beauty because it is something prized. Beauty is esteemed, and as Dostoevsky states, beauty will save the world. This beauty is not contained within one culture but moves beyond culture and transforms culture. It does this by speaking to the entirety of who we are. Icons are seen; they are touched and venerated. They exist in churches and homes. They exist when we encounter one another in love and a spirit of forgiveness, humility, and repentance.

Icons are images of reality for Orthodox Christians. Following the Triumph of Orthodoxy in 843, the Church commemorates the restoration of icons on the first Sunday of Great and Holy Lent, commonly known as the Sunday of Orthodoxy. On this day, the proclamation is read and Orthodox process with icons around their churches. The reason for this is not just to reenact a historical event, but to affirm the nature of icons in the Church. Lossky went as far as to say that "icons were the expression of Orthodoxy as such."[7] Icons are affirmed in the Orthodox life. They are mediums for prayer and devotion, penitence and supplication. Icons represent a spiritual reality. Many critics of icons argue that they are not realistic in their portrayals, but in this criticism they miss the point. Icons provide the Christian with a gateway to Christ, the Theotokos, and the Saints. When an Orthodox Christian stands before the image, they are transformed, as they stand before the archetype, all of which brings about closer union with Christ. "The icon is both the way and the means; it is prayer itself."[8]

Icons move beyond *theoria*. They affirm a divine reality where humans can participate. Making an icon of Christ, one makes an icon of God. Making an icon of a saint, one makes an icon of the telos of mankind. Icons affirm that reality is both spiritual and material. These are not separate areas but areas that interact with one another. Spiritual realities are experienced in the material world and the material world is transformed in this interaction.

Icons facilitate a harmony of all of Plato's cosmology. The structure, as properly interpreted, was never abandoned. The Orthodox interpretation placed a God who is unknowable in His essence but knowable in His energies in the center, instead of the One. This God has attributes and key among them is love. This God forms other beings out of this love through an act of will, not simply emanations. These beings are also objects of the divine love and are called to love one other. This love is divine participation and known as *theosis*. It is participation in the divine light; it is seen and known. It transfigures man. Icons therefore move beyond Plato. The cave allows for a framework of understanding that more to life exists, but icons provide engagement with that world and populate that world with others and divine love. Icons reveal the telos of mankind.

## NOTES

1. Lossky, *Orthodox Theology*, 24.
2. Lossky, *Orthodox Theology*, 25.
3. Met Hilarion Alfeyev, *Orthodox Christianity, Volume III*, 108.
4. Florensky, *Iconostasis*, 63.
5. Ouspensky, *Theology of Icon*, 469.
6. Ouspensky, *Theology of Icon*, 469.
7. Hussey, *The Orthodox Church in the Byzantine Empire*, 34.
8. Ouspensky and Lossky, *The Meaning of Icons*, 39.

# Appendix A

## *Recommended Works*

The aim of this work is to demonstrate the evolution of Platonic thought and the reception of that thought into Christianity. Ultimately, Orthodox Christianity moved beyond Plato's realm of *theoria*. Initially Christians tried to utilize the language of the dominant culture to express the truths revealed to them. The term *theoria* grew but eventually it was abandoned in favor of a new term that did not include the baggage of Platonic understanding. This term is *theosis*. I have shown how *theosis* is ultimately tied in with the icon, as it reveals the value of incarnation in the Christian cosmology, one that rejects Plato's realm of the forms as the true telos of man. In doing so, there were many conversations that I only briefly touched on that are of vital importance to the study of icons, Orthodox Christianity, and the concept of *theosis*. Given the differing audiences who will be attracted to this work, I wanted to provide a few avenues for further research and interest to those who are beginning their personal or scholarly pursuits along these lines. To that end, I am providing a list of recommended works that should aid those who desire further study on the topics addressed. Each of the works addressed below are also cited in either the bibliography or further readings. I would encourage anyone who is interested in these topics to peruse these sources for further research, but I would like to highlight the contribution of these selected works as a great place to start any further study on the topics addressed in this work.

## PLATO'S RECEPTION INTO CHRISTIANITY

Andrew Louth, *The Origins of the Christian Mystical Tradition: From Plato to Denys*. Louth's position is one that is most akin to mine and his work serves as an accessible and brilliant treatment of the Patristic understanding of Plato.

Vladimir Lossky, *Dogmatic Theology: Creation, God's Image in Man, and the Redeeming Work of the Trinity*. Lossky is a bit heaver to digest, but this along with nearly any other work that Lossky has can help anyone who wishes to understand the philosophical and mystical mind of the early church.

Robert J. O'Connell, *Plato on the Human Paradox*. O'Connell's work does a great job demonstrating the motivation behind Plato's cosmology.

Fr Stephen De Young, *Religion of the Apostles: Orthodox Christianity in the First Century*. This work is short and rather accessible. De Young's work, while not addressing Plato, should help anyone interested in understanding the mindset of the early church. He demonstrates the worldview of Second Temple Judaism.

## USE OF ICONS AND THEIR MEANING

Leonid Ouspensky, *Theology of the Icon, Volume II*
Leonid Ouspensky and Vladimir Lossky, *The Meaning of Icons*
Jim Forest, *Praying with Icons*
Aidan Hart, *Beauty Spirit Matter: Icons in* the *Modern World*
Fr Matthew Garrett, *Sanctify Those Who Love the Beauty of Thy House*

These works take a slightly different tactic on how one would approach an icon. Ouspensky, Hart, and Garrett are iconographers, so they provide an insider's perspective on the process and meaning of icons.

## THEOSIS

Norman Russell, *Fellow Workers with God: Orthodox Thinking on Theosis*. This is a great work dedicated to the concept of *theosis* and its development.

In addition to these works, I highly recommend any number of patristic writings found in this work. It is in the writings of the Church Fathers themselves that we see the development of the philosophical concepts laid out, and they were the ones who helped to shape and guide Orthodox Christianity as it is lived today.

# Appendix B

## *Further Reading*

Andreopoulos, Andreas. *Gazing on God: Trinity, Church, and Salvation in Orthodox Thought and Iconography*. Cambridge, UK: James Clarke & Co, 2013.

———. *Metamorphosis: The Transfiguration in Byzantine Theology and Iconography*. Crestwood, NY: St. Vladimir's Seminary Press, 2005.

Aristotle. *The Basic Works of Aristotle*. New York: Random House, 1941.

Berger, Peter L., and Thomas Luckman. *The Social Construction of Reality: A Treatise in the Sociology of Knowledge*. New York: Anchor Books, 1966.

Boosalis, Harry. *Holy Tradition*. Waymart, PA: St. Tikhon's Monastery Press, 2013.

Bunge, Gabriel. *The Rublev Trinity*. Yonkers, NY: St. Vladimir's Seminary Press, 2007.

Chesterton, G. K. *Orthodoxy*. Nashville, TN: Sam Torode Book Arts, 2008.

Clement of Alexandria. *Loeb Classical Library Clement of Alexandria*. Cambridge, MA: Harvard University Press, 1919.

Cressy, David. *Birth, Marriage, and Death: Ritual, Religion, and the Life-Cycle in Tudor and Stuart England*. Oxford: Oxford University Press, 1999.

Crow, Gillian. "The Orthodox Vision of Wholeness." In *Living Orthodoxy in the Modern World*, by Andrew Walker and Costa Carras, 7–23. Crestwood, NY: St. Vladimir's Seminary Press, 1996.

Daley, Brian, S.J., ed. *Light on the Mountain: Greek Patristic and Byzantine Homilies on the Transfiguration of the Lord*. Yonkers, NY: St. Vladimir's Seminary Press, 2013.

Damick, Andrew Stephen. "The Inevitability of Re-enchantment: Jonathan Pageau." *Ancient Faith*, 2021. https://www.ancientfaith.com/podcasts/orthodoxengagement /the_inevitability_of_re_enchantment_jonathan_pageau_part_1 (accessed 2023).

———. "Is There Really a Patristic Critique of Icons?" *Ancient Faith*, 2013. https: //blogs.ancientfaith.com/orthodoxyandheterodoxy/2013/05/23/is-there-really-a -patristic-critique-of-icons-part-5-of-5/ (accessed 2023).

———. *Venerating the Virgin: Orthodox Christian Reflections for Protestants. Ancient Faith*, 2012. https://blogs.ancientfaith.com/orthodoxyandheterodoxy/2012/07/06 /venerating-the-virgin-orthodox-christian-reflections-for-protestants/ (accessed 2023).

Damick, Andrew Stephen, and Stephen De Young. "The Queen Stood at Thy Right Hand." *Ancient Faith*, 2020. https://www.ancientfaith.com/podcasts/lordofspirits/the_queen_stood_at_thy_right_hand (accessed 2023).

Davis, Leo Donald. *First Seven Ecumenical Councils: Their History and Theology*. Collegeville, MN: Michael Glazier Book/The Liturgical Press, 1983.

Duffy, Eamon. *Stripping of the Altars: Traditional Religion in England, 1400–1580*. New Haven, CT: Yale University Press, 1992.

Evans-Pritchard, E. E., *Theories of Primitive Religion*. Oxford: Clarendon Paperbacks, 2004.

———. *Witchcraft, Oracles, and Magic among the Azande*. Oxford: Clarendon Paperbacks, 1976.

Gonzalez, Justo. *The Story of Christianity, Volume 1: The Early Church to the Dawn of the Reformation*. San Francisco: Harper San Francisco, 1984.

———. *The Story of Christianity, Volume 2: The Reformation to the Present Day*. San Francisco: HarperCollins, 1985.

Hallam, Gregory. "Art for Christ." *Ancient Faith*, 2019. https://www.ancientfaith.com/podcasts/voicefromisles/art_for_christ (accessed 2023).

Hart, Aidan. "Designing Icons (Pt.8): The Theology behind Iconographic Perspective." *Orthodox Arts Journal*, 2013.

———. "The Nature of Divine Beauty." *Orthodox Arts Journal*, 2019.

Hayes, Julia Bridget. "Revisiting the Patristic Theology of the Icon, Part 1: Setting Aside our Western Assumptions." *Ikonographics*, n.d.

Holy Theotokos of Iveron Orthodox Church. "Hawaii's Myrrh-Streaming Iveron Icon." *Orthodoxhawaii.org*, n.d. https://www.orthodoxhawaii.org/icons (accessed 2023).

Hopko, Thomas. *The Orthodox Faith, Volume 2*. Yonkers, NY: St. Vladimir's Seminary Press, 1981.

———. "Sunday of Orthodoxy." *Hexaemeron.org*, 2010. https://www.hexaemeron.org/reverence-of-icons (accessed 2023).

"The Icon of Saint Anna." *OrthoChristian.com, 2015*. https://orthochristian.com/88061.html (accessed 2023).

James, William. *Writings, 1878–1899*. New York: Library of America, 1992.

———. *Writings, 1902–1910*. New York: Library of America, 1987.

Justiniano, Silouan. "Icon Painting as Participation: Interview with Cornelia Tsakiridou, Part I." *Orthodox Arts Journal*, 2023.

———. "Imagination, Expression, Icon: Reclaiming the Internal Prototype." *Orthodox Arts Journal*, 2017.

Kelly, J. N. D. *Early Christian Doctrines*. New York: Harper One, 1978.

Krueger, Derek. *Byzantine Christianity (A People's History of Christianity)*. Minneapolis, MN: Fortress Press, 2006.

Lindberg, Carter. *The European Reformations*. Oxford: Wiley-Blackwell, 2010.

Lossky, Vladimir. *In the Image and Likeness of God*. Crestwood, NY: St. Vladimir's Seminary Press, 1974.

Louth, Andrew. "Orthodoxy and Art." In *Living Orthodoxy in the Modern World*, by Andrew Walker and Costa Carras, 159–78. Crestwood, NY: St. Vladimir's Seminary Press, 1996.

MacCulloch, Diarmaid. *Tudor Church Militant: Edward VI and the Protestant Reformation*. London: Penguin Books, 1999.

Marshall, Sherrin. *Women in Reformation and Counter-Reformation Europe: Private and Public Worlds*. Bloomington: Indiana University Press, 1989.

Metropolitan Joseph. *Liturgikon: The Book of Divine Services for the Priest and Deacon, 4th Edition*. Englewood, NJ: Antakya Press, 2021.

Metropolitan Hierotheos of Nafpaktos. *Patristic and Scholastic Theology in Perspective a Comparative Study*. Levadia: Birth of the Theotokos Monastery (Pelagia), 2023.

Meyendorff, John. St. Gregory Palamas and Orthodox Spirituality. Crestwood: St Vladimir's Seminary Press, 1974.

——————. *A Study of Gregory Palamas*. Crestwood, NY: St. Vladimir's Seminary Press, 1964.

Nes, Solrunn. *The Mystical Language of Icons*. Grand Rapids, MI: Eerdmans, 2009.

Origen. *Classics of Western Spirituality: Origen, an Exhortation to Martyrdom, Prayer, and Selected Works*. Translated by Rowan A. Greer. Mahwah, NJ: Paulist Press, 1979.

Orthodox Hawaiian Iveron Icon Association. *The Wonderworking Iveron Icon of Hawaii. Oohiia.org*, n.d. https://www.ohiia.org/the-iveron-icon (accessed 2023).

Ortner, Sherry B. "On Key Symbols." In *A Reader in the Anthropology of Religion*, edited by Michael Lambek, 151–60. Malden, MA: Blackwell, 2008.

Ouspensky, Leonid. "The Meaning and Content of the Icon." In *Eastern Orthodox Theology: A Contemporary Reader*, by Daniel B. Clendenin, 33–64. Grand Rapids, MI: Baker Academic, 2003.

Ozment, Steven. *When Fathers Ruled: Family Life in Reformation Europe*. Cambridge, MA: Harvard University Press, 1983.

Pageau, Jonathan. "The Nativity Icon as an Image of Reality." *Orthodox Arts Journal*, 2018.

——————. "Sacred Symbol, Sacred Art." *Orthodox Arts Journal*, 2015.

Parker, John. "A Discussion with Jonathan Pageau." *Ancient Faith*, 2018. https://www.ancientfaith.com/podcasts/lordsendme/a_discussion_with_jonathan_pageau (accessed 2023).

Pelikan, Jaroslav. *The Christian Tradition, Volume 1: The Emergence of the Catholic Tradition (100–600)*. Chicago: University of Chicago Press, 1971.

Percival, Henry. *Council of Chalcedon (A.D. 451)*. Edited by NewAdvent. Vols. Nicene and Post-Nicene Fathers, Second Series, Vol. 14. Buffalo, NY: Christian Literature Publishing, 1900.

——————. *Council of Ephesus (A.D. 431)*. Edited by NewAdvent. Vols. Nicene and Post-Nicene Fathers, Second Series, Vol. 14. Buffalo, NY: Christian Literature Publishing, 1900.

————. *First Council of Constantinople (A.D. 381).* Edited by NewAdvent. Vols. Nicene and Post-Nicene Fathers, Second Series, Vol. 14. Buffalo, NY: Christian Literature Publishing, 1900.

————. *Second Council of Constantinople.* Vols. Nicene and Post-Nicene Fathers, Second Series, Vol. 14. Buffalo, NY: Christian Literature Publishing, 1900.

————. *Seven Ecumenical Councils.* Edmond, OK: Veritas Splendor, 2013.

Plato. *Timaeus and Critias.* Suffolk: Penguin Classics, 2008.

Popkin, Richard H., ed. *Columbia History of Western Philosophy.* New York: MJF Books, 1999.

Proclus. "Proclus: The Elements of Theology." Internet Archive, n.d. https://archive .org/details/proclus-the-elements-of-theology_202109 (accessed 2023).

————. "The Six Books of Proclus, the Platonic Successor, on the Theology of Plato." Internet Archive, n.d. https://archive.org/details/the_six_books_of_proclus _2102_librivox (accessed 2023).

Pseudo-Dionysius. *Classics of Western Spirituality: Pseudo-Dionysius, the Complete Works.* New York: Paulist Press, 1987.

Roper, Lyndal. *The Holy Household: Women and Morals in Reformation Augsburg.* Oxford: Oxford University Press, 2001.

Russian Icon Collection. "Holy Icons of Our Lady of the Sign." *Russianicon.com,* 2017. https://russianicon.com/holy-icons-lady-sign/ (accessed 2023).

————. "The Myrrh-Streaming Icons in Russia." *Russianicon.com,* 2020. https:// russianicon.com/the-myrrh-streaming-icons-in-russia/ (accessed 2023).

Russian Orthodox Cathedral of St. John the Baptist of Washington, DC. "Iveron Myrrh-Streaming Icon of the Mother of God." *Stjohndc.org,* n.d. https://stjohndc .org/en/brother-munios/iveron-myrrh-streaming-icon-mother-god (accessed 2023).

————. "Jose Munoz-Cortez." *Stjohndc.org,* n.d. https://stjohndc.org/en/brother -munios/jose-munoz-cortez (accessed 2023).

Scarisbrick, J. J. *Henry VIII.* Berkeley: University of California Press, 1968.

Spade, Paul Vincent. *Five Texts on the Medieval Problem of Universals.* Indianapolis: Hackett, 1994.

St. Basil the Great. *On Christian Doctrine and Practice.* Popular Patristics Series 47. Crestwood, NY: St. Vladimir's Press, 2012.

————. *On the Holy Spirit.* Popular Patristics Series 42. Yonkers, NY: St. Vladimir's Press, 2011.

————. *On the Human Condition.* Popular Patristics Series 30. Crestwood, NY: St. Vladimir's Press, 2005.

————. *St. Basil Collection.* Philadelphia: Aeterna Press, 2016.

St. Cyril The Great. *Five Tomes against Nestorius.* Philadelphia: Aeterna Press, 2014.

————. *St. Cyril Selection: Commentary upon the Gospel According to St. Luke, the Catehetical Lectures of St. Cyril, Three Epistles of St. Cyril.* Philadelphia: Aeterna Press, 2016.

St. Ephrem the Syrian. *Hymns on Paradise.* Crestwood, NY: St. Vladimir's Seminary Press, 1990.

St. John of Damascus. "Expositions of the Orthodox Faith, Book 3, Chapter III, Concerning Christ's Two Natures, in Opposition to Those Who Hold That He

Has Only One." In *Collection: Barlaam and Ioasaph, Exposition of the Orthodox Faith, on Holy Images, on the Trinity*, by St. John of Damascus, 271–74. Philadelphia: Aeterna Press, 2016.

———. "Expositions of the Orthodox Faith, Book 4, Chapter XVI, Concerning Images." In *St. John of Damascus Collection*, by St. John of Damascus, 350–52. Philadelphia: Aeterna Press, 2016.

St. Nektarios Kefalas. *Collected Works, Volume 13: The Ecumenical Councils.* Jerusalem: Virgin Mary of Australia and Oceania, 2022.

St. Nicholas Center. "History of the Myrrh-Streaming Icon." *Stnicholascenter.org*, n.d. https://www.stnicholascenter.org/who-is-st-nicholas/stories-legends/modern-miracles/weeping-icons/weeping-icon-michigan-city/history-myrrh-streaming-icon (accessed 2023).

Wallace, Anthony F. C. *Modernity and Mind: Essays on Culture Change, Volume 2*. Lincoln: University of Nebraska Press, 2004.

Ware (Metropolitan Kallistos of Diokleia), Timothy. *The Orthodox Church: An Introduction to Eastern Christianity, New Edition*. New York: Penguin, 2015.

Watt, Tessa. *Cheap Print and Popular Piety, 1550–1640*. Cambridge, UK: Cambridge University Press, 1991.

Wells, Colin. *Sailing from Byzantium: How a Lot Empire Shaped the World*. New York: Delta, 2006.

Zelensky, Elizabeth, and Lela Gilbert. *Windows to Heaven: Introducing Icons to Protestants and Catholics*. Ada, MI: Brazos Press, 2005.

# Bibliography

"25th Anniversary of Martyrdom of Br. José Muñoz-Cortes Commemorated at Jordanville." *OrthoChristian.com*, n.d. https://orthochristian.com/149240.html (accessed 2022).

Albert the Great. *The Classics of Western Spirituality: Albert and Thomas, Selected Writings.* New York: Paulist Press, 1988.

Alfeyev, Met Hilarion. *Orthodox Christianity, Volume I.* Yonkers, NY: St. Vladimir's Seminary Press, 2011.

———. *Orthodox Christianity, Volume II.* Yonkers, New York: St. Vladimir's Seminary Press, 2012.

———. *Orthodox Christianity, Volume III.* Yonkers, New York: St. Vladimir's Seminary Press, 2014.

Anderson, Christabel Helena. "Painting as Prayer: The Art of A. Sophrony Sakharov." *Orthodox Arts Journal*, 2021.

———. "Seeking Perfection in the World of Art: The Artistic Path of Father Sophrony." *Orthodox Arts Journal*, 2019.

Andreopoulos, Andreas. *Gazing on God: Trinity, Church, and Salvation in Orthodox Thought and Iconography.* Cambridge, UK: James Clarke & Co., 2013.

———. *Metamorphosis: The Transfiguration in Byzantine Theology and Iconography.* Crestwood, NY: St. Vladimir's Seminary Press, 2005.

Aquinas, Thomas. "The Summa Theologiæ of St. Thomas Aquinas." *New Advent*, 1920. https://www.newadvent.org/summa/ (accessed 2023).

Aristotle. *The Basic Works of Aristotle.* New York: Random House, 1941.

Athanasius of Alexandria. *Saint Athanasius of Alexandria Selection.* Philadelphia: Aeterna Press, 2016.

Athanasius. *On the Incarnation.* Yonkers, NY: St. Vladimir's Seminary Press, 2012.

Augustine. *The City of God.* Translated by Marcus Dods. New York: Random House, Inc., 1993.

———. *The Confessions of St. Augustine.* Translated by J. G. Pilkington. New York: Liveright Publishing Corp., 1943.

———. "On the Trinity." In *Nicene and Post-Nicene Fathers*, First Series, Vol. 3, by Augustine, edited by Philip Schaff, translated by Arthur West Haddan. Buffalo, NY: Christian Literature Publishing, 1887.

Baggley, John. *Doors of Perception: Icons and their Spiritual Significance.* London & Oxford, UK: Mowbray, 1987.

———. *Festival Icons for the Christian Year.* Crestwood, NY: St. Vladimir's Seminary Press, 2000.

Bennett, Jamey. "Should Orthodox Christians Get Their Icons Blessed?" *Ancient Faith*, September 26, 2013. https://blogs.ancientfaith.com/orthodoxyandheterodoxy/2013/09/26/should-orthodox-christians-get-their-icons-blessed/ (accessed 2023).

Berger, Peter L. *The Sacred Canopy: Elements of a Sociological Theory of Religion.* New York: Anchor Books, 1967.

Berger, Peter L., and Thomas Luckman. *The Social Construction of Reality: A Treatise in the Sociology of Knowledge.* New York: Anchor Books, 1966.

Berkeley, George. "The Principles of Human Knowledge." Edited by Jonathan Bennett. *Earlymoderntexts.com*, 2017. http://www.earlymoderntexts.com/assets/pdfs/berkeley1710.pdf (accessed 2023).

Bigg, Charles. *The Christian Platonists of Alexandria.* London: Forgotten Books, 2012.

Bigham, Steven. "On the Origin of Ὁ ῺΝ in The Halo of Christ." *Orthodox Arts Journal*, June 2016.

Bjeletich, Elissa, and Caleb Shoemaker. *Blueprints for the Little Church: Creating an Orthodox Home.* Chesterton, NY: Ancient Faith Publishing, 2016.

Bonaventure. *The Journey of the Mind to God.* Indianapolis: Hackett, 1990.

Boosalis, Harry. *Holy Tradition.* Waymart, PA: St. Tikhon's Monastery Press, 2013.

———. *Person to Person: The Orthodox Understanding of Human Nature.* Waymart, PA: St. Tikhon's Monastery Press, 2018.

Bourdieu, Pierre. *The Logic of Practice.* Stanford, CA: Stanford University Press, 1990.

———. *Outline of a Theory of Practice.* Cambridge, UK: Cambridge University Press, 2008.

Bucur, Bogdan Gabriel. *Scripture Re-Envisioned: Christophanic Exegesis and the Making of a Christian Bible.* Leiden: Brill, 2019.

Bunge, Gabriel. *The Rublev Trinity.* Yonkers, NY: St. Vladimir's Seminary Press, 2007.

Calvin, John. "Institutes of the Christian Religion." *Bible Study Tools*, n.d. https://www.biblestudytools.com/history/calvin-institutes-christianity/book1/chapter-11.html (accessed 2023).

Chesterton, G. K. *Orthodoxy.* Nashville: Sam Torode Book Arts, 2008.

Clement of Alexandria. *Clement of Alexandria Collection.* Philadelphia: Aeterna Press, 2016.

———. *Loeb Classical Library Clement of Alexandria.* Cambridge, MA: Harvard University Press, 1919.

Clendenin, Daniel B. *Eastern Orthodox Theology: A Contemporary Reader.* Grand Rapids, MI: Baker Academic, 2003.

Climacus, John. *The Ladder of Divince Ascent.* Mahwah, NJ: Paulist Press, 1982.

"Confession/Absolution." *EasternOrthodoxChristian.com*, April 16, 2023. https://www.easternorthodoxchristian.com/confession (accessed 2023).

Cook, Mary Alice. *Community of Grace: An Orthodox Christian Year in Alaska.* Chesterton, IN: Conciliar Press, 2010.

Cressy, David. *Birth, Marriage, and Death: Ritual, Religion, and the Life-Cycle in Tudor and Stuart England.* Oxford, UK: Oxford University Press, 1999.

Crow, Gillian. "The Orthodox Vision of Wholeness." In *Living Orthodoxy in the Modern World*, by Andrew Walker and Costa Carras, 7–23. Crestwood, NY: St. Vladimir's Seminary Press, 1996.

Cunningham, Mary B., and Elizabeth Theokritoff. *Cambridge Companion to Orthodox Christian Theology.* Cambridge, UK: Cambridge University Press, 2008.

Daley, Brian, S.J., ed. *Light on the Mountain: Greek Patristic and Byzantine Homilies on the Transfiguration of the Lord.* Yonkers, NY: St. Vladimir's Seminary Press, 2013.

Damick, Andrew Stephen. "What John Calvin Really Thought about Icons in the Catholic Church." *Ancient Faith*, 2017. https://blogs.ancientfaith.com /orthodoxyandheterodoxy/2017/10/10/john-calvin-really-thought-icons -church/ (accessed 2023).

———. "The Inevitability of Re-enchantment: Jonathan Pageau." *Ancient Faith*, 2021. https://www.ancientfaith.com/podcasts/orthodoxengagement/the_ inevitability_of_re_enchantment_jonathan_pageau_part_1 (accessed 2023).

———. "Is There Really a Patristic Critique of Icons?" *Ancient Faith*, 2013. https: //blogs.ancientfaith.com/orthodoxyandheterodoxy/2013/05/23/is-there-really-a -patristic-critique-of-icons-part-5-of-5/ (accessed 2023).

———. *Orthodoxy and Heterodoxy.* Chesterton, IN: Conciliar Press, 2011.

———. "Venerating the Virgin: Orthodox Christian Reflections for Protestants." *Ancient Faith*, 2012. https://blogs.ancientfaith.com/orthodoxyandheterodoxy /2012/07/06/venerating-the-virgin-orthodox-christian-reflections-for -protestants/ (accessed 2023).

Damick, Andrew Stephen, and Stephen De Young. "Eating with the Gods." *Ancient Faith*, 2021. https://www.ancientfaith.com/podcasts/lordofspirits/eating_with_the _gods (accessed 2023).

———. "The Queen Stood at Thy Right Hand." *Ancient Faith*, 2020. https:// www.ancientfaith.com/podcasts/lordofspirits/the_queen_stood_at_thy_right_hand (accessed 2023).

Danielou, Jean, and Henri Marrou. *The Christian Centuries: A New History of the Catholic Church, Volume One: The First Six Hundred Years.* New York: McGraw-Hill, 1964.

Davis, Justin. *Pietism and the Foundations of the Modern World.* Eugene, OR: Pickwick Publications, 2019.

———. *Schleiermacher and Palmer: The Father and Mother of the Modern Protestant Mindset.* Eugene, OR: Pickwick Publications, 2019.

Davis, Leo Donald. *First Seven Ecumenical Councils: Their History and Theology.* Collegeville, MN: Michael Glazier Book and Liturgical Press, 1983.

Davydov, Philip, and Olga Shalamova. "Interview with Serbian Iconographer Todor Mitrovic: on the Dialogue between the Sacred and Secular Arts." *Orthodox Arts Journal*, 2016.

De Young, Stephen. *Religion of the Apostles: Orthodox Christianity in the First Century.* Chesterton, NY: Ancient Faith Publishing, 2021.

De Young, Stephen, and Andrew Stephen Damick. "Bodies and the Bodiless." *The Lord of Spirits.* Chesterton, NY: Ancient Faith Publishing, 2021.

Doniger, Wendy. *The Implied Spider: Politics and Theology in Myth.* New York: Columbia University Press, 2011.

Dostoevsky, Fyodor. *The Brothers Karamazov.* New York: Everyman's Library, 1990.

Duffy, Eamon. *Stripping of the Altars: Traditional Religion in England, 1400–1580.* New Haven, CT: Yale University Press, 1992.

———. *Voices of Morebath: Reformation and Rebellion in an English Village.* New Haven, CT: Yale University Press, 2001.

Durkheim, Emile. *The Elementary Forms of the Religous Life.* New York: Free Press, 1965.

Eliade, Mircea. *The Myth of the Eternal Return: Cosmos and History.* Princeton, NJ: Princeton University Press, 2005.

———. *Patterns in Comparative Religion.* Lincoln: University of Nebraska Press, 1996.

———. *The Sacred and the Profane: The Nature of Religion.* San Diego: Harcourt Brace, 1987.

Eliade, Mircea, and Joseph M. Kitigawa. *The History of Religions: Essays in Methodology.* Chicago: University of Chicago Press, 1959.

Eriugena, John Scotus. *Periphyseon (The Division of Nature).* Washington, DC: Dumbarton Oaks and Editions Bellarmin, 1987.

Eusebius. *Ecclesiastical History.* Translated by C. F. Cruse. Peabody, MA: Hendrickson, 1998.

Evans-Pritchard, E. E. *Nuer Religion.* Oxford: Oxford University Press, 1956.

———. *Theories of Primitive Religion.* Oxford: Clarendon Paperbacks, 2004.

———. *Witchcraft, Oracles, and Magic Among the Azande.* Oxford: Clarendon Paperbacks, 1976.

Florensky, Pavel. *Iconostasis.* Crestwood, NY: St. Vladimir's Seminary Press, 1996.

Forest, Jim. *Praying with Icons.* Maryknoll, NY: Orbis, 2017.

Fortounatto, Mariamna, and Mary Cunningham. "Theology of the Icon." In *Cambridge Companion to Orthodox Christian Theology*, edited by Mary Cunningham and Elizabeth Theokritoff, 136–50. Cambridge, UK: Cambridge University Press, 2008.

Freud, Sigmund. *Totem and Taboo.* New York: W. W. Norton, 1950.

Garrett, Matthew. "Theological Layers in Iconography." Des Plaines, IL: Pastoral School of Chicago and Mid-America, 2018.

Geertz, Clifford. *The Interpreptation of Cultures.* New York: Basic Books, 1973.

Gergis, Emmanuel. *Cyril of Alexandria's Christological Dialogue on the Incarnation of the Only Begotten.* London: Agora University Press, 2020.

Gerostergios, Asterios. *St. Photios the Great.* Belmont, MA: Institute for Byzantine and Modern Greek Studies, 1980.

Gonzalez, Justo. *Story of Christianity, Volume 1: The Early Church to the Dawn of the Reformation.* San Francisco: Harper San Francisco, 1984.

———. *The Story of Christianity, Volume 2: The Reformation to the Present Day.* San Francisco: HarperCollins, 1985.

Gregory of Nyssa. *On the Soul and the Resurrection.* Crestwood, NY: St. Vladimir's Seminary Press, 1993.

Gregory the Sinaite. "Discourse on the Feast of the Holy Transfiguration of the Lord." In *Light on the Mountain: Greek Patristic and Byzantine Homilies on the Transfiguration of the Lord*, translated by Brian E. Daley, 325–50. Yonkers, NY: St. Vladimir's Seminary Press, 2013.

Guroian, Vigen. *The Orthodox Reality: Culture, Theology, and Ethics in the Modern World.* Grand Rapids, MI: Baker Academic, 2018.

Haigh, Christopher. *English Reformations: Religion, Politics, and Society under the Tudors.* Oxford, UK: Oxford University Press, 1993.

Hallam, Gregory. "Art for Christ. " *Ancient Faith*, 2019. https://www.ancientfaith.com/podcasts/voicefromisles/art_for_christ (accessed 2023).

Hart, Aidan. *Beauty Spirit Matter: Icons in the Modern World.* Wales: Gracewing, 2014.

———. "Designing Icons (Pt.8): The Theology behind Iconographic Perspective." *Orthodox Arts Journal*, 2013.

———. "The Nature of Divine Beauty." *Orthodox Arts Journal*, 2019.

Hayes, Julia Bridget. "Revisiting the Patristic Theology of the Icon, Part 1: Setting Aside Our Western Assumptions." *Ikonographics*, n.d.

Heidegger, Martin. *The Essence of Truth: On Plato's Cave Allegory and the Theatetus.* London: Bloomsbury, 2022.

Hill, Robert C. *Reading the Old Testament in Antioch.* Leiden: Koninklijke Brill, 2005.

Holy Theotokos of Iveron Orthodox Church. "Hawaii's Myrrh-Streaming Iveron Icon." *Orthodox Hawaii*, n.d. https://www.orthodoxhawaii.org/icons (accessed 2023).

Hopko, Thomas. "Sunday of Orthodoxy." Hexaemeron.org, 2010. https://www.hexaemeron.org/reverence-of-icons (accessed 2023).

———. *Lenten Spring.* Crestwood, NY: St. Vladimir's Seminary Press, 1983.

———. *The Orthodox Faith, Volume 1: Doctrine and Scripture.* Yonkers, NY: St. Vladimir's Press, 1981.

———. *The Orthodox Faith, Volume 2.* Yonkers, NY: St. Vladimir's Seminary Press, 1981.

———. *The Orthodox Faith, Volume 3: Church History.* Yonkers, NY: St. Vladimir's Press, 1981.

Hsia, R. Po-Chia. *Social Discipline in the Reformation Central Europe, 1550–1750.* New York: Routledge, 1989.

Hussey, J. M. *The Orthodox Church in the Byzantine Empire.* Oxford: Oxford University Press, 2010.

"The Icon of Saint Anna." *OrthoChristian.com*, 2015. https://orthochristian.com/88061.html (accessed 2023).

James, William. "The Psychology of Belief." In *Writings, 1878–1899*, by William James, 1021–56. New York: Library of America, 1992.

———. *The Varieties of Religious Experience.* New York: Simon & Schuster, 1997.

———. *Writings, 1878–1899.* New York: Library of America, 1992.

———. *Writings, 1902–1910.* New York: Library of America, 1987.

Justiniano, Silouan. "Imagination, Expression, Icon: Reclaiming The Internal Prototype." *Orthodox Arts Journal*, 2017.

———. "Icon Painting as Participation: Interview with Cornelia Tsakiridou: Pt. I." *Orthodox Arts Journal*, 2023.

———. "The Pictorial Metaphysics of the Icon: Part II." *Orthodox Arts Journal*, January 2016.

Karant-Nunn, Susan C. *The Reformation of Feeling: Shaping the Religous Emotions in Early Modern Germany.* Oxford: Oxford University Press, 2010.

———. *The Reformation of Ritual: An Interpretation of Early Modern Germany.* New York: Routledge, 1997.

Kelly, J. N. D. *Early Christian Doctrines.* New York: Harper One, 1978.

Kierkegaard, Soren. *Philosophical Fragments/Johannes Climacus.* Princeton, NJ: Princeton University Press, 1985.

Kimbrough, S. T. *Orthodox and Wesleyan Scriptural Understanding and Practice.* Crestwood, NY: St. Vladimir's Seminary Press, 2005.

Krueger, Derek. *Byzantine Christianity (A People's History of Christianity).* Minneapolis: Fortress Press, 2006.

Lahav, Ran. *Stepping Out of Plato's Cave.* Hardwick, VT: Loyev Books, 2016.

Langer, Susanne K. "Logic of Signs and Symbols." In *A Reader in the Anthropology of Religion*, edited by Michael Lambek, 131–38. Malden, MA: Blackwell, 2008.

Lewis, I. M. *Ecstatic Religion.* Middlesex: Penguin, 1971.

Lindberg, Carter. *The European Reformations.* Oxford: Wiley-Blackwell, 2010.

Lossky, Vladimir. *Dogmatic Theology: Creation, God's Image in Man, and the Redeeming Work of the Trinity.* Yonkers, NY: St. Vladimir's Seminary Press, 2017.

———. *In the Image and Likeness of God.* Crestwood, NY: St. Vladimir's Seminary Press, 1974.

———. *The Mystical Theology of the Eastern Church.* Crestwood, NY: St. Vladimir's Seminary Press, 1944.

———. *Orthodox Theology: An Introduction.* Crestwood, NY: St. Vladimir's Seminary Press, 1978.

———. *The Vision of God.* Crestwood, NY: St. Vladimir's Seminary Press, 1963.

Louth, Andrew. *Greek East and Latin West: The Church AD 681–1071.* Crestwood, NY: St. Vladimir's Seminary Press, 2007.

———. *Introducing Eastern Orthodox Theology.* Westmont, IL: IVP Academic, 2013.

———. *Maximus the Confessor.* London: Routledge, 1996.

———. *The Origins of the Christian Mystical Tradition: From Plato to Denys.* Oxford: Clarendon Paperbacks, 1981.

———. "Orthodoxy and Art." In *Living Orthodoxy in the Modern World*, by Andrew Walker and Costa Carras, 159–78. Crestwood, NY: St. Vladimir's Seminary Press, 1996.

MacCulloch, Diarmaid. *Tudor Church Militant: Edward VI and the Protestant Reformation.* London: Penguin Books, 1999.

Malinowski, Bronislaw. *Magic, Science, and Religion and Other Essays.* Long Grove, IL: Waveland Press, 1992.

Marshall, Sherrin. *Women in Reformation and Counter-Reformation Europe: Private and Public Worlds.* Bloomington: Indiana University Press, 1989.

Mathewes-Green, Frederica. "12 Things I Wish I'd Known." *Ancient Faith*, 2020–2023. https://blogs.ancientfaith.com/frederica/12-things (accessed 2023).

Matthew the Poor. *Orthodox Prayer Life: The Interior Way.* Crestwood, NY: St. Vladimir's Seminary Press, 2003.

Maximus the Confessor. *Classics of Western Spirituality: Maximus Confessor, Selected Writings.* New York: Paulist Press, 1985.

———. *On the Cosmic Mystery of Jesus Christ.* Crestwood, NY: St. Vladimir's Seminary Press, 2003.

Metropolitan Joseph. *Liturgikon: The Book of Divine Services for the Priest and Deacon, 4th Edition.* Englewood, NJ: Antakya Press, 2021.

Metropolitan of Nafpaktos Hierotheos. *The Mind of the Orthodox Church.* Levadia, Greece: Birth of the Theotokos Press (Pelagia), 1998.

———. *Patristic and Schlastic Theology in Perspective: Based on the Spoken Teachings of Father John Romanides.* Levadia, Greece: Birth of the Theotokos Monastery (Pelagia), 2008.

Meyendorff, John. *Byzantine Theology: Historical Trends and Doctrinal Themes.* New York: Fordham University Press, 1979.

———. *St. Gregory Palamas and Orthodox Spirituality.* Crestwood, NY: St. Vladimir's Seminary Press, 1974.

———. *A Study of Gregory Palamas.* Crestwood, NY: St. Vladimir's Seminary Press, 1964.

Mitralexis, Sotiris, Georgios Steiris, Marcin Podbielski, and Sebastian Lalla. *Maximus the Confessor as a European Philosopher.* Eugene, OR: Cascade Books, 2017.

Morris, John W. *The Historic Church: An Orthodox View of Christian History.* Bloomington, IN: AuthorHouse Publishing, 2011.

Moser, David. "Sunday after Nativity: Joseph the Betrothed." *OrthodoxChristian.com*, n.d. https://orthochristian.com/89552.html.

Najim, Michel. *Services of Initiation into the Holy Orthodox-Catholic and Apostalic Church.* La Verne, CA: Antiochian Orthodox Institute, 2017.

Najim, Michael, and Patrick B. O'Grady. *Services of Initiation into the Holy Orthodox-Catholic and Apostalic Church.* La Verne, CA: Antiochian Orthodox Institute, 2017.

Nes, Solrunn. *The Mystical Language of Icons.* Grand Rapids, MI: Eerdmans, 2009.

Nietzsche, Friedrich. *The Gay Science.* Garden City, NY: Dover, 2020.

Norwich, John Julius. *A Short History of Byzantium.* New York: Vintage, 1999.

Nouwen, Henri J. M. *Behold the Beauty of the Lord: Praying with Icons.* Notre Dame, IN: Ave Maria Press, 2004.

O'Connell, Robert J. *Plato on the Human Paradox.* New York: Fordham University Press, 1997.

Oleksa, Michael J. *Alaskan Missionary Spirituality.* Yonkers, NY: St. Vladimir's Seminary Press, 2010.

Oman, Charles. *The Byzantine Empire.* Yardly: Westholme, 2008.

O'Meara, Thomas. *Albert the Great: Theologian and Scientist.* Chicago: New Priory Press, 2013.

Origen. *Classics of Western Spirituality: Origen, an Exhortation to Martyrdom, Prayer, and Selected Works.* Translated by Rowan A. Greer. Mahwah, NJ: Paulist Press, 1979.

———. *Sacred Writings of Origen.* Altenmünster: Jazzybee Verlag, 2016.

Orthodox Hawaiian Iveron Icon Association. "The Wonderworking Iveron Icon of Hawaii." *Ohiia.org*, n.d. https://www.ohiia.org/the-iveron-icon (accessed 2023).

Ortner, Sherry B. "On Key Symbols." In *A Reader in the Anthropology of Religion*, edited by Michael Lambek, 151–60. Malden, MA: Blackwell, 2008.

Ouspensky, Leonid. "The Meaning and Content of the Icon." In *Eastern Orthodox Theology: A Contemporary Reader*, edited by Daniel B. Clendenin, 33–64. Grand Rapids, MI: Baker Academic, 2003.

———. *Theology of the Icon, Volume II.* Crestwood, NY: St. Vladimir's Seminary Press, 1992.

Ouspensky, Leonid, and Vladimir Lossky. *The Meaning of Icons.* Crestwood, NY: St. Vladimir's Seminary Press, 1982.

Ozment, Steven. *When Fathers Ruled: Family Life in Reformation Europe.* Cambridge, MA: Harvard University Press, 1983.

Pageau, Jonathan. "The Cave in the Nativity Icon." *Orthodox Arts Journal*, 2013.

———. "Iconography Shows us the Pattern of Reality." *Orthodox Arts Journal*, 2020.

———. "The Inevitability of Re-enchantment." Edited by Ancient Faith. *Orthodox Engagement*, 2021.

———. "The Nativity Icon as an Image Of Reality." *Orthodox Arts Journal*, 2018.

———. "Sacred Symbol, Sacred Art." *Orthodox Arts Journal*, 2015.

Pageau, Matthieu. *The Language of Creation: Cosmic Symbolism in Genesis.* CreateSpace, 2018.

Palamas, Gregory. *The Triads.* Mahwah, NJ: Paulist Press, 1983.

Parker, John. "A Discussion with Jonathan Pageau. " *Ancient Faith*, 2018. https://www.ancientfaith.com/podcasts/lordsendme/a_discussion_with_jonathan_pageau (accessed 2023).

———. "In Defense of the Dionysian Authorship." Orthochristian.com, n.d. https://orthochristian.com/86817.html (accessed 2023).

Patitsas, Timothy G. *The Ethics of Beauty.* Maysville, MO: Road to Emmaus Foundation, 2020.

Pelikan, Jaroslav. *The Christian Tradition, Volume 1: The Emergence of the Catholic Tradition (100–600).* Chicago: University of Chicago Press, 1971.

———. *The Christian Tradition, Volume 2: The Spirit of Eastern Christendom (600–1700).* Chicago: University of Chicago Press, 1974.

Pentiuc, Eugen J. *The Old Testament in Eastern Orthodox Tradition.* Oxford: Oxford Univeristy Press, 2014.

Percival, Henry. *Council of Chalcedon (A.D. 451).* Edited by NewAdvent. Vols. Nicene and Post-Nicene Fathers, Second Series, Vol. 14. Buffalo, NY: Christian Literature Publishing, 1900.

————. *Council of Ephesus (A.D. 431).* Edited by NewAdvent. Vols. Nicene and Post-Nicene Fathers, Second Series, Vol. 14. Buffalo, NY: Buffalo, 1900.

————. *First Council of Constantinople (A.D. 381).* Edited by NewAdvent. Vols. Nicene and Post-Nicene Fathers, Second Series, Vol. 14. Buffalo, NY: Christian Literature Publishing, 1900.

————. *Second Council of Constantinople.* Vols. Nicene and Post-Nicene Fathers, Second Series, Vol. 14. Buffalo, NY: Christian Literature Publishing, 1900.

————. *Seven Ecumenical Councils.* Edmond, OK: Veritas Splendor, 2013.

Peterson, Jordan B. *Maps of Meaning: The Architecture of Belief.* New York: Routledge, 1999.

Pettegree, Andrew. *Reformation and the Culture of Persuasion.* Cambridge, UK: Cambridge University Press, 2005.

Philo. "On Creation." Earlychristianwritings.com, n.d. http://www.earlychristianwritings.com/yonge/book1.html (accessed 2023).

————. *The Works of Philo.* Peabody, MA: Hendrickson Publishing, 1993.

Plato. *Five Dialogues: Euthyphro, Apology, Crito, Meno, Phaedo.* Translated by GMA Grube. Indianapolis: Hackett Publishing, 1981.

————. *Middle Platonic Dialogues: Cratylus, Euthydemus, Menexenus, Meno, Parmenides, Phaedo, Phaedrus, Republic, Symposium, Theaetetus.* Translated by Benjamin Jowett. Independently published, 2021.

————. "Phaedrus." Edited by Benjamin Jowett. *Classics.mit.edu*, n.d. http://classics.mit.edu/Plato/phaedrus.html (accessed 2022).

————. *Republic.* Translated by Desmond Lee. New York: Penguin Classics, 2007.

————. *The Symposium.* London: Penguin, 1999.

————. *Theaetetus.* Indianapolis: Hackett, 1992.

————. *Timaeus and Critias.* Suffolk: Penguin Classics, 2008.

Plotinus. "Plotinus: The Six Enneads." Internet Archive, n.d. https://archive.org/details/in.ernet.dli.2015.460836 (accessed 2023).

————. "The Six Enneads." Edited by Stephen Mackenna and B. S. Page. Classics MIT, n.d. http://classics.mit.edu/Plotinus/enneads.2.second.html (accessed 2020).

Pomazansky, Michael. *Orthodox Dogmatic Theology.* Platina, CA: St. Herman of Alaska Brotherhood, 2021.

Popkin, Richard H., ed. *Columbia History of Western Philosophy.* New York: MJF Books, 1999.

Proclus. "Proclus: The Elements of Theology." Internet Archive, n.d. https://archive.org/details/proclus-the-elements-of-theology_202109 (accessed 2023).

————. "The Six Books of Proclus, the Platonic Successor, on the Theology of Plato." Internet Archive, n.d. https://archive.org/details/the_six_books_of_proclus_2102_librivox (accessed 2023).

Pseudo-Dionysius. *Classics of Western Spirituality: Pseudo-Dionysius, the Complete Works.* New York: Paulist Press, 1987.

Roper, Lyndal. *The Holy Household: Women and Morals in Reformation Augsburg.* Oxford: Oxford University Press, 2001.

Rose, Seraphim, Fr. *Nihilism: The Root of the Revolution of the Modern Age.* Platina, CA: St. Herman of Alaska Brotherhood, 2020.

Russell, Norman. *Fellow Workers with God: Orthodox Thinking on Theosis.* Crestwood, NY: St. Vladimir's Seminary Press, 2009.

Russian Icon Collection. "Holy Icons of Our Lady of the Sign." *Russianicon.com,* 2017. https://russianicon.com/holy-icons-lady-sign/ (accessed 2023).

———. "The Myrrh-Streaming Icons in Russia." *Russianicon.com,* 2020. https://russianicon.com/the-myrrh-streaming-icons-in-russia/ (accessed 2023).

Russian Orthodox Cathedral of St. John the Baptist of Washington, DC. "Iveron Myrrh-Streaming Icon of the Mother of God." *Stjohndc.org,* n.d. https://stjohndc.org/en/brother-munios/iveron-myrrh-streaming-icon-mother-god (accessed 2023).

———. "Jose Munoz-Cortez." *Stjohndc.org,* n.d. https://stjohndc.org/en/brother-munios/jose-munoz-cortez (accessed 2023).

Sahas, Daniel J. *Icons and Logos: Sources in Eight-Century Iconoclasm.* Toronto: University of Toronto Press, 1986.

Sahlins, Marshall. *Islands of History.* Chicago: University of Chicago Press, 1987.

Saint Athanasius of Alexandria. "Against the Heathen." In *Saint Athanasius of Alexandria Selection,* by Saint Athanasius of Alexandria, 3–46. Philadelphia: Aeterna Press, 2016.

Sardella, Dennis J. *Visible Image of the Invisible God: A Guide to Russian and Byzantine Icons.* Brewster, MA: Paraclete Press, 2022.

Scarisbrick, J. J. *Henry VIII.* Berkeley: University of California Press, 1968.

Schmemann, Alexander. *For the Life of the World.* Yonkers, NY: St. Vladimir's Seminary Press, 2018.

———. *Introduction to Liturgical Theology.* Yonkers, NY: St. Vladimir's Seminary Press, 1966.

———. *Liturgy and Tradition: Theological Reflections of Alexander Schmemann.* Edited by Thomas Fisch. Crestwood, NY: St. Vladimir's Seminary Press, 1990.

———. *A Voice for Our Time: Radio Liberty Talks, Vol 1.* Yonkers, NY: St. Vladimir's Seminary Press, 2021.

Shuttleworth, Mark. "Theosis: Partaking of the Divine Nature." *Antiochian.org,* n.d. http://ww1.antiochian.org/content/theosis-partaking-divine-nature (accessed 2023).

Smith, Jonathan Z. *Map Is Not Territory.* Chicago: University of Chicago Press, 1978.

Smith, Wilfred Cantwell. *The Meaning and the End of Religion.* Minneapolis: Fortress, 1991.

Spade, Paul Vincent. *Five Texts on The Medieval Problem of Universals.* Indianapolis: Hackett, 1994.

St. Basil the Great. "Address to Young Men on Reading Greek Literature." In *St Basil Collection,* by St. Basil the Great, 738–54. Philadelphia: Aeterna Press, 2016.

———. "Letters." In *St. Basil Collection,* by St. Basil the Great, 259–735. Philadelphia: Aeterna Press, 2016.

———. *On Christian Doctrine and Practice.* Popular Patristics Series 47. Crestwood, NY: St. Vladimir's Press, 2012.

———. *On the Holy Spirit.* Popular Patristics Series 42. Yonkers, NY: St. Vladimir's Press, 2011.

——. *On the Human Condition.* Popular Patristics Series 30. Crestwood, NY: St. Vladimir's Press, 2005.

——. *St. Basil Collection.* Philadelphia: Aeterna Press, 2016.

St. Cyril the Great. *Five Tomes against Nestorius.* Philadelphia: Aeterna Press, 2014.

——. *St. Cyril Selection: Commentary Upon the Gospel According to St. Luke, the Catehetical Lectures of St. Cyril, Three Epistles of St. Cyril.* Philadelphia: Aeterna Press, 2016.

St. Ephrem the Syrian. *Hymns on Paradise.* Crestwood, NY: St. Vladimir's Seminary Press, 1990.

St. John of Damascus. "Expositions of the Orthodox Faith Book 3 Chapter III Concerning Christ's Two Natures, in Opposition to Those Who Hold That He Has Only One." In *Collection: Barlaam and Ioasaph, Exposition of the Orthodox Faith, on Holy Images, on the Trinity,* by St. John of Damascus, 271–74. Philadelphia: Aeterna Press, 2016.

——. "Expositions of the Orthodox Faith Book 4 Chapter XVI Concerning Images." In *St. John of Damascus, Collection,* by St. John of Damascus, 350–52. Philadelphia, PA: Aeterna Press, 2016.

——. *Fathers of the Church Volume, XXXVII: Saint John of Damascus.* Jackson, MI: Ex Fontibus Company, 2015.

——. "Oration on the Transfiguraiton of our Lord and Savior Jesus Christ." In *Light on the Mountain: Greek Patristic and Byzantine Homilies on the Transfiguration of the Lord,* edited by Brian Daley, S.J., 203–32. Yonkers, NY: St. Vladimir's Seminary Press, 2013.

——. *Three Treatises on the Divine Images.* Crestood, NY: St. Vladimir's Seminary Press, 2003.

St. Justin Martyr. "Discourse to the Greeks." In *Ante-Nicene Fathers, Vol. 1,* edited by Alexander Roberts, James Donaldson, and A. Coxe Cleveland, translated by Marcus Dods. Buffalo, New York: Christian Literature Publishing, 1885.

——. *Saint Justin Martyr Collection.* Philadelphia, PA: Aeterna Press, 2016.

St. Nektarios Kefalas. *Collected Works, Volume 7: Know Thyself.* Jerusalem: Virgin Mary of Australia and Oceania, 2022.

——. *Collected Works, Volume 9: On the Holy Images.* Jerusalem: Virgin Mary of Australia and Oceania, 2022.

——. *Collected Works, Volume 13: The Ecumenical Councils.* Jerusalem: Virgin Mary of Australia and Oceania, 2022.

St. Nicholas Center. "History of the Myrrh-Streaming Icon." *Stnicholascenter.org,* n.d. https://www.stnicholascenter.org/who-is-st-nicholas/stories-legends/modern-miracles/weeping-icons/weeping-icon-michigan-city/history-myrrh-streaming-icon (accessed 2023).

St. Nikolai of Ohrid and Zhicha. *The Prologue of Ohrid, Volume 1.* Alhambra, CA: Sebastian Press, 2017.

St. Porphyrios. *Wounded by Love: The Life and the Wisdom of Saint Porphyrios.* Translated by Sisters of the Holy Vocenant of Chrysopigi. Limni: Denise Harvey, 2018.

St. Proclus of Constantinople. "Sermon on the Annunciation." *OCA.org*, n.d. https://www.oca.org/fs/sermons/sermon-on-the-annunciation (accessed 2023).

St. Theodore the Studite. *On the Holy Icons.* Crestwood, NY: St. Vladimir's Seminary Press, 1981.

St. Theophan the Recluse. *The Path to Salvation: A Concise Outline of Christian Ascesis.* Safford, AZ: Holy Monastery of St. Paisius, 2006.

Tauler, John. *The Inner Way.* Philadelphia: Aeterna Press, 2015.

Temple, Richard. *Icons: A Sacred Art at the Temple Gallery.* London: Temple Gallery, 1989.

———. *Icons and the Mystical Origins of Christianity.* Longmead: Element Books, 1990.

Tertullian. *The Prescription against Heretics, Volume 3: Ante-Nicene Fathers.* Grand Rapids, MI: Eerdmans, 1951.

Tillich, Paul. *Dynamics of Faith.* New York: Harper & Row, 1957.

Turner, Victor. *The Forest of Symbols: Aspects of Ndembu Ritual.* Ithaca, NY: Cornell University Press, 1967.

Tyson, John R. *The Great Athanasius: An Introduction to His Life and Work.* Eugene, OR: Cascade, 2017.

Van't Spijker, Willem. *Calvin: A Brief Guide to His Life and Thought.* Louisville, KY: Westminster John Knox Press, 2009.

Vasilios, Archimandrite. *Hymn of Entry.* Crestwood, NY: St. Vladimir's Seminary Press, 1984.

Walker, Andrew, and Costa Carras. *Living Orthodoxy in the Modern World.* Crestwood, NY: St. Vladimir's Seminary Press, 1996.

Wallace, Anthony F. C. *Modernity and Mind: Essays on Culture Change, Volume 2.* Lincoln: University of Nebraska Press, 2004.

———. *Revitalizations and Mazewasys: Essays on Culture Change, Volume 1.* Lincoln: University of Nebraska Press, 2003.

Ware (Metropolitan Kallistos of Diokleia), Timothy. *The Orthodox Church: An Introduction to Eastern Christianity, New Edition.* New York: Penguin Books, 2015.

Watt, Tessa. *Cheap Print and Popular Piety, 1550–1640.* Cambridge, UK: Cambridge University Press, 1991.

Wells, Colin. *Sailing from Byzantium: How a Lot Empire Shaped the World.* New York: Delta, 2006.

Williams, George Huntston. *The Radical Reformation.* Kirksville, MO: Truman State University Press, 2000.

Zelensky, Elizabeth, and Lela Gilbert. *Windows to Heaven: Introducing Icons to Protestants and Catholics.* Ada, MI: Brazos Press, 2005.

# Index

# About the Author

Justin A. Davis has a degree in systematic theology and philosophy from the Graduate Theological Union and a degree in history and religious studies from the University of Missouri–Kansas City. He has also completed work on applied Orthodox theology with the Antiochian House of Studies to complement his passion for teaching undergraduates and explaining ideas that shape the world. His academic life focuses on intellectual history, including philosophy and theology, and particularly the interaction of these systems of thought with periods of great cultural change. In addition to a number of conference presentations, Davis is the author of *Pietism and the Foundations of the Western World* and *Schleiermacher and Palmer: The Father and Mother of the Modern Protestant Mindset*. He lives in the Boise area of Idaho with his wife and four children.

Milton Keynes UK
Ingram Content Group UK Ltd.
UKHW011618030624
443662UK00003B/8

9 781666 949551